Music Cultures
in the United States

Music Cultures
in the United States

An Introduction

Edited by

Ellen Koskoff

ROUTLEDGE
NEW YORK AND LONDON

Published in 2005 by
Routledge
270 Madison Avenue
New York, NY 10016

Published in Great Britain by
Routledge
2 Park Square
Milton Park, Abingdon,
Oxon OX14 4RN U.K.
www.routledge.co.uk

Snapshot 3.2: Funk by Portia K. Maultsby (p. 75–81) was completed while the author was
a fellow at the Center for Advanced Study in the Behavioral Sciences, (1999–2000)
Stanford, California.

Routledge is an imprint of the Taylor & Francis Group.
Printed in the United States of America on acid-free paper.

10 9 8 7 6 5 4 3 2 1

Library of Congress Cataloging-in-Publication Data

Music cultures in the United States : an introduction / Ellen Koskoff, editor.
   p. cm.
   Includes bibliographical references and index.
   ISBN 0-415-96588-8 (hb : alk. paper)—ISBN 0-415-96589-6 (pb : alk. paper)
   1. Music—Social aspects—United States. 2. Music—-United States—History and criticism.
I. Koskoff, Ellen, 1943–
   ML3917.U6M87 2005
   306.4'842'0973—dc22
                                                                      2004019853

To the wonderful musics and musicians in this book, and to the wonderful scholars who came to know them.

CONTENTS

INTRODUCTION

Music Cultures in the United States presents a picture of the richly varied and intricate tapestry of musical traditions now existing in the United States, reflecting the interactive nature of musical cultures and the variety of ways in which music is actually experienced in a pluralistic society. Based on Volume 3 of the *Garland Encyclopedia of World Music* (Routledge 2000), *Music Cultures in the United States* is an updated and redesigned text for use in the classroom or by anyone with a general interest in American music and its social and cultural contexts.

HOW THIS BOOK IS ORGANIZED

The volume is organized in three large sections: **Part I**, "Music in the United States: Historical, Social, and Cultural Contexts" (Chapters 1–4), presents four chapters, each of which discusses an overarching issue affecting music, its creation, performance, reception, and dissemination throughout the country. Chapter 1 presents a brief overview of the social and musical history of the United States; Chapter 2 discusses various social, political, and economic factors that affect music making; Chapter 3 examines the role of class, race, gender, and religion in the formation of social and musical identities in the United States; and Chapter 4 discusses ways in which social and musical interactions affect music as it adapts to different contexts and changing meanings.

Part II, "A Sampler of Music Cultures in the United States" (Chapters 5-9), presents the musics of various socio-cultural groups that have contributed to American musical life, beginning with

American Indian musical culture and continuing with immigrant music cultures presented roughly in the order of their arrival and development here. **Part III**, "Global Musics in the United States" (Chapters 10–11), presents informative essays on concert musics (classical and jazz) and on a wide array of popular musics found in the United States and throughout the world today.

Within each chapter, we present short, but detailed, examples of specific musical cultures, called **Snapshots**. These are small "ethnographic moments," or discussions of musical genres that have been chosen to best illustrate issues or concepts under discussion. In addition, a compact disc, with sound examples linked to the text (starting in Chapter 5), is found at the back of this volume.

At the end of each chapter, we have included review questions and projects that are both fun and instructive. Projects can be used to stimulate written research or as the basis of group discussion. In addition, important words, names, and concepts are indicated in the margins throughout the book to help you more easily find and remember information. Finally, a comprehensive glossary, bibliography, discography, videography, and index are included at the back of this volume.

Readers of this book are strongly urged to consult volume 3 of the *Garland Encyclopedia of World Music* for many fuller discussions of topics and other similar resources pertaining to the study of musical life in the United States.

WHY CERTAIN MUSIC CULTURES (AND NOT OTHERS) ARE DISCUSSED IN THIS BOOK

It would not be possible to discuss every music that has ever existed, or continues to exist, within the United States, so certain choices had to be made for this volume. We tended to privilege musics that are not always discussed in standard histories and to put less emphasis, especially in the recorded examples, on musics such as popular music, classical music, and jazz, which are readily available through other media.

We are also interested in preserving certain cultural and ethnic boundaries, without essentializing them. That is, we recognize that discussing music cultures in the United States from the perspective of a group or social identity, including categories such as race, class, or ethnicity, tends to "mark" and privilege these parameters over others that may be fluid and self-defined. Our intention here is to honor these parameters, while at the same time stressing the interactive, boundary-crossing nature of life in a pluralistic society. Thus, we wish to stress that the realities of social and musical identity are far more subtle than these categories imply, and you are cautioned to see them here as starting, but not necessarily ending, points.

ACKNOWLEDGMENTS

A book such as this is a collaborative effort and I would like to acknowledge those who have contributed to its making here. First, and foremost, I thank the many authors—and the musicians with whom they worked—whose labors enliven these pages. It is to them that this book is dedicated. I would also like to thank Richard Carlin and the publishers of Routledge/Taylor and Francis for their help in initiating this project and seeing it through to completion. The snapshot on funk in Chapter 3 was completed while the author, Portia K. Maultsby was a Fellow at the Center for Advanced Study in the Behavioral Sciences (1999-2000), Stanford, California. Love and thanks go to two student readers, Hillary Overberg and Liisa Ambegaokar Grigorov, whose eagle eyes caught many mistakes that would otherwise have gone unnoticed. Thanks also to the Smithsonian Institution's Folkways Collection and to Michael Tenzer and Robert Morris for permission to use their recent compositions here. Finally, I would like to thank my family for its continual support, love, and laughter.

Ellen Koskoff
Rochester, New York
April 2004

Part I

Music in the United States:
Historical, Social, and Cultural
Contexts

CHAPTER 1

A Social-Historical Approach to Music in the United States

Ellen Koskoff

The United States of America, the fourth largest country in the world, covers over 3.5 million square miles of land. From its highest point, Mt. McKinley in Alaska, to its lowest in Death Valley, California, this enormous land area encompasses deserts, imposing mountain ranges, polar ice caps, lush woodlands, rainforests, rich prairies, five time zones, and more than 280 million people of varying ethnicities, languages, and histories.

Unity in diversity is a common phrase often used today to describe the people and social contexts of the United States. Home to people of virtually all of the world's social, ethnic, religious, and language groups, the United States has embedded within its history, government, and national consciousness the twin ideals of democracy and equal human rights; although not always realized, these ideals have motivated much social and musical activity within its borders.

Any discussion of music in the United States must take into account the various contexts of its creation, performance, and meaning. While reading this text, ask yourself these questions:

1. What part do specific geographical, historical, and cultural contexts play in music making among highly diverse social and cultural groups?
2. How are various group and individual identities realized or marked through music and its performance?
3. How do people and their musics interact with, merge into, or separate from one another to form distinct entities?

This book answers some of these questions by examining the musical cultures of the United States through various wide-angle lenses or windows, the first framing a picture of a shared musical culture in which *similar patterns* of social structure and musical identity are discussed, the second framing another picture, of distinct musical cultures in which the focus is on issues of *difference*. Finally, issues of social and musical interaction are addressed, in which the resulting pictures are far more fluid, where identities are contested, negotiated, and continually in flux.

Remember that these frames are artificial constructions designed to highlight certain features of musical culture over others; life lived by real people "on the ground," so to speak, is often far more complex, interactive, and unpredictable. These large frames of discussion are to be taken more as guideposts than as true pictures, pointing the way to musical and social streams that continue to have implications for the people and musics of the United States today. The reader is urged to look more closely at specific chapters and especially at the individual Snapshots found throughout this volume.

THE LAND AND ITS PEOPLE TODAY

The contiguous United States extends east to west from the Atlantic Ocean to the Pacific and north to south from the border with Canada to the Rio Grande River, which forms the natural boundary between the United States and Mexico (see Figure 1.1). The Southeast United States is framed by the Gulf of Mexico; the Southwestern portion by the Pacific Ocean. Alaska, off the Northwestern coast of Canada and separated from the easternmost tip of Russia by the Bering Strait, shares far more in terms of topography, climate, and natural resources with Northwestern Canada than with the contiguous United States, while Hawai'i, forming one of the many island chains in the South Pacific, shares much with the culture of Polynesia.

The East Coast Plain, framed on the west by the Appalachian Mountains, dominates the eastern portion of the United States, while the great prairies and plains dominate the central portion. The mammoth mountain chains—the Eastern and Western Cordilleras (stretching parallel to the Pacific Ocean from Cape Horn at the tip of South America to the Aleutians in Alaska), which encompass the Sierra Nevada, Rocky, and Cascade Mountains—provide a natural north-south barrier, giving way to the lowlands and deserts of the West and Southwest coasts of the United States.

Major inland waterways include in the east the Hudson, Delaware, and Potomac rivers, which flow east into the Atlantic; the main central river system includes the Mississippi and Missouri rivers, which flow into the Gulf of Mexico; and in the west the Columbia and Colorado rivers, which flow into the Pacific. The

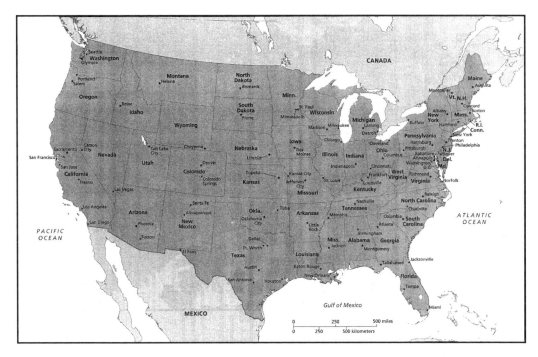

Figure 1.1
Map of the United
States

Great Lakes, which share their borders with both Canada and the United States, provide tremendous natural resources today as they did for these countries' earliest inhabitants when they dominated the inland waterways system of trade and early land ownership.

In earlier times, geographical barriers—such as imposing mountain chains and the often harsh climate at both temperature extremes—made interaction between social groups difficult; thus musical and other forms of expressive cultural exchanges were fairly limited until the nineteenth century, although American Indian groups before that time had developed extensive trade networks among themselves and with the first European traders and settlers.

Today, the United States, a federal republic, is divided politically into 50 states. In addition, it also has a number of other formal dependencies, such as Puerto Rico, the Virgin Islands, and Samoa in the South Pacific. The population of the United States reflects both its political and social history as well as current demographic patterns of immigration and settlement. The following information is based on recent census data for the United States (Crystal 1999). Although the major statistics are presented here, they do not do justice to the variety of subgroups, languages, and ethnicities embedded within these categories.

The first inhabitants—American Indians, Inuit (Eskimo), and Aleut—are today a small minority of the total population (under 5%), the majority of whom live in the Southwest, Northeast, and Plains areas. Many American Indian peoples continue to live today in rural areas or on reservations, often in very depressed economic conditions, while others, especially during the latter half of the twentieth century, have migrated to large urban areas to find work.

By far the largest portion of the population (about 75% of the total) derives from Europe, predominantly from Britain. Obviously, many aspects of our federal and local governments, social and political institutions, religions, official language, economies, and musical institutions and values derive from these nations. Sizable populations of Germans, Italians, Ukrainians, Dutch, Scandinavians, Hungarians, and Greeks also live within the United States, predominantly in urban areas, although Ukrainians and Scandinavians especially played a large part in the westward expansion and rural settlement during the eighteenth and nineteenth centuries.

The remaining approximately 20% is divided among the growing African American population (about 10% of the total), originally transported primarily from West Africa during periods of slavery; people of Hispanic origin (Mexican, Caribbean, Central, and South American), the largest growing minority population, representing about 8% of the total; and the Asian communities (Chinese, Filipino, Japanese, Indian, Korean, Vietnamese, Lao) and Pacific Islanders (predominantly Hawaiians and Tongans), about 2% of the total.

About 75% of the population of the United States lives within large urban areas, such as New York, Chicago, and Los Angeles. The overwhelming majority of the population is Christian (about 80%), with Protestants comprising about 53%. Sizable Jewish and Muslim populations as well as a growing number of Buddhists, Sikhs, and Hindus have also immigrated to the United States, especially during the twentieth century.

A BRIEF SOCIAL AND MUSICAL HISTORY OF THE UNITED STATES

The Earliest Inhabitants

The original inhabitants of the United States were the ancestors of the American Indians, who are believed to have emigrated here from what is now the westernmost portion of Russia across the Bering Strait in two great waves (ca. 18,000 B.C.E. and 12,000 B.C.E.). Centuries before the Europeans arrived, American Indian peoples had developed extensive cultures based on hunting, fishing, and small-scale farming that were sustained by a traditional life infused with music and ritual activity.

Mimetic dancing
Dancing that imitates a specific activity, such as planting corn.

Specific contexts for musical performance included ceremonies surrounding the yearly cycles of spring/summer and fall/winter activities, including hunting songs (often revealed in dreams), planting (often including *mimetic dancing*), and harvesting (thanksgiving) songs and dances, as well as shamanistic practices, including individual and community healing ceremonies. Among the Plains Indians, for example, song practices associated with medicine bundles and with war dances were common. In the Northwest, among the Haida, Salish, and Athapaskan, *potlatches* were frequently held, as well as ceremonies accompanying totem pole carving and installation. Some music, such as gambling, game, and love songs, addressed daily social and communal life, while other kinds of music commemorated historical or mythical events. Social dance songs, such as the women's shuffle dances of the Iroquois Confederacy in the northeast United States and southeast Canada, were also performed.

The traditional social structure of most American Indian communities was divided along gender and age lines, with men and women having clearly delineated and equally valued tasks and responsibilities to the group throughout their adult lives. Puberty, marriage, and death rituals were common practices ensuring safe and orderly passage into, through, and beyond life. Puberty rituals, perhaps the most extensive of the life-cycle rituals, often involved separating the young men and women from the community for a period of time, during which the elders would teach them the history and mythology of their group as well as its secret songs and ceremonies.

Many American Indian peoples, such as the Inuit (Eskimo) living in harsh northern climates, remained fairly isolated and scattered from one another, while others, such as the Plains Indians, developed by the fifteenth and sixteenth century C.E. large and powerful hunting and trading networks made up of many independent communities tied together through elaborate exchange economies. The intertribal meeting, later to develop into the powwow, became an important context for the exchange not only of food and gossip but also of songs and dances.

Although traditional American Indian song and dance were quite varied in terms of their performance contexts and meanings, musically they shared certain basic features: most of the music was vocal, *monophonic* or *heterophonic*, with frequent use of *vocables*.

No separate instrumental traditions existed within early American Indian musical cultures, although instruments such as the drum and rattle were frequently used to accompany song. The drum, especially, had deep power and significance for early communities and became in later times a source of much contention between aboriginal peoples, Christian colonists, and other settlers, who regularly banned its use.

From Colonies to Nation: 1600–1800

Although there is some evidence for early Norse contact in Newfoundland ca. 990 C.E., the first permanent European settlements in the United States were made by the Spanish in 1565 in

Potlatch
A large feast characterized by gift giving to all participants

Monophonic
One melody line
Heterophonic
One line performed in simultaneous variations
Vocables
Syllables that are phonetically related to, but have no referential meaning in, the local language

modern-day St. Augustine, Florida, and the British in Jamestown, now in Virginia, in 1607. The early visitors were mainly traders sent by various governments and business interests in Europe in hopes of establishing ties with the Indians, who could help them in the lucrative fur trade. By the early seventeenth century, American Indians in the East had a fully established economy based on fishing and hunting and had developed skills that proved essential to European survival. With the traders came also notions of private ownership and a money-based economy. Missionaries from Spain and France arrived soon after, bringing with them a radically different spiritual worldview based on the hierarchic principles of Christianity and on early modern European notions of class.

Along with the early traders and clerics came their music, their musical instruments, and their ideas of what music was—and was not. By the mid-eighteenth century, English *ballads* and other popular secular musics of the day were commonplace, as were British regimental bands, fife and drum field or marching bands, and string orchestras playing the latest *minuets* and *gavottes* from Europe to entertain the landed gentry in the southern U.S. colonies. Various forms of hymns, *psalmody*, and Christian *liturgical music* had also become commonplace within European communities in the East, promoted by singing schools that sprang up, especially in New England. Gradually, as European-derived communities began to grow and social and musical institutions began to develop, new or newly adapted music—composed and performed within the American context—also began to appear, such as Anglo American ballads, theatrical musics, and hymns composed and taught by singing masters and clerics.

Interactions between Europeans and American Indian peoples were frequent during this time. As more and more land was taken by European settlements, Indian lands began to shrink, and communities that had once roamed freely were forced to develop new forms of economy and social interaction based on European models. Furthermore, disturbed by the powerful drumming and ritual practices of many Indian groups with whom they had contact, Europeans began to ban these ceremonies, describing them as sinful and primitive.

Many revitalizing movements, such as that of Iroquoian Handsome Lake, who established the Longhouse religion in 1799, attempted to help Indian communities face the swift social, religious, and political changes (not to mention diseases such as tuberculosis and smallpox) brought by the Europeans, and much Indian music developed during the eighteenth century addressed the destruction of the Indian traditional way of life. Some musical interaction took place, such as the development of the *kaachina* ceremony

Ballad
A narrative song
Minuet
Graceful, eighteenth-century dance in slow $\frac{3}{4}$ time
Gavotte
Eighteenth-century line or circle dance
Psalmody
The singing of psalms (religious texts from the Bible)
Liturgical music
Music associated with specific rites performed as part of the Church service

(Indian/Spanish); however, most interaction was limited for many reasons, not the least of which was that European concepts of music, especially secular forms such as ballads, dances, or marching band music, and of written notation were initially unknown to the Indians, who viewed what they did as prayer, ritual, or ceremony—in other words, as religious and social, as well as "sounded," behavior.

Slavery was introduced in 1619. By 1800 over a million people, of mainly West African and Caribbean descent, were living in the United States. It would take another sixty-five years and a Civil War (1861–1865) for slavery to be abolished as a legal institution. During that time thousands of runaway slaves passed through the Underground Railroad, a system of interconnected hiding places that took them north via the Great Lakes from the United States into Canada, through cities such as Detroit, Buffalo, and Rochester, New York. Frequently African American songs such as "Follow the Drinking Gourd" (the Big Dipper, shaped like a ladle) were used as musical/linguistic codes to give directions to runaways.

The slaves imported from the coastal areas of West Africa and the Caribbean often brought with them small, portable musical instruments such as drums and gourd rattles, as well as a vast and rich tradition of song, dance, ritual, and ceremony (see Figure 1.2). Slaves were frequently separated from their families, first in Africa and then again in America, and much of the integrity and cohesiveness of their many musical cultures was lost. Furthermore, in constant fear of uprisings, slave owners frequently banned, as they had with the Indians, the use of drums and certain dances (regarded by the European gentry as indecent). Slave culture thus developed its own unique American musical tradition based on calls, cries, and other forms of vocal musics that enabled slaves to communicate their feelings as well as vital bits of information through their performance.

In the eighteenth century, as a result of various treaties negotiated in Europe between the British and French following the Peace of Utrecht in 1713 and the French and Indian War (known in Europe as part of the Seven Years War, 1756–1763), the French lost control of most of their formerly claimed territory in Canada, ceding it to Britain. Many French living in what was then Acadia (present-day Nova Scotia) were forcibly removed to the Louisiana Territory, a French-controlled portion of the southeastern United States, where they interacted with Africans and Indians primarily from the Caribbean, creating a new and vital *Cajun* culture with its own language dialects and musical traditions.

By the end of the sixteenth century, Spanish clerics had established a thriving mission culture predominantly in the upper Rio Grande Valley in New Mexico, bringing with them, either directly

Katchina
a Hopi ancestral spirit embodied by a masked dancer during ritual performances

Figure 1.2
Members of St. John's Spiritual Baptist Church in the Flatbush neighborhood of Brooklyn, New York, sing a hymn from the Church of England's *Hymns Ancient and Modern*. The Spiritual Baptist faith probably originated in St. Vincent Island in the east Caribbean, then flourished in Trinidad, but through immigrants it also thrives in New York City. Photo by Terry Miller, 1989.

Alabado
Religious ballads related to Catholic plainchant
Cajun
Cultural group formed from the interaction of French heritage settlers with native Indian and African American populations
Mestizo culture
A blending of Spanish, West African, and American Indian cultures
Corrido
Ballad
Conjunto
Ensemble music

from Spain or via Mexico, Spanish sacred music in the form of the *alabado*, and religious theatrical forms such as Christmas and Easter plays. They also frequently imported musical instruments from Europe, including organs, which were installed within their newly built churches. Secular music also traveled from Mexico and through Spanish-held territories in what is now the southwestern United States. As *mestizo* culture developed, new forms such as the *corrido* and later *conjunto* became popular along the Rio Grande and throughout the southwestern United States. European, predominantly German and Czech, immigration to Mexico also introduced various popular dances such as the *polka* and the quintessential polka band instrument, the button accordion, which became a mainstay of various later-developed Mexican and Mexican American ensembles.

Westward Expansion: 1800–1900

The nineteenth century is marked by six factors that contributed greatly to the forming of a national identity:

1. Westward expansion by Europeans to the Pacific Ocean
2. Immigration of many different European groups, as well as Chinese and Japanese
3. Building of the transcontinental railways
4. The gold rushes of the 1850s
5. Various governmental policies that involved taking Indian land, forcible Indian migration, and war
6. Discriminatory practices aimed at both American Indians and African Americans

Furthermore, the country grew through purchases of land from European and Mexican powers, so that by 1850 the United States had acquired most of its southeastern territory from France through the Louisiana Purchase (1803), Florida from Spain (1819), and much of the Southwest (Texas, California, Arizona, Nevada, New Mexico, Utah, parts of Colorado, Oklahoma, and Wyoming) from Mexico through the treaty of Guadalupe Hidalgo signed at the end of the Mexican-American War in 1848. The last large chunks of land to be added to the United States were Alaska, sold by Russia in 1867, and Hawai'i, previously an independent republic and annexed in 1898, although both would not become states until the middle of the twentieth century.

Sizable communities of Germans, Scandinavians, Italians, Ukrainians, and, in the mid- to late nineteenth century, Greeks, Hungarians, and Southern and Eastern Europeans, among others, emigrated to the United States, capitalizing on governmental offers of inexpensive farm land and land grants in the great prairie states. With these communities came their music, including sacred Moravian hymns, Lutheran *chorales*, and Orthodox Russian, Greek, and other Eastern Orthodox practices. German and Scandinavian communities, especially, modeled their musical activities after those they had enjoyed in Europe, and soon various orchestras, town bands, choral societies, *liederkranz,* and Ukrainian *bandura* orchestras were established. Italians, too, brought their own European musical culture to the New World in the form of opera, popular, and folk music traditions. And the Irish, emigrating to escape the potato famine and difficult economic conditions in their homeland, brought their rich folk song, fiddling, and Celtic dance traditions, settling primarily in the growing eastern cities.

As the major cities in the East and Midwest—New York, Philadelphia, and Chicago, among others—began to grow, large

Polka
Nineteenth-century dance from in $\frac{2}{4}$ rhythm originated in Bohermia and Poland

Chorale
Hymn tune of the Lutheran/ Protestant church, often sung in poly-phonic (multiple melodic lines) settings

Liederkranz
Singing circles

Bandura
Ukranian, long-necked lute

Celtic culture
The traditions of the *Celts*, a group of Indo-European people who settled primarily in Ireland, Scotland, and Breton (Southern France)

communities developed that could sustain middle- and upper-middle-class European-derived musical institutions such as concert halls, opera houses, theaters, and schools modeled after their European counterparts. Classical concert music began to flourish, at first based on European models but later taking on its own "American" character, based in part on the adoption and adaptation of various indigenous and newly arrived folk traditions.

In the rural U.S. South other rich traditions slowly emerged:

1. The African American spiritual and black gospel hymn, originally part of worship service but later adapted for concert use by choirs such as the Wiregrass Sacred Harp Singers (see Figure 1.3)
2. White gospel hymns, originally evolved from the *shape-note* tradition and the nineteenth-century camp meeting and produced by the hundreds by composers such as Dwight Moody (1837-1899), Ira Sankey (1840-1908), and Fanny Jane Crosby (1820-1915), among others
3. Early *blues*, based on African American musical and linguistic forms such as *field cries* and *hollers*
4. Country ("hillbilly") music, originally evolved from the Scottish and English ballad tradition that flourished there.

With the division of music into essentially urban and rural contexts, a regional/class hierarchy began to develop that had both an east-west and north-south split. Furthermore, the social and critical rhetoric of the time, found in newspapers, music journals, and other publications, began to reveal a European bias that still exists in some quarters today. Music and musical activities in the larger East Coast cities, and continuing close ties with British and other European composers and teaching methods, for example, began to be constructed as more "refined" and "sophisticated," whereas music associated with the predominantly rural southern and western areas of the United States began to be seen as "rustic," "coarse," and, in the case of fiddle music, "the devil's work." These class distinctions would become more complex and embedded within notions of American musics developed in the twentieth century.

Westward expansion resulted in the shrinking of American Indian lands and in the continued destruction of the Indian way of life. In the 1880s frequent wars broke out, between the United States cavalry and members of the Sioux nation for example. As in the East among the Iroquois a century earlier, Plains Indians developed new and creative ceremonies and rituals to counteract the destruction of their material and spiritual lives. Perhaps the best known was the short-lived Ghost Dance religion that emerged in the 1880s. This movement espoused revivalist beliefs in the coming of a new world free of white men, without sickness or hunger, and marked by the

Shape note hymns
Type of notation in which the shape of the note head indicates the pitch of the note

Blues
African American song form that developed in the late nineteenth century, often featuring a 12-bar melodic structure

Field cries
Vocalized chants used to communicate in the fields while performing manual labor

Hollers
Unaccompanied songs used in conjunction with work

Figure 1.3
Henry Japeth Jackson of Ozark, Alabama's, Wiregrass Sacred Harp Singers explains the four-shape note system (fasola) at a workshop during Kent State University's annual folk festival. Photo by Terry Miller, 1989.

return of the buffalo. Misinterpreted as war dances, Ghost Dance ceremonies were banned and interactions between the army and the Sioux grew worse, culminating in the devastating Indian massacre at Wounded Knee in 1890.

In the mid- to late nineteenth century, two events—the completion of the transcontinental railroad and the gold rushes (spawning their own repertoire of ballads)—established new patterns of immigration and social and musical exchange. Chinese and Japanese workers were brought to the United States in the 1850s to work as miners and later to help complete the railway. With them they brought Asian religious beliefs and practices as well as their own classical, theatrical, dance, and folk music traditions.

Changing Patterns in the Twentieth Century

Perhaps the major factors affecting the growth (and, occasionally, the demise) of musical traditions in the United States during the twentieth century were as follows:

1. The development of mass media and related technologies
2. The commodification of folk, popular, and religious musics
3. New patterns of immigration resulting in the influx of large groups of people, predominantly from Southern Europe, Asia, and the Caribbean, especially between 1880 and 1920, which brought about new governmental policies concerning

immigration, the status of citizens, and the construction of "ethnicity" and "multiculturalism" through revivals and other forms of cultural display

4. The development of an American-defined classical music tradition
5. The rapid growth of institutions that supported the collection, study, and teaching of American-born musics

Certainly the invention of the radio in the late nineteenth century and the rise of recording and broadcasting technology in the late nineteenth and early twentieth centuries, along with the completion of the transcontinental railroads and highways, made it easier for people and their musics to travel and to interact over greater geographic, linguistic, and social distances. Now it was not necessary to make music yourself or even to travel to the local concert hall, church, powwow, or square dance to hear musical performances. By the mid-twentieth century listeners could experience music from all over the world through recordings and even witness its performance at home through the medium of television.

Perhaps one of the most profound social and musical changes that occurred when this new technology was introduced was that—for the first time in human history—musical sound itself (not just its abstraction in the form of notation) could be captured and materialized in the form of a recording. This made it far easier for people to conceptualize music as a "thing" rather than as human social and interactive behavior, for people to "own" music, and, ultimately, for music and its performance to become a commodity within the rapidly changing capitalist economies of the modern world. Of course, this technology also made new sounds possible and far more available to many more people and thus became a source of new creative techniques for composers, performers, and other musicians. At the beginning of the twenty-first century it is possible, through electronic media such as CDs, audio- and videocassettes, computers, and other digital formats, for anyone (with the economic means to do so) to listen to, download, even edit any recorded music from any part of the world.

A major wave of immigration at the end of the nineteenth century through World War I (ca. 1880-1918) also changed the face of the United States. Although smaller communities had emigrated from the seventeenth century onwards, large groups of Ashkenazi Jews from Eastern Europe and Russia, Chinese primarily from Canton, and Muslim Arabs from the Middle East began arriving in large numbers at that time, settling primarily in large urban areas such as New York, Chicago, and Detroit. With them they brought not only their folk and dance traditions but also liturgical, theatrical, and classical musics. Many Jews, for example, who had been cantors or instrumental musicians in Eastern Europe, joined newly established symphony orchestras. Others, such as Irving Berlin (1888-1989) and Al Jolson (1886-1950), quickly found their way to *Tin Pan Alley*, to the burgeoning film industry in Los Angeles, or to the *vaudeville* stage. Still others, such as the Brooklyn-born Richard Tucker (1914-1975), became famous opera stars.

The first half of the twentieth century also saw the development of African American styles, such as gospel music (through the efforts of Thomas A. Dorsey [1899-1993] and others); the blues of Muddy Waters (1918-1953), Bessie Smith (1894-1937), and countless others; the ragtime of Scott Joplin (1868-1917); and early jazz forms performed and recorded by King Oliver (1885-1938) and Jelly Roll Morton (1885-1941) developed in large urban areas such as New Orleans, Chicago, and Kansas City. And, of course, in the white rural South, the trend of "hillbilly," "cowboy," or country music, made popular by the recordings of Jimmy Rodgers (1897-1933) and the prodigious Carter Family, among many others, would spread through radio programs such as *The Grand Ole Opry* and ultimately merge with the blues in midcentury to form early rock and roll.

Hispanic music, too, began to emerge as a growing force, especially in the southern ballad tradition (*corrido*) and in popular dance music as increasing numbers of people from Mexico and the Caribbean entered the United States and began to establish communities. Dances, such as the *habanera, son,* rumba, mambo and cha-cha-chá from Cuba, Puerto Rico, Haiti, and other Caribbean islands, performed in venues such as the Palladium Ballroom in New York City by bandleaders Xavier Cugat (1900-1990) and Tito Puente (1925-2000), among others, became wildly popular in the 1940s and 1950s, especially in large urban areas such as New York and Los Angeles.

The new wave of immigration, as well as newfound economic and social mobility for African Americans, however, soon ushered in a wave of conservatism. Laws and practices such as the quota system (1921-1965) and the "separate but equal" doctrine (established in 1896 to keep public facilities such as schools, restaurants, and so on segregated by race; overthrown in 1954) restricted the immigration and mobility of certain groups—most notably Chinese, Japanese, Jews, African Americans, and American Indians. Discriminatory practices and acts of violence against these and other groups were common. By midcentury, however, American Indian peoples had become citizens through the 1942 Citizens Act.

One outcome of a new ethnic and political consciousness in the United States in the mid-twentieth century was the renewal of interest in roots and in old-time, Old World, or traditional musics. This interest crystallized in the 1950s and 1960s in the form of revivals, festivals, and other forms of cultural display where members of different groups could perform old musics in new settings for new

Tin Pan Alley
The nickname given to the New York neighborhood where most popular music was published and so to the music itself

Vaudeville
Theatrical entertainment of the late nineteenth–early twentieth century, usually featuring a variety of acts, including musicians, dancers, and other entertainers

Ragtime
African American piano music, characterized by a syncopated melody placed against a regular bass

audiences (see Figure 1.4) and where largely white, young, middle-class audiences could come together to participate in group musical experiences, such as hootenannies and sing-ins, where various governmental policies such as school segregation, the Vietnam War, or the authority of their parents could be protested. Folk singers, such as Pete Seeger, Joan Baez, and the Kingston Trio, became not only national singing stars, but also national heroes to a younger generation of idealistic "flower children."

Classical music traditions in the United States during the twentieth century also developed in unique ways. Interested in separating culturally from Europe and in forming authentic American forms and institutions, certain "nativist" composers, such as George Frederick Bristow (1825-1898) and Louis Moreau Gottschalk (1829-1869), among others, were beginning to speak of the need to establish independent musical identities.

By the early twentieth century, U.S. composers such as Edward MacDowell (1860-1908), Henry F. Gilbert (1868-1928), and Arthur Farwell (1872-1952) were consciously incorporating American Indian and African American songs into their classical compositions, one example being Gilbert's symphonic poem, *Dance in Place Congo* (1906-1908), based on African American tunes performed by southern blacks during the Reconstruction period following the Civil War.

Perhaps the best-known U.S. composers in the 1920s and beyond whose works are most clearly defined as American are

Figure 1.4
A typical Appalachian string band, consisting of *(left to right)* banjo, two guitars, fiddle, mandolin, and guitar, performing at the National Folk Festival near Cleveland, Ohio. Photo by Terry Miller, 1984.

Charles Ives (1874-1954), Virgil Thomson (1896-1989), and Aaron Copland (1900-1990), whose works painted musical pictures of an idealized America in midcentury. Examples are Ives's *Three Places in New England* (1904-1914) and the *Concord Sonata* (1911-1915), Thomson's music to accompany the film *The Plow That Broke the Plains* (1936), and Copland's ballets *Appalachian Spring* (1944) and *Billy the Kid* (1938). Truly revolutionary musics, notations, and technologies were to come later, generally between 1950 and 1970, in the new, electronic musics of John Cage (1912-1992), Milton Babbitt (b. 1916), Elliott Carter (b. 1908), and Morton Subotnick (b. 1933).

Finally, as educational institutions began to develop and grow, so too did an interest in music scholarship: the collection and study of the musics not only of the great European masters through their own notations but also of the many groups of people who had migrated to the United States, through ethnographic fieldwork based primarily on the oral/aural tradition. Collectors such as Sir Francis James Child and Cecil Sharp (British American ballads and folk materials), Frances Densmore (American Indian materials), and Alan and John Lomax (early blues, ballads, and much else) contributed greatly to our understanding of music as human social behavior as well as beautifully organized sound.

Some Lingering (and Unifying) Effects of European Social and Musical Hegemony

Despite the rich and ever-increasing variety of social, cultural, and religious groups that have always been a part of the cultural portrait of the United States, European (primarily British) language, political, social, and economic structures have largely prevailed into the twenty-first century. With them have also come European-derived discourses surrounding the dissemination and production of music in the New World.

For example, the primary scholarly divisions and canonization of music into classical, folk, and popular musics that dominated the formal teaching of music in the twentieth century in major institutions such as the Juilliard School and the Peabody and New England Conservatories of Music, as well as major university music schools such as those of Michigan, Illinois, Indiana, California, and Rochester (Eastman School of Music), continue to define music as a largely European-derived, class-based phenomenon. However, as Timothy Rice has pointed out in his introduction to the *Garland Encyclopedia of Music,* Volume 8, *Europe,* these artificial divisions were largely invented as a European nationalist strategy in the nineteenth century to distinguish among the cultivated, literate, and monied elite (classical), the agrarian-based rural peasant class (folk), and the urban working middle class (popular). Such distinctions, still perpetuated today in U.S. educational institutions, as well as in the display bins of the large book and recording retailers, tend to further perpetuate other class-based distinctions such as literacy, education, and economic standing—clearly privileging musical notation over the oral/aural tradition, "formal" music learning over "informal," and the material aspects of music making, such as the use of (ever more complicated and expensive) musical instruments, over the solo voice. European notions of music—and even the word *music* itself—however, initially had little to do with American Indian or early immigrant ideas of sound as ritually and spiritually rooted in social and ceremonial life, or as efficacious in bringing about a successful hunt, the growth of crops, or a healthy baby.

CONSTRUCTING AND PERFORMING MUSICAL IDENTITIES TODAY

Rainbow/Mosaic
The idea that U.S. society is made up of many different cultures that exist side-by-side, maintaining their own identities

Melting pot
The idea that U.S. society is made up of many different cultures that have "melded" together to form a common cultural experience

Various metaphors—"rainbow," "salad bowl," "mosaic"—have frequently been used to describe the ethnic, racial, and social diversity of the United States. Among them, perhaps the term *melting pot,* taken from Israel Zangwill's (1864-1926) 1914 play of the same name about the Jewish immigrant experience, is the most enduring if not the most accurately descriptive of actual life and social interaction. The social history of the United States is, rather, marked as in many modern nation-states by the ebb and flow of nationalism—constructed predominantly during war or difficult economic times, when individual or group identities are minimized and discriminatory practices are more in evidence—and pride in diversity, seen most often during periods of relative economic ease, when specific social identities are valorized, and often commodified, and an interest in civil rights becomes more prominent.

In constructing many national identities over the centuries, the United States has frequently concentrated on, negotiated, or polarized different ethnic/racial groups, especially in relation to the overarching hegemony of primarily western and northern European "mainstream" culture. In certain contexts such as music festivals and contests, this polarization served positively to highlight distinctive features of specific groups that distinguish them within the mosaic or rainbow of North American culture as a whole. More frequently, however, such discriminations have served a negative purpose, resulting in the restriction and subjugation of certain groups, most notably American Indians and African Americans. These ethnic tensions have had a major impact on the growth and development of musical styles, genres, and institutions.

For example, the black/white racial divide has historically created artificial but divisive barriers to musical interaction and to the recognition especially of African American and Hispanic contributions to a complete musical portrait. The lasting effects of slavery in the form of discriminatory practices, such as those preventing black performers from playing in certain contexts, are still, albeit perhaps more subtly, affecting the ways in which black and white performers are received and accepted today, although late-twentieth-century forms such as rock and rap have catapulted many African American performers to international stardom.

Perhaps another way of understanding how music and social identity work together is to see all forms of identity, even nationalistic ones, as constantly in flux and continuously negotiated in the context of everyday and ritual life (see Figure 1.5). For example, although we may conceptualize the United States as a vast array of ethnic, social, religious, and other kinds of groups, members of such groups, in the context of everyday life, freely cross social borders, creating different kinds of cultural boundaries that are far more fluid, permeable, and changeable. Music can be seen as a marker of certain aspects of one's identity at any given moment and is often used by individuals or groups to help define themselves in relation to others and as a means for others to define them as well. A German American brass band marching down the street during Oktoberfest, for example, may be an important marker demonstrating a German community's pride in its ethnicity, but each individual member of this community may be many other things besides a German American (such as a Lutheran, a woman, a white person, and so on). Similarly, many teenagers in the United States enjoy contemporary popular music, and their identity as "punks" or "nerds" can rest on

Figure 1.5
Latin-flavored street music in New York City. Photo by Terry Miller, 1981.

the strength of what band(s) they favor. Years later, those same teenagers may look back on those musical and identity choices as childish or silly.

In his work with different musical communities, Mark Slobin (1993) has suggested that we begin to rethink our notions of musical and social identity as fixed and simplistic, instead seeing them as constructed over a lifetime, based on the interaction and relative importance of several factors, including one's ethnicity, nationality, religion, gender, affinity groups, and many others, elements that carry different weight or meaning at specific times (see also Koskoff 1980; Figures 1.6 and 1.7). And because we are all social and musical beings who interact with others, there is always the potential for identities and musics to intermingle and cross borders, creating new groups, new musics, and new interactions. Thus as we move into the twenty-first century we should not be surprised to see new musical and social forms develop, such as Northwest Indian brass bands, Celtic revivalists who are Jewish (and *klezmer* clarinetists who are not), African American classical composers, and female percussionists, as well as such unlikely musical combinations, such as American Indian gospel, or Christian rock, because these combinations are natural within the rich and complex contexts of social and musical plurality that have always and continue to define the United States today.

REVIEW

Important Terms and People to Know

French and Indian War
Ghost Dance
Handsome Lake
heterophonic
monophonic
"nativist" composers
potlatch
revivals
social dance song
social structure
The Melting Pot
vocable
Wounded Knee

Some Review Questions

1. What are some of the general factors that have influenced the creation, performance and meanings of music in the United States?

Figures 1.6 and 1.7
Young Cambodian girls and boys sing and dance at the National Heritage Festival, Washington, D.C., 1980. Social identities such as gender and age are frequently performed through music and dance. The girls in Figure 1.6 use specific movements and gestures that define them as young (probably unmarried), graceful, and refined women, while the boys in Figure 1.7 perform using the single-headed *skor chhaiyaim* drums and masks, denoting their status within Cambodian culture as young and powerful men. Photos by Terry Miller.

2. Compare and contrast some of the ideas that American Indians and Europeans held about music and its uses at the time of first contact.
3. What were some musical practices banned or vilified by Europeans in the United States? Why?
4. What major factors promoted the growth of musical traditions in the nineteenth century?
5. How did the invention of the radio and other recording and broadcasting devices forever alter the dissemination of musical traditions and the understanding of music itself?
6. What did American classical composers do to try to forge an American musical identity in the twentieth century? Who was the most successful?
7. What is the legacy of slavery and other discriminatory practices on the ways in which music developed in the United States since the end of the Civil War (1865)?
8. How and why is music such a powerful marker of individual and social identity in the United States?

Projects

Each of these could be used for either a class presentation or a written assignment:

1. Interview the oldest member of your family, perhaps one who came from another country, and find out what kinds of music he or she enjoyed as a child.
2. Look through your local phone book and find the listing of places of worship in your town or city. Go visit a church, temple, mosque, etc. and see what happens musically.
3. Find an "ethnic" restaurant in your town or city and while you are enjoying a meal there, listen to the music that is playing in the background. Is it from the same social, ethnic, cultural group of the people who own the restaurant? If so, talk to the owner about this music, where it comes from, why it's important, etc., or do some research on it in the library.
4. Go to your local book or record store and explore the bins containing American Music. How are they organized? How are they prioritized? How are they marketed?

CHAPTER 2

Institutions and Processes Affecting Music in the United States

Barry Bergey, Anthony Seeger, David Sanjek, Charlotte J. Frisbie, Kai Fikentscher, and Robert Fink

The many musics of the United States express the beliefs and values of a wide variety of individuals and communities. To understand the totality of music in the United States today, we must look beyond the musics themselves to a broader picture of the contexts in which these musics are made and understood. These include political and economic factors such as governmental and other public policies toward music, technologies surrounding music production, and the marketing of music today. Specific musical genres and ethnographic scenes are presented as Snapshots in this chapter and throughout the rest of the book as examples of these concepts.

GOVERNMENT AND PUBLIC POLICY

The impact of public policy on music cannot easily be untangled from a general consideration of the historical relationship between government and the arts. Not until after World War II was there a serious attempt on the part of the government to create a federal arts council. The National Endowment for the Arts was not established until 1965, and its creation reflected a decentralized approach to public support for the arts. Its function was not to create or enact a public arts policy, such as a ministry of culture might, but to fund artistic organizations and artistic activity at arm's length through an independent, peer-panel system. The level of support for this arts agency remains minuscule: less than 1/100th of 1% of the federal budget.

Although public policy on the arts has been notable more for its absence than its presence, other governmental instruments—including cultural preservation projects, work relief endeavors, foreign policy and exchange programs, governmental arts centers, and national artistic ensembles—have affected artists. Indirect aspects of policy, such as regulations in the form of tax laws, broadcast and Internet restrictions, postal rates, and copyright legislation, also apply. Although the public support of music reflects no single coherent cultural strategy, a historical survey reveals three areas of governmental involvement: regulation, conservation, and presentation.

Regulation of the Arts

Governmental involvement with the arts in the United States took its earliest form as legislation establishing the right of private ownership of artistic products and ideas.

Copyright

Copyright
The protection of an individual's intellectual or creative property for a period of time, defining the rights for its dissemination through various media as well as proscribing penalties for those who infringe on an individual's rights

In the United States *copyright* was established by the Constitution (framed in 1787, effective March 4, 1789); Article One, Section Eight granted Congress the legislative power to "promote the Progress of Science and useful Arts, by securing for limited Times to Authors and Inventors the exclusive Right to their respective Writings and Discoveries."

An 1870 statute mandated the Library of Congress as the sole repository for copyright materials, and all previously accumulated registrations and deposits were transferred there. Deposited materials were increasingly utilized as part of the library's general collection. In 1972 a revision of the copyright law expanded coverage to include recorded materials. As a result, the library's Recorded Sound Division, established in 1939, grew exponentially. By 1996, approximately two million recordings had gone on deposit in the newly named Motion Picture, Broadcasting, and Recorded Sound Division. Currently, copyright provides for the protection of intellectual or creative property, extending to 70 years beyond the life of the creator. In the case of music, it addresses the right to copy, print, sell, arrange, record, or publicly perform a work. Infringement of copyright can be penalized by injunction, exacting financial remuneration for the copyright owner, fines, and in some cases imprisonment. Copyright serves political and social systems, based on individual ownership and an artistic marketplace, but does not sufficiently address the concept of collective ownership. The Universal Copyright Convention (UNESCO Convention), concluded at Geneva in 1952 and later revised, provides the basis for international copyright agreements.

The age of the Internet and digital transmission of materials has inspired governments to extend copyright protection. In December

1996, representatives of 160 countries met in Geneva and reached agreement on treaties affecting copyright issues. Among other provisions, these treaties would protect owners from computer-generated copies of musical recordings from the Internet. (It is still necessary for these treaties to be ratified by legislative bodies of the various countries.) In 1998 World Intellectual Property Organization (WIPO) also initiated a process of identifying and examining the intellectual property needs of traditional knowledge holders, including their traditional cultural expressions. Responding to concerns about digital replication, the U.S. Congress also passed the Digital Millennium Act in 1998, extending copyright coverage to the digital era, making it illegal to bypass anticopying measures.

Conservation of the Arts

Copyright laws in the United States in effect created the first significant repositories of musical materials. However, technologies new in the nineteenth century, combined with a growing interest in the study of culture, led to an era of documentation of musical performance, often supported by government in the name of preserving the cultural patrimony.

American Indians

Anthropologists and folklorists in the 1890s were beginning to explore the importance of music in human culture. The invention of the cylinder phonograph and its commercial availability in 1889 opened up the possibility of documenting and reproducing musical performances for the purpose of study and entertainment. (For more on recording technology, see below.) Anthropologist Jesse Walter Fewkes, field-testing a recording device on a visit to the Passamaquoddy Indians of Maine in March 1890, made the first recording of Native American music. His interest was in documentation "as a means of preserving the songs and tales of races which are fast becoming extinct" (Fewkes 1890:257)

The earliest governmental documentation of American Indians came about as an offshoot of geological and geographic surveys. The Smithsonian Institution's Bureau of Ethnology was established in 1879 for this purpose. However, the staff of the bureau was small, and much work was done by unsalaried consultants, many of whom were self-educated. Alice Cunningham Fletcher, a pioneer student of Indian music, studied a variety of tribes of the Great Plains, collaborating with Francis La Flesche, son of an Omaha chief (Figure 2.1).

Frances Densmore, inspired by Fletcher, became the most prolific documenter of Native American music of the early twentieth century. Between 1907 and 1941 she recorded nearly 2,000 cylinders of music from 37 cultures, and wrote nearly a dozen monographs and numerous articles on Indian music. Reared in Red Wing,

Figure 2.1
The Indian Bear Dance. Many Americans learned about Native American culture by means of Currier and Ives lithography such as this.

Minnesota, and trained as a classical pianist, Densmore believed that the music she collected could become a basis for new American compositions. Her work resulted in significant publications on Chippewa and Teton Sioux music.

The implications of recording and preserving Native American musics, especially by non-Natives, began to come to light in the mid-twentieth century when many Native American groups began to seek ways to recover important cultural artifacts. Snapshot 2.1 describes an important court case concerning the repatriation of a medicine bundle, an important sacred item used in the performance of the Navajo Nightway Ceremony. This case centers on who may own, sell, or distribute Native artifacts and for what purpose, and was the first jury trial held under the criminal code of the Native American Graves Protection and Repatriation Act (NAGPRA) of 1990. This case illustrates the role of government in providing protection for "objects of cultural patrimony," which often include music, musical instruments, and other materials central to musical performance.

Snapshot 2.1: A Navajo Medicine Bundle Is Repatriated

The Native American Graves Protection and Repatriation Act was enacted in 1990 to achieve two objectives: to protect Native American human remains, funerary objects, sacred objects, and objects of cultural patrimony presently on federal or tribal lands; and to repatriate Native American human remains, associated funerary objects, sacred objects, and objects of cultural patrimony currently held or controlled by federal agencies and museums. The law and subsequent regulations provide methods for identifying objects, determining rights of descendants, and retrieving and repatriating that property to Native Americans. As such, it can be viewed as human rights legislation.

In 1996, a court case in New Mexico tested the legal protection afforded by NAGPRA to "objects of cultural patrimony" or items having ongoing historical, cultural, or traditional importance central to the Native groups covered by the law. These cultural items are of such importance that they may *not* be alienated, appropriated, or conveyed by any individual group member. The test case, *Richard N. Corrow v. United States of America* (Frisbie 1987, 1993), was the first jury trial in the nation under the criminal provisions of NAGPRA. The combined efforts of the FBI, the National Park Service, the U.S. Fish and Wildlife Service, and the Bureau of Indian Affairs resulted in the arrest of Richard Nelson Corrow, age 54, for trafficking in protected cultural items and for possessing bird feathers protected by the Migratory Bird Treaty Act.

Briefly, the case focused on Ray Winnie, a well-known Navajo ceremonial practitioner (medicine man, chanter, or *hataali*), who lived in Lukachukai, Arizona. Winnie died in 1991 without making provisions for the transmission/disposition of the *jish* (or medicine bundle) he used when performing the *Nightway*, one of the major nine-night sacred ceremonials during which masked deities—the *Yé'ii*[s] or *Yeibichei*—may appear. *Jish* are considered to be sacred and alive by Navajos. As comparable to "living gods," they require appropriate care at all times, whether in use in ritual settings or in storage. While a number of options exist among Navajos for the acquisition, transmission, and disposition of *jish*, it is understood that medicine bundles should not be sold to non-Navajos involved in making a profit by buying and selling "esoteric art" in the international marketplace. Instead, the sacred, living medicine bundles belong in the hands of qualified Navajos who live within the boundaries of the four sacred mountains.

Corrow, owner of Artifacts Display Stands in Scottsdale, Arizona, and a buyer/seller of Navajo religious items, traveled to Lukachukai, Arizona, after Winnie's death and visited his 81-year-old widow, Fannie, in her hogan in the presence of her granddaughter and other family members. After several visits, Fannie showed Corrow some of her husband's ceremonial equipment, among which was the Nightway *jish*, which included twenty-two ceremonial masks. Corrow said he wanted to buy the *jish* and some other items in order to give them to a younger Navajo man in Utah, who was learning the Nightway. After negotiation, in August 1993 Corrow paid $10,000 to Fannie Winnie for the Nightway *jish*, five headdresses, and other items.

In November 1994 the owners of East-West Trading Company in Santa Fe contacted Corrow, saying they had a wealthy Chicago surgeon interested in buying a set of Nightway masks. The alleged

Jish
medicine bundle
Nightway
One of the Navajo's major nine-night sacred ceremonials
Yé'ii[s]
Supernatural beings, giants
Yeibichei
God impersonators

buyer was James Tanner, who in reality was an undercover agent for the National Park Service who was helping in the federal investigation of questionable activities at the East-West gallery. Photographs of Corrow's recent purchase revealed eagle and owl feathers on several of the ceremonial items. Agent Tanner agreed to pay $70,000 for the Nightway *jish,* with $50,000 to go to Corrow and the remainder to the store's co-owners. After Corrow arrived in Santa Fe with two suitcases and one cardboard box on December 9, 1994, he was apprehended and charged with trafficking in Native American cultural items and selling protected bird feathers. The store's owners were also apprehended for making an illegal sale involving feathers of protected birds.

The trial in Albuquerque's U.S. District Court of New Mexico began with pretrial hearings on April 11, 15, and 19; the jury trial followed from April 22 through 25. Testimony focused on the cultural patrimony status of the Nightway *jish* and other aspects of Navajo religion and traditional law, especially the diversity of Navajo options for transmission and disposition of medicine bundles. Paula Burnett, assistant U.S. attorney, led the prosecution, and Alonzo J. Padilla, the defense; Judge James A. Parker presided. Among the government witnesses, in addition to federal agents involved in investigative aspects of the case, were Alfred Yazzie, a well-respected Nightway chanter who also works for the Navajo Nation Historic Preservation Office; Harry Walters, Navajo anthropologist and director of the Ned Hatathli Cultural Center Museum at Diné College; and myself. The defense called Fannie Winnie and some members of her family, as well as two singers, Jackson Gillis and Billy Yellow, from Monument Valley, and a younger Navajo, Harrison Begay, said to be learning the Nightway. The jury found Corrow guilty of trafficking in objects of cultural patrimony and of possessing protected feathers. At his hearing on July 2, in accordance with penalties facing first-time NAGPRA offenders, he was sentenced to two concurrent five-year probationary terms and 100 hours of community service to benefit the Navajo Nation.

On September 26, 1996, the Nightway medicine bundle was repatriated, first through a transfer ceremony in the U.S. District Attorney's Office in Albuquerque. After the transfer, the medicine bundle traveled back to Blue Canyon, Arizona, where it went through an all-night cleansing and welcoming home ceremony on September 26 and 27 before being returned to Wilbert Williams of Deer Springs, the maternal grandson of the chanter who had first acquired the bundle. Finally, after needed repairs, the *jish* was put back into use during a nine-night Nightway ceremonial in Blue Gap, October 4 through 11, the final phase of repatriating this particular medicine bundle.

On October 21, Corrow appealed his conviction to the U.S. Court of Appeals, Tenth Circuit, Denver; his appeal was accompanied by the brief from the Antique Tribal Art Dealers Association. The Denver Court upheld the District Court's decisions (Case No. 96-2185, published July 11, 1997). On December 31, 1997, Corrow filed another appeal, this time with the U.S. Supreme Court. On February 23, 1998, that court, without comment, denied his request, thus finally bringing this case to an end.

Charlotte J. Frisbie

Non-Native Music

Documentation of musics other than those considered "aboriginal" was somewhat slower to occur. The accumulation of musical items at the Library of Congress as a result of the copyright law necessitated the accommodation of physical and bureaucratic structures for musical materials, including the establishment of a separate music section in 1897. No less important in the library's early history was the vision of such leaders as Herbert Putnam, Librarian of Congress from 1899 to 1930, and Oscar Sonneck, hired to be the chief of the Music Division in 1902.

The Archive of American Folk-Song was established in 1928, Robert Winslow Gordon, a scholar of folklore, a folk song collector, and a freelance writer, was named director. During his tenure he collected music in a number of states, and he continually experimented with new technological advances in recording equipment. In 1931 the distinguished folk song collector John A. Lomax contacted the Library of Congress to inquire about borrowing recording equipment to record African American work songs in Texas prisons. Lomax had made some of the earliest English-language American cylinder recordings of music when recording cowboy songs between 1906 and 1910 for his publication *Cowboy Songs and Other Frontier Ballads* (1910), the first collection of American folk songs with both printed texts and music. From the Archive of Folk-Song in 1933, John Lomax, and his son Alan (see Figure 2.2), received a shipment of equipment, first to record on cylinders and then on disks. The Lomaxes collected material for the Archive and for their book *American Ballads and Folk Songs* (1934). During the Depression years, material collected through WPA and other work projects also found their way into the Archive, including the fruits of a collecting expedition in the South by Herbert Halpert conducted for the WPA Federal Theater Project in 1939.

The Recording Laboratory was created in 1940 to accommodate the Archive's recording and duplicating ventures, plus commercial recordings, radio recordings, electrical transcriptions, and WPA-generated recordings. It began to play a more active role in musical programs at the library, including the release of a series of albums,

Figure 2.2
Alan Lomax performing at the Asheville Mountain Music Festival, c. 1940. The Lomax Collection, Library of Congress

Folk Music of the United States. In succeeding years there was a decline of staff fieldwork, but there was an increase in acquisitions through duplication, gifts, purchases, and transfers from other federal agencies. The recording series and documentation-equipment loan program continues today.

In 1976 the American Folklife Preservation Act established the American Folklife Center at the Library of Congress with a mandate to preserve and present American folklife. This legislation provided the first official definition of folklife: "The traditional expressive culture shared within the various groups in the United States: familial, ethnic, occupational, religious, regional" (Loomis 1983:26). The Archive of American Folk-Song, renamed Archive of Folk Culture in 1981, became part of the American Folklife Center, which initiated

Folklife
The traditional expressive culture shared within the various groups in the United States: familial, ethnic, occupational, religious, regional

several broad-based fieldwork projects, most of them documenting music as one facet of the project.

The Federal Cylinder Project, initiated by the Center in 1979, was intended to preserve and disseminate earlier ethnographic recordings, many of them made under the auspices of the Bureau of Ethnology. Tribal groups have benefited from the repatriation of rare and in some cases forgotten musical repertoires inscribed on wax. The Archive of Folk Culture has holdings that include 53,000 sound recordings, 1,250,000 manuscripts, 220,000 photographs, 450 moving-image materials, and 26,000 printed items (Jabbour 1996b).

The Music Division of the Library of Congress, having actively solicited composers' manuscripts, maintains an extensive collection of European and American works. Special private trust funds, the first of their kind in the federal government, have allowed the library to purchase important work, acquire five Stradivarius instruments, maintain resident chamber ensembles (such as the Juilliard Quartet), sponsor ongoing musical programs, and commission new works (including Aaron Copland's *Appalachian Spring*). The Music Division contains over eight million items, with strong collections of chamber music, opera, popular music, and American musical theater.

Presentation of the Arts

Direct federal support of artists and artistic presentations in any significant way is a development of the late twentieth century. The first governmental support of musicians actually occurred through the subsidy of military bands. The U.S. Marine Band, organized in 1798 and conducted by John Philip Sousa from 1880 to 1892, predated by two years the government's move to the District of Columbia (Figure 2.3).

Direct federal support of the arts advanced like the mythical slow train through Arkansas: Riders on this train were said to comment that the train would have to speed up to stop. George Washington remarked that "the arts and sciences are essential to the prosperity of the state and to the ornament and happiness of human life," but Senator Jacob Javits, during hearings in 1965, the year of the creation of the National Endowment for the Arts, noted: "Federal concern with the arts goes back a very long way—way back to George Washington's time. We have not done too much about it" (Mankin 1976:62). The birth of an arts-funding agency within the U.S. government culminated a long period of gestation marked by debate about the government's proper role with regard to the arts.

The National Endowments for the Arts and Humanities

On September 29, 1965, President Lyndon Johnson signed a bill creating the National Endowments for the Arts and Humanities. The

Figure 2.3
John Philip Sousa,
c. 1900. Courtesy:
University of Illinois
Archives, RS 12/9/54,
http://door.library.uiuc
.edu/sousa/online.htm

National Endowment for the Arts (NEA) budget of 1966 was approximately $2.5 million. (As a comparison, in the same year, the Ford Foundation, a private "charitable" trust, announced it would disburse $85 million for symphony orchestras alone.) The NEA was set up to allocate money by artistic discipline in the form of matching grants to nonprofit organizations and individuals using a peer-panel system of review. The budget of the National Endowment for the Arts during the tenure of its second chairman, Nancy Hanks (1969-1977), increased tenfold. From 1980 until 1996, the NEA budget varied between $150 and $174 million. By 1974 the NEA Music Program had created a subcategory, Jazz/Folk/Ethnic Music, and in 1976 Jazz and Folk Music were split into separate categories. Although allocated a small budget, the Folk Arts Program under Bess Lomax Hawes, daughter of John A. Lomax, dispensed a powerful and far-reaching philosophy of cultural equity, which combined elements of conservation and presentation. Hawes has said, "The folk arts need what the fine arts need: chances to be heard and seen, a reasonable financial return for effort, a knowledgeable and informed audience, an opportunity to reach children and young people, tough aesthetic criticism, respectful attention to matters of documentation and history" (1985) A policy of funding was developed to support the traditional and folk arts of small cultural communities. In addition to supporting festivals, workshops, tours, and documentation of traditional artists, the Folk Arts Program developed the National Heritage Fellowships to honor master traditional artists and initiated artistic apprenticeships to aid in the perpetuation and refinement of endangered artistic skills.

Nationally subsidized radio also plays a minor role in the support of music. The federally appropriated budget for the Corporation for Public Broadcasting, a conduit for federal funds to nonprofit radio

Music Cultures in the United States

and television stations, was $340 million for 2001. While National Public Radio (NPR) has increased its listenership, the emphasis in programming has been on news and public affairs. The new and expanded audience for public radio stations seems to exhibit a greater eclecticism when it comes to musical taste, and individual stations exercise great independence in their core programming. Listeners—once patrons of Western classical music—no longer accord this music a privileged position; instead, they seek varied programming, including folk, jazz, rock, world, country, bluegrass, and new age styles.

The Smithsonian Institution

Although George Washington had in his farewell address of 1796 recommended the establishment of a national institution of learning, it was not until the 1830s that federal plans for such an entity took shape. With a bequest of £104,960 (then worth $508,318.46) from James Smithson, the Smithsonian Institution was founded in 1846. It was the original home of the Bureau of American Ethnology. Technically a public-private hybrid, it receives about 85 percent of its funding from the government.

Founded in 1967, the Smithsonian Folklife Festival presents traditional artists performing, demonstrating, and interpreting their work on the National Mall. The Bicentennial celebration of 1976 included a summer-long folklife festival featuring music, craft, and foodways artists from across the United States, as well as around the globe. Today the annual festival attracts an average of a million attendees to this two-week event.

In 1977 a separate Office of Folklife Programs was established at the Smithsonian. This office, later renamed the Center for Folklife Programs and Cultural Heritage, has conducted field research and documentation, published books and audiovisual materials, and established an internal archive. In 1987 the Smithsonian acquired the Folkways Records catalogue and archive of Folkways's founder Moses Asch, including more than 2,000 recordings of traditional musicians and speech. The Smithsonian Folkways label continues to release new recordings, some in conjunction with festival programs, focusing largely on traditional folk music.

The Smithsonian's Division of Performing Arts, continuing independently, developed programs in jazz, chamber music, country music, American musical theater, and African American expressive culture. In addition to conferences and resident ensembles of jazz and chamber music, this division released significant series of historic recordings. In 1983 it was disbanded, but aspects of its program continue. Also, the Division of Musical Instruments, located within the National Museum of American History, has one of the largest collections of musical instruments in the world.

Public Policy at the Turn of the Twenty-First Century

The 1990s ushered in a period of reexamination and debate with regard to public policy and the arts. Court cases involving recorded samples and control of previously recorded material called into question the concept of individual ownership and copyright. Issues regarding individual ownership of musical content or style and the appropriation of musical traditions of other cultures by pop musicians were debated. Some writers opposed the writing, recording, mechanical reproduction, and copyrighting of music as the ultimate agents of commodification and reification of culture, while lawmakers attempted to broaden copyright protection to include new technologies such as the Internet. A few legislators, however, challenged the assumption that taxpayers should support the arts, however parsimoniously. With a new political dynamic in the U.S. Congress, the 1996 budget for the NEA was reduced by 40 percent to $99 million (38 cents per citizen), and the staff was reduced by almost half.

Just as issues related to nationalistic self-identity and sovereignty provided some of the impetus for the creation of policies on the arts, political realignments called into question the desirability of using culture as a diplomatic tool. The dismantling of the Arts America Program of the United States Information Agency in 1996 virtually ended any serious government sponsorship of musical groups or arts programs abroad.

However, there is a renewed interest in issues related to the role of arts in education. The Goals 2000: Educate America Act did not include the arts as a core subject when standards were originally conceived in 1989. The move toward establishing educational standards and testing for them is still vigorously debated, but the Music Educators' National Conference has been very active in developing and striving to implement standards in music. Music is now one of four arts disciplines described in *National Standards for Arts Education: What Every Young American Should Know* (1994).

Barry Bergey

TECHNOLOGY, MEDIA, AND MUSIC

The sounds of music cannot be separated from the technology involved in their conception, performance, transmission, and audience reception, because the technology is an integral part of the sounds themselves. By "technology," I mean a manner of accomplishing a task, especially using technical processes, methods, or knowledge.

With the exception of the unamplified human voice, unaccompanied or accompanied by naturally occurring objects such as stones or sticks used as musical instruments, some technology is involved in the production of all music. Virtually every aspect of the music of

America has been affected by technological changes during the past 500 years.

In the precolonial period, prior to 1492, North American Indians employed a variety of technologies in the manufacture of musical instruments. The acoustic knowledge and skill used to produce even an apparently simple rattle, flute, or drum should not be underestimated, even though the production may require few implements and no machines. Many decisions made in the manufacture of a traditional instrument are based on past experience and experimentation. Technology need not be complex to have a profound influence on musical sounds.

During the first 300 years after 1492, most parts of North America were colonies of European powers. Their colonial status affected both their technology and musical styles. Colonialism is partly characterized by the dominant relationship between the colonial power and its subject colonies in which the colonies provide raw materials to the mother country and purchase finished products from it. Most colonies were prohibited by law from a number of manufacturing activities. Their economic dependency was often paralleled by a cultural dependency. The musical dependency of North America on Europe (especially England, France, and Spain) continued even after the United States became independent in the eighteenth century. Until the mid-nineteenth century, most of the musical genres and performance styles of the wealthy were imported from, or directly imitative of, the mother countries. The less wealthy rural dwellers often passed their traditions within the community, made their own instruments out of materials at hand, and transmitted their music without music publishers or imported instruments.

Enslaved Africans and American Indians often continued to practice earlier musical traditions on a reduced scale in the framework of large and terrible changes in their lives and in the face of religious and secular influences from European settlers, missionaries, and military forces. Because of regional isolation, personal preference, and artistic innovation, the musical instruments of rural North America varied widely from place to place and instrument maker to instrument maker.

Instruments

Some European immigrants to North America brought with them skills with which they set up industries in the United States. For example, makers of keyboard instruments came as early as the late 1700s, but they did not begin to transform the existing European technology until the 1830s. The establishment of the United States as a nation, with copyright and patents stipulated in its Constitution, was an important factor in the independent development of musical technology within that country.

With the nineteenth century came the industrialization and standardization of many musical instruments and the replacement of certain ensembles by new ones. The history of the piano is especially significant because of the large numbers manufactured and sold, the stimulus piano sales gave to the sheet music publishing industry, and the role it has long played in music education. Encouraged to innovate by the system of patents and the possibility of profits, nineteenth-century U.S. innovations in piano technology (the one-piece metal frame being probably the most important) transformed the industry from one based in England and France to one based in the United States, just as much of manufacture of keyboards (acoustic and electronic) in the late twentieth century would move the center of production to Asia.

The piano was capable of playing many genres, from European classical music to locally popular barroom dance music, and it was found in many middle-class homes as well as in churches, brothels, bars, and other venues in which musical performance was a significant feature (but not necessarily the entire focus) of the events taking place. The automatic, or player, piano, which played the encoded contents (long rolls of perforated paper or cardboard), was one of the earliest and most accurate sound recording devices developed in the nineteenth century. The development of the piano has acoustic, technical, and social components, all of which influence the use of the instrument today.

Electric amplifiers and loudspeakers, which improved rapidly after World War II, developed along with new instruments. Important among these were the electric guitar and the electric keyboard. The electric guitar was more than an amplified guitar; its design permitted a number of performance styles that were not previously possible. In addition to the amplification of the strings themselves, the electronic signals produced by the instrument could be modified in a number of ways that added to its flexibility. The electronic keyboard is also capable of many sounds impossible to produce on the instrument from which it evolved.

The digitalization of sound waves sparked another wave of instrument invention that transformed the conceptualization, performance, and analysis of music. The music instrument digital interface (MIDI) synthesizer permitted musicians to compose on the keyboard with virtually unlimited sonic capabilities, play back their compositions, and even print certain kinds of scores. And more recently, digitization has modified the conceptualization of both composers and producers, the production of the sounds, some performance spaces, and some of the media through which music can be transferred—increasingly over telephone lines on the Internet. It has also led to lawsuits (particularly in the area of digital quotation or sampling in some genres) and to the redefinition of intellectual property in music and other domains.

Sound Carriers and Dissemination

For our purposes, "dissemination" means simply how the sounds get from the performer(s) to the audience(s). It is easy to contrast the transmission of a musical piece by oral/aural face-to-face transmission with the impersonality and wide scope of the Internet, but transmission needs to be considered as a continuum in which many of its forms may be used at the same time by different members of a community. Technology may add new dimensions and possibilities, but older forms often continue, albeit at a reduced rate: children still teach their playmates clapping rhythms in schoolyards, even as they learn other music from books prepared by music publishers and taught in school music classes, or from audio recordings, radio, television, and the Internet. Innovations do not necessarily replace earlier traditions; they are used to create new ones.

> **Dissemination**
> The means of transmitting a musical performance from its creator(s) to an audience

Sound Recording Before the Twentieth Century

The most significant technological development in North American music was certainly the invention of the audio recorder, with its subsequent evolution through a number of different technologies to the compact disc (CD) and Internet. The history of the development of recorded sound, from its initial invention toward the end of the nineteenth century to its ubiquitous presence at the start of the twenty-first century, is an important area for ethnomusicological and historical research on the impact of technology on music specifically and on culture in general.

To summarize a complex history, in 1877 Thomas Edison created a recording device consisting of a rotating tinfoil cylinder into which he sang "Mary Had a Little Lamb"; he then played it back. Edison considered his invention of principal interest to businesses: for dictating letters, recording important events (such as deathbed statements), and entertainment. He did not, at the outset, consider prerecorded music to be a particularly important use of the machine; other inventors, however, quickly saw the potential of prerecorded entertainment. Early audio recordings were not all of music. Popular subjects included vaudeville recitations, speeches, humor, and other nonmusical items. As a disk might cost as much as a worker's weekly wage, early recordings were often used in slot machines. The first musical star with a "big hit" was Enrico Caruso (1873-1921), whose recordings were the first to sell over a million copies in the twentieth century.

The Far-Reaching Influence of Recorded Sound

The recording industry developed steadily with the help of a number of technological innovations, including electric (rather than direct) recording, the standardized 78-rpm disk, the 45-rpm single, the 33⅓-rpm long-playing record, the audiocassette, and the compact disc (see more on the music industry below). By the 1950s the impact of recorded sound on all aspects of music—musicians, composers, performers, performance spaces, and audiences—was tremendous. Some analysts have argued that recordings enabled people to hear musical sounds in entirely new ways and created new attitudes toward performances of all kinds.

The invention of recording technology certainly stimulated the comparative study of music and the development of ethnomusicology. Most musicology, to the extent that it existed, was based on the study of written documents. Only with the invention of the cylinder recorder was it possible to reliably fix and then study sounds that had no scores. Only when sound was a transcribable onto physical objects could it become part of museum collections and the subject of reanalysis and dissemination.

The new recording technology not only created new possibilities, it imposed certain limitations. Early cylinder and disk recorders had a great impact on performers and their musical performances (see Figure 2.4). Both the cylinder and Emile Berliner's disks shared a common feature: They had limited fidelity and could only play three to five minutes of music at a time. Musicians therefore had to distill their performances into that limited period. Thus dance tunes that might have been played for fifteen minutes and long ballads that might have gone on for more than ten minutes were reduced to

Figure 2.4
Edison cylinders, c. 1900. Photo courtesy Frank Hoffmann

Music Cultures in the United States

about three minutes. Until the development of the long-playing (LP) record, the medium served popular music better than longer classical pieces. A number of other performance traits can be traced to the early history of recording technology.

The widespread adoption of recorded sound had a profound influence on the lives of performers. At the same time as they opened new opportunities for some musicians, recordings certainly had a negative effect on others. Many performers began to make their living as studio musicians, while others were put out of work by the replacement of live performers with jukeboxes and other playback devices.

Recorded sound had a huge impact on audiences as well as on musicians and the academic study of music. North Americans soon became accustomed to listening to music from a machine, far from the performers. Performances became "mediated" in the sense that there was an intermediate stage between their production and the audience's hearing them, and also objectified and subject to repeated listening, collection, sale, archiving, rediscovery, and reissues.

Radio, "Talking Pictures," and Television

The invention of wireless transmission was transformed into full-blown commercial radio broadcasting in the 1920s, with the some of the earliest stations established in that decade. Like early recordings, early radio programming was quite varied, but it quickly focused more and more on music. Radio stations presented a variety of musical forms, and as early as 1922 country or "hillbilly" music was featured on a number of stations. Nashville's WSM's *Barn Dance* began in 1925 and later achieved international renown as the *Grand Ole Opry*. Because the programming was free, many people first heard traditions they came to enjoy and even to perform on radio broadcasts. By the late 1930s, the majority of radio programming consisted of popular and "light" music.

The trio of radio, audio recordings, and music publishing soon became closely linked, as music publishers, record companies, and artists realized the promotional value of radio play. What people heard on the radio they often wanted to buy for their home listening. The different parts of the entertainment industry did not agree, however, on the distribution of radio income to artists and music publishers. The history of radio reveals repeated conflicts between the networks and the music publishers. In the United States, regulation by the Federal Communications Commission (FCC) has also played an important role in shaping music through a number of its rulings on programming.

Radio had some unintended influences on vocal performance style, for example, the development of "crooning." Radio engineers found it easier to amplify a soft voice than to modify a loud one, and so a combination of microphone technology and radio practice strongly influenced the growth of the soft-voiced crooning style by vocalists from the 1920s on. Musicians learned to exploit the possibilities of evolving microphone, radio, and loudspeaker technology as the century wore on, but they may have been encouraged to do so by technicians and the limitations of their equipment.

In addition to inventing the cylinder recorder, Thomas Edison developed a machine that combined sound and moving visual images at the end of the nineteenth century. But it was not until the 1930s that cinema films with sound tracks became commonplace. Film music soon became an important part of the production, both as background sound and as part of the feature itself. Film sound tracks, issued on recordings and for a while also in the form of sheet music, were very popular from the beginning and continued to be so throughout the century.

Although invented in the 1920s, television became a mass medium only in the 1950s, a time of tremendous expansion of television into homes and its appropriation of the lion's share of the audience during the evening hours. Although music never became the central focus of television as it had been for radio, some influential shows, such as the *Ed Sullivan Show*, introduced new artists (Elvis Presley, the Beatles, and others) to large audiences. Cable television—whose signals are distributed by cable rather than transmitted through the air—and home satellite dish reception were other technological breakthroughs that permitted programmers and viewers access to a larger number of channels. This opened the door for more varied programming and for the real emergence of television as a music medium.

The use of television as an independent musical medium—one in which the visual aspects of the performance have a compositional and interpretative significance of their own—began with MTV (Music Television), distributed by cable television, and spread to other cable channels. MTV went far beyond the televised performances that typified earlier televised music events and began to present elaborate visual dramas that depicted the content or the mood of the song rather than just the images of the performing musicians. Like other innovations before it, MTV inspired some performers and producers and influenced some audiences to imagine music in a new way, and video became a staple of the popular music industry.

Computers and Music

In the 1980s the use of home computers became widespread. At first the technical limitations of computers prevented most of them from being very useful for the production or dissemination of music. By the 1990s, however, various computer formats had emerged that suggested some larger long-term changes in the way musical sounds are produced, assembled, and distributed. One of the innovations was the MIDI, which primarily influenced the conceptualization and performance of music. Another was the compact disc read-only memory (CD-ROM), which enabled programmers to present music, text, photographs, and moving images on a single computer disc. The emergence of the World Wide Web (WWW) on the Internet enabled computer users to access sound, photographs, and moving images, download them, and manipulate them in a variety of ways. Distributing sounds through the Internet is considerably faster than mailing a compact disc to a store to sell to a consumer, and every indication is that the dissemination of music will be once again transformed by a technological innovation. Yet all of these developments have posed new problems for the existing music industry, which continues to be transformed by technology. (For more on the music industry, see below.)

From the first manufacture of instruments to the use of computers for the production and dissemination of musical sound and images, technology has been an intimate part of musical conceptualization, performance, and evaluation. Because of this, technology employed in musical performances must be considered as carefully as the structures of the sounds themselves in order to understand what music is today, how it became what it is, and where it might be taken in the future.

Snapshot 2.2 discusses the development of two related American musical genres, disco and house music, each of which is highly dependent on technology, especially that which focuses on the production processes of music. In these genres, the technology itself, and the people who control it, become the major performers and artists.

Snapshot 2.2: Disco and House Music

In contrast to much rock and pop music, in which aspects of musicianship in performance are central and generally given priority, disco and postdisco dance music highlight the production process itself—exemplified in the roles of producers, recording engineers, and disc jockeys. In contrast to the world of pop music (and, to an extent, of hip-hop), the central performers are the disc jockey and the dancers rather than the singers and musicians. In this performance environment, music is as physical as it is audible, involving, in the deejay booth, twin turntables, a mixer, and vinyl records, and on the dance floor, the human body as chief musical instruments.

Disco

After 1970, American popular dance music can be summarily viewed as the development of disco music, and disco's evolution, during the 1980s and 1990s, into three main categories of dance music: club, house, and hip-hop. Disco, house, and hip-hop are thus related forms of twentieth-century American popular dance music. As such, they belong to a continuous history of American social dance that begins with the Charleston in the 1920s and to an even longer continuum of African American expressive culture.

Disco is a category of 1970s dance music, derived from the abbreviation for discotheque as the main venue of its performance and consumption. Before disco evolved into a stylistic category that eventually included dance routines as well as fashion and hair styles, the term referred to a new musical context, pioneered in New York underground dance venues by disc jockeys (deejays) catering to primarily minority (African American/Latino) and gay audiences. The roots of the disco phenomenon are located at the intersection of underground dance clubs and gay sensibilities and, more specifically, in gay black clubs of New York City in the late 1960s/early 1970s. Using two turntables and a repertoire of mainly soul, funk, and Latin records (before 1975, only 45-rpm singles and 33-rpm album cuts were available), deejays at that time began to create an uninterrupted flow of music at dance parties in nightclubs, lofts, and bars, following the example of Francis Grasso at New York's Sanctuary, in 1970 the first notoriously gay discotheque in America. Grasso's innovation, later called disco blending, became a standard for seamless mixing of prerecorded music for uninterrupted dancing that was copied and refined by other downtown disco deejays (such as Walter Gibbons, who went on to remix the first commercially available 12-inch single, Double Exposure's "Ten Percent") and uptown deejays such as Kool Herc and Grandmaster Flash, two of the pioneers of hip-hop.

Disco dance parties were held either as private, members-only events or for a more general clientele, largely by and for segments of urban society that identified themselves as being on the margins of the American mainstream. These segments consisted largely of gays, African Americans, Latinos, and women, who collectively had been largely closed out of the increasingly white, sexist, male-dominated rock music industry.

With the appeal of discotheques, such as Sanctuary, Salvation, Gallery, Le Jardin, The Loft, and Better Days, New York City became the world's disco capital during the early 1970s, with more than 200 discotheques in Manhattan alone inviting thousands of weekly dancers by the end of the decade. Following the success of disco-hits (a term introduced by *Billboard* in 1973) such as Manu Dibango's "Soul Makossa" (1973), the Hues Corporation's "Rock the Boat" (1974), and George McCrae's "Rock Your Baby" (1974), radio stations such as WKTU changed to a disco format, while

Disco
A popular dance style that developed in the 1970s that centered on dance clubs where deejays played continuous sequences of records to allow for uninterrupted dancing

disco records began to sell so well as to compete with the sales of rock and pop singles and albums. Celebrities lined up to get into Studio 54, arguably the most famous Manhattan discotheque of that period.

Between the early and mid-1970s, with the help of radio and television exposure across the United States and Europe, disco became one of the most popular sounds of the decade. Originally based on up-tempo rhythm-and-blues-based funk and soul music (for example, MFSB's "Love Is the Message" [1974]) and popular Latin repertoire (for example, Barabas's "Checkmate" [1975]), disco's development as both style and commerce increasingly involved electronic instruments such as synthesizers and drum machines and European producers (for example, Donna Summer's "I Feel Love" [1977] was produced by Giorgio Moroder).

In 1975, disco music began to be issued in a new format, the 12-inch single. This deejay-friendly medium established the deejay as remixer who, through rearranging, editing, and finally rerecording dance music versions for club play, became an important marketing tool for record companies eager to profit from the disco boom. In the process, discotheques became test labs for new dance music; advance copies of records were given to deejays before their commercial release to test audience responses on the dance floor.

Disco's most profitable venture was the November 1977 release of the film (and its best-selling sound track) *Saturday Night Fever,* produced by Robert Stigwood and featuring John Travolta and the music of an Australian pop trio, the Bee Gees. Comparable to the dance crazes associated with 1930s jazz and 1950s rock and roll (both African American musical styles gaining mainstream acceptance only after their popularization by Caucasian stars such as Paul Whiteman and Elvis Presley), disco's popular success came at the price of rendering its sociocultural origins invisible: both John Travolta's character in the film and the Bee Gees were neither gay nor of African descent.

The economic success of disco as America's most important mass sound of the 1970s raised the ire of the mainstream rock/pop establishment, based in no small measure on the association of disco with male homosexuality and ethnic minorities. As some rock musicians jumped on the disco economic bandwagon (examples of recordings are the Rolling Stones' "Miss You" [1978], Rod Stewart's "Do Ya Think I'm Sexy?" [1978], and Queen's "Another One Bites the Dust" [1980]), others joined efforts to combat the "disco craze." On July 12, 1979, at a time when *Rolling Stone* magazine published advertisements for "Disco Sucks" tee-shirts, rock radio deejay Steve Dahl organized a public burning of hundreds of disco records at Comiskey Park in Chicago.

By 1980, a glut of disco products coincided with an economic recession that decimated the ranks of recording companies, including those who had invested in disco acts. Disco, controversial because of its emphasis on bodily pleasures and the associated sexual, social, and ethnic connotations, lost its economic clout. In the early 1980s, the term *disco* rather quickly disappeared from the media discourse and public life. The recording industry, chiefly through *Billboard* magazine, replaced *disco* with the more neutral terms *dance music* and *club music*.

At this point, while disco's original urban core clientele continued to dance to disco, funk, and soul records at underground venues known for their primarily gay patrons (in both racially segregated and mixed settings), the attention of America's mainstream media and their audiences was caught by punk and new wave, and, from the mid-1980s onward, by hip-hop. By this time, discotheques had become referred to as clubs, and disco music had been renamed club, underground music, or simply dance music. As an abbreviation, *club* eventually came to stand for the venue as much as the music, just as disco had done before. However, these 1980s terms had the advantage of not being nominally associated with disco, thus leaving open issues of musical style and associated audiences.

The stylistic flexibility of this period is reflected in the eclectic repertoire of influential club deejays such as Afrika Bambaataa, who developed followings in community centers in the Bronx as well as at the Mudd Club in downtown Manhattan. While his 1980 single "Planet Rock," a reworking of Kraftwerk's "Trans-Europe-Express" (1977), enlarged audiences for rap and electro-funk, his downtown colleague Larry Levan (Figure 2.5), residing at the Paradise Garage club on the Lower West Side, became the most influential deejay in New York, with a repertoire ranging from Philly soul (for example, the songs of MFSB and First Choice), to German electronic music, to Caribbean pop, to songs by the Who ("Eminence Front" [1982]), the Clash ("Magnificent Dance" [1980]), and Marianne Faithfull ("Why D'Ya Do It" [1979]). In the process, the Paradise Garage, which had been voted "Most Favorite Disco" at a record industry convention in 1979, became an underground dance venue with a national and international reputation, with Levan acquiring the nickname "The Father" from his disciples among New York's growing deejay circles.

House Music

House music
Dance music created electronically in home studios to accompany dancing in clubs

House music is generally viewed as the electronic offspring of disco music. As with disco and club music, the name refers to a location rather than to stylistic traits. Accordingly, *house* is the abbreviation of the Warehouse, an influential Chicago dance venue where a

Figure 2.5
The late Larry Levan
in the deejay booth
at The Choice, New
York City, 1989.
Photo by Tina Paul.
Reproduced with
permission.

Bronx-born deejay, Frankie Knuckles, acquired the nickname
"Godfather of House." Knuckles was referred to the Warehouse,
where he worked between 1977 and 1983, by his friend and mentor
Larry Levan, who had declined the offer to relocate in order to
remain resident deejay at the Paradise Garage. House also refers to
the location of its production: in contrast to disco, which was produced inside the recording studio, house music began as home-
made music. This points to changes in music technology associated
with the then-emerging home recording industry that blurred the
line between the recording technology of the recording studio and
the playback technology of the deejay booth.

Disco deejays have been instrumental in lengthening disco tracks
from three-minute pop songs to extended versions as long as six-
teen minutes. But whereas the typical disco production used studio
musicians, technology, and professional production standards,
house music pioneers such as Frankie Knuckles, Farley "Jackmaster
Funk," Chip E., Jesse Saunders, Steve "Silk" Hurley, DJ Pierre,
Marshall Jefferson, and Larry Heard, who were influenced by the
music of European artists such as Kraftwerk, Manuel Göttsching,
Depeche Mode, and Gary Numan, emphasized electronic technology and sounds that had recently become available and accessible
with the establishment of MIDI standards and the growth of the
home recording industry. Accordingly, the sound of house music
was characterized initially by the use of cheap analog and, later,

more costly digital electronic equipment, including synthesizers, samplers, drum computers, and sequencers. Although early Chicago house records evidence a rough, unpolished, and minimalist sound related to the do-it-yourself approach of its producers, this technology eventually helped house deejays to become producers, remixers, and recording artists in their own right. In the 1990s, Frankie Knuckles became one of the highest-paid remixers, one of the first deejays to receive a major label contract as recording artist, and, in 1998, the first deejay to receive a Grammy Award as best remixer, itself a newly established award category.

Chicago clubs, such as the Warehouse, the Powerplant, and the Music Box, were as important to the initial exposure of house as were radio shows on WGCI and WBMX by the Hot Mix 5, a disc jockey collective formed in 1981 by Kenny Jason and Farley Keith Williams (Farley "Jackmaster Funk"). Like their club-based colleagues Frankie Knuckles and Ron Hardy, they mixed and produced music on 12-inch singles that were released on local independent recording companies, primarily Larry Sherman's Precision and Trax labels and Rocky Jones's DJ International company. In the late 1980s, as house gradually branched out to other urban dance scenes, several subcategories emerged, including acid house, deep house, hip house, and, later, garage and speed garage. The latter two terms, popular with British deejays, honor the Paradise Garage, as they refer to the inspiration of New York club music produced after its closure in 1987. Since then, the economic center for house has shifted from the United States to the U.K., where acid house, into the 1990s, turned into rave and techno music in the hands of British house producers, such as Jazzy M, Babyford, CJ Mackintosh, Paul Oakenfold, and Danny Rampling. Under the name techno, European derivations of British acid house have since become the soundscape in dance clubs all across Europe.

Kai Fikentscher

MUSIC PUBLISHING

If the dissemination of music through the air may be considered the most traditional form of music transmission, music publishing is probably the second oldest. The publication and sale of song books, hymnbooks, and scores in North America dates back to the eighteenth century. During the nineteenth century and into the early twentieth century, sheet music and song books were the most important media for disseminating popular and religious songs as well as other forms of music. Such publications were abundant and provide an important source for the study of American music before the advent of the recording industry. Songs from the musical theater, vaudeville songs, and a large variety of genres were published and disseminated with piano transcriptions. Some music publishers sent groups of musicians on tour to promote their copyrighted books, anticipating by decades the practice of popular music groups going on tour to promote their record companies' recordings. The growth of music publishing paralleled the growth of music education in North America. Here a dissemination technology awaited an educational movement. Some form of music education—especially vocal training and piano lessons—came to be considered part of general education, and particularly appropriate for women.

Music publishing was more than just a means for disseminating music. It was also a big business—a mass medium. Some of Stephen Foster's songs sold over one hundred thousand copies each in the 1850s (Figure 2.6). Music publishers became a powerful force in the entertainment industry of the late nineteenth and early twentieth centuries, and their influence can be seen in the copyright law of 1909, which protected composers and print music publishers but did not include a provision for performers and audio recording. During the twentieth century the sales of audio recordings gradually exceeded the sales of sheet music, and music publishers increasingly became the administrators of intellectual property rather than actual disseminators of published music.

Anthony Seeger

By the early twentieth century publishers had developed sophisticated means of getting their material before the eager public that

Figure 2.6
Stephen Foster

Tin Pan Alley
A nickname given to the area of New York City where many music publishers had their offices during the early decades of the twentieth century; more generally, the popular music produced by these publishers

Pay for Play (Payola)
The practice of paying performers to sing particular songs to generate popular interest in them

Song pluggers
Professional marketers employed by music publishers to promote songs, either by performing them in music stores or by encouraging popular entertainers to include them in their performances

filled vaudeville theaters and other venues of public amusement. Those Manhattan-based publishing companies that collectively came to be known as *Tin Pan Alley* made use of popular entertainers who performed their material in return for above- or under-the-table compensation, a practice that came to be known as *pay for play* or *Payola*. Pictures of performers were displayed on the covers of sheet music, or firms would offer them the exclusive right to perform a particular composition in their acts. On other occasions, a performer would receive credit and compensation as one of a song's writers even if he or she had no formal musical skills whatsoever. Professional marketers, known in the industry as *song pluggers*, hawked their clients' wares (sometimes written by the pluggers themselves) through a variety of means that included public performance in music stores or planting individuals in theaters who "requested" predetermined material by popular performers.

Even the new technology of motion pictures was employed for promotional ends. Illustrated reproductions of song lyrics, reproduced on slides, were offered to theater owners free of charge during the first decade of the century. This led to the advent of the public "sing-along," and publishers frequently commissioned songs written exclusively for this format. Whatever the means of merchandising, music was becoming a more and more profitable commercial commodity, a fact underscored by the rising costs of promotion. By the middle of the 1890s, it cost as much as $1,300 to launch a single song. Fewer than half of those individual compositions made back their investment, and only one out of every 200 songs secured a profit.

American Society of Composers, Authors and Publishers (ASCAP)

Despite the fact that the 1909 revision of the Copyright Act instituted payment for public performance, few composers or publishers took advantage of that fact because no codified system was in place to ensure reimbursement. In 1913, six writers and publishers, including the preeminent theatrical composer of the day, Victor Herbert, banded together to rectify the matter and founded the American Society of Composers, Authors and Publishers (ASCAP). Convinced that no single individual or corporate entity could monitor all potential performances of its intellectual property, the membership pooled its interests and, by combining its individual catalogues into an inclusive body of compositions, proposed to require any users of that music to take out a license for the entire repertoire. The result was, in effect, a private organization for the enforcement of a public law and the principle of performing rights.

In order to guarantee ASCAP's legal standing, the membership sued several establishments that it felt used music without appropriate compensation. The first case, *Church v. Hilliard* (1914), took on the hotel industry on behalf of a nonmember publisher, the John Church Company (Ryan 1985:19-20). The case alleged that the performance of John Philip Sousa's "From Maine to Oregon" in the dining room of New York City's Hotel Vanderbilt constituted a for-profit occasion even if no special admission charge was required to hear the composition. The hotel countered that music was no more than a portion of the establishment's general environment. The courts ruled in favor of the John Church Company. To reinforce this claim and circumvent a local court's overturning of *Church v. Hilliard,* ASCAP, in the person of Victor Herbert, sued Shanley's Cabaret of New York City, where it was alleged his composition "Sweethearts" was sung on more than one occasion to dinner guests. While a lower court ruled in Shanley's favor, the case was officially decided for Herbert and the other defendants by the Supreme Court on the basis of the dramatic-work licensing provision of the copyright law. In 1917, the U.S. Supreme Court justices declared that the public performance of music contributed to the ability of an establishment to make profits even if no special admission was charged for that music. ASCAP now possessed a legal precedent, and the performance license became a boon to writers and publishers.

At the same time, ASCAP's membership was a select, and far from representative, sample of the nation's writers of music. Being admitted required a publisher to have been in business for no less than a year, and a writer had to have had no fewer than five of his works "regularly published," an obscure attribution meaning that it had been released by an ASCAP member. Applicants were then required to solicit the sponsorship of two members of the ASCAP board before they finally received the approval of the membership committee. Needless to say, this series of obstacles restricted the organization to a body of like-minded individuals. As a result, ASCAP possessed a virtual lock on all compensation for public performances of music. This led, as shall be seen, to recurring battles with other portions of the entertainment industry.

The Music Industry Today
The music industry has undergone many changes since the end of World War II. Three of the most crucial are as follows:

1. The absorption of independent record labels by multinational media conglomerates
2. The introduction of sophisticated technologies that render preexisting formats obsolete
3. The synergistic interfusion of diverse media by Fortune 500 corporations to maximize the means by which music, and other forms of entertainment, are sold

In effect, what was once an enterprise dominated by a large number of independent entrepreneurs has succumbed to the kind of gigantism that rules the global economy unabated by either the desires of the consumer or the political will of government bodies. The small-scale operations that began to come into being during the 1940s and proliferated thereafter have succumbed one after the other to the superior capabilities and substantial profit margins of the major record labels.

At the present time, four companies (Sony/BMG, Universal Music Group, Warner Music Group, and EMI) account for virtually 80 percent of global record sales. They therefore dictate what the public will be able to hear. For the major companies, the currently operating independent companies serve two principal purposes: to act as systems for career development whereby new artists develop audiences and illustrate their potential marketability; or to present those forms of music or individual artists that will never command the interest of the majority of the record-buying public. While it is inarguable that more music can be purchased at the present time than ever before, the question remains whether the bottom-line mentality of multinational conglomerates, for which music is but one of many products, will ever be able to serve the needs of progressive or experimental musicians, let alone the purveyors of those indigenous forms of expression, such as blues, jazz, gospel, and bluegrass to name a few, that they consider to be outmoded or inaccessible.

David Sanjek

While much attention is paid to the marketing of popular musics in the United States, how is classical music sold? Snapshot 2.3, a small ethnography describing a trip to Borders Books and Music, illustrates that marketing strategies (quite unlike those used for popular musics) are also employed for the distribution of Western classical music in the United States today.

Snapshot 2.3: Marketing Classical Music

Let's go shopping. Most North American devotees of classical music would deny that the packaged goods on display in the classical section of a record store represent the essence of art music. But "art for art's sake" means little in a megastore, where the values and structures of meaning associated with the historic canon of Western classical music confront directly the power of late capitalist mass marketing.

Most scholars of consumer culture agree that the distinctive features of a mass market—mass production, national distribution of standardized products, the creation of distinctive corporate logos, media advertising—first came together in late-nineteenth-century

America. Nationally advertised brands either displaced locally distributed staples (Uneeda Biscuit, Ivory Soap) or created huge new markets for previously exclusive luxury items (Eastman Kodak, Ford). Music, in its live performance both a locally produced staple and an elite luxury, had to undergo a fundamental transformation to be mass marketed: The invention of sound recording provided the impetus for music's national distribution and branding. One of the most recognizable brand logos in the early mass-market days was RCA's mascot "Nipper," the dog transfixed by His Master's Voice as it emerged from the gramophone's horn. But 78-rpm disks had technical limitations: three minutes per side meant that an opera recording, spread over fifteen disks that could cost a month's salary, was still a luxury item. These bulky "albums" were marketed on a small scale to consumers already socialized into the appreciation of locally produced art music in performance.

Mass marketing and distribution of classical music had to wait until after World War II, when the economies of scale made possible by magnetic tape recording and the long-playing record (LP) led to the first true mass consumption of art music. In the fifty years since the introduction of the LP in 1948, national retail chains and the huge multinational media conglomerates that supply them have thoroughly transformed the way Western society consumes and values classical music. We have moved from a system of social relations, controlled by networks of patronage, personal instruction, and group interaction, to a system of objects, controlled by advertising, mass marketing, and individual consumption. At the record store, in the neatly stacked rows of brightly packaged shiny discs, we confront the system of (classical music) objects in all its disorienting complexity. Sometimes this system of objects passively reinterprets traditional art music ideology for the commodity age, but just as often it dramatically disrupts many of classical music's most cherished beliefs.

In the mass market system of (consumer) objects, commodities are not simply useful things; thanks to brand advertising, they signify, and in consuming them we consume meaning as well as value. The function of marketing and advertising is not just to sell goods but to construct their meaning, to imbue commodities with signifying power. Consumption as "invidious display" is an old idea, with many obvious applications to the history of Western classical music. On the other hand, the prospect that the cultural meaning of music in an industrialized mass society could be constituted primarily through consuming musical works in (mass-marketed) commodity form—buying and listening to recordings—has caused intense anxiety. From an ethnographic perspective the interference between classical music as idealized in cultural tradition and as materialized in a system of mass-marketed commodities provides crucial data. A preliminary ethnography of the classical section of Borders Books and Music in Rochester, New York, taken on the afternoon of October 14, 1997, documents a real, if low-key, conflict between the remnants of classical music's performance culture and what we might call CD culture.

Actually, in its large-scale structure the system of musical objects constructed by Borders and its suppliers reinforces some key aspects of classical music traditions. Like almost any store that expects significant traffic in classical music recordings, Borders rigidly segregates classical music from all other types of music. At the largest record stores, the classical section is often acoustically sealed off from the rest of the store and decorated more conservatively, with a simulacrum of more luxury. This retail strategy translates the claims for aesthetic autonomy made on behalf of Western art music into material terms, even inflecting them with the same slight tinge of class consciousness. (The separate space of classical music is also the locus of an ersatz gentility.) This separate section only exists because a select few stores devote a wildly disproportionate amount of floor space to classical music; its very appearance is limited to a network of boutiques where consumers can indulge the fiction that their extremely exotic taste is still at the center of the world's musics.

As you enter the large rectangle of the record department, the classical music section is on your left. (Studies show that consumers overwhelmingly turn to the right as they enter a new space; as in the world at large, no one wanders into classical music by mistake.) Classical music extends halfway up the left-hand wall and halfway along the far wall; it is bisected by racks of videotapes in the far left corner. Along that back wall it abuts the jazz section, sensibly enough; jazz is the "black classical music" and is rapidly approaching classical music's canonicity, aestheticism, and cultural marginalization. But the rest of the classical section is bordered by a riot of exotic and flagrantly "nonclassical" musics: soundtracks, yes, but also reggae and world music, rap, electronica, ska, funk, and soul.

This strange border zone becomes clear only after you have traversed the entire store, which reproduces the generic landscape inside the mind of a typical upper-middle-class consumer quite precisely. Along the right (dominant) wall is pop-rock, by far the largest section, arranged alphabetically by artist. Facing off uneasily against the rock colossus along the left wall is classical, also arranged alphabetically. Between are "borderline" exotic and dance musics—African, Latin, Asian—that occupy the same marginal place in the system of musical objects as in the Western musical imagination.

The bulk of classical recordings is organized by composer, reinforcing the traditional Western emphasis on individual creativity and "genius" quite handily. (The overwhelming recorded preponderance of a few "great" composers goes without saying.) This materialized canon of the great composers is physically segregated from mongrel classical recordings categorized in other ways. Past the video racks are budget recordings, operas (by title, not by composer), recordings of famous and historical performers, collections by instrument type and by chronological period, and, farthest from Bach and Beethoven, "greatest hits" albums and collections organized on extramusical themes.

But only half of these thematic collections are in the bins; the rest are prominently displayed in special fixtures. If the bins largely reinforce traditional classical music values, these display racks are where those values take a beating. Of the several kinds of marketing displays visible at Borders on this afternoon, two show "CD culture," the new system of musical objects, under construction most clearly.

Towering garishly over the understated wooden bins is a large rotating metal stand. Its 12- by 4-inch slots are filled with identically styled CDs, whose intentionally crude bright yellow and red covers grab the eye. Each CD bears a cartoon figure holding up a poster/blackboard, on which is chalked *Beethoven* [Bach, Brahms, Romantic Music, Puccini] *for Dummies.* The *Classical Music for Dummies* (Pogue and Speck, 1997) series is a collaboration between EMI Records and IDG Books, which first used the *X for Dummies* rubric to sell instructional computer books, and it recasts classical music's vaunted cultural autonomy in a new, unflattering light. "Classics for the Rest of Us!" the covers announce, echoing a famous slogan coined for the Apple Macintosh; classical music is still an autonomous realm, but the prospective consumer is now located firmly outside its suddenly rather exotic and geeky precincts. Here classical music has become Other.

Classical Music for Dummies turns the notion of "high" art upside down. Art music is difficult, not like great art or literature, but difficult like badly written computer manuals, and these CDs, which include some rudimentary educational software, provide a "Fun and Easy Way" to master it. Nobody buys *Windows 95 for Dummies* because he or she actually feels stupid; we are responding to the promise that the stripped-down knowledge it contains is purely instrumental (in other words, "I don't really care about this, just tell me what I need to get the job done"). The idea that connoisseurship of art music could be reduced to such pure instrumentality ("Get to Know the Real Rimsky-Korsakov and Have the Ultimate Listening Experience") erases music for music's sake from the system of objects. Within the system, all music, like all computer equipment, is functional.

However ironic its outsider attitude toward art music's aesthetic of disinterested intellectuality, *Classical Music for Dummies* does at least leave the canon in place: almost every title is devoted to the work of one famous composer. But scan the classical section's most prominent display case, devoted to new major label releases, and an even more disorienting picture emerges. This is the first rack you see as you enter the section, and in October 1997 it was completely under the control of Polygram's Deutsche Grammophon subsidiary, providing a particularly clear picture of one conglomerate's view of the system of musical objects. The canon is in ruins: Of the thirty-five slots, only seven used a composer's name to attract the eye, and most of those were reissues. Most trumpeted a celebrity performer, usually a singer or violinist, with the music a distinctly secondary consideration. (Fully six slots went to a single Pavarotti collection; three to Cecilia Bartoli; two to Bryn Terfel; eight other slots were selling either a voice or a violin.) Media tie-ins abounded: a new recording of Vivaldi's *Four Seasons* was linked to the Weather Channel, while another release echoed late-night TV infomercials by offering *The Only Opera CD You'll Ever Need* ("hundreds of excerpts on one incredible CD!").

And thus the new system of (musical) objects displaces the old system of social relations. Should we mourn? In one sense, "Western classical music" does reveal itself as another fragile indigenous musical culture, as vulnerable as any to the destructive encroachment of technology and capital. But I would argue that the system of musical objects is ultimately liberating. If we move out of the embattled classical section and browse among those other musics, we can find a new anticanon of serious music, a new set of sociomusical relations mediated quite happily by technology and commodity exchange, and a hardy growth of that perennial, art. CD culture is alive and well.

Robert Fink

REVIEW _____

Important Terms and People to Know

American Folklife Center
American Society of Composers, Authors and Publishers (ASCAP)
Bureau of American Ethnology
Classical Music for Dummies
Copyright
Frances Densmore

Disco
Federal Communications Commission (FCC)
Jesse Walter Fewkes
Alice Cunningham Fletcher
House Music
Jish
Frankie Knuckles
John A. and Alan Lomax
Mediated music
National Endowment for the Arts and Humanities (NEA, NEH)
National Heritage Fellowships
Native American Graves Protection and Repatriation Act
  (NAGPRA)
Smithsonian Institution
Tin Pan Alley
Warehouse

Review Questions

1. What are the major differences between the regulation, conservation, and preservation of the arts, especially music?
2. How has the United States government both restricted and enabled the regulation, conservation, and preservation of music to occur throughout its history?
3. What major technologies have had the most impact on the production and dissemination of music in the nineteenth century? In the twentieth century? Today?
4. What economic, social, and political factors influence the music we hear on the radio?
5. What roles do labeling, illustrating, and titling musical media have in their marketing?

Projects (Written or Oral)

1. Listen to the radio for a few hours each day. Try different stations and times. What are you hearing? What choices are available? Not available? Is there any music that does not appear on the radio at all?
2. Visit a record store and choose two very different kinds of musical genres. Examine where they are placed in the store and how they are organized within the various bins. Examine the jewel-box covers, print materials accompanying the recordings, and other illustrations. Compare and contrast the two genres. What does this tell you about the values associated with each?

3. Visit the American Folklife Center, The Smithsonian Institution, and/or the Library of Congress (all in Washington, DC) either in person or through the Internet and check out the various archives and other collections of recorded American music materials you find there.
4. Talk to the oldest member of your family and find out what technologies were available in his or her childhood. How does that compare to what is available today?

CHAPTER 3

Social and Musical Identities

Adelaida Reyes, Ann Dhu McLucas,
Ronald Radano, Susan C. Cook, Terry E. Miller,
Tamara Livingston, Portia K. Maultsby,
Susan Fast, and Jennifer Rycenga

Issues of individual and group identity have always had historical significance and continue to affect the musical lives of those living in the United States today. Although there is considerable mobility and interaction within and among identities, with some more freely chosen than others, all affect music and music making.

Your socioeconomic class, for instance, might influence whether or not you take private music lessons as a child; your race, ethnicity, or gender might direct you toward or away from certain musical instruments, genres, or learning opportunities; and your religion might be a major factor in the kinds of music you experience throughout a lifetime.

Four categories of social identity are presented in this chapter:

1. Class
2. Race
3. Gender
4. Religion

In each section, the author traces the importance of these factors in the development of musical and social life within this country. Specific snapshots have been chosen to illustrate the relationship between each social category and the musical practices, often stressing the interaction of categories, such as race and class, or gender, race, and religion.

We are not suggesting that these constructed social categories necessarily define or pigeonhole individual people into neatly wrapped, essentialist boxes. Identities are both self- and other-defined, as are musical paths and choices, but they need not totally govern one's life. Thus, the categories of identity presented here are not to be taken as fixed or immutable, but rather as suggestions of the varied personal and social factors that often affect music and music making in this country.

THE NATURE OF IDENTITY

Who are we? This question arises from a profound human need for identity that comes to being when consciousness of difference begins. In the United States, the question draws added significance from the country's history as a nation-state. Though born out of a successful rebellion against the British and ultimately taking a different form of government, the United States adopted the basic civic features from the English model. One did not have to be born American; one could become an American through citizenship. Diversity, therefore, was not an unintended consequence of migrations from Europe, Asia, and Africa, nor merely an accident of history, but part of the ideological foundation of the new nation-state. No wonder, then, that throughout the United States, the question "Who are we?" resounds, because the constituent populations change as do the replies, depending on the intellectual climate, the temper of the times, and the tools that become available to those who ask and those who respond.

Identity can be examined in terms of two basic components:

1. Human agency
2. A medium through which to express it

First, identity requires a minimal pair—a self and an other (whether an individual or a group)—because identity is not only a statement of *who* a group is and what it identifies itself as, it is also a statement that expresses *to* someone an identification with and difference from an other on some grounds. Second, identity is conveyed through something perceivable: an object, an act, a music, an art, a language, a banner that serves as label, insignia, diacritic, or emblem. These tag a human group and, in the literal sense of identity as sameness or oneness, they in turn assume the identity of the group. Those who pledge allegiance to the American flag, for instance, proclaim their American identity. The piece of cloth with stars and stripes imprinted on it is rarely described as simply a piece of colored cloth; it is identified as an American flag.

Some objects or forms of behavior mark identity more readily than others. Language, for example, is highly indicative because it penetrates all areas of daily life and because it has referential meanings. Music, less pervasive in daily life than language, more flexible as a vehicle of or instrument for meaning, is more ambiguous as a marker. It therefore requires more deliberate action from human agents, more interventions—from history, language, convention—to fulfill its assigned function. Thus, the effectiveness of national anthems to symbolize national identity, for example, is enhanced by their texts, usually patriotic in nature.

Sometimes the focus is on markers. The singing of a national anthem and the raising of a flag at the Olympic Games, for example, signal the national identity of a victorious athlete or team. Sometimes the emphasis is on *ascription*, on who people say they are or on what identity they impute to the things they create. The significance now given to ascription is partly an acknowledgment of the multiple identities that contemporary life imposes and requires. Depending on context, for example, immigrants may insist on their Americanness, or they may insist on their dual identity as hyphenated Americans. The tango, for example, is frequently identified as Vietnamese by Vietnamese at their New Year's Day celebrations in the United States; it is identified as Latin American in most other American contexts.

The current emphasis on ascription is also a corrective to earlier practices in which outsiders to a group unilaterally imputed—or denied—identity. "Negro," for example, was a label imposed on African Americans by colonialists without the consent of those they were labeling. It ascribed to "Negroes" an identity based on race while denying them an identity as American citizens.

Changes in form and/or function of one or more of the components reflect the dynamic nature of identity. "We Shall Overcome," a song widely recognized as a symbol of the Civil Rights movement and the Black Power movement, was originally a Christian church hymn. In 1972, in New York City's East Harlem, its function was broadened to become a rallying cry, sung weekly at processions organized to mobilize the community in its fight against drugs. Subordinating their differences in ethnic identity to their shared identity as members of the East Harlem community, African Americans and Latinos who organized and attended the rallies sang the strophes of "We Shall Overcome" alternately in English and in Spanish to signal their unity and dedication to a common cause. In each of these cases, the same song, with some modification, was used by different groups for different (though related) purposes in different contexts. Similarly, the West Indian carnival in New York, with its elaborate costumes, steel drum bands, and dances that hark back to the Caribbean homeland, is recognized by both the West Indian and outside communities as distinctively West Indian in form despite some fundamental changes in function. Once a pre-Lenten event, the carnival is now both a proud symbol of West Indian identity and part of West Indians' celebration of Labor Day, an American national holiday.

The tension between the unum (one) and the pluribus (many) in the American motto "E pluribus unum" has always been a fundamental dialectic in American life. On the level of ideology pluralism reigned, but its realization has always been problematic. Changing metaphors have reflected the difficulties. The homogenizing melting pot that celebrates oneness induced by assimilation has given way to the mosaic, the salad bowl, and the rainbow. The diversity that these recent metaphors celebrate finds expression everywhere: in ethnic festivals, in performances of music and dance, and in other types of cultural expression that are public manifestations of ethnic pride.

The continuing influx of new immigrants and the constantly changing social milieu continually call for new ways of reconciling aspirations toward oneness and the strong desire of immigrant groups to perpetuate their cultural identity. Identity is a concept that changes in the way it is manifested, studied, and interpreted. It implies diversity: at the very least, a self and an other. It implies interaction: at the very least, a self acknowledging and being acknowledged by an other. It implies an object or behavior, something perceivable, through which the message of identity may be conveyed and understood. And it implies conventions and dynamic processes that habitually engage these components with each other on the basis of perceived likeness and difference.

Adelaida Reyes

THE IMPORTANCE OF CLASS

> **Class**
> The socioeconomic group to which an individual belongs

The socioeconomic group to which an individual belongs—his or her *class*—is a strong determinant (though certainly not the only one) in decoding the meaning of a particular kind of music created or enjoyed by that person. In surveying the wide variety of genres and styles of music in the United States, it is clear that social class has a great deal to do not only with the creation of music but also with its consumption, meaning within society, and modes of study.

Music serves as a potent symbol that carries a generally agreed on meaning for the members of a particular group, even though that meaning may not be clearly articulated by any one member of the group. The meaning is carried in both the actual sound of the music and in the social networks that are necessary to sustain its creation and performance. In the case of oral traditions, for example, which must be transmitted face to face, the music comes "packaged" with the person who transmits it; therefore, its meaning is always socially determined and socially relevant. In contrast, the advent of the middle class brought the commercial exchange of music for money; its clients multiplied from the single patron of feudal times to a concert audience, simultaneously creating a wider gulf between the musician and the audience with whom the musician no longer had a personal relationship.

Perhaps most important, and a recurring theme in American music, were (and are) the special problems that the exercise of democratic ideals bring to an art form transplanted from an aristocratic Europe. What music is accessible to the populace? How do citizens become educated to "higher" aesthetic experiences? What is the appropriate music for a democracy? Composers, educators, music businesspeople, and occasionally even politicians have grappled with these questions. Even the history of patronage by the elite classes has recently been characterized as having a "democratizing spirit" (Locke 1993).

Just as pervasive an influence as democracy is that of commercialism, which became a factor in American music making as early as the mid-eighteenth century with the advent of the singing schools. Singing masters—such as the Boston tanner William Billings or the farmer, liquor merchant, and horse breeder Justin Morgan—traveled from town to town to teach music; often of the working class, they nonetheless taught the children of both middle and upper classes. Equal parts of idealism, aesthetic concern, and entrepreneurial spirit motivated the peripatetic singing masters.

Early on, the democratic ideal of educating the masses to appreciate art music was intertwined with commercialism as it became apparent to publishing companies and instrument manufacturers that the educational market would be a lucrative one. This alliance, formed in the early nineteenth century, perhaps earliest in Boston, under the guidance of composer and educator Lowell Mason, is still with us today, especially in the music industry's various interactions with public schools. A new level of commercialism that uses the notion of class to target particular audiences is that of geodemographics and lifestyle analysis in which the profile of each subgroup is ascertained, and radio or television advertising uses music to reach that subgroup. At the other end of the spectrum, contemporary art music, which since the early nineteenth century has been developing an ideology of individuality, has narrowed its audience to an elite few and must therefore survive on charitable donations by powerful institutions or individuals.

The pervasiveness of the commercial side of our society touches music of virtually every class. For example, the songs of the rural working class, created in oral traditions, have been appropriated to make money for those who "discovered" them, and classical music is used for the marketing of almost anything to almost anyone. But, consumption of music as a product is only part of the overall picture. Music is also being created, and although the percentage of active creators of music compared to passive consumers is quite low —Charles Seeger estimated less than 1% (Seeger 1957)—the class associations of the creators range from the working-class and middle-class "garage-rock" bands to the highly educated classical composers of the conservatory, with increasing links between the two groups as rock composers become interested in further training and sometimes turn toward universities.

During hard economic times, music has provided a viable alternative to factory jobs or manual labor. Benny Goodman and many other Depression-era swing musicians escaped the grinding labor experienced by their parents and siblings by cultivating their musical talents, often turning professional at early ages. The WPA Federal Music Project, as well as the short-lived attempts of the New York composers of the 1930s such as Aaron Copland, Marc Blitzstein, Elie Siegmeister, and others to organize themselves around social causes in the Young Composer's Group and the Composer's Collective, provided outlets, if not much remuneration, for art music composers.

Does the urge to create music fall along class lines? That we have music created by all classes would seem to speak against the idea that one class has dominance in the area of creation. The type, quantity, and commercial viability of music of different classes may vary considerably, but the urge to create exists everywhere.

Some Intersections of Music and Class

Music of the Elite: Opera and Concert Music

Class consciousness in nineteenth-century music was most clearly displayed in the newly opened urban opera houses and concert halls. Eighteenth-century opera in the colonies and the new nation was originally a genre in the tradition of British ballad opera, one that embodied a middle- and lower-class satire of aristocratic conventions. As in Britain, the American public for this sort of opera ranged from working class to elite, and as the genre developed into English-language comic opera, the plots and the music continued to provide something for each layer of society (Ahlquist 1997:9). In addition, these works were often performed as "afterpieces" to the popular plays of the day, which were likewise attended by many levels of society.

Reception varied between cities and more rural areas: Audiences in small communities, such as small southern and western towns and mining camps, were surprisingly heterogeneous in class makeup and were open to the wide variety of entertainment that made its way to the western outposts of the developing country. City audiences tended to be more stratified, with the positioning of the classes literally on display in the various tiers of theaters, or largely segregated by class, as people congregated in different theaters to witness, variously, Italian or English opera, minstrel shows, melodrama, and so on.

The most infamous of the incidents arising from the class differentiations and the tensions arising from them was the Astor Place Riot of May 1849, "an altercation ostensibly prompted by a feud between the British actor William Charles Macready and the American actor Edwin Forrest, but in reality a class conflict: the rich versus the poor, the aristocracy versus American democrats" (Preston 1993:141). As the Astor Place Theater had been built exclusively by the upper class to house its favorite Italian opera, with many discouragements offered to the middle- and lower-class general public (such as uncomfortable seating with bad sight lines to the stage), the resentment that boiled over into the streets was in hindsight hardly a surprise. By the late nineteenth century, according to Deane Root, New York theaters were situated along class and ethnic lines in three general zones according to the ethnic composition and income level of their neighborhood and the programs they characteristically offered (Root 1981:174-175).

Music of the Nineteenth-Century Working Class: Minstrel Shows

At the other end of the social and entertainment spectrum of the mid-nineteenth century—although sometimes sharing the same stages as opera—were the minstrel shows. Growing out of strong working-class roots in rural celebrations and urban rowdiness, and a long British American tradition of white men blackening their faces for both theatrical and folk presentations, the blackface minstrel show appeared in more or less crystallized form in the 1840s, performed and composed mainly by white men of urban origin. It thrived through the 1870s, when it was absorbed into vaudeville and other forms, but in both the United States and Britain as late as the 1980s it put forth late-blooming offshoots designed to satirize class divisions: "The original foursome of undifferentiated musicians expanded into a line in which customary position corresponded roughly to class identification. The end men, who always played tambourine and bones, were lower class . . . the middleman, or interlocutor, served as a bogus mouthpiece for the high culture" (Saxton 1975:9-11; see Figure 3.1).

Minstrel show
A theatrical performance in which white performers portrayed stereotypical African American types, featuring music, dance, and comedy

Work Songs and Songs About Work

In addition to the music of the minstrel shows, the clearest examples of music made by and for the working class are labor songs, which have comprised a large and variegated strand of our national heritage from the beginning. Classification of these songs is fluid; crosscutting the occupation of the singer-composer are issues of whether the song is descriptive or accompanies work, whether it has entered an oral tradition or is the expression of a single moment in time, and whether it is descriptive or political (or sometimes both).

Work songs
Songs that either accompany or describe work, such as songs sung while picking cotton or laying railroad tracks

Country Music

The popular genre of country music intersects the world of work songs. (See more on country and Western music in Chapter 11.) The major themes of country music are work, freedom, and alienation, appearing in approximately one sixth of all Top 20 selections.

Country music
The commercial offshoot of traditional Southern music; music designed to appeal to a working-class identity

Figure 3.1
The Ethiopian Serenaders, a typical early minstrel performing group. Note the banjo player (center), the two endmen (bones on left, tambourine on right), and—an unusual feature—the melodian player (4th from left). Courtesy David A. Jasen

Country music is itself a commercial offshoot of the traditional song and instrumental music of the South, formerly carried on in an oral tradition. Consequently, from the start country music was an eclectic mix, which included ancient British ballads, Americanized versions of these, sacred songs, minstrel tunes, rudimentary blues, and songs of many sorts absorbed from the commercial popular music industry over the years (Figure 3.2). Over the century it has grown from a homegrown and heartfelt music, expressing working-class identity, into a commercial music, produced by others to appeal to a working-class identity, whether or not its listeners are actually working class. The symbolic meaning of country music as the declared favorite music of New England-educated, upper-class President George H. W. Bush, as making him more "of the people," is unmistakable (Malone 1990).

Folk Music and the Folk Revival

The "invisible musics," which have persisted for centuries in pockets of oral tradition all over the United States, have surfaced into the visible, commercial market at various times in the history of this country. In doing so, they have often crossed class lines in interesting and complex ways. The minstrel shows, for example, had their roots at least in part in oral tradition, although probably less of the southern blacks they pretended to portray than of the British-Irish American

Folk music
The traditional songs and dance music of a group of people, usually passed through oral transmission from one performer to another

Figure 3.2
Hank Williams in a publicity photo, c. 1950. Williams was a major figure in the post World War II country music boom. Courtesy Southern Folklife Collection, University of North Carolina at Chapel Hill

men performing in them. The middle-class white composers and performers of minstrelsy (until after the Civil War, when blacks also formed minstrel troupes) used music derived from that of the rural working class to entertain audiences of the urban working class.

In the early history of the recording industry, the market for "race" and "hillbilly" records (commercial designations for music aimed largely at rural black and white working-class audiences, respectively) used performers from those classes. But the profits from the recordings went almost solely to the middle-class producers who hired the traditional performers. In the case of hillbilly music, some performers went on to develop country music and later became well-paid stars. In the 1950s, the "smoother" and usually white performers often covered the songs of earlier black and white performers. This practice went on quite visibly in rock and roll, where performers like Elvis Presley and the Beatles became wealthy, as well as in the folk revival, where the Kingston Trio, Pete Seeger, and others sang songs collected from traditional performers for radio, recordings, and college performances. Although the intent of record producers of the folk revival was perhaps not as crassly commercial as that of rock and roll's producers, the shift in values and class lines was probably even sharper. Rock and roll was a translation of a largely black working-class music into an urban white working-class music, which later spread to the youth of every class. The folk revival took the music of rural whites and blacks and purveyed it directly to the elite, college-educated youth (Cantwell 1993:40-43).

For example, in tracing the career of folk revival singer Pete Seeger from his early days of idealism with his radical singing collective, The Almanac Singers, to his later commercial popularity, Robert Lumer writes: "Ironically, the folk music alternative to commercial mass music could only be popularized by making it a commercial music, ultimately changing its nature" (1991:53). Seeger himself was a Harvard dropout, son of the well-known composer-musicologist, Charles Seeger—hardly a man of the working class or "peasantry" (Figure 3.3). Nor were the many college students who followed Seeger, the Kingston Trio, Joan Baez, Judy Collins, and others into the folk revival. "Why American college students should want to express the ideas and emotions of the downtrodden and the heartbroken, of garage mechanics and millworkers and miners and backwoods farmers, is in itself an interesting question. But there is certainly good reason for students today to find the world brutal and threatening, and one suspects that when they sing about the burdens and sorrows of the Negro, for example, they are singing out of their own state of mind as well" (Montgomery 1960:118). For at least some of these students, the folk revival meant a complete change in lifestyle and the adoption of some of the values that were seen to go with folk culture: less reliance on money and its accumulation; more concern with community; pursuit of participatory, not vicarious, recreation; and political goals that resisted centralization of power while taking into account global and ecological concerns.

Anne Dhu McLucas

Snapshot 3.1 examines revivals and their relationship, primarily to American middle-class values and basic belief systems. Although many of us are familiar with the folk music revival of the 1960s, revivals take place in many varied musical and social contexts, such as the revival of the Russian balalaika orchestra presented here.

Figure 3.3
Pete Seeger, pictured in an illustration from the early '60s used in Folkways Records advertisements.
Courtesy Smithsonian/ Folkways Archive

Snapshot 3.1: Revivals

Music revival
A social movement to restore musical styles or musical instruments from a previous time that are believed to be in danger of disappearing

Social movements calling themselves "music revivals" are a prominent feature of the twentieth-century musical landscape. Music revivals have occurred in the United States, Canada, Germany, England, Brazil, India, Russia, Scotland, and elsewhere. Their focus is as wide-ranging as their geographical spread; they span from the revival of a single instrument—the harpsichord, the Northumbrian small-pipes, the lute—to the re-creation of entire popular, indigenous, or art music traditions—traditional jazz, American folk song, early music.

Music revivals are defined as social movements that strive to restore musical systems that have disappeared (or are believed to be disappearing) for the benefit of contemporary society. What distinguishes music revivals from musical fads or trends is the overt political and cultural agenda expressed by revivalists themselves. Through the re-creation of a past music system, revivalists position themselves in opposition to the contemporary cultural mainstream, align themselves with a particular historical lineage, and offer a cultural alternative in which legitimacy is grounded in claims of authenticity and historical fidelity.

The most important tenet of revivalist ideology is the historical continuity (*how long* a type of music has been performed) and authenticity (is this tradition found among the *true practitioners* of the musical style) of the revivalist practice. In the case of indigenous music revivals, the term *folk music* is often employed to refer to music with a long history outside consumer culture that contains the essence or seeds of a national cultural expression. In other types of revivals, authenticity is based on written source interpretation or on the re-creation of certain recorded performances. In revivalist discourse, historical continuity is often used to imply authenticity and vice versa, and both in turn are used to imply positive social value. Exactly how these concepts are mapped onto the repertoire, instrumentation, playing style, and interpretation of revivalist music will vary, but what is notable is that these values and distinctions are made, debated, and defended.

The educational aspect of revivals is another characteristic trait; once the aesthetic code referencing historical continuity and authenticity has been determined and reified through performance, recordings, and written and spoken discourse, it must be passed on to novice revivalists in order to ensure the correct maintenance of the tradition. Core revivalists also engage in efforts to educate the general public, such as lecture-demonstrations, public television appearances, and recordings, in the hope of gaining new converts as well as to foster a widespread appreciation of their music.

Music revivals are almost always initiated by a group of individuals who feel a strong affinity for and commitment to the musical tradition. Almost invariably they are scholars and collectors, and many are amateur musicians as well. Using their connections with institutions, the recording industry, radio, and television, they frequently act the role of cultural producer in promoting the revival.

Core revivalists are responsible for formulating the tradition's repertoire, stylistic features, and history. In the process an aesthetic code is constructed on what is believed to be a stylistic common denominator derived from individual performances and/or written and oral sources. This is transformed into the essence of the style that is then used to judge revivalist performances. Although aspects of this transformation may be historically verifiable, what core revivalists really do is create a new ethos, musical style, and aesthetic code strongly influenced by their revivalist ideology and personal preferences.

The revivalist community is reinforced through participation in activities such as organizational meetings, informal gatherings, concerts, festivals, and competitions. It is at these events that revivalists meet each other face to face to share repertoire and playing techniques, to discuss the strengths and weaknesses of artists within the tradition, to actively learn and experience the revivalist ethos and aesthetic code at work, and to socialize among other insiders. These events are fundamental to a revival's success, because they supplement what can be learned from recordings and books with lived experiences and direct human contact. As the community grows, it tends to diversify, and factions may arise that challenge dominant revivalist assumptions. The ebb-and-flow nature of revivalist experience is mirrored by the way the revivals themselves go through a cycle of boom and bust before they break down completely.

An industry consisting of nonprofit and/or commercial enterprises catering to the revivalist market, including concert promotions, sales of recordings, newsletters, pedagogical publications, instruments, and supplies, may develop. Public success and longevity of musical revivals depend in part on the strength and vitality of such industries, although problems can arise when revivalist concerns for authenticity compete with industry demands for marketability.

The Balalaika Orchestra Revival in the United States

A brief overview of the balalaika orchestra revival in the United States serves to illustrate some of the most prominent features of music revivals. The transformation of the balalaika, a triangular, three-stringed Russian folk instrument, into a concert instrument began with its discovery by nobleman Vassily Andreyev in the 1880s (Belevich 1988). Intrigued by its sound, Andreyev engaged a luthier to build a balalaika suitable for concert performances. In a

Balalaika
Three-stringed, triangular-bodied Russian folk instrument
Domra
A round-bodied Russian folk instrument played with a pick

short time, Andreyev had mastered the instrument and was giving concerts that dazzled elite Russian society. Inspired by his success as a balalaika soloist, he decided to create an orchestra consisting of balalaikas and *domra*s of various sizes. Andreyev and his balalaika ensemble were so well received at home that they began to tour abroad, appearing in concert halls in Paris, London, and Berlin. In 1910 and again in 1911 Andreyev's group gave concerts in the United States. Balalaika orchestras formed by Russian and East European emigrés and supported by the Russian Orthodox Church soon arose in St. Louis (1910), Chicago (1911), New York (1912), Philadelphia (1920), and Detroit (1926). These groups strove to pass on the teachings of Andreyev to their peers and children, thereby celebrating their Russian heritage.

In Russia the October Revolution (1917) brought about radical political changes; among these was the use of the balalaika orchestra as a means of furthering socialist ideology. Professional balalaika orchestras modeled after Andreyev's group were developed and supported by the Soviet state. Although these groups were presented by the Soviets as representative of regional folk music, they were composed of highly trained professionals who strove for a technical virtuosity and precision that rivaled Western art music. Nevertheless, these groups were and continue to be looked upon as role models for balalaika groups in the United States and elsewhere.

The burst of activity stimulated by Andreyev's visits to the United States came to an end with World War II, and the ensuing McCarthy era forced many groups to restrict their activities. During this time Russian instruments were difficult to find, and anything having to do with Russian culture was viewed with suspicion. By the early 1960s, however, the political climate was beginning to change, and younger generations of Russian Americans became interested in reviving the balalaika orchestra from the early twentieth century. The appearance of long-playing recordings of orchestras helped to stimulate interest. Old instruments were dug out of attics, and veterans from the old orchestras, including Sergei Larionoff, Luke Bakoota, and Mark Selivan, were sought out to guide their efforts and interests. The revival began with the foundation of the Balalaika and Domra Society of New York in 1961, founded by veteran performers Mark Selivan, Jack Raymond, and Alexander Kuchma. These revivalists were not interested in reviving Russian folk music as it existed in peasant villages. Instead their aim was to revive the balalaika orchestra as it was conceived of by its founder, Vassily Andreyev.

By the late 1970s a number of different balalaika orchestras and performers were operating throughout the United States. It was felt that the creation of a national organization would bring these disparate groups together and serve as a clearinghouse for importing Russian instruments, books, and music, so the Balalaika and Domra Association of America was created in 1978 by musicians Lynn Carpenter, Charley Rappaport, and Steve Wolownik. The group produces a regular newsletter and sponsors annual conventions. Most years, instrumentalists from Russia and/or East Europe are invited to act as teachers and performers, thus allowing novices to learn from accomplished performers of the tradition. The conventions are an important aspect of maintaining the revivalist community, which has grown from a small group of Russian emigrés and their descendants to include both Slavs and non-Slavs alike (Figure 3.4).

Musical revivals are both a middle-class product of and a reaction against modernity. The appearance of a great number of revivals across the globe is a generalized response within the middle sectors of a society to specific local and historical crises. The fluidity and dialectical nature of revivals, however, make each one a unique phenomenon in time and space, appropriate for that culture at that point in history. Music revivals, then, provide fertile ground for the study of music as a site for social action and political contention in times of social stress and for the study of the articulation of class identity through musical performance.

Tamara E. Livingston

Figure 3.4
"Rodina" Balalaika and Domra Convention, University of Illinois, Urbana, 1993. Photo by Bibs Ekkel.

THE IMPORTANCE OF RACE: EARLY BLACK/WHITE INTERACTIONS

Among the many social determinations of musical meaning in the United States, none has proven more powerful and enduring than that of race. At the onset of the new millennium, music's racial aspect carries forward the burden of its long memory, charting the extent of specifically black and white relations. The relationship of race to music is so fundamental to the American experience that it identifies a crucial linkage or even an archetype. What we may call the racio-musical dynamic not only informs modern notions of color and difference; it can be traced to the very seat of their formation over 200 years ago.

As an ideology, the concept of race would seem inextricably related to all musical categories and artists, from folk to classical, from Madonna to Aaron Copland. Typically, however, the extent of racial influence is downplayed in favor of more "colorless" distinctions of personality and style. Indeed, most Americans, and particularly those of the white majority, fail to recognize race's impact on music, except when it intervenes directly in representation and judgment. The appeal of Paul Whiteman in the 1920s and the public fascination with rap artists such as Vanilla Ice stand as exceptions to a rule of musical racelessness, which defers discussions of difference to the realm of African American artistry. Accordingly, the innovations of rap, jazz, gospel, and blues are not only representative American forms but color-coded ones, subsumed under the broad category of "black music."

The designation of African American music as quintessentially racial emerged out of the trajectories of colonial relations taking shape in the early modern era. While already a concept existing in Europe before the Renaissance, *race* acquired its specific, modern meaning by the seventeenth century, replacing the vague category of *nation* that had previously distinguished people of color from Europeans and European Americans. Africans in particular were singled out as the weakest of humanity's links, to the point at which the black phenotype became widely acknowledged as a signifier of intellectual and moral inferiority. By the late eighteenth century, the social weaknesses of blacks were deemed irreversible and endemic to the "species," an assumption that helped to justify the practice of slavery.

The appearance of a racially determined "Negro music," in its turn, took shape within this setting as it simultaneously proposed a critical challenge to a facile racialist orthodoxy. While providing sonic evidence of the difference between black and white, "Negro music" also complicated race-based distinctions because of its formation within the common ground of American cultural expression. As will be seen, the power of black music can be understood

Music Cultures in the United States

historically as something that emerged as much from this inherently unstable racial economy as it did from qualities typically attributed to the music itself. The magnitude of its power eventually carried into other realms, suffusing American social and intellectual perspectives (including those of musical scholarship) with a discernible racial cast.

Early References to "Negro Music"

Occasional references to "Negro music" provide insight into the European comprehension of African performances and, in turn, into how this understanding helped to determine racio-musical categories. Musical practices, when acknowledged, were typically framed within a discourse that characterized the array of discrete performance practices as so many versions of "noise." These fragmentary references to singing, instrumental playing, preaching, and bodily movement appeared as passing asides, such as the comment in a letter by Lady Oglethorpe from 1736 that referred to the "dismal and incessant blare" of an African slave playing a conch horn (Head 1893).

By the 1830s, reports of "Negro music" had become conspicuous, marking its transformation from a prior noise. These commentaries appeared in a variety of public and private sources that brought to wide attention a new awareness of a formally coherent African American performance. As public acknowledgments of musical form, the depictions were significant, reflecting the changing attitudes of white Americans who were now sometimes led to acknowledge the humanity of African Americans. Typically, these portraits took two forms. The first reflected the antislavery sentiments of the abolitionist movement, which represented black song in its slave narratives and newspapers as the tragic expression of a noble people caught in struggle. The second depicted black music as a debased kind of primitive glee, staged in performance by white men in blackface (the minstrel show). While tracing dramatically different social figures, the representations shared in their caricatures a reliance on stereotypes of authenticity and folk nature.

With the emergence of a recognizable "Negro music" in the 1830s, however, singing masters began working assiduously to stress performance practices that appeared to favor white significations. The departure from the West African call and response form and the new emphasis on harmony, together with the broadscale institutional efforts to remove blacks from white congregations (commencing already by the 1810s), worked to craft a racio-musical defense against the encroaching "noise" of blackness. While slave and free singing had most likely already reflected recognizable distinctions based on the peculiar concentrations of African and European musical peoples, a new ideological separation heightened these distinctions and, most likely, prompted the invention of new ones out of the existing intercultural matrix.

Spirituals and the Rise of Modern "Black Music"

By the 1860s, the twin social forces of blackface minstrelsy and southern slave song had converged in public performances and representations. Rendered publicly as *spirituals*, these songs would be celebrated as the wondrous achievements of a possessed people, representing a kind of miracle of sound. (See more on spirituals in Chapter 7.) First described by northern visitors to the Sea Islands around 1860, the songs would grow in popularity, soon to be documented in the form of published lyrics and notations that circulated among northern and southern people. By the 1870s the songs were being sung professionally by blacks themselves, most notably by the Fisk University Jubilee Singers, whose famous tours of the United States and Europe made black music a common symbol of pleasure and leisure in Western societies (Figure 3.5).

Significantly, these renderings of black music were not actual slave songs but rather second-level representations of the already inauthentic expressions that had evolved interculturally within the particular locales of southern plantations. Refigured in notation and performed according to practices introduced by northern white teachers, the spirituals of the Fisk singers and other singing groups identified yet another level of racially based cultural interplay that spoke to a legacy of interracial involvement. Nonetheless, these

Figure 3.5
The Jubilee Singers of Fisk University, c. 1875.

Music Cultures in the United States

hybrids would carry meaning across black and white cultures, informing practices as they were repeatedly recast within the particular circumstances of communities across the nation. Later specifications, notably the rhythmic qualities *hot, rag, jazz,* and *swing,* contributed additional levels of meaning to the musical formation of racial difference.

By the turn of the twentieth century, black music had come to define the difference between black and white, even as its actual history betrayed repetitions of cross-racial influence. It was this sound that W. E. DuBois named black people's gift to America, a form whose paradoxical racial markers revealed the true source of its affective power (DuBois 1992 [1903]). Indeed, the emotional potency of black music derived not from some mythic concentration of racial essence but from its instability as a racial marker. It offered to African Americans a sense of "blackness" accessed ironically through the interracial American whole, as it provided for European Americans the imagination of a national completion that also maintained racial separation.

Ronald Radano

Snapshot 3.2 illustrates the connection between African American identity during and following the Civil Rights Movement in the twentieth century and the musical forms that developed at that time. Funk, perhaps more than any other music of its time, expressed the powerful feelings and beliefs of African American urban culture and has continued to provide a space for these expressions.

Snapshot 3.2: Funk

Funk is an urban form of dance music that emerged in the late 1960s, crystallized and peaked in the 1970s, and expanded in new directions in the 1980s. Its sound resonated the energy of black working-class communities, and its message, the rhetoric of Black Power and black America's response to the post–Civil Rights era. The 1960s Great Society legislation, affirmative action programs, and Black Power movement raised expectations among African Americans for a better life. Yet society's support for these programs began to wane in the mid-1970s at a time when changing economic conditions led to massive unemployment and poverty in innercity communities.

> **Funk**
> Post-1960s black musical style that combined a strong political message along with a wedding of rock instrumentation with black rhythms

The ubiquitous optimism that once prevailed in African American communities slowly changed in response to unfulfilled expectations. While some members of the new middle class expressed ambivalence about progress, the poor and unemployed verbalized their disillusionment at the system that failed them. The term *funk* captured these feelings. As a musical style, funk represented the resilience and creativity of African Americans under changing social conditions, becoming an expression of social change, cultural liberation, and musical experimentation.

The pioneers of funk were revolutionaries who created a musical genre that broke rules and crossed musical, class, and racial boundaries. It was the interracial and intergender group Sly and the Family Stone from San Francisco that led the way by redefining the direction of black popular music. This self-contained group (members sang and played instruments) introduced the technology from rock (wah-wah pedal, fuzz box, echo chamber, vocal distortion, and so on) to the tradition. They also fused a blues-rock flavored guitar ("Sex Machine" [1968]) with syncopated horn riffs and blues- and jazz-inflected horn solos laid over a polyrhythmic "groove" established by the "Godfather of Soul," James Brown. Another innovation of Sly and the Family Stone was the revolutionary style of bassist Larry Graham. Graham exploited the instrument's melodic and rhythmic capabilities by pulling, plucking, thumping, and slapping the strings to produce a distinctive percussive style heard in the 1969 recordings "Stand!," "Hot Fun in the Summertime," and "Thank You (Falettinme Be Mice Elf Agin)."

Sly and the Family Stone epitomized the spirit, chaos, and contradictions of the late 1960s and early 1970s. Influenced by the civil rights movement and the ideology of Black Power, Sly Stone spoke out against social injustice, promoted universal harmony and candidly addressed racial issues, revealing his political consciousness as a black man in America. His politically conscious lyrics, eclectic sounds, infectious energy, and hippie image attracted multiracial audiences from all social and economic backgrounds. This form of racial integration engendered themes of universal love and world peace that became codified and promoted through the music of black artists and white folk groups. In the early 1970s, however, messages of Black Power and "let's party" began to overshadow themes of universal love and world peace. These themes revealed the response of African Americans to the changing economic and social conditions of the innercity poor and working classes. In innercity communities, funk became a major form of cultural expression, and it provided some hope for the poor and working classes that saw little, if any, potential for improved conditions.

In black clubs, the poor and working-class blacks temporarily escaped from the uncertainties and pressures of daily life, partying to funk music. The "Dayton street funk" style of the Ohio Players, for example (Figure 3.6), became popular among these groups. According to bass player Marshall Jones (1997), their songs captured the flavor and drew on the vocabulary of black street culture. Other groups, such as Kool and the Gang, created a celebratory atmosphere by adding party sound effects to their music that inspired black folk to "hang loose" on the dance floor

Figure 3.6
The Ohio Players, who
created the Dayton
street funk style.
Courtesy Archives of
African American Music
and Culture, Indiana
University.

("Funky Stuff" [1973], "Jungle Boogie" [1973], and "Hollywood Swinging" [1974]).

Positioned between the black working and middle classes were African American college students. In a field study on the musical preferences of these students, many indicated that they favored funk because they could "chill," "party," and "be themselves" (Maultsby 1982; 1983). On predominantly white campuses, funk provided a source for personal rejuvenation and reconnected black students to their cultural roots. These students experienced exclusion and an inhospitable environment and that their feeling of alienation increased after the assassination of Martin Luther King, Jr. Determined to influence change, African American students negotiated the implementation of black studies curricula, the recruitment of African American faculty and staff, and the establishment of black student unions, cultural centers, and all-black dormitories. Retreating from mainstream pressures, funk music created an atmosphere for unrestricted social interaction and an expression of "blackness."

Although funk music appealed primarily to African American communities in the early 1970s, some groups had crossover appeal. Continuing the tradition of Sly and the Family Stone, Earth, Wind and Fire encouraged society to care for its children and to find peace on earth and meaning in life through understanding and love. Despite the crossover success of Earth, Wind and Fire and occasional crossover singles from Kool and the Gang and other groups, funk largely disappeared from the mainstream in the second half of the 1970s. Contributing factors were the rise in disco music as a competing form, a slower tempo that made funk incompatible with the dance styles of whites, restrictive programming policies of Top 40 radio, and racially segmented marketing practices of record labels. In contrast, funk became central to social settings in African American communities as an outlet for frustration and a uniting force in an era of social change. This music dominated the programming of many black-oriented radio stations, the turntables in nightclubs, and the stage in performance venues.

By the mid-1970s, funk and other styles of black popular music had begun to evolve in new directions. This development paralleled the government's move toward fiscal conservatism, society's shift in views on the 1960s equal rights legislation, and the expression of disillusionment and ambivalence about progress among African Americans. In "Funky President," singer James Brown criticized President Richard Nixon for his social and economic policies. He explained that while stock prices rose and taxes increased, jobs disappeared in the black community, leaving black people drinking from paper cups. Addressing the working-class and poor blacks, Brown declared: "We gotta' get over, before we go under." A year later, the O'Jays in "Survival" desperately pleaded for assistance to pay rent and buy shoes for a baby because they were broke and "one step away from the bread line."

George Clinton (Figure 3.7) took party-funk to another level when he formulated the P-funk concept, defined by a philosophy, attitude, culture, and musical style. Grounded in the ideology of Black Power, P-funk advocated self-liberation from the social and cultural restrictions of society. It created new social spaces for African Americans to redefine themselves and celebrate their blackness. P-funk had its own language, fashion, dances, and mythical heroes and villains, who Clinton presented as cartoon and black science-fiction characters. The mastermind and producer of five P-funk groups (Parliament, Funkadelic, Parlets, the Brides of Funkenstein, and Bootsy's Rubber Band), Clinton combined these cultural components to create stories about black people and black life from a black perspective.

The P-funk sound drew elements from the blues, rhythm and blues, jazz, funk, and psychedelic rock. The tempo of songs encouraged black people to be cool and laid back. Therefore, they were slower than the music of non-P-funk groups, centering on 88 beats per minute and rarely exceeding 104, as opposed to the 96 to 120 beats per minute of other funk groups. Clinton also broadened the scope of funk by introducing new approaches to varying moods, textures, and timbres that symbolized concepts of heterogeneity and spontaneity in black cultural expression.

Figure 3.7
George Clinton, originator of P-funk. Courtesy Archives of African American Music and Culture, Indiana University.

In the 1980s, funk developed in new directions. New trends in popular music and the popularity of disco music following the 1978 release of the film *Saturday Night Fever* forced many funk musicians to include pop elements in their productions. The reliance on synthesizers in the production of disco influenced the reconfiguration of funk groups. Changing technology as well as recording budget restrictions compelled many funk bands to reduce their personnel by replacing bass and horn players and other musicians with synthesizers to remain competitive.

Several of the 1970s groups, including the Isley Brothers, Brothers Johnson, and Rick James, successfully incorporated advanced technology to modernize their funk sound. Others, such as Kool and the Gang, Slave, and Dayton, changed musical directions by adding lead vocalists to the group in addition to disco and pop elements over the funk groove. Some funk groups had difficulty redefining their musical direction. The group Dayton, for example, reached its maturity in the transitional period between disco and funk. Dayton's use of advanced technology resulted in a more sophisticated sound with less obvious funk roots.

New crossover funk sounds came out of Minneapolis. The multi-talented Prince created an eclectic repertoire and musical style rooted in R&B and rock. He expanded the tradition by introducing an erotic brand of synthesized funk in the albums *Dirty Mind* (1980), *1999* (1982), and *Purple Rain* (1984). Another Minneapolis group, The Time, created a new style of synthesized dance funk employing flavorings reminiscent of Graham Central Station and high-tech production techniques (*What Time Is It?* [1982] and *Ice Cream Castles* [1984]).

The 1980s represented a transitional period not only for funk musicians but the broader African American community as well. The economic downside and President Ronald Reagan's gradual dismantling of affirmative action programs created chaos in innercity communities. The second recession (1980–1982), ongoing fiscal and social conservatism, and the accumulative impact of deindustrialization thrust poor and working-class blacks into severe poverty marked by high unemployment and overcrowded, dilapidated, rat-infested dwellings. Moreover, the relocation of the black middle class to the suburbs and integrated neighborhoods left these communities without traditional leadership and financial resources.

Funk Philosophy and Style

Funk as a cultural style defined an image that portrayed a lifestyle and communicated a philosophy. It is manifested in the persona adopted by groups, the fashions they wore, artwork on album jackets, and elaborate stage props.

The Ohio Players, for example, chose their name and constructed an image from the street life of Dayton. On album jackets and in live performances, they dressed in tuxedos, furs, hats, diamond rings, and other fashionable street attire from the 1970s and 1980s. They also used extensive stage props to create the ambience of city street life. In contrast, Earth, Wind and Fire constructed an image of spirituality using Egyptian symbols that connected them with the ancient past. They dressed in sequined white and bright-colored costumes, and their stage props depicted ancient spiritual sources. These visuals and the people of different racial and ethnic backgrounds that appeared on many of Earth, Wind and Fire's album jackets conveyed themes of universality and world peace.

George Clinton's groups, Parliament and Funkadelic, adopted images that mirrored both the P-funk philosophy and themes for each album. They dressed in outlandish costumes such as sheets, diapers, hot pants, bell-bottom pants, furs, sequined tops, space outfits, sunglasses, and masks. Moreover, live performances featured elaborate props accompanied by sound, lighting, and stage effects that transformed the stage into imagined places, including outer space, where a huge spaceship landed on the "planet of funk." Stage performances of George Clinton, Earth, Wind and Fire, and the Ohio Players advanced funk to another level and influenced the productions of musicians of subsequent decades.

The funk sound, image, and stage performance of the music represented a rejection of mainstream values and norms. In the 1970s and 1980s, many African Americans from all socioeconomic classes created new spaces for unrestricted black expression in the "land of funk," where they responded to the pressures of daily life in an "integrated" society by affirming and celebrating their black identity.

Portia K. Maultsby

THE IMPORTANCE OF GENDER

Gender as an analytic category and interpretive focus has become increasingly central to music research of all kinds. The concept of gender is generally understood to describe the means or systems by which cultures and social groups create, display, transmit, and enforce biological sexual difference; that is, *gender theory* describes how a culture makes sense of what it means to be male and female. Given the almost universal practice of patriarchy, which gives some men power over all women and many other men, gender roles typically enact and thereby perpetuate unequal power relations. Thus

Gender theory
How a culture makes sense of what it means to be male and female

behaviors and other social practices described as masculine are not only different from those identified as feminine but typically carry more cultural prestige and power.

In the United States, the ideologies of masculinity frequently incorporate a fear of the feminine, because femininity, like the female sex, is still less socially valued and valuable. Such gender imbalance further shapes other cultural relationships, especially assumptions about social power and worth. The influential Cartesian theory that the mind and body represent two opposing forces accords greater significance and importance to the rational mind—typically understood as "masculine"—over the irrational and "feminized" body. Similarly, notions of the "civilized" and civilization have been masculinized, and male "primitives," including most men of color, have been placed in subordinate or feminized positions regardless of their biological sex.

Gender roles, while often portrayed as dichotomies or opposites, are highly mutable and frequently contradictory, changing over time and place and in response to social realities of all kinds. Although gender roles may be understood as normative and self-evident by their cultural practitioners, the explication and interpretation of the gendering process require great care and contextualization to understand how power relationships function and change on a day-to-day basis and over time. For example, men and women may share roles and attributes and regularly or occasionally take part in certain behaviors or activities typically assigned to the other sex. However, some gender transgressions may be more permissible than others, depending on other sociopolitical realities. Acknowledging and exploring gender dynamics allows scholars to see behaviors and activities—music making among them—as socially and culturally shaped and shaping rather than biologically determined and essential.

Gender Ideologies in Nineteenth- and Early Twentieth-Century Music Making

Although musical practices themselves reinforce sociocultural hierarchies of power, music making in the United States has historically been a feminized activity. Due largely to the constructions of nineteenth-century gender ideologies, in which middle- and upper-class men and women were understood as acting in separate and unequal arenas (often described as "public" and "private" spheres), certain kinds of music making and music appreciation came to be understood as activities appropriate to middle- and upper-class femininity as "feminine accomplishments." Training in female seminaries, colleges, and even within public coeducational universities identified music—typically singing or playing the piano within the home and teaching amateurs—as women's work, not unlike embroidery, quilting, or the later academic discipline of home economics.

Furthermore, certain kinds of music became associated with moral uplift, which similarly was a white woman's purview, given her position as the guardian of domesticity and goodness within the middle- and upper-class home. Men required practical training in business and agriculture; the arts and other recreational pursuits were luxuries left to women with class privilege who had the resources of leisure time and money.

Particular musical activities, such as the powerful roles of conductor or composer of large-scale symphonic and operatic repertoires, remained largely off-limits to women of all classes as well as to nonwhite or working-class men. Women, who challenged these practices and sought public careers as performers or composers, often did so at great personal cost. "Acting like a man" rendered a female musician open to criticism regarding her femininity and sexuality; those who persisted in masculine careers often found themselves judged "abnormal."

With the growing power of the nineteenth-century suffrage movement in the United States, antiwomen attitudes in general became more prevalent and fears about the feminization of culture more acute. Similarly, the turn of the twentieth century witnessed the earliest scholarly discussions of homosexuality and homosexuals, or "gender inverts" as Richard Kraft-Ebbing (1840-1902), a German neuropsychaiatrist, called them. This gave rise to homophobic and misogynistic beliefs that attempted to counter fears of music making as a female, and thus effeminizing, activity.

The granting of suffrage in the United States in 1920, along with other political and educational reforms, helped bring about real changes in many women's lives. Although white middle- and upper-class women were frequently the greatest beneficiaries of these changes, as the twentieth century progressed, women gained greater—if rarely full—parity with men in many public and professional arenas of music. Women composers of modern concert music, for example, were no longer a rarity, and a number, including Amy Beach and Louise Talma (Figure 3.8) in the United States, attained recognition.

Research on Music and Gender

Concert Music

Some of the earliest works that made women's music making a central focus were biographical studies of women composers and performers of European American concert music. Further research recovered the lives and activities of African American women in the United States, exploring how they negotiated the cultural constructions of femininity as well as race within the privileged concert repertoires. Four notable biographical studies are those of U.S. composers Ruth Crawford (Tick 1997), Amy Beach (Block 1998), and Pauline

Figure 3.8
Louise Talma (1906–1996) was an
active composer in the neoclassical
style, as well as a prominent
teacher. Photo from the collections
of the Library of Congress.

Oliveros (Mockus 1999), and early feminist musicologist Sophie
Drinker (Solie 1993a). All four studies provide complicated explica-
tions of gender, sexuality, racial ideologies, class privilege, and
national identity as central to specific musical practices, the writing
of music history, and the musical lives of their subjects. The careers
and writings of male composers of "classical" music have also provided a means for exploring various relationships between masculinity and musicality and musical style.

Not unlike feminist scholars who challenged the systems of cultural prestige by celebrating quilt making, romance novels, and
other aspects of "woman's culture" that had been ignored, music
scholars began to examine and reinterpret undervalued repertoires
of European American music, such as so-called parlor or salon music
and magazine music, and venues, such as settlement houses, where
women exercised a great deal of power or where women acted as primary consumers.

Apart from the examinations of women's lives and activities,
other studies have explored how aspects of music life and culture
have been talked and written about in ways that show the gendering
of music within larger social frameworks and practices. Such critical
interpretations of these discourse strategies include how modern
music maintained its masculinity in the face of feminized culture,
how technology has become a masculine domain that has influenced the consumption of hi-fi stereos in the 1950s as well as the
current accessibility of electronic and computer music composition,

and how the academic fields of music study perpetuates exclusive if not misogynistic practices.

Popular Musics

The postmodern critic Andreas Huyssen (1986) has suggested that in the West mass culture—or practices and activities associated with popular taste—presents another feminized cultural space. Popular culture, by definition, does not partake of the timelessness associated with "high art," itself a historically constructed category, but rather embodies novelty, changeability, faddishness, and malleability, all attributes often associated with women and contributing to their lesser cultural value (Levine 1988). This perspective can be borne out in music studies in which popular musics have only recently received the kind of scholarly attention presumed for so-called classical or concert repertoires. The term *popular music* is used here in the most inclusive way possible to encompass a wide variety of traditions and repertoires that have been judged outside the normative limits of concert and classical Western music, for example, Anglo American balladry, sheet music and popular song, blues, jazz, rock and roll, country, klezmer, and so on.

> **Popular music**
> Traditions and repertoires outside of the limits of Western classical or concert music, including rock and roll, ballads, country, klezmer, and other styles

Popular musics, in order to be indeed popular and populist, have often relied on amateur music making, industrialization, and changing mass media, such as the growth of the sheet music industry, mass production of the parlor piano in the last decades of the nineteenth century, and the emergence of recorded sound technology in the early twentieth century. The domestic venues of popular music often encouraged female participation, and thus women found opportunities as creators of popular song or even as public performers within popular entertainments such as vaudeville. Women still participated in clearly gendered and frequently sexualized ways visible in the kinds of repertoire chosen, how they learned repertoire, and the kinds of roles they might play on stage (Figure 3.9). However, while adhering to gender norms, situations could arise that demonstrate the malleability of gender and suggest how women may adapt or redefine notions of masculinity and femininity in their participation. For example, in a family without sons, a firstborn daughter might join her father as a singer, or during times of war, when male musicians are drafted, female instrumentalists might find greater—and unusual—opportunities for public performance.

Female popular music instrumentalists often faced the same kinds of prohibitions as women performers of so-called high art repertoires. Singing and playing the piano remained the most appropriate ways for women to take part in popular musics, and singers, male or female, were frequently not accorded the same prestige as instrumentalists were. Women who played the saxophone, drums,

Figure 3.9
The Amazon chorus was an innovation of mid-nineteenth-century popular theater that provided the largely male audience with a mass display of the female form. This image, which was printed in the *National Police Gazette* on 15 November 1884, had the following caption: "Walking into their Affections: How a manager at Tombstone, Arizona, utilized his pretty waiter girls as Marching Amazons."

upright bass, or other "masculine" instruments faced almost insurmountable difficulties in pursuing professional careers except within the context of all-women ensembles. Rock music's emphasis on electric guitar and drums—both instruments still largely viewed as inappropriate for girls to learn—continues to mark it as a music men make and women listen to. Even women singers who pursue the masculinized vocal genres of rap, heavy metal, or punk encounter opposition coming from their attempts to cross gendered musical lines. An increasing reliance on MIDI technology in popular music also raises questions of gender in contemporary technology-based musical education, because this technology is often perceived as a masculine domain. Regardless of its challenges and limitations, popular music, in its many varieties and musical possibilities, remains particularly attractive and accessible to women.

The popular traditions of blues, gospel, and rhythm and blues (and later hip-hop and rap) provided women, most often African American, with continued career opportunities, although ones still marked by race and gender. Some of the earliest popular recording stars in the United States were black women blues singers whose success and performative power called into question their repertoires, which might seem to perpetuate images of women as passive victims. Similarly, women as gospel performers, although often prohibited from preaching in the pulpit, might find their music making a place of power from which to reconstruct gender behaviors. Rap is frequently depicted in the mainstream popular press as an undifferentiated kind of music almost exclusively voicing black male aggression and misogynist violence, but female rap artists have constantly presented alternative models of black femininity (Figure 3.10). While relying on rap's musical and textural modes, these female creators subvert beliefs about femininity and musicianship, masculinity and racial difference, and call into question simplistic and reductive approaches to rap as a musical category.

Jazz has attained significant scholarly and cultural prestige, and compensatory histories have argued for the important contributions of women performers, arrangers, and composers. More recently, scholars have begun to explore jazz's complicated racial meanings and roles in the changing ideologies of black manhood and white masculinity as well as addressing the complicated issues facing black women, whose public presence has often been controversial.

Country music has provided a way for male and female performers, typically white, to challenge class presumptions. Although widely popular with listening audiences, country music remains a marginalized genre, a music often satirized for its lack of class status and its connection with the undervalued and "backward" South. Indeed, country music's initial self-definition in the 1930s as "country and western" was a means to legitimate its lower-class roots through connections with the then-popular western cowboy hero, whose positive image of masculinity replaced that of the uneducated southern hillbilly. Recent scholarship demonstrates how country music provides another means to explore the multiple intersections of gender, class, and race. Women both as consumers and as popular performers continue to rework and negotiate the multiple oppressions of their lives, often creating powerful subversive strategies in the face of the contradictions of gender.

Rock music, loosely defined, has been an especially powerful kind of popular music in this century, one that allows for many explorations regarding the connections between music and identity.

Figure 3.10
Queen Latifah, a prominent and highly successful rap artist since the early 1990s, has advocated equality and unity within the black community through her music. Photo by Randee St. Nicholas, courtesy the BMI Archives.

While women have played enormously important roles as performers and consumers of rock-based musics, as with most other traditions, rock remains a male-dominated field as well as an industry that is still largely controlled by white Americans.

Likewise, within the emerging field of popular music study, scholars have overwhelmingly focused on rock-based genres to the exclusion of other genres and popular musics existing before 1960. Some of the earliest scholarship on rock music came from sociologists who recognized the importance of this new kind of popular music in the courtship activities of adolescents. More recently, scholars have examined the ways in which rock music helps individuals construct and identify themselves as sexualized and gendered beings (Figure 3.11). Several recent scholarly collections have specifically brought gender to the forefront by examining connoisseurship, consumption, and the musical sounds themselves.

Susan C. Cook

Men, as well as women, are gendered; that is, they are taught through the rules and codes of their cultures the appropriate ways to be masculine within specific contexts. Nowhere is the display of the male gender as evident as in the performance of rock music, where sexuality is frequently enacted through musical performance. Snapshot 3.3 examines the often nuanced construction of masculinity through the music of Led Zeppelin and the performances of its star singer, Robert Plant, and guitarist, Jimmy Page.

Figure 3.11
Poison (right to left): Bret Michaels, singer; Bobby Dall, bass; Rikki Rockett, drums; C. C. Deville, guitar), who reunited for a reunion tour in 1999, typified the glam side of the heavy metal scene in the late 1980s and 1990s. Photo courtesy the BMI Archives.

Music Cultures in the United States

Snapshot 3.3: Led Zeppelin and the Construction of Masculinity

The group Led Zeppelin (1968-1980) is often cited as the progenitor of heavy metal or hard rock, genres of music that have been dominated by male performers. The prevalent view of gender construction in this music has focused attention on the ways in which both visual images and musical sounds reinforce stereotypical notions of masculinity. As Simon Frith and Angela McRobbie characterized it in their influential 1978 article "Rock and Sexuality," these performers and their music can be "aggressive, dominating, and boastful, and they constantly seek to remind the audience of their prowess, their control" (1990:372). Frith and McRobbie, and many others since, have referred to this kind of music as "cock rock" because of its celebration of machismo and masculine sexuality. Many metal performers, Led Zeppelin's Robert Plant among them, choose to bare their chests in performance and to wear tight pants that emphasize their genitals, flaunting their biologically male physical attributes by putting these on display for their audiences. Typical performance gestures, such as taking a wide-legged firm stance or picking up the microphone stand and walking around with it, have been interpreted as demonstrations of male strength and power.

The guitar player—or better, the guitar "hero"—is central to hard rock and metal and has also been linked with the notion of masculine power and control. Typically, the guitarist is a virtuoso player, whose mastery of the instrument can also be interpreted as signifying dominance and control over it. The electric guitar has also often been thought of as a metaphor for the phallus because of its shape and the position in which it is often held (slung around the hips) and because the way in which it is played suggests masturbation. The sound of much of the music—very loud and rhythmically insistent—has also often been associated with masculine sexuality, the loudness suggesting, again, domination and power; the rhythmic insistence, male thrusting during intercourse. Metal singers display power through the use of high, strained registers and plenty of distortion, the latter of which especially can be viewed, as Robert Walser has expressed it, as "a signal of extreme power and intense expression by overflowing its channels and materializing the exceptional effort that produces it" (1993:42).

These powerful images of masculinity, as well as the relationships among band members, especially between singer and guitarist, acted out in performance have been described as opportunities for male bonding not only among band members but, as Deena Weinstein (1991) has pointed out, among band members and the males in their audiences. The enactments of power and control have been thought to be especially compelling for young men and further, to young *white* men (almost all metal performers are white as well), less so for women. Lyrically, the songs often celebrate male sexuality (in a tradition largely taken over from the blues), create escapist fantasy narratives, or explore spiritual life through a mixture of Christian, Eastern, ancient, and other religious themes and symbols.

One of the quintessential "cock rock" songs is surely Led Zeppelin's "Whole Lotta Love," the lyric of which (mostly taken from bluesman Willie Dixon's song "You Need Love") is about sexual gratification. It is not so much the lyric that has attracted attention, however, as it is Plant's performance, which, with its generally intense expression, moans, and screams, can be read as an enactment of sex, complete with orgasm. Because Plant is biologically male, and because there are references in the lyrics to his maleness and his partner's femaleness, this song is generally viewed as a boastful, arrogant display of heterosexual machismo. The riff, one of guitarist Jimmy Page's most famous ones, seems to reinforce the idea that this song is being sung from a masculine perspective, each beat of the measure articulated by a stroke on the guitar, the regularity and speed of these gestures suggesting, perhaps, male thrusting during intercourse, as well as the approach of sexual climax.

But this is quite a superficial reading. First, the nearly hysterical emotional landscape suggested by Plant's singing has traditionally been associated with women, not men; although this is an essentialist idea, it is nonetheless the way in which hysterical behavior has traditionally been coded—it is not a behavior associated with men who are "in control." Second, there are several points, not simply one, throughout the song at which Plant would seem to reach climax, and this idea of multiple climaxes also suggests a feminine identity for Plant. The insistent riff subsides twice during the song as well, making way for an experimental section of electronic music in the first instance and a guitar solo in the second.

Another consideration of gender construction in "Whole Lotta Love" is that in some cases—perhaps many—the song is not understood in isolation but within the context of other Led Zeppelin songs. While the band is known for producing some of the heaviest rock music ever, their recorded output also includes a considerable number of acoustically based songs or songs in which acoustic and electric elements are blended. In other words, while the group was interested in creating an identity that included macho posturing, this identity is not monolithic and is not understood, at least by avid fans, in isolation. The acoustically based love song "Tangerine," for example, suggests intimacy and vulnerability in its musical as well as lyrical narrative.

Equally problematic are the visual images in this band. Although Page, for example, certainly enacts elements of the typical macho "cock rocker" figure, his appearance often contradicts this image. Page's machismo poses are always uneasily negotiated through his slender, lanky frame, the delicacy of his features, the way in which he so often bends his body inward in collapse as he plays, signifying the "frailty" that journalistic writers have commented on. Quite aside from the sometimes frilly or glittery clothes that he wore, or his curling-ironed long hair, his body, face, and elfin gestures have an androgynous quality that is difficult to ignore.

The relationship between Page and Plant on stage is certainly partly about male camaraderie and competition. The two often engaged in a kind of sparring during which Page would play a musical gesture on his guitar that Plant was then expected to imitate. The gestures would become increasingly higher, often driving Plant past the uppermost reaches of his vocal range, and eventually forcing him to concede failure to Page. Sometimes, however, this kind of rivalry gave way to Plant's urging Page on during a guitar solo, responding to his musical gestures with moans and sighs, imploring Page to "push, push," suggesting that he stretch himself further in terms of musical direction. These exchanges also have interesting possibilities in terms of gender construction, because they cast Plant in the role of feminine other to Page's masculine guitar hero: Plant begs Page for more, for him to push harder, and responds to Page's musical gestures as if they were a lover's caresses.

Much has been said about how the majority of the audience for heavy metal is male and how the music and images reproduce hegemonic constructions of white suburban male identity. But the culture of heavy metal cannot be so unproblematically interpreted in terms of gender. As Robert Walser reports (1993), by the late 1980s, nearly half of the audience for heavy metal was female. In the ethnographic study of Led Zeppelin fans that I conducted (Fast 2001), a third of the people who responded were women, all of whom were avid fans. Many of these women find the music and images erotic, and many appropriate the demonstrations of "masculine" power for themselves, finding the images and music empowering, not frightening (as Frith and McRobbie [1990] suggested they were to women). Walser (1993) also reports that there is significant interest in heavy metal by gay men, who view some metal videos as erotic fantasies.

Some imagery and lyrics in metal are decidedly misogynistic, and the arguments I make here are not intended to excuse or justify those that are. Rather, I would call for a closer examination of images and music, a differentiation among various performers in terms of their constructions of gender, and interviews with those who consume the music and images in order to understand what and how they relate to the genre.

Susan Fast

In approaching any given faith, one can ask a number of questions about a particular group's values and uses of music. Following are nine such questions, posed here as dichotomies: two opposing positions, each pair representing the ends of a continuum. Each set of dichotomies reflects a basic defining issue of primary importance to social, cultural, and religious identity in the United States.

A Model for Examining Religious Beliefs and Musical Practices

The Mainstream/Folk Continuum

Mainstream religious denominations tend to be highly centralized and standardized and are found over a broad geographical area. Most are of foreign origin; they are sometimes described as "historical churches." Typical examples include the Roman Catholic Church, the Orthodox traditions, and the main bodies of the Lutheran, Methodist, Presbyterian, Episcopal, and other such denominations. Folk churches, perhaps better described as sects, tend to be small in scale, restricted in geography, and idiosyncratic in practice, if not in belief. A great many faiths fall somewhere between these two, with characteristics of both. For many reasons, the music found at the folk end of this scale tends to be of greater interest to researchers than that at the mainstream end.

The Urban–Rural Continuum

The urban-rural dichotomy—perhaps more useful in the past than in the present as a result of demographic changes especially since World War II—nevertheless retains some relevance, especially in terms of music. Urban churches, especially the larger mainstream congregations, are more likely to have instruments, in particular large pipe organ installations, and choirs. In the nineteenth century, it was also common in urban churches to accompany singing with a violoncello, and the old European Baroque custom of thorough bass accompaniment persisted in such churches until the late nineteenth century. Although rural folk churches have become part of the urban environment because of migrations, rural churches are unlikely to have more than a piano, pump organ (in the past), or electronic organ. Archaic performance practices such as lining out, singing from shape-note notation, and chanted sermons are more likely found in isolated rural areas than in towns or cities. The term *rural* can denote both churches located in vast agricultural areas such as Illinois, where mainstream historical churches dominated and those in isolated areas, such as Appalachia, where independent local sects predominate.

Mainstream religions
Major religions that tend to be highly centralized in structure with standardized rituals; examples include the Roman Catholic and Episcopal churches

Folk religions or sects
Religions that are smaller in scale than mainstream religions, restricted in geography, and following individual practices and beliefs

Lining out
The practice of a songleader singing a musical phrase and then the congregation repeating it

Shape note notation
A method of notating hymns in which the shape of the note indicates the pitch to be sung

---

The Black/White Continuum

Although the United States is ostensibly an integrated society, it tends to remain segregated in terms of religious association. Few churches, none of them mainstream, would exclude members of any race or ethnicity, but in practice, churches are either white, predominantly white, or black. Black denominations—primarily Baptist and Methodist—formed out of historically white denominations after the Civil War, and by the end of the nineteenth century newly founded sects proliferated. Black and white styles of worship tend to remain distinctive, especially in terms of performance practices and repertoire. For example, both white and black churches perform types of gospel music, but despite their having common roots, these have become completely differentiated. In presentday America, however, many traits hitherto considered black have been absorbed by white society, and one can now encounter white and mixed choirs singing and behaving like black choirs.

The Upper-/Lower-Class Continuum

Although one might hope that religious doctrines would overcome class differences, people still prefer to associate with others of similar class and lifestyle. Churches tend to reflect the ethnic, economic, and political orientations of the secular world. Fair or not, many people associate particular denominations with particular classes because these stereotypes have been more or less true. Ethnic-based denominations or congregations, even when associated with otherwise broad-based mainstream groups, tend to retain traits from the homeland. Consequently, one encounters a Korean Presbyterian church, a Hungarian Jewish temple, an English Lutheran church, a Polish Catholic church, or an African American Islamic mosque. Many of these faiths worship with distinctive musical traditions.

In terms of class, few churches are clearly based on a single economic category, but members of the working and professional classes do tend to gravitate toward separate congregations of like membership, and this factor often determines the style of worship as well. People sometimes refer to "country club" or "silk-stocking" churches, or to emotional congregations as "holy rollers."

The Restraint/Emotion Continuum

The degree of emotional expression during worship may say nothing of individual sincerity but often says a great deal about culture and tradition, because such behaviors are learned within one's own socioreligious context. Most denominations and sects follow typical patterns of behavior that usually correlate with socioeconomic status, ethnic background, and sometimes geographical origin. At the restrained end of the scale one finds many of the historical denominations, especially those originating in the British Isles and northern Europe. For the most part, orthodox Christian faiths, Judaism, and especially the Asian-derived religions are also restrained. At the emotional end are those faiths that are described as "pentecostal" or, in the case of black churches, "sanctified." Here one encounters the "gifts of the spirit," including glossolalia (speaking in tongues) and being "slain in the spirit."

Emotional expression is typically found wherever evangelism is strong, and music has long been an important tool for encouraging conversion. At the extreme end of the scale one encounters music that brings the worshiper to a state of ecstasy or even trance through repetition and extreme volume combined with emotional words encouraging surrender to the Lord. Although both are Baptist, a member of a Missionary Baptist church is much more likely to exhibit emotional behavior than a Primitive Baptist, as the former sect is evangelical and the latter sect is predestinarian, eliminating any appeal to conversion. Similar to this scale is one that considers impersonal aloofness at one end and a personal relationship with God at the other. Such aloofness may derive from a more philosophical, intellectual, or abstract approach to religion, whereas the personal view is well expressed in the gospel hymn "What a Friend We Have in Jesus."

The Elaborate/Plane Continuum

Virtually all liturgies require music. In the most elaborate rituals there is a great variety of music, from congregational hymns and responses to chants sung by the priest and choir. In less elaborate rituals only fragments of the Mass remain, such as a Kyrie response, a foreshortened Gloria, and a spoken Creed. At the other end of the scale are patterns that, though fixed, are not liturgical in any historical sense, as well as worship patterns that strive for spontaneity. Much of this seeming spontaneity, however, derives from long-standing and more-or-less fixed patterns of behavior.

The "Primitive"/Modern Continuum

The term *primitive,* far from being pejorative, is usually interpreted by practitioners as meaning "in the manner of the first-century Christians" and is worn as a badge of honor by a number of American sects espousing this idea, especially the Primitive Baptists (also called "Hardshell Baptists" because of their alleged refusal to consider alternative—that is, "modern"—ideas). Strict primitives admit no practice unless explicitly endorsed by precept or example in the Bible's New Testament. Only four rites are allowed: baptism, foot washing, communion, and marriage.

At the primitive end of the scale one is likely to find unaccompanied singing; archaic practices such as lined hymnody and chanted preaching; and a rejection of such modern practices as Sunday School, missionary activity, or the use of printed bulletins. Typically, these sects are male dominated, following the Apostle Paul's comments in his epistles on the subordinant place of women. Perhaps the most "primitive" people in the United States are the Old Order Amish, who shun musical instruments, gasoline-powered vehicles, electricity, and modern dress.

At the modern end of the scale are churches that exist in the modern world both socially and technologically. Some churches, such as those of Roman Catholicism, have willingly dispensed with the use of Latin and Gregorian chant in favor of the vernacular and newly composed tunes, sometimes accompanied by guitars. The extreme end includes churches where so-called political correctness has been institutionalized, especially through the degendering of standard prayers (for example, in the Lord's Prayer, changing "Our Father" to "Our Father/Mother") and hymns (for example, adding "Faith of Our Mothers" to "Faith of Our Fathers").

The terms *conservative* and *liberal* might appear to be synonymous with *primitive* and *modern,* but the former terms more likely connote attitudes toward doctrine, lifestyle, and politics than to musical practices. Modern churches may allow somewhat exceptional practices such as dance, drama, mediated music, and the performance of long, concerted works such as cantatas, oratorios, and masses by classical composers.

The Composed/Improvised Continuum

At the performance end of the scale, people perform musical compositions created, in most cases, by others; at the self-expression end, people use some aspect of a composition—perhaps the melody—as the departure point for their own emotional expression through the medium of often improvised music. The concepts are fundamentally different, because a performer is self-consciously aware of being a medium for someone else's thoughts and can contribute only minimally to the performance. Concerned about performance issues, musicians may experience anxiety, regrets about wrong notes, uncertainty about reception, and a desire to behave appropriately in terms of dress, gesture, and overall demeanor. In some traditions, especially those of Asia, performers must chant the sacred texts with exactitude.

At the opposite end of this continuum, musical expression is confident, without concerns for right or wrong notes or for obeying the wishes of the original composer; the self-expressive performer uses the music merely as a medium for conveying sincerity of feeling and concern for the souls of others. In a broadly generalized sense, this is a fundamental difference between white and black worship in the United States.

The Otherworldly/Worldly Continuum

The atmosphere for worship is created by both physical and conceptual elements. Religions and denominations that strive for otherworldliness favor buildings that remove the worshiper from the ordinary world through sheer size, and through the use of stained glass windows, statuary, murals, icons, elaborate altars, officiants dressed in sacred vestments, flickering candles, and the smell of incense. The most sensuous buildings are those of the various Orthodox traditions and Roman Catholicism, although Episcopal cathedrals strive for this as well. Musical expression, too, tends to be ethereal, especially through the use of otherworldly heightened speech, whether the drone and melody of Greek Orthodox chant or the monophonic Gregorian chant of Roman Catholic churches of the recent past. These denominations prefer to re-create the architecture and decoration of buildings from their geographical origins, giving the United States many styles prefixed with "neo" (for example, neo-baroque, with the churches' vaulted ceilings painted to look like heaven itself).

At the worldly end of the scale are church buildings called meeting houses, built as simply as possible, lacking stained glass, adornments, and even basic Christian symbols other than perhaps a cross and a print of Warner Sallman's *Head of Christ*. Most often associated with austere, Calvinistic sects such as the Old Regular Baptists, such buildings may double as dining halls or meeting rooms. No attempt is made to isolate the worshiper from the secular, which is easily seen through the clear windows. Officiants wear the same styles of clothing as those worn by worshipers, including slacks and open-collared shirt or skirt and blouse. Singing tends to be unelaborated, often unaccompanied. Otherworldliness is conceptual; a baptized member is no longer "living in the world," and preaching may take the elder into an altered state, even a trance, during which the Lord speaks through him. Worldliness and unworldliness coexist in different ways at each end of this spectrum.

The musics practiced in the endless variety of religions of the United States embrace historical styles as well as express migration patterns from Europe, Africa, Central and South America, and Asia. Music serves many roles, from an edifying cultural experience to a way of expressing one's profoundest feelings about the nature of life, salvation, and the afterlife. The field is so rich because most churchgoers recognize the necessity of making their own music, in contrast to the general population, which more often experiences music through the media. Although the mainstream denominations offer few surprises for researchers, as one moves to the "folk" end of the spectrum, the limitless musical inventiveness of American worshipers becomes apparent.

Terry E. Miller

In the early twentieth century, large groups of Chinese, Japanese, and Korean peoples began to immigrate to the United States. Along with music, art, and other cultural expressions, they brought the religious beliefs and practices of Hinduism, Buddhism, and Taoism from East Asia. These philosophies and religious systems had a profound effect on American culture and continue today to influence our twenty-first century worldview, as is shown in Snapshot 3.4.

Snapshot 3.4: The Influence of Asian Religious Ideas on American Music

Asian religious ideas pervade American music even more than Asian musical influences do. This surprising cross-cultural narrative weaves together strands of orientalism, war, imperialism, commerce, counterculture, and immigration.

The religious traditions of Asia—Hinduism, Buddhism, and Taoism—have reached North America in three principal ways. Countercultural contact came first, enabled by translations of major Asian religious texts. Second, increased contact between Asian nations and the United States occurred via cultural and intellectual exchanges as well as through commerce and war, starting from the mid-nineteenth century. While such contact fueled orientalism around Asian religions, ongoing human contact exposed these ideas to diverse groups of Americans, including soldiers, businesspeople, and jazz musicians. Third, Asian religions have become established, institutionally and culturally, through immigration to North America. The most recent immigrants, particularly from Tibet, have had the widest musical impact.

But why have religious concepts had musical influence? The perceived body/mind dualism of Western traditions is offset by the concrete religious practices, such as meditation and yoga, encouraged in Asian religions. Immanent Asian cosmologies that locate the sacred in matter as well as spirit encourage different philosophic approaches to time, sound, and form.

Countercultural movements go against the grain of the dominant culture. In religious terms, in North America after European conquest, this has meant rejection of Christianity (and, to a lesser extent, Judaism). Buddhism and Hinduism serve as perfect foils for this impulse, presenting highly literate traditions with cosmological presuppositions radically different from those of monotheism. Ideas like karma, *samsara* 'reincarnation', *moksa* 'enlightenment', and nirvana derive from the concept that ignorance of our true situation is what blocks spiritual progress—not sin or human guilt.

The epochal breakthrough for countercultural Buddhism and American music came with John Cage's (1912-1992) attendance at D. T. Suzuki's (1870-1966) Columbia lectures of the early 1950s. Cage's interest in Asian religions began in the 1940s, when he had a student, Gita Sarabhai, who conveyed that in her Indian tradition "the purpose of music is to sober and quiet the mind, thus making it susceptible to divine influences" (Revill 1992:90). Cage read the aesthetic writings of Ananda Coomaraswamy (1877-1947), particularly on the theory of *rasa* (the Indian aesthetics of representing emotional states), and the sayings of Ramakrishna; these Hindu influences were applied in Cage's *The Seasons* (1947).

Adopting D. T. Suzuki's brand of Zen Buddhism yielded an austere removal of expression and personality from music. Letting sounds exist for themselves, apart from human intentions, was something Cage learned directly from Suzuki. Zen offered Cage the means for excising personality: discipline. Drawing on the Taoist *I Ching*, Cage developed "a means as strict as sitting cross-legged, namely the use of chance operations" to generate sound. This resulted in the role of the composer shifting "from that of making choices to that of asking questions" (Fields 1986:196).

Cage's transformation culminated with the famous *4'33"*, a composition in which a pianist approaches the piano but plays nothing for the designated length. The piece consists of the ambient sounds in the concert hall and the questions in the minds of the listeners. The removal of ego was central for Cage. He had long sought to erase the distinction between music and noise, resenting composers' imposition of their agendas upon the givenness of sound.

Because jazz musicians often found greater respect outside of the United States, international jazz tours became a jazz institution from the 1920s onward. After World War II, these tours increasingly included Asian countries, particularly Japan. World War II and the Korean and Vietnam Wars also created increased contact between working-class soldiers and Asian thought; one enduring result of this is the proliferation of martial arts in North America.

The musical and spiritual journey of John Coltrane can be viewed from the perspective of Asian influences. In 1957, his life and career endangered by excessive drug use, Coltrane went "cold turkey" and claimed to have experienced a spiritual awakening. By 1958 he was practicing yoga, eating health food, and reading Eastern philosophy. His explorations were public knowledge by 1962: Coltrane came to know Indian sitarist Ravi Shankar, even naming his son Ravi.

This combination of Asian religious ideas with modal improvisation can be heard in all of Coltrane's music of the 1960s, but it is most explicit on the album *Om*. The composition evokes world music by using *mbiras*, gongs, and low-voiced chanting, while

Mbira
A South African plucked idiophone, featuring short steel "tongues" attached to a soundbox

remaining essentially an avant-garde jazz improvisation. But the focus of the piece is on a specifically Hindu idea: the idea of *Om,* in Coltrane's words, "the first vibration—that sound, that spirit which set everything else into being. It is The Word from which all men and everything else comes, including all possible sounds that men can make vocally. It is the first syllable, the primal word, the word of Power" (Hentoff 1968). This description is saturated with Hindu philosophy. The recited words, preceded and followed by an intensely chanted *Om,* convey the ritual intent of the piece: the search for universals in sound. This "universalism" is reflected in the album cover art, which displays "The Omulet," an amulet of flower power and religious eclecticism.

Om was released in 1965, in the midst of 1960s radical activism, from the Civil Rights movement to the anti-Vietnam War activities. Some critics, like Black poet/activist Amiri Baraka, criticized the album for being "apolitical." Coltrane's search for a universal religious meaning in music pulls away from both the narrative specificities of Christian mythology and the history of Black struggles in the United States. It offered instead a more open-ended message, one of universalism, that was reflected in others '60s philosophical movements, such as the rise of the Hippies.

Likewise, the different perspective on time that Asian religious traditions offered was less linear in its direction. Western thought tends to view time as progressive; we are moving toward a goal, constantly improving, and building on the past; Asian thought tends to view time as more circular and subjective, without as much emphasis on progress. The connection to meditative practices, including yoga, which employ this Asian sense of time, is evident in the structure of Coltrane's compositions on *Om.* The combination of discipline and freedom needed in improvisational musics, and the articulation of that dynamic in Indian thought, was attractive to many jazz musicians, especially those who, for ideological reasons, were looking outside European traditions. Like John Cage, Coltrane attempted to substitute the perceived universalism of sound in Asian traditions for the finitude of musical ego. Coltrane's influence put jazz musicians in the vanguard of introducing Asian thought into popular music.

The invasion and occupation of Tibet by China in the 1950s created a diaspora of Tibetan Buddhist (Vajrayana) practitioners to India, the United States, Canada, and Europe. In North America in particular, Tibetan teachers have established teaching institutes that combine transmittal of Vajrayana Buddhism with the political cause of Tibetan freedom. The establishment of the Naropa Institute by Chögyan Trungpa in Boulder, Colorado, in 1974 was a signal event in this still-developing movement; John Cage was on the faculty in its first year.

The influence of Tibetan Buddhism on American music has come through musicians who have embraced the political cause of Tibet's restoration. The Free Tibet Concert, held in Golden Gate Park in San Francisco in 1996 and featuring The Smashing Pumpkins and Rage Against the Machine, is one high-profile example of this. Another prominent instance is found in the Beastie Boys' rap setting of "Bodhisattva Vow." Ensemble member Adam Youch credits a brief meeting with the Dalai Lama as the inspiration for this composition and for Youch's own conversion to Buddhism.

Jennifer Rycenga

REVIEW

Terms and People to Know

Vassily Andreyev
Authenticity
John Cage
George Clinton
Cock rock
John Coltrane
Country music
Essentialism
Fisk University Jubilee Singers
Folk music revival
Funk
Gender ideology
Led Zeppelin
Minstrel show
Om
Oral tradition
Orientalism
"Primitive"
Pete Seeger
Sly and the Family Stone
Social identity
Spirituals
D. T. Suzuki
Work song
Zen Buddhism

Review Questions

1. What is the nature of identity? How is it manifested in music creation, performance, and reception?

2. What has been the role of class, race, gender, and religion in the development of musical traditions in the United States historically? Today?
3. What other social categories affect music making in the United States (i.e., age, geographical region, etc.)?
4. What is "folk music"? What is "popular music"? What is "classical music"? How have the definitions and uses of these terms changed historically?
5. What is the relationship between music and cultural politics? How does music express, validate, or subvert cultural politics?

Projects (Written or Oral)

1. What is your own musical and social identity? How has it affected your musical life? Find a friend, family member, classmate, or anyone else who is not of your class, race, gender, or religion and talk with him or her about the role of music.
2. Research the use of music as political protest during the 1960s and 1970s (or at any other historical moment) in the United States. How did the music and its performance express protest (i.e., lyrics, costuming, performance style)?
3. Is music marketed toward specific class, race, gender, or religious groups? If so, how? (Go back to the book/record store and find out.)

CHAPTER 4

Musical and Social Interactions

James R. Cowdery, Victoria Lindsay Levine,
Judith A. Gray, Barbara Benary,
Jody Diamond, Amy Ku'uleialoha Stillman,
and Steven Cornelius

We live in a highly diverse, pluralistic society, in which a variety of social and musical interactions are always possible. This has enabled us to develop musical cultures that are, at times, identified by strong cultural boundaries, and at other times, highly integrative products of creative social and musical fusions and mergers (Figure 4.1). Many of the genres of music we experience today, such as country and western, rock, and certain concert musics, are the result of musical and social mixtures that created new forms and meanings for music. This chapter discusses the process of musical acculturation and synthesis (the borrowing, adaptation, and/or merging of different musical and social elements) as they have occurred in various contexts within the United States as disparate peoples have moved and settled close to each other, and have shared their lives and musics.

Two examples underscore the issues that can arise in today's musical world:

The folk festival presenter on the phone was telling our band something we had heard before. Yes, we played Irish traditional music, which she was interested in presenting. Yes, we had studied the music thoroughly, and we could play it in an authentic manner. Yes, we had built up a good-sized local audience, so people would come to hear us. But, no—we weren't Irish. We didn't even act like Irish musicians, who (according to her) projected a proper reverence for their traditional music and culture. We conducted ourselves on stage like the middle-class American college students we were, speaking and behaving in ways that were grounded in our own culture and experiences. The name of our group, How To Change a Flat Tire, evoked the

Figure 4.1
Fusions and border-crossings of all kinds occur naturally between and among musical cultures. Here, Ken Zuckerman, a western classically trained musician, plays on the *sarod*, a North Indian solo instrument. Zuckerman, who has studied under Ali Akbar Khan for more than twenty-five years and is recognized world-wide as a master of the sarod, is the Director of the Ali Akbar School in Basel Switzerland. Photo courtesy of Heiner Grieder, 1997.

culture that produced The Velvet Underground and The Mothers of Invention, not the one that produced The Chieftains and The Boys of the Lough.

Finally, despite our ability to play our instruments in a recognizable (if rather generalized) Irish style, we insisted on experimenting with complex group arrangements that she considered unsuitable for the simple, pure folk music of our mentors. We were appropriating a music that was not rightly ours and treating it, she felt, with disrespect. Our music smelled of privileged Americans plundering and debasing the fragile heritage of a culture of poor farmers and laborers. Of course we disagreed, and we tried to explain ourselves: we felt that we were Americans playing Irish music in a way that made cultural sense to us and to our American audience. (The festival presenter must have felt some of the ambiguity of the situation herself, because she ended up hiring us for her folk festival —and changing her mind the next day.)

Anthony Barrand, who was born and raised in England and moved to the United States as a young man, provides another point of view, involving the traditional English outdoor seasonal rituals known as morris dancing. When his group of American morris dancers performs in the United States, with their repertoire of tunes and dances from England and new ones derived from traditional models, he resolutely tells curious onlookers that what they are watching is *American* dancing. Although the original style, tunes, and dances came from England, their offering is an American event, not an English one; to characterize it otherwise would be to suggest that the activity was independent of the context of its performance.

In their own ways, both of these examples involve the idea that affect and meaning are not simply artifacts of their original cultural contexts: They also are processes that are inextricably intertwined with the time, place, and community in which they currently occur. Indeed, the very concept of "original culture" is a problematic one. In the mid-twentieth century, some ethnomusicologists who had revisited sites of earlier fieldwork to find once-meaningful practices discarded in favor of mass-mediated popular culture propounded a gloomy prophecy of cultural decay: the beautiful old traditional genres and styles were being abandoned for drab modern ones, and eventually the world's wonderful diversity would disappear, replaced by one big, gray cultural monolith (Lomax 1968:4). But this theory misses two important points: eventually, some people will not remain satisfied with insipid cultural forms (witness, for example, the rise of punk, rap, and other defiant musics out of the bland, safe commercialism of disco in the 1980s); and any perception of an original, static culture is a mirage. Throughout human history, people have created, explored, and developed music in ways that respond to the vital nature of all cultures.

Musical practices have evolved in relation to cultural dynamics in North America in various ways, often involving the generation of new musical genres, repertoires, and styles. While examples may not always represent a literal crossing of political or geographical borders, they share a movement away from some prior physical and/or psychological location of musical practices and meanings toward a new meeting place mapped by new cultural developments and demands. And in comparing physical borders to conceptual ones, we must remember that although—both may become war zones—conceptual space always has room for a new region, delineated with a new border.

Borrowing the language of horticulture, these metaphoric crossings may be seen in two general categories: transplanting and hybridizing. If a tree is *transplanted* from one ecosystem to a new one, it may or may not be able to thrive at all; if it does, it may have to adapt in one or more ways to its new climate. Such transplantings can be done formally, as in the conscious introduction of a plant from a different habitat, or they may occur informally, as in the accidental stowaway seeds that brought certain nonindigenous wildflowers to North America from Europe.

Hybridizing involves mergers of species—usually intentional—that create new and genetically viable ones. Such hybridizing may take place in the mind of one person, such as a classical or jazz composer who is influenced by elements of other musics, or it may be the result of cross-cultural contacts, such as the myriad African

Original culture
The idea that certain cultural traditions that were once practiced can be restored or revived in their original form, and are worthy of being preserved exactly as they were once performed

Transplanted (musical style)
Moving one musical style/form/element from one tradition to an unrelated one, and the adaptation(s) that occur following this transplanting

Hybrid (musical style)
Merging two previously unrelated musical styles/forms/elements to create a new one

American genres that arose from the interaction of African rhythmic and formal practices with the European harmonic system.

And, as we have already seen, issues of appropriation and power may come into play in both hybridizing and transplanting. What does it mean to use someone else's music? Are various musics just collections of sounds, like colors on a painter's palette, to be combined at the whim of the artist?

TRANSPLANTING MUSICS

Barrand was not the first person to institute morris dancing in North America. When the English musician and folklorist Cecil Sharp visited the United States in the mid-1910s to teach and collect folk songs, he enlisted May Gadd, a young Englishwoman, to help to establish the Country Dance and Song Society of America. Gadd presided over the teaching of morris and country dancing in the northeast United States for almost fifty years through various venues, notably at Pinewoods Camp near Plymouth, Massachusetts. In the late 1960s the Pinewoods Morris Men took their dancing to the streets of Cambridge, Massachusetts, bringing their music and dancing to the public in a replication of morris events in England. Numerous American morris groups descended from Gadd's teaching have followed, including Barrand's Marlboro Morris Men in Vermont, touring for local street performances in the spring just as the morris groups in England have done for several generations. Since the mid-1970s some of these American groups—like the Marlboro Men—have started to develop new dances and tunes as well, ensuring a thriving creative pulse (Barrand 1991).

Therefore, this transplanting involved a certain amount of formal, institutional support. A host institution was found or founded, teachers were hired, and people who wanted to participate gravitated to the established centers, perhaps later establishing their own centers elsewhere. This relative formality mirrors the comparatively formal nature of morris events, in which a set number of dancers and a solo musician perform carefully rehearsed musical and choreographic compositions. The creation of new tunes and dances—a practice that is still somewhat controversial among more conservative practitioners—takes place within this established framework. Similarly, Scottish highland bagpipe regiments have been organized throughout the United States, each with a specific name and leader, performing set repertoires of tunes played in unison and precisely executed marching formations, with much difference of opinion concerning the desirability of composing and playing new tunes. More broadly, ethnomusicology programs such as those at Wesleyan University in Connecticut or the University of California in Los Angeles have established performing groups in African, Asian, and other world musics, hiring master musicians from abroad as teachers.

These activities have sometimes spawned new local groups as well, such as the Boston Village Gamelan in Massachusetts, which performs traditional Central Javanese gamelan music, and Gamelan Son of Lion in New York City, which performs new compositions by American and other composers.

The Irish tradition adapted by How To Change a Flat Tire had been transplanted to North America in a less formal way. Immigrants from Ireland who played the music brought their songs and instruments along when they could, sometimes as their most prized possessions from home. When an Irish emigrant named Francis O'Neill arrived in Chicago in the late nineteenth century, he found a thriving community of players of this music. O'Neill became a key early collector of Irish dance music, publishing two large volumes of traditional tunes that are still in use today by musicians. He also became the head of Chicago's police force, and he used this position to nurture and expand the Irish music community. (During his tenure as superintendent, it was much rumored in Ireland that a good man who was a skilled player of traditional music and was able to emigrate would have little trouble landing a job on the Chicago police force.) And New York City became the home of virtually whole transplanted musical communities from Ireland in what was later called a golden age of Irish music in New York in the first three decades of the twentieth century (Miller 1996).

While the transplanting of Irish traditional music was sometimes nurtured by institutions such as the New York Gaelic League or the Chicago police force, it was not at all dependent on them. To extend the horticultural metaphor, it was more like the spreading of wildflowers than the cultivation of gardens. Again, the informality of the process reflects the informality of a typical Irish music session, in which any number of musicians—playing any suitable instruments with varying degrees of proficiency—can participate freely, spontaneously embellishing the melodies in accordance with each one's individual skill and temperament. The same structural informality can be found in the music making of certain other transplanted cultural groups in North America—Caribbean and South American, for example—echoing the relative informality of the musical transplantation process itself. Of course, these are not sharp generic distinctions: one may encounter informal sessions among Scottish highland pipers and morris dancers, and one can find structured, formal presentations of Irish, Caribbean, and South American musics. But the relationships between the usual methods of transplantation and the usual structures of musical events are notable.

Whatever the degree of formality involved, immigrants brought their music to North America, and it thrived there as long as it continued to be valued, sometimes going through periods of decline and renewal. Africans who were sold as slaves brought their music, too, but their captivity proved as harsh to their music as it was to their bodies and souls, so adaptation was the only key to survival. North American slaveholders, concerned that the African culture—most notably represented by a long tradition of drumming as both an expression of religious belief and as a means of communication—would lead to insubordination or worse, forbid drumming among their slaves and banned cultural events that replicated African ones. Only in a few isolated pockets—for example, in and around New Orleans—could true transplantations of African music actually thrive.

Snapshot 4.1 presents a picture of Afro-Cuban sacred music in the United States. Born from the fusion of West African and Spanish/Cuban musics and contexts, Afro-Cuban music was transplanted to large urban centers, such as New York, Los Angeles, Chicago, and New Orleans in the United States, where it has influenced both sacred and popular musics for decades.

Snapshot 4.1: Afro-Cuban Sacred Music in the United States

Afro-Cuban music has been evolving since the arrival of the first African slaves in Cuba in the sixteenth century. The music is a product, to varying degrees, of the assimilation and reintegration of rhythms, melodies, harmonies, and instruments from various African ethnic groups—ranging geographically from Bantu-speaking peoples of Angola to the Mandinga of Senegambia—with those of the European continent. In terms of Cuban musical heritage today, the most influential of these African peoples have been the Yoruba and the Congolese.

At the heart of Afro-Cuban music, and common to all the musical styles to be discussed here, is the adherence to a rhythmically based timeline (a continuously repeating rhythmic/metric motive) broadly referred to as *clave* (Figure 4.2). Indeed, *clave*—or variations on that principle, such as 6/8 bell, *tresillo, cinquillo,* or *baqueteo*—constitutes a fundamental building block of Afro-Cuban music. The word *clave* translates as clef, key, or keystone. It variously refers to sticks used to play rhythmic patterns, the patterns themselves, or the concepts underlying the performance of those patterns. In short, *clave*'s structure, with its highlighting of on- and off-beat pulses, provides a grid or backdrop for rhythmic drive and melodic invention.

Clave
Literally clef, key, or keystone. In Afro-Cuban music, the rhythmic patterns that underlies most compositions

African-derived sacred musics constitute the purest Afro-Cuban traditions currently being performed in the United States. Although there has been considerable flow of musical ideas outward from these styles into secular genres, secular innovations have had virtually no impact on sacred styles.

By far the best-known sacred music is that associated with the religious system variously known as Regla de Ocha, Lucumí, or—

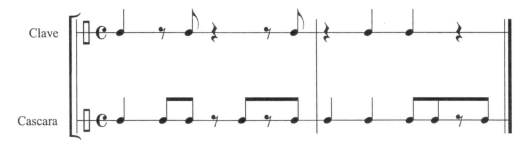

Figure 4.2
Timeline played by the *clave*.

most commonly to nonpractitioners—Santería. Within Santería, ritual music making—as expressed through song, drumming, and dancing—acts as a doorway through which the religion's deities (*orishas*) are praised and invoked through the phenomenon of possession trance.

As generally practiced, Santería is based on beliefs from the Yoruba people of West Africa. In many but certainly not all of Santería's temples, Yoruba religious concepts have been influenced by or even merged with those of Catholicism and occasionally Kardecian spiritualism. Ceremonial music making can be divided into two distinct genres: *bembé* and the more formal *güemilere*. In addition to drums, the music ensemble may include shakers and bells. All participants are involved in responsorial singing, and dance is also an essential part of any ceremony.

Although the earliest documentation of Santería in the United States dates from the 1940s, the religion was practiced in relative obscurity until the waves of North American immigration prompted by the 1959 Cuban Revolution. It was also in 1959 that the first African Americans—who went to Matanzas, Cuba, for the ceremony—were initiated. The first stateside initiations probably took place in New York in the early 1960s.

Cuban musicians and the Santería initiates Julio Collazo and Francisco Aquabella, who came to the United States in 1957, are generally credited as catalysts for the development of North American ceremonial music making. Yet, although their activities attracted interest from musicians outside the religious culture, the two men taught the music to relatively few North Americans. Until the early 1980s, most North American musicians relied on secondary sources for their information.

Since 1981, the emigration from Cuba of important musicians such as Orlando "Puntilla" Rios and Lazaro Galarraga, the growth of public music and dance classes, and workshops based in Cuba have provided North Americans ample opportunities to work with master musicians.

By the 1990s, Latino and non-Latino musicians and practitioners could be found in virtually every major North American city.

Santería
Afro-Cuban religious tradition, derived from the African Yoruba religion and its interaction with European and other religious traditions
Orisha
Deity or god in the Santería religion

Today, the largest religious community resides in Miami, but there are extensive populations in New York, Los Angeles, and San Francisco as well.

The most common American ceremonial music style is *bembé* (also known as *drum and güiro*), which is itself a merging of two distinct Cuban genres: *bembé* and *iyesá*. In Cuba, *bembé* and *iyesá* have their own instrumentation and rhythmic foundation, but in North America, both rhythm genres are performed with the same instrumentation within a single ceremony. The ensemble consists of an iron bell or *guataca* (hoe blade), which provides a timeline; one to three gourds (known variously as *güiros* or *shekeres*), which provide rhythmic support; and one to three conga drums, which function as support or lead instruments.

Other ceremonies, called *güemilere, tambore,* or *toque,* use an ensemble of three double-headed *batá* drums. The most elevated ceremonies require the use of *fundamento* ("baptized") *batá* drums. Although in the 1960s there were perhaps no *fundamento batá* in North America, by 1998 there were as many as twelve such sets, a number of which were owned by North American drummers, in different cities throughout the United States

In both *bembés* and *güemileres,* the ritual is directed by a song leader (*akpwon*) who leads practitioners in call-response singing. The songs, which are in the *Lucumí* language (evidently a mixture of various Yoruba dialects), are designed to honor the *orishas.*

Steven Cornelius

guataca
Literally "hoe blade." A percussive instrument used to mark the basic timeline in *bembé* music
güiros or shekeres
Gourds; rhythm instruments used in *bembé* music
Batá drum
A double-headed drum used in Santería religious ceremonies; *fundamento batá* drums are "baptized" for use in the most sacred ceremonies
Akpwon
Song leader in Santería ceremonies

HYBRIDIZING

As suggested in Snapshot 4.1, African and musical elements, forms, and practices could sometimes survive through adaptation. Ecstatic singing and dancing—even trance and spirit possession—might be sanctioned if they were framed in Christian worship. Some slaves, for example, mastered European instruments and genres for the entertainment of their captors, incorporating various African musical practices for their own recreation. Many slave owners came to believe that such religious and recreational usages contributed significantly to their slaves' contentment, lessening the possibility of rebellion. Field hollers and other kinds of work songs founded on African models seemed to spark more spirited labor among the slaves, invigorating workers and increasing output, so these genres were allowed to develop and thrive.

LeRoi Jones (Amiri Baraka) has noted that only first-generation slaves were African; their children were American (Jones 1963). Similarly, second-generation slave music in North America was seldom purely a transplanted African form; it was African American, a hybrid. Today the story of African American music is one of the richest accounts of hybridization in recorded history, involving the development of blues, jazz, and the foundations of virtually all contemporary popular music.

Musical hybridization has often been the result of close contact between ethnic groups—perhaps literally involving intermarriage, or sometimes just due to proximity in residence and work. The minglings of Scottish and French communities produced distinctive musical styles and repertoires in Nova Scotia and Québec, just as interactions among Scottish, Irish, and English immigrants generated new songs, tunes, and techniques in Appalachia and New England. *Tejano* music arose along the U.S. border with Mexico, reflecting the cultural mixing and social tensions of the region. (For more on Tejano music, see Chapter 8.) The music that became known as jazz, with its particular mixtures of African American performing styles and European instruments and harmonic practices, largely developed in the Creole community of New Orleans, where blacks and whites fraternized more freely than they could in most other parts of the world. Sometimes such interethnic developments have involved a commingling of older and newer forms: contemporary klezmer music, for example, arose out of contacts in the United States between jazz players and immigrant European Jewish traditional musicians, just as salsa evolved among jazz musicians and immigrants from Cuba and other Caribbean and South American countries.

Here the picture starts to get more complex, as we start to perceive hybrids mixing with hybrids. We can see, for example, Appalachian music leaving the high mountains in the early twentieth century as hillbilly music (also known as old time or, in a more recent development, as bluegrass) and joining forces with early rhythm and blues to become country and western, with mid-century jazz to become western swing, or with rock and roll to become rockabilly music. We can see the music of transplanted French Canadians combining with the local African American traditions in Louisiana to become Cajun music and further recombining with rhythm and blues to become zydeco.

First Nation cultures are also a part of this picture: witness the development of Native American fiddle traditions and the many mixtures by Native American musicians of genres and elements of their older traditions with country, rock, jazz, folk, and new age musical styles. Here, musical hybridization creates a contemporary identity rooted in older values and practices, in a sense saying: we are thriving in the modern world, while our heritage continues to nurture and inspire us. Snapshot 4.2 shows how these developments articulate historically situated redefinitions of identity in response to changing social situations.

Snapshot 4.2: Musical Interactions Among American Indian Peoples

Social and musical interaction occurs between and among all people living within a common geographical area. Before contact with Europeans, American Indian peoples interacted for centuries with each other; following the arrival of the French, Spanish, and English, among others, interactions between Indian and non-Indian peoples often took place within the context of Christian missionization. More recently, American Indian groups have joined to create new contexts for the performance of Indian identity. These interactions show a variety of adaptive strategies used by American Indian peoples to both renegotiate and maintain traditional beliefs within new social and musical environments.

The Powwow

Pantribal traditions
Musical (or other) tradition adopted across several different communities

Powwow
Multifaceted, intertribal celebration, including music, dance, and feasting. Derived from *pauau*, an Algonkian name for curing rituals

Pan-Indianism, pantribalism, and intertribalism are terms used to describe a Native American strategy for effecting musical and cultural change. This strategy involves the adoption by one community of a musical repertoire indigenous to another, in a process that facilitates the renegotiation of ethnic boundaries and perpetuates native concepts, beliefs, values, and aesthetic expression in new social or geographical environments. Many Native Americans choose to participate in one or more pantribal musics; at the same time, they may maintain their indigenous music in separate contexts. There are several examples of pantribalism in the history of Native American music, including the repertoires associated with the Ghost Dance and the Native American Church. Currently, the most popular and widespread pantribal music belongs to the powwow.

The powwow is a multifaceted, multivalent intertribal celebration with historical roots in the rituals of nineteenth-century men's organizations among the Plains Indians, including the Inloshka, Hethuska, and Iruska Societies of the Kansa, Omaha, Ponca, and Pawnee tribes. The ceremonies performed by these organizations celebrated acts of heroism carried out by experienced warriors and included music, dance, and feasting. These ceremonies spread throughout the Plains during the second half of the nineteenth century and developed into the Grass Dance, Omaha Dance, or Crow Dance. In the late nineteenth century, some tribes performed the Grass Dance in conjunction with the Ghost Dance or Sun Dance; other tribes blended it with the Drum or Dream Dance ceremony.

By the early twentieth century, the Grass Dance had combined components of several ceremonies with newly created elements, and the style of the music and dance, as well as associated concepts and practices, had begun to diverge between the Northern and Southern Plains tribes. At the same time, European Americans were using the term "powwow" to refer to Indian council meetings or other assemblies. (The word "powwow" derives from "pauau," an Algonkian name for curing rituals.) Native Americans gradually adopted this word to describe the music and dance event that had grown out of the Grass Dance, and by the 1950s the word "powwow" was widely used.

The federal government initiated the Indian relocation program in 1949, offering incentives to Indians who moved from reservations to urban areas. This move brought together people of widely separated tribes and stimulated the development of the powwow. The involvement of non-Indian hobbyists, particularly during the 1960s, and the Indian Awareness movement of the 1970s further contributed to the growth and spread of powwows. Today they occur virtually every weekend throughout Indian country, on reservations as well as in urban centers. The participants are men, women, and children of all ages, from tribes all over North America and from diverse educational and socioeconomic backgrounds. A dynamic, dramatic, and innovative expressive form, the powwow has become a mainstay of Indian life and culture and is a powerful manifestation of Indian identity.

Powwow organization and structure differ somewhat from place to place, according to local concepts and traditions. Ideally, powwows are held outdoors, but during the winter months, school gymnasiums, community centers, or indoor sports arenas offer comfortable alternatives. Longer powwows held outdoors during the summer months usually involve encampments and provide an opportunity for joyous family reunions and homecomings. Powwows vary in length from one evening to a week, depending on the season and location of the event. Powwows may be sponsored by families, tribes, civic organizations, or student associations, and they are held for various reasons, from fund-raising for charitable causes to honoring a family member. Scholars have often characterized the powwow as a secular event, but this is contradicted by its origin in religious ceremonialism, by certain ritual practices (such as the treatment of fallen feathers), and by the spirituality many participants express.

Northern Plains Powwows

Northern Plains powwows begin with a Grand Entry, or parade entrance of the participants into the dance circle. The parade is led by an honor guard, composed of local American Indian veterans, who carry the American flag into the dance ground. The Grand Entry is accompanied by a special parade song; spectators stand during the Grand Entry to honor the dancers. After the posting of the colors, a Flag Song is performed, as dancers and spectators stand. Many tribes have their own Flag Song that honors the American flag with an Indian-language text set in Plains musical style. Next, an invocation is offered in an Indian language as well as in English, reflecting either Native American or Christian religious beliefs. A member of the organizing committee welcomes the participants and introduces the principals, which include the Host Drum, Head Man Dancer, Head Lady Dancer, Arena Director, and Announcer. At large powwows there may be additional principals, such as a Head Boy Dancer, Head Girl Dancer, and Princess (who represent the sponsors of the event). After these preliminaries, the main program begins.

The powwow focuses on the intertribal War Dance, also known as Grass Dance, Omaha Dance, Wolf Dance, or Intertribal Dance. In the War Dance, many dancers perform simultaneously, each with his or her own spontaneous choreography. Although each dancer wears a unique outfit and uses individualized dance steps, seven main styles are recognized: Men's Straight, Men's Traditional, Men's Grass Dance, Men's Fancy Dance, Women's Traditional, Women's Jingle Dress, and Women's Fancy Shawl. Intertribal Dances are interspersed with other dances, including the Sneak-up Dance, which pantomimes warriors sneaking up on and fighting with an enemy, social dances (Round Dance, Rabbit Dance, Crow Hop, Two-Step, or Owl Dance), and exhibition dances, performed by one or two dancers at a time, such as the Hoop Dance. When members of a tribe from outside the Plains culture area are present, they may perform dances from their indigenous repertoire as exhibition numbers.

At certain points during the event, Honor Songs and Giveaways or Specials take place. Honor Songs are performed in memory of one or more relatives, or to honor a specific person or family present at the event; those being honored dance around the arena, accompanied by family and friends. Giveaways involve the distribution of gifts and express appreciation for an individual, family, or group. After the program has proceeded in this manner for some time, contest dances may be held, in which dancers classified by age, sex, and style of outfit compete for prizes. The program concludes around midnight.

The music featured at powwows derives from Plains Indian styles; new War Dance songs are composed regularly, and the repertoire changes continually. The fundamental powwow musical ensemble is called a drum group, or simply a drum, and includes three to six or more singers. They use a nasal, extremely tense vocal style with heavy pulsations on sustained tones and slides at phrase endings. Powwow singers must have clear, loud voices, in order to be heard above the drum and the dancers. Most War Dance songs start high and cover an octave or more in range. Song texts consist primarily of fixed *vocable* patterns, but some lines of lexical text (actual words) may be inserted, particularly in Flag and Honor songs. Occasionally songs with English-language texts are performed, primarily at urban powwows and in social dance songs. The drum was initially a male ensemble, but many women now sing with drum groups and compose War Dance songs.

The scales in powwow songs tend to use four or five pitches. Melodies usually start high and descend by steps, a contour scholars call *terraced descent*. Standard War Dance songs employ a *strophic* (incomplete repetition) *form*. The strophe begins with a push-up or lead, a brief introduction performed by the song leader and then repeated or seconded, with some variations, by the other singers. The second half of the strophe, or chorus, contains two or more phrases, sung *heterophonically*; the chorus is then repeated. The strophe may be diagrammed as AA'BCBC; the phrase endings of the lead, second, and subsequent phrases are articulated by certain melodic and rhythmic patterns. One strophe is repeated several times, and at the end of the song, the final two phrases of the chorus are reiterated as a coda or tail. Variations on this basic form are found in Crow Hop and some other contest songs.

The musical instrument most characteristic of the powwow is the large bass drum; the drum group sits in a circle around the drum, and each singer plays it with a padded stick. The drumbeat slightly precedes the melodic beat, a rhythmic complexity that the singers maintain throughout a song (drum groups from outside the Plains culture area do not always adhere to this practice). In War Dance songs, the drum supports the underlying pulse of the song in steady duple beats. Occasionally the drummers perform a series of honor beats or heart beats, in which the first beat of a duple pair is heavily accented. Other powwow instruments include an eagle bone or metal whistle, carried by some male dancers, and bells worn on dancers' outfits.

Victoria Lindsay Levine
Erik D. Gooding

Vocable
Nontranslatable syllables, such as *he*, *ya*, *ho*, *we*, that are phonetically related to but have no specific meaning in the local language

Terraced descent
A melody that begins high and then descends gradually by steps

Strophic form
A song in which two or more lines are sung to the same melody or rhythmic pattern

Heterophony
The simultaneous performance of many variations of a single melody line

Christian Hymnody

The presence of Christian hymnody within Native American communities is a reminder of the history of contact between indigenous groups and European American culture. Whether it was originally imposed from without or absorbed through conversion, example, and personal relationships, Christianity was foreign to the Western Hemisphere; correspondingly, students of Indian traditions have tended to look upon Christian elements as evidence of acculturation or hybridization. But this, like all generalizations, conceals complex interrelationships.

There were, of course, many intermediate forms of contact, each with musical implications. In some cases, Christianity was simply a precarious overlay on the native culture. But over the course of five centuries, the European-introduced religion has become more intertwined in the daily lives of some Indian people (sometimes, but not always, to the exclusion of traditional ways). In a public television program aired in 1994, for example, the governor of one of the southwestern pueblos, noting that pueblo people had initially pretended to convert in order to survive, raised the question: "At some point, did we forget we were pretending?"

There are, then, in Indian communities, many varieties of Christian-derived music as well as Christian-influenced musical traditions that no longer are attached very directly with Christian worship. Some music practices, such as the use of prepared hymnals, originated outside native communities, but intended for use by Christian Indian people, even those in remote areas. The resulting mingling of traditions is apparent, for example, in *The Utkiaguik Inupiat Hymn Book*, printed in Mexico in 1959, a compilation of non-Indian religious songs translated into an indigenous language. The hymnal, edited by the Reverend William Wartes, missionary to the north Arctic slope from 1951 to 1958, consists of English-titled, Inupiat-texted songs such as "In the Sweet Bye and Bye," "Rock of Ages," "O Little Town of Bethlehem," "Is My Name Written There," and "The Old Rugged Cross."

Music and Nativism

Musical style is influenced by song genre. Songs adopted from other traditions—and serving as a template for new compositions—in many cases retain stylistic features not otherwise found in songs of communities in which they are subsequently used. Such is the case, for example, with Ghost Dance and peyote songs.

The *Ghost Dance* was a revivalist religion, the first manifestation of which came around 1870 with the preachings of Wodziwob, a Northern Paiute prophet, at traditional gatherings. The interest in Wodziwob's ideas spread to many tribes in California but disappeared rather quickly among the Paiute themselves. The more well-known religion began with the visions that came to another Paiute man, Wovoka, around 1887. He subsequently prophesied the reunion of all Indian people, living and dead, in a regenerated world, free to live without sickness or death according to traditional ways; white people would disappear, the buffalo would return. Emissaries going from tribe to tribe spread the word to many Great Basin as well as Plains communities, together with the songs and decorated shirts that went along with the dance rituals. The Plains Ghost Dance observances, misunderstood by non-

Ghost Dance
A revivalist religion that developed among Native American peoples in the late nineteenth century that prophesied the reunion of all Indian people, living and dead, in a regenerated world

Indians as war dances, led to the tragedy of Wounded Knee in 1890 where Sioux ghost dancers were killed by U.S. soldiers.

The Ghost Dance songs found on recordings or transcribed in the 1896 Ghost Dance monograph by James Mooney (1973 [1896]) all have the paired phrase structure and limited range characteristic of songs from the Great Basin. Most songs are short and, unlike many Indian song genres, fully texted rather than based on vocables. They are usually sung unaccompanied. Although no longer sung within a ritual context, Ghost Dance songs remain in the memory of some singers. See particularly the accounts of the Great Basin Ghost Dance [Naraya] songs known by Emily Hill and Dorothy Tappay, two Wind River Shoshone women who worked with ethnomusicologist Judith Vander (1997).

The peyote religion, centered on the eating of hallucinogenic peyote cactus "buttons," was introduced from Mexico to the southern plains around the 1880s and spread from there in all directions. It was formally incorporated in Oklahoma in 1918 as the Native American Church. A syncretic religion, peyotism draws on a combination of native beliefs and practices with some added Christian symbolism. Songs are a major and distinguishing portion of the ritual.

The night-long ceremony that takes place in a special tipi includes groups of four songs by every person present (or by their designated representative), each song repeated four times. Four special songs are sung by the ceremony leader at designated times during the night: the Opening Song, Night Water Song, Morning Sunrise Song, and Closing Song. Peyote songs are sung by individuals who accompany themselves by shaking a gourd rattle decorated with characteristic peyote motifs and colors; the person to the right of the singer also accompanies the songs with a rapid, even drumbeat on a small water drum made from an iron pot. (During intervals between the songs in a set, the drummer may press a thumb into the moistened head of the drum, thus tightening it and making the drum pitch rise.)

Peyote song texts consist primarily of vocables, with a characteristic ending formula: "he ne ne yo way." Like Ghost Dance songs, peyote songs typically have paired phrases. In many communities, this repertoire exists completely separately from songs of very different styles that are more traditional for that group.

New Musics

New circumstances, new occasions, and new technologies come to people in all cultures. Such changes over time frequently find expression in music. Similar to its definition in Western classical music circles, however, the term "contemporary music" does not

Peyotism/Native American Church
Religious ceremonies introduced to Native Americans from Mexico in the late nineteenth century, centering on the eating of hallucinogenic peyote cactus "buttons"

include all varieties of newly created American Indian music. It does not simply mean "newly composed music;" instead, "contemporary" is usually applied to nontraditional genres, to musical categories not exclusively linked to Indian culture: folk music, rock and roll, country and western, New Age, and reggae, for example. Such music is produced by everything from full orchestra to accordions, saxophones, and electronic keyboards.

The involvement of Indian musicians in these kinds of music is underscored by Greg Gilbert's (1994) *A Guide to Native American Music Recordings*; one third of its entries are devoted to what he calls "Crossover Music Styles": adult acoustic alternative, blues, chicken scratch, children's, classical, comedy, country, country and western, educational, folk (and fiddle), gospel, jazz, Native American flute, New Age, rap, reggae (and ska), rock (alternative and standard), rockabilly (and rhythm and blues), and world beat. And many of the recordings that have won the Indie [Association for Independent Music] awards in the "Aboriginal" or "Native American" categories are in crossover genres: Jerry Alfred's "Etsi Shon" and Joanne Shenandoah's "Matriarch," for example. Recordings are submitted to the sponsoring association by record labels and voted on by members of the associations or by category specialists, few of whom are probably of native background.

Questions about definitions and boundaries come up periodically concerning art, literature, and especially, music created by Native American people: is a given composition "Indian music," particularly if it makes no use of or allusions to traits typically associated with Indian songs, such as vocables, drums, rattles, and so on? Is the definition dependent on musical content or on the ethnicity of its creators and performers, or on some combination of traits?

These questions become still more complex when we look at audiences and marketing. Some of the contemporary genres are directed principally to non-Indian audiences. New Age recordings, for example, are often flute-based "reveries" with titles that suggest dreaming or visions, ceremonies, spiritual journeys, and the like. Every element from cover art to album title to information about the artists may be shaped with an eye toward an audience (and potential market) among those who reach out for connections with the natural world and who perceive non-European American people as having privileged contacts with that world. Given that there are many New Age recordings by non-Indian musicians, the question remains whether those recordings by native composers and performers are best classified as "Indian music" or as New Age music *by* Indian people. At this point in time, there may be as many different answers as there are composers and performers of the genre. But the category under which a potential customer finds a recording has real economic consequences for the musicians.

Other crossover genres, while utilizing nonindigenous instruments and repertoire, for example, still speak primarily to an Indian audience. Among them are songs using all the musical devices of mainstream rock and roll but filled with in-group references that affirm what is particularly "Indian." A classic case is the 1960s–1970s political rock of the group called XIT: "Nothing Could Be Finer Than a 49'er" on the album *Relocation* uses the mainstream rock genre to praise a specifically Indian social dance type. The text includes references to a classic Forty-Nine Dance song about a "one-eyed Ford." The rock song fades out at the end, until the listener can hear a drum group actually performing that Forty-Nine Dance song. The success of the song depends on the audience's familiarity with both repertoires. A parallel situation occurs with the comedy "Indian Chipmunks" recordings; the humor lies in the juxtaposition of popular culture references, tunes, and texts ("Peter Cottontail," here entitled the "Yuk-a-day Rabbit Dance") with Indian musical devices such as vocables and in-group allusions to powwow behavior. Those who are amused solely by the use of the high-pitched voice of Alvin Ahoy-Boy and his cohorts miss much of the humor.

Judith A. Gray

CONSTRUCTED MUSICAL IDENTITIES

In addition to transplantation and hybridization, other types of musical interaction also occur in various social and cultural contexts. *Heritage*, for example, cannot always be so clearly defined. Many North Americans grow up without any particular feeling of belonging to a specific ethnic group, and some who do eventually find that the range of expression provided by their ethnic background is not sufficient for their needs. Such people may be satisfied by the mass-mediated music that is easily available to them, or they might construct a different sense of belonging, founded more on choice than on family history or mainstream allegiance. They might gravitate toward what Mark Slobin has called *affinity groups*: communities bound together not by ethnicity but by attraction to particular cultural practices, such as music (1993).

Affinity groups can generate their own musical hybrids. Young white musicians who were more attracted to African American genres than to European-based popular musics contributed significantly to the development of rock and roll. Most of the participants in the folk revival of the 1950s did not grow up with Appalachian or other traditional musics. They discovered these musics as young adults, were attracted to them, and developed their own musical styles, drawing on what they learned from them. Sometimes such affinity-driven musicians go deeper into the cultures that produced

Heritage The specific cultural "inheritance" that is attached to an individual through ethnicity or cultural background

Affinity group A community bound together not by ethnicity but by attraction to particular cultural practices, such as music

their adopted music—studying or apprenticing with Appalachian or African American musicians, for example—and they may reach high levels of technical and expressive proficiency.

From the idea of affinity we can branch into more complex kinds of musical borrowings. Groups like The Chicago Art Ensemble, for example, combine the instruments and techniques of jazz with African instruments and experimental improvisational forms to evoke a broadly based cultural identity, rooted equally in African, African American, and contemporary experimental musics. A number of jazz groups include instruments (and sometimes players) from Africa, the Caribbean, or South America, suggesting a kind of black identity that spans geographic boundaries. Some composers of contemporary folk, popular, and new age music take this kind of generalized identity even further, combining instruments and techniques from every corner of the earth as an articulation of a pan-human identity: the harmonious juxtaposition of sounds from different cultures becomes a metaphor for peaceful coexistence in a utopian global village.

Classical Music Composers

Constructed identity takes on another dimension when we consider the border crossings of North American classical composers. (I use the word *classical* more to indicate the usual venues for performances of this music than to tag all of these composers with one label; there is little consensus among them regarding identifications like classical, art, serious, concert, and so on.) Wishing to develop a specifically American compositional voice, mid-twentieth-century composers like Aaron Copland and Roy Harris sometimes borrowed American folk tunes for their compositions (Copland's use of the Shaker song "Simple Gifts" in his 1944 ballet *Appalachian Spring* is a well-known example), but more often they brought abstractions of what they perceived as folk elements into their music, inspired by what Béla Bartók and other European composers had done with elements of their own countries' folk traditions. Like these Europeans, they wanted to forge a uniquely American sound that was identifiably rooted in European classical traditions—a generalized national identity within a larger, established genre.

Other composers have a less nationalistic agenda, but are attracted to the fresh palette of sounds offered by instruments, forms, and techniques from other cultures. Such composers may gravitate toward the kind of institutional ethnomusicology programs described above, where they can find such instruments and people who can play them. Lou Harrison, for example, was so inspired by his studies of Indonesian gamelan music that he founded his own American gamelan group and composed a sizable repertoire of new music for it, often with parts for European instruments and voices as well. Harrison didn't imagine that he was articulating a Javanese American identity; rather, he envisioned something akin to the kind of harmonious blendings sought by the contemporary folk, popular, and new age composers, but with a classical sensibility (see Snapshot 4.3). European classical music has a long history of adopting and adapting instruments from other cultures—string instruments from Arabic countries, percussion instruments from Turkey, and so on—so composers like Harrison often see their work as a natural development rather than as a clever curiosity.

While composers like Aaron Copland and Roy Harris expanded the range of Western classical music to include a distinctive American voice by incorporating elements of American traditional musics, composers like Harrison and his teacher, Henry Cowell, took a less regional stance, making room for influences from any and every part of the world. Rooted in Western classical music, they worked to broaden its scope from within.

Other composers have come from different cultural roots, establishing antihegemonic subcultural voices that contest the supremacy of European classical traditions while still making some use of their affective powers. Jazz composers like Ornette Coleman have created works that develop an authentically African American sound within Western classical music. The rock guitarist and composer Frank Zappa combined forces with classical musicians for a number of his projects, even collaborating with the celebrated conductor and composer Pierre Boulez. Working in the opposite direction, some heavy metal guitarists have assiduously studied classical music theory and compositions—particularly the works of Baroque composers like Vivaldi and Bach—to broaden their scope for composing and improvising.

Nor is classical music the only genre to inspire such cross-pollinations: Fred Wei-han Ho, for example, brings his jazz background to the forging of a contemporary Asian American musical voice, sometimes combining Chinese and jazz instruments and styles to produce compositions and performances that can be heard as an enrichment of both musics' expressive capabilities and as a challenging—even subversive—articulation of subcultural identity.

Snapshot 4.3 looks more closely at the interactions between Indonesian gamelan music and classical music composers in the United States, showing a wide variety of social and musical interactions that have both enriched Western composers and their Indonesian counterparts. Despite the small size of the Indonesian community in this country, Indonesian musics have had a sizeable impact on concert musics in the United States since the late nineteenth century.

Snapshot 4.3: Indonesian Music and the American Composer

In 1947, 300 seamen on a Dutch vessel jumped ship in New York. Claiming to be Indonesian citizens, they sought asylum. At that time the United States did not recognize the Republic of Indonesia (and would not until 1949), so their status was problematic. Robert Delson, now an attorney-at-law to the American Indonesian Chamber of Commerce, represented the crew, who were eventually able to settle in America, where they formed one of the few small communities of Indonesians living on the continent—quite possibly the first such immigration from a soon-to-be born nation.

The number of Indonesian citizens living in the United States is small compared to populations from other Southeast Asian countries such as the Philippines. However, the influence of Indonesian music, especially on Western classical composers, has been great. Indonesian gamelan music has fascinated musicians in the United States since the late nineteenth century. This ensemble, consisting of various tuned *metallophones*, gongs, strings, drums and other *idiophones*, has also been an inspiration for many western composers.

A major force in the expansion of Indonesian gamelan music in the United States has been the work of American composers. Some of the earliest and most influential were Henry Cowell, Lou Harrison, and Canadian Colin McPhee. Sometimes referred to in earlier decades as "Orientalists," these composers approached the assimilation of gamelan music into their own work in various ways. McPhee arranged Balinese pieces for Western instruments and used Balinese motifs in his compositions. Harrison adapted Javanese forms, built gamelan instruments with partner William Colvig and in his many compositions often mixed them freely with Western instruments (Harrison 1988), using *just intonation* as a bridge between Javanese and diatonic tuning systems. Henry Cowell, though not approaching Indonesian music so closely or directly, was nonetheless influential through his interest in Indonesian-inspired musical ideas and his insistence that his students, among them Harrison and John Cage, be open to all forms of music. Cage, though just as sympathetic to Asian influences as Harrison, composed only one piece for gamelan (Cage 1987).

Succeeding generations of musicians were more thoroughly trained in Indonesian performance techniques; this affected the nature and intention of their work and led to new directions in American composition for Indonesian and Indonesian-style instruments. Some American composers, already immersed in their own contemporary styles, brought those to bear when composing for gamelan.

Gamelan Son of Lion in New York City (Figure 4.3), started in 1976, was one of the earliest gamelan composers' collectives.

Metallophone
A xylophone with metal (as opposed to wooden) bars
Idiophone
"Self-sounder"; musical instruments whose principal sound is the vibration of the primary material of the instrument itself, such as gourds or rattles
Just intonation
Tuning of a musical instrument based on the "true" acoustic relationships among the intervals, as opposed to "tempered" scales where adjustments are made to accommodate Western harmony or other considerations

Figure 4.3
Gamelan Son of Lion's
repertoire includes a
number of pieces
employing pitched hub-
caps as portable gongs.
Photo by unknown,
1986.

Founders Barbara Benary, Daniel Goode, and Philip Corner, along with other composer-members, produced an extensive repertoire of pieces shaped by current ideas in experimental music, including process composition, minimalism, and indeterminacy. Some of their repertoire has been documented in Benary's four volumes of scores (1993a, b, c, 1995) and Corner's Gamelan Series of over 400 process pieces published by the American Gamelan Institute. Goode's "Eine Kleine Gamelan Music," which has been played all over the world in many instrumentations (including a version with computer), shows evidence of his various influences. The use of small repeating patterns with shifting emphasis is characteristic of much minimal music, the use of written instructions that lead the players to create their own parts in real time is indicative of process music, and the use of gongs to punctuate large phrases is found in most gamelan music.

Near the end of the twentieth century, there was an increased interest in compositions for gamelan and orchestra, such as *Kreasi Baru* by Robert Macht and, in 2000, *Dandanggula* by I. M. Harjito. This is another indication that gamelan is gaining more acceptance as a classical orchestra ensemble accessible to American composers —one with musical as well as cultural attributes.

Another important development is the collaboration of Indonesian and American artists on works that have been performed in both Indonesia and the United States. In some cases Indonesian artists created new works for specific U.S. groups; in others the teacher–student relationship was expanded to one of collegial artistry in which new pieces were created that were "equally informed by both traditions" (Ziporyn 1992:30). Following the Festival of Indonesia in 1991, three Indonesian composers—Rahayu Supanggah. I Wayan Sadra, and A. W. Sutrisno—had residencies with American gamelan groups; each produced a piece and a recording. Percussionist Keith Terry has worked with Balinese choreographer I Wayan Dibia on the work "Body Cak," combining the interlocking rhythms of Balinese *kecak* (a theatrical unaccompanied choral style based on a kind of Balinese trance music) with body sounds. Los Angeles-based composer Elaine Barkin has co-composed pieces with Balinese artists Nyoman Wenten and Komang Astita. Jarrad Powell and Gamelan Pacifica of Seattle have worked with Javanese and Balinese composers and shadow theater masters, including Indonesian composer Tony Prabowo and writer Goenawan Mohamad.

Many American gamelan groups play Indonesian music, learned from either Indonesian artists or from North Americans with extensive experience in Indonesia. At the same time, these ensembles, as well as others playing Indonesian or American-built instruments, have served as an experimental ground for dozens of North American composers writing in various musical styles for the instruments. Over the years, a considerable body of American new music repertoire has been developed and presented. An organization whose mission is to document both the new works and the sources that inspired them is the American Gamelan Institute (AGI; www.gamelan.org), founded in 1981 by Jody Diamond. AGI maintains an international archive of scores, recordings, and monographs representing gamelan in all forms and in 1984 began the publication of *Balungan,* a journal devoted to "gamelan, Indonesian performing arts and their international counterparts."

Certainly one of the most successful groups playing Balinese music in the United States is Gamelan Sekar Jaya (Figure 4.4), founded in 1979 and currently based in El Cerrito, California (www.gsj.org). This ensemble is very active in both education and performance. A number of people have directed the ensemble, some of whom have gone on to establish other ensembles around the continent. These include cofounders Michael Tenzer and Rachel Cooper; Evan Ziporyn, who co-founded Gamelan Galak Tika at the Massachusetts Institute of Technology (M.I.T.) in Cambridge; and Sekar Jaya's current leader, Wayne Vitale. Tenzer, Ziporyn, and Vitale are also composers who have explored the wealth of possibilities of

Figure 4.4
Gamelan Sekar Jaya in a concert of music and dance of Bali. Photo by Richard Blair, date unknown.

writing music for Balinese instruments. They have used composition as a way to delve further into Balinese traditions, in contrast to composers such as Schmidt or Corner, who took Javanese ideas in other directions. Sekar Jaya always works with top Indonesian artists—musicians, dancers, composers, and choreographers—all of whom spend extensive time with the group. Sekar Jaya is also notable for having toured their Balinese and American repertoire in Bali as well as around North America.

What accounts for the popularity of gamelan in the United States, particularly on the part of American performers of gamelan? Direct contact with an art form of a culture other than one's own is certainly a compelling way to learn something about that culture, so gamelan provides a rich cross-cultural experience. Many American gamelan players, however, admit that the experience is as much social as musical. For some, the social aspect of playing music with a group of people is more important than musical study or connections to Indonesia. The social nature of gamelan playing may fill a special need that Americans have for community and for a group where ideally everyone's contribution is equally important regardless of individual skill.

Gamelan and other Indonesian-born performing arts have clearly found a home in North America. American gamelan musicians continue to find new uses and contexts for the traditions they have both studied and created. The various ways in which North

Americans interact with Indonesian arts has evolved from the first Indonesian performers on tour, to the ethnomusicologists and musicians who studied with Indonesian master artists, to the composers who invented instruments and groups to play them. In the future, Americans will no doubt continue to appreciate and study Indonesian traditions as well as to create more of their own, each generation honoring its parents while exploring new worlds.

Jody Diamond
Barbara Benary

APPROPRIATION AND POWER

In the wake of World War II, the United States saw a considerable resurgence of parochialism—xenophobia, bigotry, and class resentment—underscored by the anticommunist fervor of the House Un-American Activities Committee (HUAC). In 1948 Pete Seeger, Lee Hays, Fred Hellerman, and Ronnie Gilbert—four musicians who deplored such conservative developments—began singing together informally. They soon became The Weavers, and by 1950, they had become a successful performing group, playing acoustic guitar and banjo and singing songs from various parts of the United States as well as from other countries. Their first hit record, "Goodnight Irene," presented a song by the African American musician Huddie Ledbetter (publicly known as Lead Belly). Subsequent successes included "Wimoweh," a song that the South African composer Solomon Linda had based on a traditional Zulu chant; "Tzena Tzena," an adaptation of a Yiddish folk song; the Appalachian "On Top of Old Smoky"; and "The Hammer Song" ("If I Had a Hammer"), composed by Hays and Seeger. The overall message was eminently antiparochial: all men are brothers, and music is a particularly potent and attractive vehicle for the unification and empowerment of the world's oppressed peoples (Cantwell 1996).

But why should these comfortably middle-class young white Americans appoint themselves the spokespeople for the earth's oppressed? They had acquired record deals and concert and television engagements, they were pleasant and safe-looking, and their performances projected a feeling of good clean fun, not angry defiance. Certainly they believed that their relatively privileged position in society enabled them—even compelled them—to use their prominence to champion the voiceless masses, and in a dismal episode in American popular music history, they were hounded out of the music business by HUAC in 1953. But despite their best intentions and subsequent persecution, in retrospect one might ask whether the result of the Weavers's efforts was real social redress or just the commercial commodification of other peoples' songs, involving the inevitable dilution of meaning caused by replacing the cultural context in which the songs arose with a sanitized, mass-mediated one. When considerations of political, social, and economic power enter the picture, musical border crossings can take on a new dimension.

The case raises more questions than it answers. Pete Seeger went on to become a significant figure in the Civil Rights and antiwar movements of the 1960s and continues to address social issues in song well into old age. He scrupulously honored his sources—for example, tracking down Solomon Linda's widow to ensure that she shared in the proceeds from "Wimoweh"—and he often donated his own profits to activist social organizations. Does this in some way mitigate the fact that he was also a commercial entertainer, using mass media to spread his message and songs? Further, Seeger is not a true "folk" musician; he wasn't raised in Appalachia. Does it matter that his father was a distinguished musicologist instead of a coal miner?

Consider the white rhythm and blues musicians in the 1950s who recorded cover versions of songs by black musicians, reaping financial rewards from the racist radio and television stations who wouldn't present African American artists but were happy to turn a profit from their songs. Until comparatively recently, the American mass media consistently have tried to put a white face on any successful black music. Benny Goodman was dubbed the king of swing; Elvis Presley the king of rock and roll (the term "rock and roll" was itself a kind of white subterfuge for supplanting the racially loaded term "rhythm and blues"). But whatever the motives of music business operatives, these artists were all drawn to their professions through a sincere love of the music. Why shouldn't they follow their affinity and garner financial rewards if they could? Can we define absolutely the point beyond which affinity becomes appropriation?

The issue of power is salient. African American musicians have long played the musics of neighboring white communities—barn dances, polkas, popular songs, and so on—as well as their own community's music, but that was because they needed to do so in order to eke out a living as musicians. Listening to Alan Lomax's recordings of Sid Hemphill's group in Mississippi in 1942, it is hard to believe that the personnel was the same from one song to the next, so complete was their ability to render local white music as well as their own African American traditions. These musicians appear to have had a real affinity with all of the music they played, but one cannot ignore the fact that they needed to be able to satisfy a broad range of clientele in order to survive as musicians. By contrast, white musicians have usually performed African American music out of choice rather than necessity. As some of these musicians have pointed out, their participation does not deplete a resource: they are not taking music away from anyone—indeed, they may help to increase audiences for the music they espouse, leading listeners back to their original sources.

In Snapshot 4.4, issues of appropriation and power dominate the description of Polynesian music and island exoticism outside Hawai'i. From the discussion of song lyrics that demean the Hawaiian language to the analysis of movies that promote an orientalizing Hawaiian eroticism, this example, perhaps more than any other in this chapter, most directly points to economic gain as the motivating factor in colonialism and cultural appropriation.

Snapshot 4.4: Hawaiian Music Outside Hawai'i

The presence of Polynesians on the U.S. continent is tied in with historical and cultural trajectories of colonization. The Hawaiian Islands were annexed as a territory in 1898 and attained statehood in 1959. Following decades of international rivalry, an administrative partitioning of the Samoan archipelago brought American Samoa under U.S. jurisdiction in 1899; Western Samoa attained independence in 1962. Because kin ties override political boundaries, American Samoa has served as an entry point to the United States for all Samoans, as well as for islanders from Tonga and other locales.

Throughout the twentieth century, Polynesian traditions also figured in American cultural consciousness. Continental conceptions of exoticness, intensified by the geographic remoteness of the islands, were initially formulated in the accounts of early explorers and subsequent travelers, including literary lions Robert Louis Stevenson, Mark Twain, and Jack London; themes of an idyllic paradise were also taken up in film and television production. Several waves of national popularity of Hawaiian music have facilitated exposure for other Polynesian traditions.

In the late 1800s and early 1900s, Hawaiian music became known outside Hawai'i through two means. First, travelers who visited Hawai'i wrote descriptive accounts of performances that emphasized their exoticness, the aura of which has remained an important marketing tool in the tourism industry. Second, troupes began touring the United States and Europe, starting with the 1893 World Exposition in Chicago, where hula dancers entertained daily on the Midway Plaisance for six months. Another troupe spent several months at the 1905 Exposition in Buffalo. The Columbia and Victor record companies began commercial recording of Hawaiian music in 1905. Although performers were recorded in Honolulu by teams of traveling engineers, the recordings enjoyed national distribution and sales; remarkably, Hawaiian music was not marketed as "race" or "ethnic" music.

The Panama-Pacific Exposition, held in 1915 in San Francisco, was the event that launched unprecedented interest in Hawaiian music on the continent. Live performances stimulated widespread interest in the islands' repertoire and instruments. The debut of the song "On the Beach at Waikiki" at the Panama-Pacific Exposition is credited with sparking a national fad for Hawaiian songs. Its English-language lyrics play on the first line repeated in each of five verses; literally meaning "quick, let's kiss," the line is not directly translated in the song. Its representation of Hawaiian maid as siren is made explicit in the fourth verse: "'*Honi kaua, a wikiwiki,*' she was surely teasing me, So I caught that maid and kissed her on the beach at Waikiki."

Sherman Clay, a San Francisco music publisher, published Hawaiian sheet music and song folios starting in 1916 until the mid-1930s, making the repertoire available to continental buyers and giving Hawaiian songwriters access to broader distribution. Compared to song folios published in Honolulu, Hawaiian language songs, especially the strophic songs known as *hula ku'i* (literally, "interpretive hula that combines old [that is, indigenous] and new [that is, Western] components"), were frequently replaced in continental publications with songs in AABA format containing English-language lyrics, known as *hapa haole* (literally, "half foreign" [that is, English]) songs, some of which were never published in Honolulu.

Popular songwriters, based in New York's Tin Pan Alley music publishing district, were attracted to the vogue in Hawaiian songs. (For more on Tin Pan Alley, see Chapter 2.) Through the late 1910s and 1920s, Tin Pan Alley songwriters churned out songs with Hawaiian and other generic South Seas settings (Figure 4.5). These songs capitalized on romanticized stereotypes of Hawai'i as a visitor destination. Written from a male perspective, the lyrics extolled female hula dancers with suggestive innuendo of sexual liaisons awaiting lonely travelers. Exotic distance was further increased with the use of nonsense phrases intended to mimic the Hawaiian language, evident in titles like "Oh, How She Could Yacki Hacki Wicki Wacki Woo (That's Love in Honolu [sic])" and "Down on Ami Ami Oni Oni Isle." This corpus of songs established the use of the thirty-two-bar popular song form (AABA) among subsequent Hawai'i-based songwriters of *hapa-haole* songs. Many of these songs were performed on continental vaudeville and variety stages, and they were also recorded commercially by Hawaiian musicians.

The national fad for Hawaiian music in the wake of the 1915 Panama-Pacific Exposition also sparked interest in two instruments, the *'ukulele* and the so-called Hawaiian guitar. Demand for instruments and classes across the continent led to a proliferation of instrument manufacture and sales, studios offering instruction, and pedagogical publications. Hawaiian composer Ernest Ka'ai published a 'ukulele method book in Honolulu in 1916. Numerous titles followed in the 1920s and 1930s. Among continental instructional

hula ku'i
Literally, "interpretive hula that combines old (Hawaiian/indigenous) and new (Western) components"

hapa haole
Literally, "half-foreign" (English-language) songs, based on popular Tin Pan Alley song forms

'ukulele
Small, 4-string, guitar-like instrument

Figure 4.5
"They're Wearing
Them Higher in
Hawaii," a typical
popular Hawaiian-fla-
vored pop song of the
teens. Courtesy David
A. Jasen

Figure 4.5 "They're Wearing Them Higher in Hawaii," a typical popular Hawaiian-flavored pop song of the teens. Courtesy David A. Jasen

Hawaiian or "steel" guitar
Guitar held on the lap, tuned to an open chord, and noted with a metal (steel) bar

books, the quantity of non-Hawaiian songs gradually surpassed Hawaiian songs, showing evidence for a separation of the instruments from the repertoires with which they originally came to prominence.

The Hawaiian guitar sound originated as a technique of melodic picking while stopping strings with a metallic bar on a guitar held across the lap; invention of the technique is most often credited to Joseph Kekuku, a Hawaiian schoolboy, in 1885. Various modifications were made to the guitar to enhance the sound, including the addition of aluminum resonators, substitution of steel for wood in the body, electrical amplification by the late 1920s, and pedals that allowed players access to multiple tunings—all factors that led to the designation *steel guitar*. The sustained sounds produced by electrically amplified instruments became iconically associated with tourist entertainment between the 1930s and 1960s. This sound also led to the adoption of the instrument and its playing techniques by honky-tonk country musicians in Nashville from the 1940s.

Amateur interest in the steel guitar across the continent led to the formation of associations that continue to promote the instrument and, through it, Hawaiian music. Many groups, such as the Hawaiian Steel Guitar Association, have Internet Web sites publicizing their activities and newsletters. Despite efforts to mentor young players, however, the steel guitar's close connection to tourist entertainment has led subsequent generations of Hawaiians to eschew the instrument, leading one scholar to conclude that its popularity at the end of the twentieth century is anachronistic (Junker 1998:390).

Fascination with the South Seas was taken up in Hollywood films beginning in the 1920s. Production numbers often involved native consultants and performers in the background, such as in *Bird of Paradise* in 1932 and especially its remake in 1951, *Waikiki Wedding* in 1937, and *Song of the Islands* in 1942. The 1963 release of *Blue Hawaii,* starring Elvis Presley (and his follow-up *Paradise Hawaiian Style* in 1966), fostered yet another wave of popularity for Hawaiian music. Films were an important means of exposure for repertoire; the song "Sweet Leilani," composed by Harry Owens, became Bing Crosby's first million-selling hit, won an Academy Award in 1937 for best song, became an iconic musical referent of Hawai'i, and subsequently became a staple of Hawaiian entertainers.

In the wake of World War II, which ended in 1945, two factors contributed to strengthening the presence of Polynesian performance traditions on the U.S. continent. First, new levels of nostalgic interest in the islands emerged among soldiers returning from stations throughout the Pacific. Film, television, and radio producers catered to this interest: the *Hawaii Calls* radio show broadcast from Honolulu had as its continental counterpart in the *The Arthur Godfrey Show,* which included resident Hawaiian entertainers in the cast. Second, migration from the islands of Hawai'i and Samoa led to the establishment of communities of residents seeking wider educational and employment opportunities, particularly in the Los Angeles and San Francisco areas of California. Within these communities, studios offering dance instruction catered to homesick islanders. These community-oriented studios contrasted with studio enterprises in the 1920s and 1930s that offered limited lessons and routines for specific purposes (parties, cruises, and so on) to nonislander clientele.

Throughout the 1950s, continental interest in the islands also contributed to a phenomenon known as "tiki culture." In part a reaction to the escalating Cold War and the advent of space exploration, tiki culture celebrated fabricated notions of primitivism, using Polynesian wood carvings as symbolic totems. The phenomenon spawned restaurants across the country that offered fanciful mixed cocktails, a mixture of Polynesian and Chinese cuisine, and tropical decor that included thatched walls, glowing volcanoes, vine-covered waterfalls, and torches; tiki-themed decor carried over into motels and apartment complexes as well.

The musical component of tiki culture crystallized in a 1957 album, *Exotica,* by pianist Martin Denny. Its characteristic features included lush accompaniments provided by exotic percussion, Latin rhythms, and tropical bird calls (performed by musicians in the combo). Although "exotica" music is not indigenously Hawaiian per se, musicians drew liberally on Hawaiian repertoire. Among the popular numbers that appeared repeatedly were Hawaiian-language songs adapted to instrumental versions, such as "Hawaiian War Chant" (*Kaua i ka Huahua'i*) by Leleiohoku; "Hawaiian Wedding Song" (*Ke Kali Nei Au*) and "Song of the Islands" (*Na lei o Hawai'i*) by Charles E. King; and "Pearly Shells" (*Pupu o'Ewa*), adapted by Webley Edwards and Leon Pober, along with English-language songs such as "Beyond the Reef" by Jack Pitman, "Lovely Hula Hands" by R. Alex Anderson, and "Sweet Leilani" by Harry Owens. A seemingly obligatory "Hawaiian" album can be found in the discography of many lounge instrumental music recording artists of the 1950s and 1960s, including Leo Addeo, Ray Coniff, Enoch Light, country guitarist Marty Robbins, and 101 Strings. Hawaiian music profited by the national popularity of tiki culture, just as attention on Hawai'i was enhanced by its admission to statehood in 1959.

Related to the proliferation of tropical-themed restaurants was another major hallmark in Polynesian entertainment: the pan-Polynesian revue. These productions feature live performance of music and dance from related Polynesian societies—Hawai'i, Tahiti, New Zealand Maori, Samoa, and occasionally Tonga and Fiji—in a now-standardized narrative "journey through Polynesia." The origin of these revues is as yet undocumented, but their early history is associated with tourist venues in Hawai'i, which included Waikiki hotels and especially the Polynesian Cultural Center theme park, opened on O'ahu's north shore in 1963 by the Mormon Church. The multiple-island format, adopted elsewhere in the Pacific Islands, appeared on the continent as well, in tropical-themed restaurants and nightclubs such as the Don the Beachcomber and Trader Vic's chains, the South Seas restaurant in Hollywood, Duke's in Malibu, and Disney amusement parks in California and Florida. Performers recruited from the islands often served as community cultural resources and instructors; instruc-

tional studios and established troupes are populated with entertainers who have remained after their contracts expired.

The so-called pan-Polynesian approach of presenting multiple
Polynesian traditions continues today, especially among troupes
who work in commercial entertainment venues. However, because
the majority of teachers are most knowledgeable about only one of
the traditions that they teach (usually Hawaiian), the extent of
repertoire in circulation from the other traditions—Samoan,
Tahitian, Maori—is somewhat limited. Traveling frequently to
Tahiti and New Zealand to learn new repertoire is not financially
feasible for most teachers. Thus, for many troupes, the repertoire
taught consists of routines that teachers themselves learned as performers from each other or from instruction sheets obtained
through mail-order sources.

Amy Ku'uleleialoha Stillman

If there is one issue running throughout this chapter, it is that of
social and economic power, which may be related to race or, more
broadly, to the social stratification of people and genres. Here are
some questions we might ask as we consider this issue:

- Does a person's pursuit of a musical affinity have the result—
  intended or not—of usurping a more authoritative musician's
  share in the marketplace?
- Does it change the original meaning of the music in ways that
  neutralize potentially controversial expressions and reduce the
  impact of vital cultural symbols?
- What kinds of power structures are involved, and how do they
  interact?

Some maintain that scholars must be wary of imposing their
own moral judgments on musical practices; others insist that it is
their duty to recognize and censure inequities wherever they find
them. Certainly, it is important for those involved in the study of
musical border crossings to contemplate questions such as these,
and it is just as important to refrain from oversimplifying our per-
ceptions of situations in order to answer them.

James R. Cowdery

REVIEW

Important Terms and People to Know

Clave
Constructing musical identity
Drum group
Fancy Dance style
Mary Gadd

Gamelan
Gamelan Sekar Jaya
Ghost Dance
Grass Dance
Lou Harrison
Hawaiian steel guitar
Hybridizing musical identity
Morris Dancing
Music affinity groups
Pan-Polynesian revue
Pantribal musics
Peyote songs
Powwow
Salsa
Santaria
The Weavers
Tiki culture
Traditional Dance style
Transplanting musical identity
'Ukulele
Vocable

Review Questions

1. What are the major differences between transplanted, hybridized, and constructed musical and social identities? Give at least two examples for each process and explain why you have labeled them as such. How would you categorize the four Snapshots presented in this chapter and why?

2. How do identities change in new musical and social contexts? What is the role of social construction in the creation and maintenance of new musical identities?

3. Are there differences in the ways in which social and musical interactions occur between classical and popular musics? Between popular and religious musics? If so, what are they? Give specific examples from the chapter.

Projects

1. Choose a contemporary genre of music that you really like and do some research on its origins, changes in style, and presentation today. Do you see any evidence of musical interaction, fusion, or bordercrossing? What was the motivation for this musical process? What was the outcome?

2. Listen carefully and transcribe (write out in musical notation) a piece of contemporary popular music. Can you trace different elements of the music to earlier styles, or other influences that have affected its sound?
3. Talk to a friend, relative, or stranger and write up a small "oral history" of his or her musical affinity groups. How do these relate to his or her "given" social and musical categories (see Chapter 3).
4. What are your musical affinity groups? Why do you have them and how have they affected your musical tastes and actions?

Part II
A Sampler of Music Cultures in the United States

CHAPTER 5

American Indian Musical Cultures

Charlotte Heth, Victoria Lindsay Levine, and Erik D. Gooding

American Indian peoples comprise a variety of social, linguistic, and musical groups, from the Choctaw living in the forests of the southeast to the Navajo of the great southwestern deserts; from the powerful Six Nation Iroquois Confederacy in western New York to the Eskimo/Inuit of northern Alaska (Figure 5.1). Despite a wide variety of languages, physical environments, and musical cultures, however, most American Indians share a common history of European interaction and of rapid social and economic change brought about by European immigration and expansion. Various revivals of traditional musics, such as accompanied the Longhouse tradition in the early nineteenth century and the development of new rituals over the past one hundred years, such as that associated with the Ghost Dance religion and the Native American Church, address these concerns, while contemporary musical forms, such as rock and country and western music, have also attracted Native musicians.

HISTORY AND WORLDVIEW

The first Americans (also called the American Indians, or Native Americans) have for centuries valued music as integral to their lives. Creation narratives, migration stories, magic formulas, and ancient ceremonial practices tell of music. Archaeologists have found Indian musical instruments and pictographs of singing and dancing from as early as 600 C.E. and from areas as far apart as the mounds of the Southeast and the cliff dwellings of the Southwest. Although styles

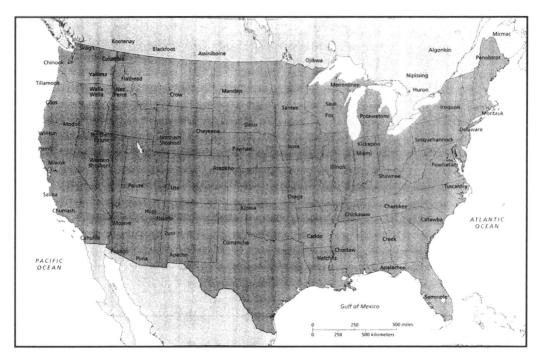

Figure 5.1
Map of the United States showing locations of Native American tribes.

differ within tribal groups and among individuals, the variety of the music is infinite, due largely to its constant recreation and renewal.

The migration of Native peoples over time has encouraged musical interaction and exchange. Historically, North America was a great and open hunting and fishing ground for many native peoples. They came together for subsistence and farming activities, marriage, religious, ceremonial, or trading purposes, often ignoring national and state boundaries and formal tribal borders created largely after white occupation. In the nineteenth century, the U.S. government forced Indian peoples to leave their ancestral homelands, later establishing reservations and allotments. In the twentieth century, Indian people began leaving their reservations, migrating in the 1930s to work on commercial farms and later in the 1940s to work in industries and to join the armed forces. Starting in the 1950s, government agents urged many Indians to relocate and moved them, for job training, from all parts of the United States to big cities in the West and Midwest. One way they made their lives happier in the cities was to form powwow clubs and social dance clubs with other urban Indians, often from different tribes (see Chapter 4). By the end of the twentieth century, Indians had begun to travel back and forth between cities and their homelands for family and ceremonial events specific to their own tribal groups.

Sacred narratives, legends, music, and dance enable today's Native American people to carry on those ceremonies and traditions critical to Indian life. Originating from the Creator, other deities, guardian spirits, and animal spirits, or from respected human story-tellers and composers, their ceremonies are simultaneously ancient and modern. They rely on memory and reenactment, not written words, thus transcending generations and cultural boundaries. Even traditional apparel and dance regalia tell stories about the makers, wearers, and symbols important to the nation, tribe, village, clan, family, or individual. We find in studying these spoken histories, song texts, and sacred narratives—often called myths, creation stories, or Indian literature—that they are much more than extraordinary tales. These oral histories concern the land and the spirits of the land, the important animals and plants, the history of the people, and their religious and moral beliefs. The worldview embodied in the stories tells us how various Indian peoples look at their lives in relation to the rest of the world. These philosophies frequently control how the people represent themselves through music and dance. This overview provides general background information on issues and concepts in American Indian music. A brief history of research on Native music is followed by a survey of musical characteristics, song texts, musical origins and sources, social and gender considerations, and learning and tradition in American Indian music.

SCHOLARSHIP ON AMERICAN INDIAN MUSIC

To our knowledge, although Native peoples have always valued music highly, its significance was largely overlooked by most early writers: the travelers, missionaries, and soldiers who thought it quaint, comical, savage, or hard on the ears. After these very early accounts, we proceed to the era of the curiosity seekers, usually amateurs who visited various tribes and recorded their songs. Throughout much of the nineteenth century, authors transcribed Indian songs from memory and published them in various reports and journals in Europe and the United States. In the last two decades of the nineteenth century and in the early twentieth century, musicologists and scientists began collecting and analyzing Indian music. These early collectors provided the academic world with theories on "primitive" music and also gave the world's composers new melodic and rhythmic material for works based on Indian themes. Some of the composers who later used Indian music as the basis for composition were Victor Herbert (1859-1924), Frederick Burton (1861-1909), Edward MacDowell (1861-1908), Arthur Farwell (1872-1952), Henry F. Gilbert (1868-1928), Thurlow Lieurance (1878-1963), Charles Wakefield Cadman (1881-1946), and Charles Tomlinson Griffes (1880-1920). After 1900, comparative musicologists such as Natalie Curtis (1875-1921), Helen Roberts (1888-1985), George Herzog (1901-1983), and Frances Densmore (1867-1957) started systematically collecting and analyzing Indian music of many tribes and nations. The most prolific of these authors was

Densmore, who from 1903 until 1959 published more than 120 books, monographs, and articles on American Indian music. Since the 1950s, ethnomusicologists who focused their research on Native American music have included David McAllester, Ida Halpern, Alan Merriam, Bruno Nettl, Charlotte J. Frisbee, James Howard, William Powers, and many others. Yet the importance of American Indian music is found not in its impact on modern scholarship and composition, but in the traditions and values it expresses to and for Indian people.

MUSICAL CHARACTERISTICS

Responsorial song
A song in which a leader sings a line or verse, and then the group responds.
Multipart songs
Songs with more than one vocal line
Vocable
Nontranslatable syllables, such as he, ya, ho, we, that have are phonetically related to, but have no specific meaning in the local language

In Indian music, the voice is the most important instrument. Vocal music includes solo pieces, responsorial songs in which the leader and chorus take turns, unison chorus songs, and multipart songs, some with rattle and/or drum accompaniment. Although most singers use a drum to set the beat and cue the dancers, rattles and sometimes whistles are also common. The singers perform for the most part in their native languages, but many songs include vocables (nontranslatable syllables, such as he, ya, ho, we, and so on) that are used to carry the melody.

Usually the songs begin with a soft, slow, stately drum beat and get louder and faster throughout the song. Hard and soft drum beats, accented patterns, rattle and drum tremolos, and shouts enliven the performance. These often signal important words, repeats, and changes of movement or direction for the singers and dancers. Many of these musical characteristics—the words, the number of repetitions, the instruments, and the way the singers work together—come from a particular worldview and depend largely on the dance or ceremony being performed.

Many of the most ancient and unchanging songs are not intended to be sung in public or translated for the uninitiated. Indian people reserve these songs for ceremonial occasions, which are often sacred and secret. They usually do not allow them to be recorded or made available for study. In contrast to these songs, ritual speeches performed at public ceremonial events often sound musical because they employ rhythm and melody not found in everyday language. These are not usually secret, because any speaker of that particular Indian language can understand them. Often the speakers refer to the event that is happening and explain its significance. For example, during his ritual speech preceding a Stomp Dance, a Cherokee speaker might discuss singing, dancing, being happy, and shaking turtle shell rattles all night.

Often historical and current events take their place in songs. Probably the best known Navajo song is "Shi' naasha'," composed in 1868 to mark the Navajos' release from four years of internment at Fort Sumner, New Mexico (1864–1868; Musical Example 5.1). The text expresses the people's joy in returning to their homeland. Unlike many other Navajo songs, almost every syllable in the text is translatable. The words of the first verse may be freely translated as

I am walking, alive
Where I am is beautiful
I am still walking (lonely, sad, or nostalgic).

In "Shi' naasha'," vocables are used only to indicate the beginning and ending phrase of each section; the same vocable phrase, "he ya he ne ya," also marks the end of the song.

Many tribes and nations have composed flag songs or national anthems in their own languages and styles. These are performed at the beginning of a powwow or other traditional event. The songs are treated seriously: All the people stand, the men remove their hats, and no dancing occurs. The free translation of the Sioux "Flag Song" (in Lakota) is

The flag of the United States will fly forever;
Under it the people will grow and prosper;
Therefore have I (fought for my country).

Its form is typical of Plains songs, and the vocables occur in the same way they do in the Rabbit Dance, discussed below.

The subjects of songs tend to reinforce important aspects of culture. The first of nine San Juan Pueblo Butterfly Dances, a ladies' choice partner dance performed in the spring, speaks of how the corn is growing, starting from the sprout, and describes the green leaves, the red flower, and finally the white ear (see Figure 5.2). It

Figure 5.2 Butterfly Dance performed by Pueblo Indians, c. 1933. Courtesy Western History/Genealogy Department, Denver Public Library.

Wasa
The entrance or processional part of a ceremony, performed before the dance proper begins

gives thanks to Mother Earth, who produced that ear. The first section of the song is the wasa or "entrance," sung entirely in vocables. The second section, the dance proper, not only contains vocables but also includes Tewa words about growing corn.

The placement of words in songs can occur in a number of ways: whole texts, words sprinkled throughout, alternating phrases or verses with vocables, and words performed in improvisatory fashion. A Northern Plains Rabbit Dance with English words employs a typical placement for texts in Plains powwow songs:

A vocables (leader)
A vocables (chorus echoes leaders)
B vocables (all)
C text (all):
Hey Sweetheart, I always think of you
I wonder if you are alone tonight hai yai
I wonder if you are thinking of me
Hai yai we ya hai ya.
D vocables (all)

The entire song is then repeated, beginning with the second A section.

In the Cherokee Stomp Dance, the call-response style allows the leader some freedom to improvise. After each song in the cycle is established with vocables, the leader moves temporarily into a higher register and can improvise if he likes. He can add Cherokee words, the chorus can harmonize briefly, the melody can be altered, and the dancers can clap hands and add special hand and arm motions as they face the fire. The leader does not have to add words; he can sing the entire song with vocables if he so desires. The songs in the cycle are separated by shouts that are also part of the music. One Cherokee song with words speaks of the Stomp Dance, the particular song being used and its ancient origin, the tobacco, and the group assembled at the Stomp Ground. Another song talks about the song itself, how it starts quickly, and how beautiful it is. A few singers have incorporated American popular tunes and words into social dance songs, such as "Jambalaya" and "Sugar in the Morning" for the Navajo, "Dixie" for the Hopi, and "Amazing Grace" (in a Buffalo Dance song) for Jemez Pueblo.

ORIGINS

The origins of Native American music are many and varied. Some are described as coming from creation stories, individual inspiration, dreams, visions, personal or group experiences, purposeful composition, collaborative efforts, reworking time-tested models, buying, selling, inheriting, or misappropriating. Indian composers and singers cite many examples of music being taught or given by supernatural means. For example, Changing Woman, a central character from Navajo mythology, is the architect for the creation of the world and sings the world into being. The Navajo songs performed by the Singer (a ceremonial leader) can reunite or restore the order of the universe and appease the forces of evil. The Lakota people trace the Pipe Ceremony and Buffalo Calf Pipe Song to White Buffalo Woman, who taught the ceremony to the people, then departed, later being transformed into a white buffalo.

On the Plains, songs were often described not as taught but as given to humans by guardian spirits such as the fox. The warriors who founded the Lakota Fox Society (see Snapshot 5.1), for example, followed the sound of singing to an old fox who taught them the first songs and rules for their men's association. These songs were theoretically learned in one sitting. Some Indian people still fast and seek visions that may include songs taught by animal or other guardian spirits. Furthermore, songs can be inspired by the sounds of nature: rivers, winds, or animals. Singers often talk of catching songs. In addition, songs are given, sold, or exchanged with other people for many reasons, such as when ceremonial activities and objects are transferred, people are initiated into societies, power is transferred, or in recognition of honor and friendship.

Snapshot 5.1: Lakota Music

The Lakota are a Siouan-speaking Native American group of the Great Plains region of the United States. Today they reside on the Cheyenne River, Lower Brule, Pine Ridge, Rosebud, and Standing Rock reservations in South Dakota as well as on the Wood Mountain Reserve in Saskatchewan, Canada. For the Lakota, music, which was primarily vocal, accompanied all aspects of life. Their musical system was comprised of three broad, interrelated categories: music of the common people, music of the warriors, and music of the holy people.

The vocal quality in Lakota music is marked by tenseness, with pulsations on longer tones. This vocal quality is also influenced by the presence in the Lakota language of nasal vowels. *Glissandos* are present at the ends of phrases and of the songs themselves. Musical texture varies between solo and group singing. Lakota songs are typically *monophonic*, with women's parts approximately an octave above the men's. The music form of the Lakota song is AABCBC, and songs typically begin with an introductory line or phrase sung solo that is repeated (sometimes interrupted) by another solo singer or by the group. This is known as the "second." The song moves from the second into the main body or chorus, divided into two verses. In solo singing, the introductory line is followed by the main body of the songs.

Glissando
A rapid slide up or down the scale

Monophonic
A composition with a single melody line, without any harmonic accompaniment

Song texts consist of both words and vocables, either separate or in combination. Vocables, or nonlexical syllables, are formed from the sound system of the specific language of the singer and are primarily vowels sounds in combination with initial consonants. The melodic range is typically over an octave. The melodic contour is terraced and descending, with each phrase beginning lower than the start of the previous phrase. There is a predominance of *pentatonic* and *tetratonic* scales, with the average range being a tenth. Major seconds and minor thirds are the most common melodic intervals. Finally, most Lakota singing has a rhythmic accompaniment, provided primarily by a type of drum, but also with various types of rattles and bells that are worn or shaken by the dancers. Drum rhythm varies depending on the type of song or dance and will range from a unaccented beat to an accented 1-2 beat, to a steady tremolo.

The Lakota also employ several types of musical instruments. *Membranophones*, such as hand drums or small drums, are used typically if solo singing, and larger wooden drums or commercially manufactured bass drums with either commercially made drum heads or with hide drum heads are used to accompany group singing. Other forms of drums, such as stretched rawhides, were used as well. Several *aerophones* (flutes and whistles) were also common to the Lakota. Flutes were end-blown, and were made of certain types of wood, with varying numbers of finger holes. These were used in courting. Whistles were used in conjunction with dancing, either blown in the Sun dance, or blown over drums to encourage the singers. Rattles, which are *idiophones*, were also used in religious rituals, as well as secular dances (Figure 5.3).

Pentatonic scale
A scale having five notes
Tetratonic scale
A scale having four notes

Membranophone
A musical instrument that produces sound through the vibration of a membrane (often an animal skin), such as a drum
Aerophone
A musical instrument that produces sound through a vibrating column of air, such as a flute or whistle
Idiophone
"Self-sounder"; musical instruments whose principal sound is the vibration of the primary material of the instrument itself, such as a gong or a rattle

Figure 5.3
A traditional dancer blows his whistle over the Badlands Singers Drum at the 1994 Milk River Days Powwow, Ft. Belknap, Montana. Photo by Erik D. Gooding.

The history of the Lakota and their music from first contact to the present can be characterized as one of cultural florescence, followed by destruction, and then regeneration. The historic picture of the people of the Great Plains including the Lakota began to be documented with the arrival on the Plains of Spanish, French, English, and later, American explorers, travelers, traders, missionaries, and military. During the early years of contact the classic attributes of Plains Indian cultures were forming and flourishing: large communal buffalo hunts, the horse culture, intertribal raiding and warfare, men's societies, and tribal ceremonies.

During the early years of contact with Europeans, the Lakota had limited interactions with outsiders. These contacts brought trade goods and exposure to the tenets of Christianity—as well as diseases and epidemics. Also, other native groups introduced the horse to the Lakota during this time. With the addition of the horse and European trade goods, Lakota culture flourished during this time.

Music of the common people was an important aspect of the social life of the Lakota. From lullabies to memorial songs at funeral rites, the life cycle was accentuated by song. Courting was also assisted by the use of flutes. Various organizations, such as those women's societies based on the production of beadwork or quill work, used singing as an entertainment activity. Many children's games were accompanied by songs, and singing was a popular activity itself. Dancing was also a key social activity and was always accompanied by a variety of song forms.

The music of the warriors was related to the activities of the men. Men's warrior societies relied on song for several purposes. Songs were used to document the successes of intertribal warfare as well as to recount individual exploits, known as coups. Many of these societies accompanied their social dances with songs particular to their groups, using songs as a vehicle of group identity. Songs were also used in asking for assistance in hunting, either communal buffalo hunts or individual occurrences.

Music of the holy people played a key role in Lakota religion, both formally and informally. The dialogue between higher powers and individuals is expressed through song in important rituals, such as the Sun Dance, vision quest, Sweatlodge, Ghost Keeping, and the Hunka. Organizations and societies with religious functions, either for shamanism or curing, relied heavily on musical performance.

At the beginning of the nineteenth century, a new foreign presence came onto the Plains—the Americans. With the Louisiana Purchase in 1803 and the expedition of Lewis and Clark beginning the following year, the Lakota's time of cultural florescence and independent ways of life was beginning to end. In the early years of the nineteenth century, the United States government initiated a policy toward all Plains Indians intended to destroy their traditional cultures and force them to assimilate into the dominant American society, and measures were enacted in the mid-1800s to break down their economic, religious, political, and social systems.

During this time American expansion onto the Plains increased interaction, which was often hostile. From the 1850s to the 1880s numerous military encounters occurred, leading to the eventual confinement of the Lakota onto reservations. This period of reservation life took its toll on Lakota culture. Their economic system based on the hunting of buffalo was entirely eliminated. Christian denominations moved onto the Lakota reservations establishing churches and boarding schools, as both traditional Lakota religious and secular activities were discouraged or banned. The confinement on reservations also led to the cessation of intertribal warfare, which led to the decline of the warrior ethos, and warrior societies, which were key aspects of Lakota culture, were divested of their power.

During this period of cultural destruction, Lakota music was severely affected. The various policies enacted by the U.S. government restricted or banned performances of all three categories of Lakota music. Many forms of Lakota music were no longer performed in public or were discontinued in fear of arrest. New religious movements and their associated musical styles arrived among the Lakota during this time in response to the breakdown of their traditional culture. These included the Ghost Dance and the Peyote religion (Native American Church).

America's involvement in World War I provided a new outlet for the warrior traditions of the Lakota. Many young men joined the armed forces, and with their participation came a brief revival of these traditions. Following the war criticisms of government policies led to a reform in Indian policy. With this change in policy, rituals and traditional Lakota customs that had been driven out of public forums returned, particularly those associated with the warrior ethos. Tragically, many rituals and customs were lost with the passing of a whole generation of elders during the early 1900s.

Lakota involvement in World War II again renewed interest in early warrior society traditions. Following the war, however, U.S. Indian policy returned to the assimilation of American Indians into the general population as well as the termination of government support for certain groups. A program of relocation was also instituted that provided assistance for reservation Indians to migrate to large urban centers, including Denver, Los Angeles, Minneapolis, and Chicago.

In the 1960s and 1970s, the activism of the general U.S. population inspired by the Civil Rights movement and the Vietnam War was mirrored in its Indian population. In the following decades the U.S. government passed several policies favorable to American

Indians, including the American Indian Religious Freedom Act in 1978, the Indian Civil Rights Act in 1986, and the Indian Gaming Regulatory Act in 1988.

Today, the Lakota and other Plains peoples are experiencing a new cultural florescence, one in which music plays a highly visible and important role. One of the most visible music and dance forms today is the powwow. The powwow is a complex of features that centers on various music and dance forms that have persisted in a historical continuum from the mid-1800s to the present through a certain flexibility and adaptability that met the ever-changing needs of its participants. Today powwows express Lakota tribalism through distinct dance outfits, language, singing, and traditions.

Erik D. Gooding

MUSIC COMPOSITION

Native American composers use varying techniques to express their artistry. Some cultures encourage creativity, while others require exact duplication of music from year to year. Most tribal groups express an active need for new compositions, while also maintaining as many of the ancient songs as possible. Improvisatory techniques, particularly in call-response songs, are a type of composition. The numbers of verses and repetitions the singers can use are often based on sacred numbers. When an old song or ceremony is revived, it is often renewed or updated in some fashion.

In some communities, musicians do not compose new pieces because of the revered origin of the age-old songs. For example, a Cherokee story relates how all of their songs were originated by a monster known as Stonecoat. This cannibal monster introduced death to the Cherokee by eating the livers of unsuspecting villagers. To weaken him, the medicine men positioned seven menstruating women in his path (seven is a Cherokee sacred number). As he passed each woman in succession, he became weaker and finally was captured and burned. While he was burning in the fire, Stonecoat sang all the songs that the Cherokee will ever need for dances, magic, and curing and instructed the people as to the songs' uses. Because of this supernatural origin for music, the Cherokee usually do not compose songs, preferring to express their creativity through improvisation. The forms of music found in the Stomp Dance and various animal and agricultural songs, particularly the responsorial songs, allow for several types of improvisation in words, melodies, and lengths.

In contrast, among Pueblo singers, being able to compose new songs is often as important as being able to remember old ones. Composing can be summed up in four words: interest, tune, words, and memory, all adding up to talent. In singing both the new and older songs, the Pueblo men strive for perfect unison and faithful reproduction of songs from performance to performance. Pueblo songs are said to possess the power to lure needed game animals to the hunters who provide food, and they also have the power to regulate the agricultural cycle.

SOCIAL AND GENDER CONSIDERATIONS

In Native American musical settings, an audience is rarely defined. Most tribal members participate in dances and ceremonies, and visitors are often asked to join in. The audience reaction and interaction can therefore be determined by the extent to which the people gathered together endorse the musicians through active participation. They may join the singing and dancing or add shouts, *ululations* (high-pitched, wordless, rhythmic cries), and whistles to show approval, or may show disapproval by boycotting or other negative actions.

In many reservation or rural settings where tribal members live near each other, all or most of the community members are expected to participate in music and dance events, such as powwows, ceremonies, social dances, fiddle festivals, and hymn singings. Plains women often show approval by singing *lulus* for honor or encouragement. The lead dancer at a powwow will sometimes blow a whistle, praising the singers and calling for a repetition. If a Cherokee man does not lead the Stomp Dance well, or if he is of poor character, the women will not dance behind him with their leg rattles, and he has to leave the circle. By contrast, a young singer just learning to lead brings out all of the people to dance with him and support his efforts.

Women can participate as singers, dancers, and instrumentalists in many events, but in others they must observe custom and not partake. There are only a few dances and songs for women. In the Northeast and Southeast, there are a few ceremonial and social dances for women. In these, one or a few men provide the music, or, more recently, a women's singing group is featured. Ordinarily the women may sing softly while they dance, accompanying themselves with rattles worn on their legs. In California and the Great Basin, there are hand game songs for women by themselves. And in California and the Northwest Coast, there are many medicine songs, love songs, and other influential songs that are exclusively for women (Figure 5.4).

Dozens of ceremonies, songs, and dances throughout North America cannot be performed without women. Although the Southeastern women provide accompaniment by shaking their leg rattles for various animal, friendship, and closing dances, they have regular singing roles in the Horse and Ball Game dances. The Ojibway women's dances in Wisconsin include a section in which the men drop out and the women sing alone, highlighting the words of

Ululation
A high-pitched, rhythmic cry, similar to a yodel
Lulu
The Indian word for ululation

Figure 5.4
Singing and drumming, Helma Swan leads other family members in a Swan family song performed in honor of Oliver Ward Jr. at his Memorial Potlatch, Neah Bay, Washington, 10 October 1998. Photo by Linda J. Goodman.

the song. The Iroquois social dances also require the participation of women, particularly as dancers. Women's dances are the most popular type of song in singing contests, with all-female ensembles participating in recent times.

Both men and women of the Kashia Pomo of California traditionally sang the musical repertoire for curing, dancing, and other ceremonial activities. Both played the *double whistles*, and all accompanied themselves with *clapping sticks*. Further north in California, the Brush Dance of the Yurok, Karok, and Hupa focuses the group's energy on a sick child and the medicine woman sitting near the fire in the center of the dancing pit. The woman sings to cure the child, while male and female Brush Dancers sing and dance. The only rhythmic accompaniment is provided by the girls, whose shells and beads sewn onto their dresses and dance aprons clink in time to the music. Either men or women can sing "Light," or secular, Brush Dance songs, while a male chorus accompanies the soloist, but only men can sing the "Heavy," or spiritual songs.

Musical Example 5.2 is a Yurok Brush Dance Song, sung here by a group of men, two of whom sing alternating melodic sections against an accompaniment of vocal rhythmic pulsations. The voice at the beginning of the example is that of the ethnomusicologist, Richard Keeling, marking this as a true field recording.

Double whistle
A whistle consisting of two pipes, of different lengths, blown simultaneously

Clapping sticks
Idiophone consisting of two sticks that are beaten together percussively

Light songs
Secular songs

Heavy songs
Spiritual or religious songs

The Sun Dance of the Great Plains and Great Basin requires the presence and participation of women in various roles. Sioux women dance, carry the pipes to the sacred circle, and make sacrificial offerings. They also sing behind the drummers during the social dances, as do the Arapaho and Shoshone women. Until the 1980s, Shoshone women still remembered and sang Ghost Dance songs, although the ritual was discontinued in the 1930s.

In the Southwest, with its rich musical variety, women have many roles to play. The Navajo and Apache girls' puberty ceremonies are centered on women and their activities. In these ceremonies, women sing, dance, and interpret ritual singing. The Pueblo women are accustomed to choosing their male dancing partners for many dances and often participate equally in the Basket, Corn, Harvest, Comanche, Butterfly, Dog, and Buffalo Dances. They even serve as instrumentalists by playing a notched-stick *rasp* in the Basket Dance. The sticks that are components of the rasp itself have gender designations as male and female. The Cloud Dance at San Juan Pueblo features four pairs of women who dance as Corn Maidens, representing four colors of corn. They dance in front of the male chorus, at times entering and leaving the men's ranks.

> **Rasp**
> An idiophone consisting of a notched stick or gourd that is scraped with another object

Ordinarily, both men and women can sing lullabies. Love songs, magic songs, and curing songs often have both male and female versions. Mescalero Apache women even compose love songs. In the Bird Songs of the Southern California Indians, both men and women sing and dance in unison, playing rattles. And one cannot imagine a powwow without the participation of women as dancers and backup singers.

Music and dance can serve as metaphors for life ways. In music, as in life, women serve as leaders, equals, or supporters; they perform alone, together, with men, or subordinate to men; they make instruments, compose music, and retain, transmit, and revive songs and cultures; they serve as evaluators and critics of music, of dance, and of both male and female performers; they can be the focal points or sponsors of ceremonial and musical events; they can cure or be cured, and they can pledge themselves in music and dance to live in this world and struggle for the good of all.

LEARNING AND TRADITION IN NATIVE AMERICAN MUSIC

Native American music, outside movies and popular contemporary recordings, is little known to the general public in North America because traditional Indian musical events are rarely advertised. Often the organizers charge low admission prices, or the events are free of charge. The composers usually create their music without reading notation or using finely tuned instruments, outside purely instrumental pieces or those based on Western models, such as some hymns and fiddle tunes. Famous only locally or in "Indian Country," the best singers customarily do not take lessons in American Indian music but instead learn by participating in performances. They or their families and friends make their own instruments and special clothing and earn very little money, if any, practicing their arts.

These people and their communities organize and participate in festivals, social dances, games, special ceremonies, family and clan events, hymn singings, powwows, and medicine rites. Some Indian people live on reservations or in small towns or villages, but others live in major cities. They use the word "traditional" to cover various activities and practices. Often being traditional means adhering to the oldest norms: languages, religions, artistic forms, everyday customs, and individual behavior. More recently, the word refers to modern practices based on those norms. In other instances it may refer to a time period before technological advances. It may even indicate categories of dance, music, and dress that are derived from ancient, established practices.

Snapshot 5.2: Music of the Northeast Indians

The Northeast Indians inhabited what is now New England, the mid-Atlantic states, the tidewater zones of Virginia and North Carolina, and Canadian territory from the lower Great Lakes to Nova Scotia. The region contains two major geographical divisions: the coastal zone and the Saint Lawrence lowlands. The coastal zone includes the eastern seaboard from Nova Scotia to North Carolina; much of this area is separated from the interior by the Appalachian Mountains. The Saint Lawrence lowlands include southern Ontario, northern New York, and the Saint Lawrence and Susquehanna River valleys.

At the time of contact with Europeans, the Northeast was thickly forested with coniferous and deciduous trees, providing a rich variety of nuts, berries, and other wild fruits and vegetables as well as abundant fish and game. The climate of the region alternates between cold winters with deep snow, and hot summers; the peoples who lived in the northernmost reaches of the area employed winter survival techniques similar to those used in the Subarctic region.

Northeast Indians are culturally related to Southeastern tribes as well as to the Algonkian-speaking peoples of the western Great Lakes and Prairie regions. The dominant language families of the Northeast are Iroquoian and Algonkian. The Iroquoian languages include Seneca, Cayuga, Onondaga, Mohawk, Oneida, and Tuscarora. The Algonkian languages include Micmac, Maliseet, Passamaquoddy, Eastern and Western Abenaki (including Penobscot), and Delaware (Lenape). The coastal Algonkian languages spoken in southern New England, Virginia, and the Carolinas, such as Massachusett, Narragansett, Powhatan,

Nanticoke, and many others, have been extinct for more than a century.

Northeast Indians are descended from Woodland traditions, which developed in the eastern United States after 400 C.E. Woodland peoples grew maize, squash, beans, and other crops in addition to hunting, fishing, and gathering wild foods. Woodland settlements were semi-sedentary, and villages were moved periodically as the soil in an area became depleted. Warfare and raiding were intense during this period; many Woodland communities were protected by palisades. At the time of contact with Europeans in the fifteenth and sixteenth centuries, most Northeast Indians lived in relatively small, autonomous villages; alliances with neighboring communities were fluid and temporary. The modern tribes grew out of these informal alliances that became more permanent as a result of contact (Figure 5.5).

Figure 5.5
Young woman in jingle dress. Courtesy Brenda Romero.

Music Cultures in the United States

The League of the Iroquois

By the early seventeenth century, five of the Iroquoian tribes—the Mohawk, Oneida, Onondaga, Cayuga, and Seneca—had established a confederacy known as the Five Nations or the League of the Iroquois. Other Iroquoian groups in the region were eventually dispersed by or incorporated into the Five Nations. Some southern Siouan and Iroquoian speakers such as the Tutelo and Tuscarora began migrating to the north in the seventeenth century to escape the colonists. Around 1722 the Tuscarora were adopted by the League of the Iroquois, which became known thereafter as the Six Nations. The Tutelo were among the dislocated peoples who subsequently found homes among the Six Nations. After the Revolutionary War, some members of the League remained in their homelands, while others resettled in Ontario, depending upon which side they had taken in the war. The Six Nations Reserve was established near Brantford, Ontario, in 1847; it remains the largest Iroquois reservation in North America.

Algonkian-Speaking Peoples

The Algonkian-speaking peoples of the Northeast generally did not fare as well as the Iroquoians. Several coastal Algonkian cultures were completely destroyed during the seventeenth century by disease epidemics and warfare with the colonists; the survivors from some of these communities were absorbed by the Delaware. The Delaware lived in several independent but related bands in the Delaware River valley during the early seventeenth century; their history involves a complex series of migrations, along with repeated divisions and consolidations. Ultimately some Delaware people were absorbed by the Iroquois and others moved to Wisconsin, but most were eventually settled in Oklahoma. The Algonkian-speakers in New England and the Maritime Provinces, including the Micmac, Maliseet, Penobscot, and Passamaquoddy, have endured many changes but continue to live within their homelands. These groups were part of a political and ceremonial alliance known as the Wabanaki Confederacy, which was active from the mid-eighteenth century through the late nineteenth century.

Contexts for Musical Performance

Because the southern-coastal Algonkians suffered the most complete cultural destruction after contact, very little is known about their indigenous music. The traditional music of some other eastern Algonkians, such as the Micmac, Penobscot, and Delaware, became moribund during the twentieth century but is currently being revitalized. Iroquoian peoples continue to perform native music in a variety of contexts, including the seasonal thanksgiving ceremonies of the Handsome Lake or Longhouse religion, the curing rituals of medicine societies such as the False Face and Husk Face Societies, and the Feast of the Dead. In addition, Northeast Indians now perform a variety of pan-Indian and syncretic musical styles, Christian hymns and gospel music, and European American classical, folk, and popular music.

Musical Styles

Northeast Indians use a moderately relaxed and open vocal quality in traditional songs, emphasizing the middle or lower range. Vocal pulsations articulate phrase endings in some Northeast styles; *aspirated attacks* and releases, as well as vocal glides, are common. Northeast Indian song texts consist of vocables with some lines of lexical text; the texts are often humorous in social dance songs. Many Northeast Indian songs feature *antiphony*; the leader sings a short melodic phrase and is answered by the dancers in unblended unison, with the women doubling the men at the octave in some tribes. Some dance songs are performed as solos or duets by one or two head singers.

Diverse strophic, sectional, and *iterative* forms are used in Northeast Indian music. Songs in strophic form may have an introduction performed as a solo by the head singer; sectional songs sometimes use a phrase design that may be diagrammed as AABAB or AABABA. Many different scale types exist in the Northeast, although there is a predilection for five-tone scales. Most Northeast Indian songs employ melodic contours that descend or undulate with a descending inflection; these songs generally have an *ambitus* of an octave or more, although certain genres have a small scale and narrow range. Most dance songs have relatively simple, symmetrical rhythmic structures, although songs with small scales tend to be more complex rhythmically.

A variety of musical instruments are indigenous to the Northeast, including many kinds of container rattles. Iroquoian peoples use different rattles to accompany different genres of dance music; cow horn rattles accompany Social Dance songs, while rattles made of bark, gourds, or turtle shells are used in ceremonial music. Other idiophones used in the Northeast include striking sticks (Tutelo), rasps (Seneca*), pounding sticks* (Seneca), *plank drums* (Maliseet), and deerhide drums (Delaware). Small *water drums* are used throughout the Northeast; some double-headed hand drums are indigenous to the region, as is a kind of snare drum used in Penobscot shamanism. Drums are played with wooden drumsticks throughout this region. Several different musical instruments are indigenous to the Northeast, such as *flageolets* and flutes, which are played as solo instruments.

Iroquois Social Dance songs and Delaware Big House songs are two of the most important genres of Northeast Indian music. The

Aspirated attack
A vocalization technique that emphasizes the exhalation of breath as a means of accenting a given note

Antiphony
A call-and-response form in which a song-leader sings a line, and then the chorus responds in unblended unison

Iterative form
A song form based on a repeated melodic line

Ambitus
Range

Pounding sticks
Large sticks that are beaten against the ground to provide a percussive accompaniment

Plank drum
A drum made by placing a plank over a hole in the ground, and sounding it by beating it with sticks

Iroquois perform Social Dances during ceremonies associated with the Longhouse religion, which was founded by the Seneca prophet Handsome Lake in 1799. Longhouse ceremonies are communal expressions of thanksgiving and renewal; they are held inside a rectangular council house with a stove or fireplace at each end and two rows of benches along each wall. As it is important to maintain a good feeling throughout a Longhouse ceremony, Social Dances are performed during and after more intense, sacred rituals, to entertain and provide an element of humor. Iroquois Social Dances are similar to the Social Dances of other eastern tribes; they are performed in single-file lines or by couples and move counterclockwise around the Longhouse. The Social Dance repertoire contains about nineteen different dances, including the Standing Quiver Dance, Women's Dance, animal dances, and dances obtained from other eastern tribes, such as the Alligator Dance (received from the Seminole) or the Delaware Skin Dance.

Listen to this example of an Iroquois Social Dance, called the "Women's Shuffle Dance" (Musical Example 5.3), recorded in 1941 by William N. Fenton, who conducted fieldwork among the Six Nations of the Iroquois Confederacy in Western New York and Canada. This song, performed by George and Joshua Buck, is accompanied by a water drum and horn rattle, playing complex rhythms against a repeated melodic verse.

An evening of Iroquois social dancing usually opens with the Standing Quiver Dance, which has also been known as the Warrior's Dance, Trotting Dance, Old Man's Cane Dance, or Stomp Dance. A large number of discrete songs exist in this genre, all of which are identified by the generic title of Standing Quiver Dance. These songs are very short and fast and are performed as a set in rapid succession; the leader sings short phrases and is answered by the male dancers in unblended unison. This genre showcases the song leader's unique vocal style and quality as well as his knowledge of the repertoire. Unlike other Iroquois Social Dance songs that employ strophic and sectional forms, Standing Quiver Dance songs feature an iterative form. Melodic contours in these songs are level or undulate with a descending inflection. These songs tend to have narrow ranges, and scales with three, four, or five pitches predominate. Standing Quiver Dance songs are usually in *duple meter* and feature simple rhythmic patterns, compared to the rhythms in other Iroquois musical genres. The song texts are primarily vocables, but sometimes humorous words are added, and new texts are composed regularly. Standing Quiver Dance songs are performed without instrumental accompaniment. In form, style, and function, they resemble the Stomp Dances performed by many Eastern Woodland peoples.

The Delaware experienced dramatic culture change during the seventeenth and eighteenth centuries. By the early nineteenth century,

Water drum
A skin-headed drum whose sound chamber is partially filled with water

Flageolet
A simple, endblown flute, with two or three holes

Longhouse religion
A religion founded by Seneca prophet Handsome Lake in 1799, consisting of ceremonies performed in the rectangular council house (the so-called "Long House") that forms the social center of tribal life

Duple meter
A rhythm based on a 2-beat measure

Big House ceremony
A planting (Spring) and Harvest (autumn) ritual, lasting several nights, held in a special rectangular log cabin called the "Big House"
Vision quest
Personal visions that are recounted during the Big House ceremony

their most important religious ritual was the *Big House ceremony* that developed from an annual harvest observance combined with the performance of songs received in *vision quests*. The Big House ceremony was held in the spring at planting time and again in the fall after the corn harvest. The entire event lasted six, eight, or twelve nights and included many subrituals, each accompanied by its own musical genre. The ceremony took place inside a rectangular log cabin called a Big House; the structure had no windows and was sited east to west, with a door and a fire at each end. The sponsor of the event held a turtle shell rattle while reciting a stylized narrative of his vision experience; then he danced counterclockwise around the Big House, singing the song he had received in the vision. Those who wished to do so could dance single file behind the sponsor; the women danced in a separate line. After the sponsor had completed his performance, he passed the rattle to another participant, who presented his vision narrative and song. The ceremony ended when the rattle had been passed once around the entire circle of participants.

The Delaware vision experience was highly personal, and therefore each Delaware vision song is stylistically idiosyncratic. Big House songs use a great variety of scales, ranging from three to seven tones. The lengths of melodic phrases can vary within a song, and meter changes frequently in some songs. Several kinds of melodic contours are used, including broadly undulating lines, melodies that begin high and gradually descend, and melodies that begin low but leap upward. The visionary was assisted in his performance by two head singers, who sang the vision songs while playing a deerhide drum. Actually an idiophone, this instrument was made from a dried deerhide, which was folded into an oblong packet framed by four wooden slats and bound together with deerhide thongs. The drum was played by striking the slats with narrow wooden paddles. The last Big House ceremony took place in 1924, although vision songs remained in the musical repertoire of some Oklahoma Delawares until the 1980s.

Victoria Lindsay Levine

Songs and musical instruments are integral to the Indian peoples who created and still use them. Music pervades Indian life, starting with creation stories and ending with death and memorial songs. American Indian music is important not only because it influences modern American society, but also because it emphasizes the traditions and values of Indian people. This oral tradition has survived solely because the music and dance were too important to be allowed to die.

Important Terms and People to Know

Aerophones
Algonkian
Big House Songs
Butterfly dance
Flag songs
Idiophones
Iroquois
Lakota
Longhouse religion
Membranophones
Ritual speech
"'Shi' naasha'"
Six Nations
Social Dance Songs
Standing Quiver Dance
Stonecoat
Strophic form
Ululations
Vocables
Wabanaki Confederacy

Review Questions

1. What are some myths of the origin of American Indian music? How do they relate to Indians' basic beliefs and worldview?
2. Although vocal music predominates in American Indian culture, musical instruments are also crucial to correct performance. What musical instruments are used by American Indians and how are they used in both everyday and ritual contexts?
3. What happened to Lakota society and musical practices as a result of being put on reservations in the nineteenth century? How did things change in the second half of the twentieth century?
4. Describe some of the differences between American Indian men's and women's musical cultures, genres, practices, costuming, etc.
5. Compare the similarities and differences in music making between the Plains and Northeast (Woodlands) Indians, as illustrated in this chapter's two Snapshots.

Projects

1. Visit an American Indian community in your area or attend a powwow where many communities come together. Observe the similarities and differences in their music and social practices, interactions, and cultural exchanges.
2. Choose an American Indian group not represented in this chapter and conduct research on its musical practices. Does the group share commonalities with the groups studied here?
3. Go to your local book/record store and check out their American Indian musics. What genres can you find? How is American Indian culture marketed?

CHAPTER 6

European American Musical Cultures

Carl Rahkonen, Christopher Goertzen, Jennifer C. Post, and Mark Levy

European immigration to the United States began in the late sixteenth century and has continued until the present, with people of
European descent forming the majority population of this country.
The British, who set up permanent settlements in the seventeenth
century and claimed the fledgling colonies for the Commonwealth,
donated their language, much of their political and governmental
organization, and their musical culture to the "new world," and their
influence continues to the present day. Certainly one of the major
contributions, especially of western and northern Europe, to the
United States was a classical music system that was born in and grew
within European court and urban cultures over many centuries. So
pervasive was this influence that it was not until the early twentieth
century that classical music composers in the United States could
establish their own "American" musical forms, based in part on
materials borrowed from American Indian and African American
traditions. (See more about American concert music in Chapter 10.)
In addition, European culture contributed dance and instrumental
musics to the American mix, and the entrance of southern and eastern Europeans, including large numbers of Ashkenazic Jews, in the
late nineteenth and early twentieth centuries opened the United
States to different religious and ceremonial practices as well.

Between 1820 and 1960, an estimated fifty million immigrants
came to America, the majority from Europe, in what has been
described as "the greatest folk-migration in human history" (Jones
1960:94). Many immigrants formed their own ethnic communities
that set them apart from other groups. At the same time, they became

part of a larger American society that created a culture of unity out of diverse ethnic groups. America has been called a *melting pot*, the theory being that immigrants from all over the world become Americanized to form a homogeneous whole. But a more accurate analogy might be that of a *mosaic*, with people of diverse ethnic backgrounds mixing together and coexisting. In a mosaic, each piece retains its individual integrity but also becomes an essential part of the complete picture. As we have slowly abandoned the melting pot ideal, we have come to value diversity and even, at times, to emphasize it.

The dominant culture of the United States came from England, Spain, and France. These first immigrants established the framework within which the ethnic mosaic was created. From the very beginning, immigrants to America differed from their European counterparts. Immigrant communities were internally more heterogeneous than in the Old World. Individuals who came from various regions, from urban or rural areas, tended to set aside regional differences and coalesce into a unified community in the New World. Thus, regional identities in the Old World gave way to new ethnic identities in the New World. Non-English-speaking, first-generation immigrants were often isolated by language and thus tended to interact primarily with their own group. The music they listened to was that which they brought with them from the Old Country. Having language, religion, and music in common helped to overcome Old World regional differences.

As succeeding generations learned a common language, typically English, they communicated with others outside their group, developing a tolerance and eventually an acceptance of the surrounding American culture. The second generation, or children of immigrants, could adopt a dual identity. They would perhaps speak the language and practice Old World customs and traditions within their own ethnic community, especially with the older generation, but they could also adopt a general identity, which could be national, regional/group, religious, or occupational, or any combination of these four. These second and subsequent generations of European Americans developed an ability to shift back and forth between a specific and a general identity, depending on context. In my research with the Jerry Intihar Ensemble (Figure 6.1), a polka band from the Cambria City area of Johnstown, Pennsylvania (Rahkonen 1993), for example, I found that the region's various European American ethnic groups shared four specific identities:

They were all *United States citizens* from western Pennsylvania. (national identity).

Many had served together in the *armed services*, producing ties that transcended their ethnic backgrounds. (Group identity as veterans)

Virtually all of them were *employed in the steel mills* and shared the dangers and rewards of working in this industry. (Occupational identity)

Melting pot theory of American culture The idea that multiple cultures have come together in America to form a homogeneous whole, losing their original identities

Mosaic theory of American culture The idea that each individual culture retains its unique identity but also plays a role in completing the picture of the American culture

Figure 6.1
The Jerry Intihar Ensemble performing at the 1992 National Folk Festival in Johnstown, Pennsylvania. Photo by Carl Rahkonen.

A large proportion of them were *Catholic*, although they attended their own parishes—Slovenian, Polish, Irish, and so on. (Religious identity)

Third and subsequent generations in America face an even more formidable force of assimilation: having multiple ethnic identities due to intermarriage. We would expect becoming a homogeneous member of American society to be the end product of the melting pot, but this has hardly ever been the case. Typically, later generations *choose* an individual ethnic identity or multiple identities. By choosing their identities, the grandchildren and great-grandchildren of immigrants are better able to appreciate the overall ethnic diversity of their society.

Answer the following question: How Irish do you have to be to be Irish on St. Patrick's Day? As a class project, I had students interview patrons of Irish pubs on St. Patrick's Day, and we found that the overwhelming majority of patrons considered themselves Irish. We found on further questioning that most were actually less than half Irish, some just "having an Irish relative in the past." Being Irish on St. Patrick's Day had less to do with lineage and more to do with the enjoyment of Irish American music and customs.

With subsequent generations, there is a shift from an *immigrant identity* to an *ethnic identity*. The term *ethnic* has most frequently been applied to non-English-speaking European American immigrants. This usage has incorrectly tended to exclude Native Americans, African Americans, and to some extent Asian Americans from being

Immigrant identity
A person who identifies himself as a member of a specific immigrant group, such as an Eastern European or Italian

Ethnic identity
A person who identifies himself as being a member of a specific ethnic group, such as a Jewish American, Irish American, or African American

"ethnic." At the same time, Irish Americans have been considered ethnic in spite of being overwhelmingly English-speaking. Institutes of immigration research, which in the past have tended to concentrate solely on European Americans, have in recent years expanded their scope to include all immigrants.

INSTITUTIONS SUPPORTING ETHNIC AND MUSICAL IDENTITY

As new immigrants arrived in America, they would seek out institutions that supported their ethnic identity. One of these primary institutions was the church or temple to which they belonged. It was not as simple as being Catholic, Lutheran, Orthodox, or Jewish. Frequently, local congregations were organized specifically for their own ethnic group. For example, the Cambria City section of Johnstown, Pennsylvania, has five Catholic churches within a square half-mile, each defined by its ethnic composition. German and Scandinavian communities in North America were largely defined by the presence of their local Lutheran church parish. Members of these congregations felt at home because they held services in their original languages and they featured music from the Old Country. These churches also functioned as a focal point for social activities, providing an important outlet for the community's musicians. The local church was also central to the life-cycle and year-cycle events of the immigrants. Weddings, funerals, and initiation rites, Christmas, Easter, Passover, and similar calendar celebrations became a time to gather and reaffirm their identity as a community. Ethnic music and food were an essential part of these occasions.

In addition to their churches, many immigrant communities created their own lodges and clubs. Some were fraternal organizations based on language and ethnicity; some were based on politics within the ethnic community. For example, left-wing Finnish immigrants organized their own social clubs and halls to promote their ethnicity as well as their political views. Some clubs were based on the primary occupation of the immigrant community, such as Workers' Halls frequented by ethnic groups in one occupation. Some were commercial establishments, such as restaurants or pubs that catered to the food, drink, and music preferences of a particular ethnic group, such as the Greek American coffeehouse or the Italian American *caffe concerto*. These lodges and clubs provided a significant venue for ethnic music, particularly dance music.

Some ethnic groups, especially those with members scattered over a wide area, formed regional, national, and even international societies based on their ethnicity. Some of these societies began as fraternal organizations or mutual benefit societies, such as the Italian Catholic Federation and the Order of the Sons of Italy or grew from networks of local lodges, such as the Sons of Norway or the Finnish American Knights and Ladies of Kaleva. These societies provided benefits to their members and produced publications that kept more isolated immigrants abreast of the activities of their countrymen. The Finnish Suomi Seura ("Finland Society") publishes the journal *Suomen Silta* ("A Bridge to Finland"), which includes articles written in Finnish, English, and Swedish, and caters to the needs of Finnish immigrants not only in North America but also in Sweden, Australia, New Zealand, and elsewhere. The society supports summer workshops and clinics as well as charter flights to Finland. It provides the primary means for isolated Finnish immigrants to keep in touch with their ethnicity.

Another institution that supports and promotes ethnic identity is the ethnic or folk festival. There are literally hundreds of such festivals on local, regional, and national levels. Local festivals may originally involve a single ethnic group and grow to become a multiethnic festival of a region or community. Such is the case with the Finnish American *Laskiainen* festival of Palo, Minnesota, which was documented by the Smithsonian Institution in a film (Vennum et al. 1983). Whereas diversity of languages and religions tends to separate people, this is not the case with music and food; people tend to try the music and food of another culture before anything else. *Laskiainen* became a combination of all the ethnic traditions of the region and was appreciated by the entire community.

The National Folk Festival, sponsored by the National Council for the Traditional Arts, is the oldest of the national American festivals, beginning in 1934. Its founder, Sarah Gertrude Knott, recognized that folk festivals go through three stages: The first features "native material traditionally learned and traditionally transmitted"; the second stage includes "basic cultural offerings from [ethnic] communities"; and the third stage adds "urban and popular" materials (Knott 1953; Lawless 1960:442). Today the National Folk Festival is held in a selected American city for three years, after which that city continues on its own. These festivals typically feature the foods, crafts, and musics of the local ethnic community, as well as some nationally known performers. The Smithsonian's annual Festival of American Folklife in Washington, DC, has served the dual purpose of educating the nation about its various ethnic heritages and providing the premier performance opportunity for ethnic groups (Figure 6.2). FinnFest USA, first held in 1985, has been a primary vehicle for the rejuvenation of Finnish American identity, particularly among the second, and subsequent generations of Finnish Americans. Each summer FinnFest attracts thousands to hear lectures on Finnish American culture, sample ethnic foods, and attend concerts of Finnish and Finnish American music. What was at one time local music is now appreciated on a national stage.

Figure 6.2
A Volga German ensemble from Nebraska playing at the 1975 Festival of American Folklife in Washington, D.C. Photo courtesy the Ralph Rinzler Folklife Archives and Collections, Center for Folklife and Cultural Heritage, Smithsonian Institution.

Mode
A collection of pitches of differing importance and "weight" that can be arranged as a scale. These pitches and their ways of interacting form the basis of musical compositions. Contemporary Western music primarily features two modes (major and minor), while earlier Western and many non-Western musics employ many others, such as the pentatonic (5-tone) mode.

EUROPEAN MUSICS IN AMERICA

Members of European American ethnic groups were bound together by common language, customs, religion, and music. These common cultural traits took on added importance in the New World, becoming *symbols* of ethnic identity. As symbols they had, in many instances, greater stability here than in the Old World. Ethnic groups have tended to perpetuate customs, traditions, and music even after they had vanished in the lands of their origin. One example was the discovery of English and Scottish folk songs in the southern Appalachians by Cecil Sharp in 1916–1918.

Snapshot 6.1: British Ballads in the United States

Child Ballads and Other Folk Songs

Late in the nineteenth century, Harvard English professor Francis Child traveled to England and Scotland to seek out an old, substantial body of English-language poetry, ballads that still flourished in oral tradition. Both lyrics and music proved appealing aesthetically, as centuries of revision by generations of singers had polished both stories and melodies. The ballads also appealed to prevailing ideologies: Scholars with a romantic and nationalist bent savored tunes and poetry endorsed by history and supposedly unsullied by industrialism and other modern trends. Child published 305 texts, many in multiple variants, in *The English and Scottish Popular Ballads* (1882–1898). Scholars, following the lead of Briton Cecil Sharp, found that Child had not been looking for surviving ballads in the best places. The tradition was actually more vigorous in North America than back in Britain. This body of song, still known as the Child ballads, became the focus of folk music research in both the United States and Britain: Many hundreds of collections and analyses made this the most studied body of folk music in the world.

Child ballads are strophic (have the same music for each verse of text) and are set to melodies that usually arch upward at the beginning of the verse, then downward at the end. Although the stories the ballads tell are often melodramatic, featuring murder, unrequited love, and bloody battles, the singer usually does not express emotion when performing the song. Rhythms are straightforward, although some singers dwell on given pitches. A majority are in the major *mode*, although much scholarship deals with other modes that contrast with major. In some of these contrasting modes, the two half-steps lie relative to the tonic (the so-called church modes); others use fewer than seven pitches per octave. Indeed, pentatonic scales, more used in Scotland than in England, also are employed relatively frequently in the American South. Coffeehouse singers of the 1950s to the early 1970s often underlined the age of the Child ballads by performing ones with exotic topics and set in exotic modes, for example, "The Great Silkie of Sul Skerry" (following Child's classification, No. 113), some forms of which are in mixolydian mode (like major, but with a lowered seventh scale degree).

The texts tell stories, ones seldom tied precisely to time or place, partly through narration and partly through the voices of the characters. Verses—generally four lines long, sometimes with one or two repeated—range in number from a few to as many as several dozen. Descriptive language often follows conventions: Horses are usually "dapple grays" or "milk-white steeds," and a (fair) maid's skin is "lily white." The topics of these ballads are venerable and enduring, although neither those explicitly tied to British history nor humorous ones have fared well in America, with a few exceptions. Many ballads relate bloody, perhaps supernatural tales that offer both titillation and moral instruction. In "Barbara Allen" (Child 84, the only of these ballads that frequently reached print in nineteenth-century America), a young man flirts clumsily, alienating the very young woman he wished to impress. She spurns him, causing him to despair and die. Filled with remorse, she herself pines away. The lesson for those listening: Be careful and considerate in expressing love. In "The Golden Vanity" (Child 286), a British ship is threatened by pirates. The captain convinces a cabin boy (or carpenter boy, depending on the version) to sabotage the approaching enemy despite great personal risk. If the plan succeeds, the boy will be rewarded with great riches plus social elevation through marriage to the captain's daughter. The valiant deed is done, but the boy is abandoned to drown. The lesson: Do not trust the upper classes. In "Lady Isabel and the Elf Knight" (Child 4; Figure 6.3), a knight with a habit of seducing, robbing, then murdering young women is finally killed by one of them. In many versions, she then returns home and admonishes her parrot not to reveal the story, whereas in other versions, she is killed. The lessons are straightforward: One should not seduce (or be seduced!), rob, or murder.

Figure 6.3
"Lady Isabel and the Elf Knight," tune and text as sung by Mrs. Moore of Rabun Gap, Georgia, on 1 May 1910. Source: Bronson 1959-1972, I:45 (originally recorded by Olive Dame Campbell, and transcribed by Cecil Sharp).

Oral transmission
A song or melody that is passed from one performer to another orally (as opposed to using a notated text)

Just as a ballad's text exists in many forms, so does its tune. Samuel Bayard called these related melodies "tune families." Bayard believed that a tune family was probably descended from a single source (the original tune for a ballad), and then each individual version was slightly changed through an individual performer's variations. These could occur as the ballad was learned in *oral transmission* (one singer would perform it and others would try to imitate this original, leading to slight changes). Bayard noted that key notes (notes with a prominent position in the rhythm) and the overall shape of the melody tended to remain the same in different members of a single family, while the actual mode or rhythm might vary more greatly. An air may thus be traced through many versions practically up to the point of its disappearance—its complete transformation into another and different tune. There is also a loose linkage between text and tune. Usually the various forms of a text are set to members of the same tune family, although some examples may be sung to other tunes, and a given tune or tune family may be associated with more than one text (Figure 6.4).

Christopher Goertzen

Northern New England Ballads

Northern New England is a unique cultural region in the United States. Because of the area's physical geography, settlement patterns, and relative isolation from urban centers before the middle of the twentieth century, its musical traditions exhibit a particularly close connection between musical performance and economic and social practices.

Early northern New England residents were primarily Irish, English, and Scottish settlers who arrived from Europe and southern New England beginning in the eighteenth century. In the nineteenth and twentieth centuries, the Euro American population grew with the arrival of settlers from Canada and Europe who joined the growing rural and urban work forces; yet the region has remained strongly Anglo American. The primary livelihood for

Figure 6.4
"Lady Isabel and the
Elf Knight," tune as
sung by Agnes Conners
of Antigonish, Nova
Scotia, on 8 March
1912. Source: Bronson
1959-1972, I:57 (origi-
nally collected and
transcribed by Phillips
Barry).

many was farming, although later, as commercial enterprises
arrived, some residents moved out of the rural sphere to work in
mills, lumberyards, and other industries.

The geographical landscape that northern New England settlers
adapted to was a many-layered one. When families settled on hill-
sides and in villages, they joined neighborhoods that were dependent upon one another for support. Social obligation became a critical factor in their everyday lives, and the resulting reciprocity
turned into a pattern of farm mutuality that played a major role in
family and community survival.

Active musical traditions accompanied work and play, provided
entertainment, reinforced social roles, and contributed to the
establishment and maintenance of a cultural identity. British Isles
and North American ballads and lyric songs, popular songs and
tunes, hymns and dance pieces dominated the diverse repertoires of
the residents and were performed at events that took place regularly in families, neighborhoods, and occupational groups. Shared
musical ideas in the family or household, and among neighbors
and other members of the community, enriched each tradition.
Among these, singing played a significant role, shaping individual,
community, and regional identity. In the northern region, singing
practices continued in rural neighborhoods well into the twentieth
century until the mid-1940s when major cultural, social, and economic changes finally moved the traditions away from localized
practices and into the mainstream.

Families and neighbors gathered to sing not only for entertainment, but also in conjunction with work they shared. The same
groups that met to sing and dance regularly provided help for one
another during times of need. Thus sharing songs helped bond
families and communities. When residents assembled to share ballads, popular songs, and hymns, it was sometimes referred to as
having a sing, a *social*, or a *party*.

Listen to Musical Example 6.1, "The Glouster Witch," also known
as "Old Meg," from Glouster, Massachusetts. It is a typical ballad
with a verse and refrain set to a repeating tune. This ballad recounts
changes in the attitudes toward witches in the centuries following
the Salem witch trials in 1692. No longer seen as agents of Satan,
old women and eccentrics, such as Margaret Wesson of Glouster,
tended to be scorned, pitied, and, as in this song, ridiculed.

Songs shared in neighborhood and occupational gatherings connected event participants to song traditions shared in their ancestral homelands. The varied repertoires comprised old English and Scottish ballads, locally written songs modeled on eighteenth- and nineteenth-century narrative songs, American popular songs heard on the radio and recordings, as well as Anglican American hymns learned in church and at camp meetings.

Communal singing also took place when friends met informally to share work or at gatherings when neighbors socialized at the end of a long work week. While these gatherings were gender-specific at times, and at others were attended by young couples, more often they were broad intergenerational events. We find references in diaries and oral histories to bees for quilting, apple paring, hops picking, and corn husking, as well as to shared labor for haying and barn raising. Typically, a social time with food, dancing, and singing followed an intense period of labor, especially communal labor. In addition to dance tunes, songs, including game songs, were popular among adults at these socials. They danced to game songs such as "Go In and Out the Window" and "On the Green Carpet" in circles and lines as they moved from room to room of the large farmhouses.

Songs frequently accompanied women and men's daily work, especially on the farm, to provide relaxation while working and to ease workloads. Among women, singing as an adjunct to work is referred to more often than any other type of song. Repertoires were drawn from a wide spectrum of songs. One Springfield, Vermont, woman remembered her mother dancing around the kitchen singing her version of "The Auld Soldier."

> There was an auld soldier an' he had a wooden leg,
> He had no terbaccy, nor terbaccy could he beg,
> There was another soldier, as cunnin' as a fox,
> An he allus had terbaccy in his auld terbaccy box.
> Said the first auld soldier, "Won't you give me a chew?"
> Said the second auld soldier, "Shoot me dead if I do.
> Shtop yer drink' whisky. Go te pilin' up yer rocks,
> An' ye'll allus have terbaccy in yer auld terbaccy box."
> (Richardson 1931)

Northern New England farming families often sent men to spend winters in the woods to cut timber in preparation for the spring log drives. In the lumbercamps, men frequently assembled on Saturday evenings after a long week of work, to entertain one another with dancing, fiddling, storytelling, recitations, and songs. Anglo American songs popular in the camps included lumbering ballads with tragic themes such as "The Jam on Gerry's Rock" or "Peter Amberley," humorous songs, satirical pieces about local people and events, as well as more sentimental songs. The musical environment in some of the camps was competitive; men challenged one another to perform and encouraged some to create new songs. Ballads about tragedies reminded the singers and their audience about the constant dangers of working in the woods.

Despite the close relationship between singing and work, the use of songs to regulate work was found in limited spheres in northern New England. On the Maine coast sailors sang shanties to coordinate specific work activities on the ships, especially hoisting sails and anchors. While shanties had a critical function in the work on sailing vessels, they were also popular among lumbermen in the camps (some of whom worked winters in the woods and summers on the sea) where they were sung purely for entertainment.

Changes in the Twentieth Century

Today northern New England families and neighbors seldom socialize with songs in homes and community spaces, although social dancing continues to be popular in many rural and urban communities. The lifestyle changes that began to affect most Americans in the early years of the twentieth century have decreased opportunities for sharing in families and neighborhoods. On the farms, widespread mechanization has altered rural social practices that have in turn affected family and community repertoires and overall performance practice.

For many rural residents, active social singing has been replaced by listening. Those once active in community singing today are involved in a more passive tradition. Gradually they have become listeners—of the radio and audio recordings—and viewers—of television and videos—rather than active participants in musical events as performers. This behavior is reflected in repertoires and performance practices throughout the region.

Songs and their social function have also been altered by professional singers, and commercialization has been encouraged by the song industry. Singers in northern New England now regularly interact with musicians from other regions and countries. This naturally contributes to the development of new songs and styles. At public events where "the old songs" are occasionally presented, older singers are presented as remnants of the past, younger singers offer new and revised songs that less often repeat and recreate images of the past than comment on the present. Rather than representing broad sentiments and issues targeting an intergenerational community, they speak to listeners who comprise a single generation, or social group. The environment has changed and so have the songs that the northern New England communities support.

Jennifer C. Post

DEVELOPING NEW MUSICAL STYLES

Hybridization/ fusion
When different musical styles mix with each other to form a new one

At the same time that some musical styles were being preserved in America, new musical styles were being created by a process of *hybridization*, or fusion. Ethnic groups came into close contact with other groups and with American popular culture. When different ethnic groups in close proximity had similar kinds of music, a performing ensemble could cross over and play at the other group's social functions. Many examples of this have been documented by Victor Greene in his history of old-time ethnic music in America (1992). A large proportion of the engagements of the Intihar Ensemble, the polka band from Johnstown, for example, were at weddings or other events that mixed ethnicities: a bride, for example, might be Polish, and the bridegroom Italian. The band's repertoire included Polish, German, Italian, Greek, Irish, and Mexican pieces, which reflected the multiethnic makeup of their audiences. They performed a variety of pieces that could be appreciated by all, regardless of ethnic background. This had the overall effect of uniting their audiences despite the divergent backgrounds of individuals. Individual ethnicity became something that could be appreciated by everyone in a panethnic context. In such a context, ethnic diversity can be a unifying force, in which each person respects and values differences in others.

An additional force for hybridization has been American popular culture as spread by the mass media. This has influenced ethnic ensembles to adopt certain popular stylistic features, especially when performing in a multiethnic context. One of the best examples of this process is that of the Slovenian-style polka bands of the 1940s and 1950s. The style, popularized by Frankie Yankovic, combined old Slovenian melodies played by two accordions, with popular rhythm provided by bass, drums, and four-string banjo. During that era, its popularity stretched far beyond the Slovenian community and even that of ethnic music in general.

"Chicago is a Polka Town" (Musical example 6.2) is a typical polka, which comments on the popularity of this dance, especially in the Midwestern United States. Notice the use of the button accordion as an accompanying instrument and the repeating melody of the tune, which, like the ballad presented, is structured on four lines of text.

Immigrant ballad
A newly written song commenting on the immigrant experience

GENRES AND CONTEXTS

Although it may not have been easy to bring a musical instrument on the arduous journey to America, all immigrant groups brought vocal music with them; the voice took no space in the luggage. The music that had the most relevance to the immigrant community was that passed down by oral tradition. Of primary importance to non-English-speaking immigrants were those songs in their original languages. Subsequent generations would learn these songs; sometimes they were the only things known to them in the original language. These songs functioned as a fundamental tie to these people's ethnic language and culture heritage.

Immigrants also created new songs featuring texts about the immigrant experience, commonly called *immigrant ballads*. These songs had the double function of strengthening immigrants in their newfound situations and of relating their experiences back to their home countries. Similar to these were songs with nostalgic texts about longing for the Old Country.

It was possible to express in song certain points of view that could not be said openly in any other way. Songs frequently commented on historical or current events, politics, living conditions, labor problems, or dissatisfaction with or desire for a better life. Even lullabies or humorous songs might include commentary. Songs composed about local events or local points of view could enter a stream of tradition carrying them throughout the ethnic community in North America and perhaps to other communities.

Ethnic groups also knew a great deal of vocal music outside oral tradition, such as church carols or hymns, for which the texts, at least, appeared in hymnals or other books. Many ethnic groups in North America formed choirs and singing societies, which performed choral compositions in European classical style or classical arrangements of folk songs. These choirs and singing societies generally sang compositions in their original language, thus creating an image of national or ethnic unity.

DANCE MUSIC

Just as in the Old World, instruments accompanied song, but purely instrumental music was most frequently associated with dance. For example, even a cursory examination of transcribed ethnic fiddle music shows that the vast majority of pieces are reels, jigs, hornpipes, waltzes, schottisches, strathspeys, and polkas, all of which are dance forms. The only exceptions are instrumental song transcriptions. Originally these pieces actually accompanied dance, but today they may be heard just as frequently at fiddle contests or on the stage at folk festivals. There has been a gradual shift from being purely functional dance music, to being music that may be listened to in a variety of contexts and appreciated for its style, rather than its function.

Of all the dance forms played by European Americans, perhaps the most pervasive is the polka, and it may be the most representative form of ethnic music in America. Charles Keil and colleagues (1992:14) cite six (or more) distinctive polka styles: southwestern Chicano and Papago Pima polkas; midwestern to western German American and Czech Bohemian American polkas; eastern to midwestern Polish American and Slovenian American polkas. Richard

March (1998) includes Slovenian, Norwegian, Polish, Croatian, Bohemian (Czech), Finnish, and Dutchman (German) styles of polka just from the state of Wisconsin. Each of its various styles is immediately recognizable as ethnic and can be associated with a specific group. At the same time, all these styles embody mixtures of ethnic traditions as well as elements of popular music.

Snapshot 6.2 takes a closer look at German music in the United States and the role it played in the establishment and maintenance of a German American community from the late 1600s to the present. In addition to many song and dance forms, both sacred and secular, the polka stands out as a major contribution of German Americans to our shared culture.

Snapshot 6.2: German Music in the United States

Immigrants from Germany began arriving in the United States in the late seventeenth century and have continued in a steady stream from that time to the present. Establishing religious and social institutions in the New Country, they have continued to be active musically, contributing to the mainstream Western classical tradition as it developed in the United States as well as to the enrichment of their own communities. Many German musical traditions have thrived here, including a strong and healthy polka culture that continues to this day.

The immigration of various German-speaking groups to the United States began in the 1680s and continued into the twentieth century. Large numbers arrived in the 1850s, 1870s, and 1880s. Pre-1847 immigration consisted primarily of religious exiles ("Old Lutherans"), farmers, and landless peasants from southern and eastern Germany. Political exiles immigrated to America following the 1848 revolutions. During the eighteenth century, Pennsylvania was settled by German and Swiss immigrants speaking a variety of Middle and South German dialects that gradually became homogenized into what is popularly known as Pennsylvania Dutch. This designation includes sectarian groups such as the Mennonites, Amish, Dunkards, and Moravians, but most German Americans in Pennsylvania are Lutheran or Reformed. Early settlers used the local dialect for everyday discourse and High German in church and school. During the nineteenth century, many settled in the Midwest in areas with high concentrations of German speakers and so were able to conduct a considerable portion of their daily affairs in that language. In general, German culture today has persisted most noticeably in rural areas.

In some respects it is difficult separating German American music from the music of mainstream America. German folk music acquired traits that we associate with concepts of Western or European American music long before the musics of many other ethnic groups did. For example, much German folk music uses

Heptatonic
Seven-note scales, such as the Western European major or minor scales

Triadic movement
Based on triads, or the three primary notes of a chord

heptatonic scales, major/minor melodies with a predominance of *triadic melodic movement* with implied harmonic function. German folk music also has a relatively long history of interaction with urban culture and the widespread use of notated music.

Music is central to German American concepts of culture; musical literacy has always been highly valued and from early years was an integral part of the curriculum in German American schools. Various genres of sacred and secular music were extremely significant in the lives of nineteenth-century German Americans and were closely tied with ethnic pride and the conservation of German identity.

During the past century, functional and contextual distinctions between religious and secular music among German Americans became hazy, and today, for example, hymnody is sung at home as well as in church, and secular music is also performed in church. In many communities the secular singing society is also the church choir. Similarly, the church instrumental ensemble also functions as the community social orchestra.

German Americans had a dominant role in the development of European American symphonic music in the nineteenth century. In 1890, for example, eighty-nine of the ninety-four musicians in the New York Philharmonic were German Americans. Many orchestras, such as the Chicago Symphony, were founded by German conductors. In Texas during the 1880s, German community orchestras performed works by Wagner and Mendelssohn regularly at state festivals. The influence of Germany on European American classical music decreased after World War I, when France became the preferred location for music study abroad.

Singing Societies

The German American *choral society*, called *Liedertafel, Liederkranz, Männerchor, Gesangverein*, or *Musikverein*, was traditionally a male chorus located in an urban area, led by a classically trained director. These singing societies were established to perform elaborate four-voiced arrangements of German folk songs as well as polyphonic music by German composers in the Western classical tradition, with the intention of creating an image of national and spiritual unity of the German people. Such groups encouraged their German American members to adopt a national German identity as opposed to their regional ones. Songs previously associated with a particular region often became part of a standard repertoire. During the nineteenth century, this classicized folk song repertoire was published in religious and secular song collections and periodicals used in German American homes in rural areas. Some collections contained texts only; others included music notation for piano and voice or four-part chorus.

Choral society
A group dedicated to the performance of four-part vocal music: in German American culture, limited to men, and usually found in urban areas

Sängerbunde
Literally "singing leagues"; groups that coordinate sangerfestes (compeititions/festivals) of German choral groups

Membership in any particular choral society tended to cut across economic, social, and occupational boundaries; a singing society could include mechanics, clerks, storekeepers, and professionals. All-male choruses have been dominant, but by 1900 mixed choruses were also common. These groups have generally opened their membership to interested individuals from other ethnic backgrounds, sometimes changing the group's name from German to English to appeal to a broader population.

Singing leagues (*Sängerbunde*) were formed beginning in the 1850s to coordinate competitions and festivals (*Sängerfeste*) of singing groups on local, state, national, or international levels. Such festivals included elaborate banquets, picnics, parades, concerts, and the participation of bands and orchestras. The evening banquet at these festivals was an exclusively male activity. Songs sung between elaborate toasts were mainly student songs, many in Latin.

In general, choral societies had multiple responsibilities and functions, including performing at a variety of civic events such as building dedications, holidays, and ethnic festivals. In addition, these groups sang in church services and provided choruses for local opera, operetta, and oratorio productions. Director/conductor positions were generally salaried. A singing society in a larger city would sometimes become associated with a German American instrumental ensemble and/or drama group, with which it would collaborate on concert programs. Because their song texts tended to focus on praises of the Fatherland in the German language, the loyalties of these singing groups were questioned during World War I; this period marked the beginning of a general decline in the prestige and importance of these groups. Anti-German sentiment was created as part of the war effort; everything German fell from esteem, German language instruction was dropped in the schools, and it was forbidden to speak German in public. German music was looked down upon, and singing societies became the objects of anti-German feelings.

Religious Music

The Lutheran Church historically has been the most important social institution for many German Americans, especially those in rural areas. It has been the center for religious, educational, social, and musical activities and has had an important role in the perpetuation of the German language. From the early nineteenth century, classes for teaching hymn singing to young people were established in churches and parochial schools.

At late as 1925, the Missouri Synod of the Lutheran Church, which claims the majority of German Americans, still used German in half its parishes. It favored the return to an older, more conservative hymnody, revitalizing the rhythmic style of the Reformation.

This style of singing united various German American groups by providing a single style of music in a single dialect, High German. Beginning in the 1840s, the Wisconsin and Missouri Synods published sacred and secular music for home use, including some hymns in English translation as well as some patriotic American songs. These publications formed a cultural link among German Americans throughout the Midwest.

At the time of the Protestant Reformation, a small group of reformers known as Anabaptists was led by Menno Simons (1492–1559). This group believed that all worldliness was wicked and that one should lead an extremely plain, austere, and pious life, refusing to bear arms in the military. Followers of Menno were called *Mennonites.* "Old Colony" Mennonites use *Gesangbuchs* (song books) for the singing of unison hymns; these books contain texts only, without music notation. Hymns are sung informally in the home and on Sundays in the village meeting house. At the meeting house, each line of text is initiated by a *Vorsanger* (lead singer), who is joined by the congregation. At the end of each line, the Vorsanger adds some solo notes after the congregation has stopped singing. Old Colony Mennonite hymns are sung in unison and in free rhythm, with no harmony or metric pattern. They are basically *melismatic,* melodically ornamented versions of old Protestant chorale tunes. Over time the tune may deviate significantly from the original through the variations of oral tradition.

A young bishop in the Mennonite church, Jacob Amman, believed that the practice of *meidung* had grown lax and should be more strictly enforced. This led to a schism in the church, and Amman and his followers broke away. They became known as *Amish,* after his name, and are the most orthodox of the Mennonite groups. The Amish first arrived in Pennsylvania around 1720. They maintained their attitude of separateness from the world, settling in distinct communities apart from other German-speaking dissenting religious groups, such as the Dunkards and Moravians.

Amish church music is entirely monophonic and without instrumental accompaniment. Hymns fall into two major categories according to music style: older slow hymns in *free rhythm* and newer fast metric hymns. *Monophonic* slow hymns are often highly melismatic versions of fifteenth-, sixteenth-, and seventeenth-century secular songs, *Gregorian chants*, or *chorale* melodies. Fast tunes are generally based on German secular folk songs, well-known Lutheran hymns, American Protestant hymns, or Anglo American folk tunes with German texts. Specific composers and dates are known for a number of these fast tunes. These melodies are not used in the church service but are sung at Sunday evening sings and weekday meetings.

In Amish communities, a worship service is held Sunday mornings at a home, in a room from which all domestic furniture has

Mennonites
Breakaway Protestant religious sect that proscribes an extremely plain, austere, and pious life

Gesangbuchs
The song books used by the Mennonites

Vorsanger
The lead singer in a Mennonite congregation

Melisma
Using several notes to sing a single syllable

Meidung
The shunning of an errant member of a Mennonite congregation

Free rhythm
Without a steady, underlying rhythmic pulse

Monophonic
A single, unaccompanied vocal line

Gregorian chant
The hymns sung in the middle ages in the Christian church

Chorale
A composed multipart vocal work on a religious theme

been removed. Men and women sit on opposite sides of the room on hard, backless wooden benches. A single congregation may have a half-dozen song leaders, usually older men who take turns in leading the congregation. The *Vorsanger* announces each hymn by page number in the hymnal and sings the first syllable of the line alone. The entire group joins in on the second syllable in unison. Any member of the congregation if so moved may announce the number of a hymn and proceed to lead it. Hymns are always monophonic and unaccompanied; instruments in the home or at church in conjunction with devotional singing are strictly forbidden.

Secular folk songs are sung in Amish communities in the home and on special occasions, such as the afternoon and evening of the wedding day, or during Sunday evening "singings" for young people. The repertoire for these events includes faster metric hymns and songs. Popular ballads may be sung at the Sunday evening sings, often to the accompaniment of (officially forbidden) harmonicas. In some Amish communities, weekly Saturday night barn dances are held for young people. A typical barn dance band includes some combination of guitar, fiddle, mandolin, and harmonica. Dancing is done in sets of six to eight couples in a circle formation. There is no central caller; one person in each set calls out the various steps, which others in the set must follow. Usually young women locate themselves on one side of the barn, young men on the other. At these events English rather than Pennsylvania Dutch is usually spoken, although in general no outsiders are present.

Polka Bands

German Americans, along with Czech, Polish, and Slovenian Americans, have had a prominent role in the American polka movement. New Ulm, Minnesota, is a major German/Czech settlement noted for its wealth of bands and well-known polka musicians. In this and other regions, Sunday evening picnic concerts have been a major context for polka band music. Groups from New Ulm are known as "Dutchman" bands and tend to have an eclectic style incorporating repertoire from their Slavic American and Scandinavian American neighbors.

The "American Dutchman" style is based on instrumental dance music of southwestern Bohemia, a Czech region that has had a great deal of German cultural influence. This style is characterized by a marchlike or military quality, with instrumentation emphasizing button accordion, brass instruments, and drum set. Bands often consist of family members, whose repertoire focuses on polkas and waltzes. Song texts are often in English and relate to the American experience of European immigrants and their descendants.

In the late 1940s, many German American bands tended to emulate mainstream swing and "sweet" bands, synthesizing old-time

Swing band
Popular jazz band of the 1930s and 1940s focusing on syncopated dance music

Sweet band
A popular band oriented toward popular songs and slower dance numbers, with less syncopation

and modern American ballroom musical styles. The instrumentation of these groups included multiple saxophones, trumpets and other brass, drum set, accordions, and piano. Repertoire included two-steps, polkas, schottisches, and romantic Tin Pan Alley ballads.

Lawrence Welk (1903–1992; see Figure 6.5), who became a household name through television appearances from the early 1950s, integrated German American polkas and waltzes into the standard mainstream American dance band repertoire. His parents were Russian Germans from Ukraine who settled in North Dakota in 1892. His father played organ and accordion, and Welk soon began playing at local barn dances and weddings. His earliest recordings in the late 1920s and early 1930s were not "ethnic" at all, but standard contemporary popular tunes. His first polka recording was

Figure 6.5
Lawrence Welk on a
sheet music cover,
c. 1948. Courtesy
Dave Jasen.

made in 1939. Welk, essentially an American bandleader of "sweet" music, had an important role in mainstreaming the acceptance of polka music, even though polkas and waltzes were always a minor part of his repertoire. His style can be characterized as smooth, bouncy, and conservative, aiming to please as wide an audience as possible. His popularity lasted into the 1960s and 1970s.

Mark Levy

THE SYMBOLIC CONTENT OF INSTRUMENTS AND GENRES

One class of instrumental music not associated with dance was that of the wind band movement. Beginning in the nineteenth century, wind bands became popular all across Europe and America, and many ethnic communities formed their own bands. Typically, these bands played the same kinds of music as other wind bands of the era: waltzes, polkas (and other dance forms primarily for listening and not for dancing), marches, opera selections, and patriotic and nationalistic music.

Certain instruments have become symbolic of ethnic groups. For example, the *tamburitza* has become a primary symbol of Croatian and Serbian immigrant groups, the button-box accordion for Slovenians, the *bouzouki* for Greeks, the *hardingfele* for Norwegians, and bagpipes for Scottish Americans. Frequently these instruments were played only by a minority in the European areas from which they came: the *tamburitza* from northern Croatia and northeastern Bosnia, the *hardingfele* from the Telemark provinces of western Norway, and so on. In America they have become general symbols for the entire nationality.

Some ethnic groups may have the same or very similar instruments as symbols of their ethnicity. For example, the Czechs use the *cymbaly* and the Ukrainians the *tsymbaly*, essentially the same instrument. The psalteries played by Baltic peoples have become symbols for each of the countries where they appear: the Finnish *kantele*, Estonian *kannel*, Latvian *kokle*, and Lithuanian *kankle*.

Joyce Hakala, a veterinarian from Minneapolis, formed Koivun Kaiku ("Echo of the Birch"; see Figure 6.6) in 1984, the first Finnish *kantele* ensemble in North America. The group was an immediate hit with the Finnish American community. Although few Finnish Americans had ever even seen a *kantele*, they had all heard of the instrument and knew it was the national instrument of Finland. As such, the *kantele* had an enormous symbolic value beyond its use for the production of music. Hakala's ensemble is made up entirely of third- and subsequent generation Finnish Americans and non-Finnish individuals interested in *kantele* music. No one speaks Finnish, but they sing many songs in this language (Hakala 1997).

Tamburitza
Fretted, long-neck lute plucked with a flat plectrum, found in South Slavic areas of the Balkans

Bouzouki
Greek long-necked, multistringed lute

Hardingfele
Norwegian modified violin, with 4 melody strings and 4 strings (running under the fingerboard) that sound sympathetically

Cymbaly/tsymbaly
Trapezoidal-shaped struck zither (hammer dulcimer)

Psaltery
Bowed zither common in the Baltics, such as the Finnish *kantele*, Estonian *kannel*, Latvian *kokle*, and Lithuanian *kankle*

Figure 6.6
The Finnish American
kantele ensemble *Koivun
Kaiku* (Echoes of the
Birch) dressed in
Finnish national cos-
tumes, with their
instruments. Photo by
Charles Marabella, c.
1990. Used by permis-
sion.

Listen to Musical Example 6.3, Vigala Reinlender," which presents the Wind Wizards: Estonian Instrumental Folk Music Ensemble of Chicago, with Andres Peekna on the kantele. Here we have a tune in two parts (A and B), each part consisting of four lines repeated as in the following scheme: AABB AABB, with first the kantele and later the guitar and violin playing the tune and a simple harmony.

Although many of the same forms and genres from Europe have been preserved in America, the contexts and functions of these genres may have changed. For example, music associated with calendrical rituals of agrarian societies may now provide entertainment and sustain ethnic identity. Svatava Pirkova-Jakobson (1956) said that what were rituals in Europe have become reenacted as drama in America. Still, certain year-cycle events associated with various saints days, Christmas, Easter, Passover, and New Year continue to be a significant venue for ethnic music. Perhaps the most significant contexts for ethnic music continues to be life-cycle events such as weddings, initiation ceremonies, and funerals. Ritual songs and customs may still be performed in the New World, but they may lose their ritual significance and be performed outside ritual contexts.

THE RECORDING INDUSTRY

One of the greatest forces for the dissemination and preservation of European American music in North America has been the recording industry. Many record companies, beginning with cylinder recordings and reaching a peak with 78s, began issuing specialized ethnic series advertised in record catalogs. (See more about the recording industry in Chapter 2.)

Ethnic music was most often performed by amateur musicians for family and friends or for events held by their local ethnic communities. They performed a specialized repertoire for a specialized audience. Ethnic musicians almost always had to have some other kind of profession and performed their music as a hobby. When the best of these musicians issued recordings, their status in the community changed. In some cases they turned professional, touring beyond their local boundaries to other communities of their nationality. They might also perform for other nationalities who enjoyed a similar style of music.

 Musical example 6.4, "Dortn, Dortn, Ibern Vasserl" ("There, Across the Water"), features one of the foremost scholars and interpreters of Yiddish songs, Ruth Rubin, whose performances, recordings and scholarship chronicle the emigration of European Jews to the United States during the late nineteenth and early twentieth centuries. Many of her songs have been recorded by Smithsonian Folkways and have reached wide audiences both within and outside the American Jewish community.

Some sound recordings became best-sellers within their particular ethnic communities. When a recorded version of a genre of music became widely known in a community, it would homogenize, standardize, and popularize that musical style. This happened for two reasons. First, the community expected a particular piece, or type of music, to sound like the familiar recorded versions in live performance. Second, and more important, new musicians in the tradition would frequently learn their repertoire and style from recorded versions of the music.

With the advent of the audiocassette, recordings of ethnic music became even more pervasive, but the effect on the overall musical community moved largely back to local control. Almost any musical ensemble could produce its own cassette, which could be marketed at local performances. The impact of the cassette tape has been documented in studies by Roger Wallis and Krister Malm (1984) and Peter Manuel (1993). Sound recordings also leave us with a primary historical record of the music of various ethnic communities.

Even though the era of mass immigration from Europe has long passed, European American music is as vibrant as ever. As earlier generations pass away, there is no need to fear that their music will also pass into oblivion. There will always be someone interested in Irish fiddling, Polish polka, Croatian *tamburitza*, Finnish *kantele*, or German hymn singing, if not for its ethnic symbolism, at least for the quality of its style and the aesthetic enjoyment it provides.

REVIEW

Important Terms and People to Know

Acculturation
American Dutchman style
Assimilation
Ballad
Child ballads
Ethnic identity
Festival of American Folklife
Heptatonic scale
Immigrant ballads
Kantele
Melismatic
Monophonic
Oral tradition
Pentatonic scale
Polka
Sharp, Cecil
Singing society
Social (as a noun)
Tune family
Lawrence Welk

Review Questions

1. What sorts of activities did early European immigrants to the United States do to promote a sense of community in the New World? What role did music have in the immigrant experience during the three stages of adjustment?
2. Discuss the textual and musical characteristics of British ballads. Who were some of the scholars, collectors, and performers of ballads in this country and in Britain?
3. Discuss community life in Northern New England during the eighteenth and nineteenth centuries. What was the role of music and music making in various social contexts? What changes occurred in these communities and their musical practices during the twentieth century?
4. Why were singing societies important for the German American communities that developed during the eighteenth and nineteenth centuries? What kinds of music were performed and why were these important to the sense of German American identity?
5. What was the role of the Lutheran Church in German American communities? How did it serve to regulate musical practices?

6. How and why did certain instruments and genres become symbols of European American identity in the United States?

Projects

1. Compose your own work or love song in the style of a British ballad. Try to incorporate as many musical, textual, and performance characteristics of British and British American ballads as you can in your song and perform it for your class.
2. Interview a member of your family, a friend, or anyone you know who is an immigrant to this country from Europe and see how (or if) this person has maintained an ethnic connection with his or her home community, language, and/or music.
3. Research a musical instrument or song form that originated in Europe and was brought to the United States. What changes have occurred since its introduction to this country, especially in the twentieth century? What role (if any) did new technology and/or media play in these changes?

CHAPTER 7

African American Musical Cultures

Portia K. Maultsby, Mellonee V. Burnim,
Dena J. Epstein, Susan Oehler,
Jacqueline Cogdell DjeDje, David Evans, and
Thomas Riis

INTRODUCTION

The first African Americans were forcibly taken from their home communities, mainly in West Africa, and brought in the early seventeenth century to what would become the United States. Slaves in the cotton- and tobacco-based economy of the rural South were frequently separated from their families and supporting communities once they arrived, and they continued to be subjected to harsh and demeaning discriminatory practices after slavery ended in 1865.

Much of the early history of African Americans reflects these social and economic realities, as well as the importance of the church in reestablishing strong communities and providing various contexts for musical performance. Forms, such as early blues, and other folk traditions, as well as spirituals and early musical theater, grew from a synthesis of predominantly West African and Western European musics and developed over time into musical styles that today permeate all of American music. Jazz, blues, early rock and roll, soul, and rap, among many other styles, would not exist today without the creative contributions of African American musicians, entrepreneurs, and recording companies. In addition to these and many other forms, African Americans have also made important contributions to American theater and to classical music traditions, as performers, composers, and patrons.

African American music is among the musical styles that has had a major impact on the music of the United States. This is reflected throughout this book in the discussions of a wide range of musical styles that have their roots in African American culture. This chapter gives an overview of African American folk and popular styles through the 1970s. For other styles, see Snapshot 2.2, which gives an overview of disco and house music, and Snapshot 11.3, which discusses rap and hip-hop. African American classical music and jazz are covered in Chapter 10.

FOLK TRADITIONS

African Musical Legacy

Among the peoples of Africa, music was integrated into daily life, as a group activity rather than as a performance before a passive audience. Music accompanied all kinds of group work, regulating the pace of work and lessening the monotony. Even individuals working alone often sang about their work. Festivities were accompanied by music and dancing. Derisive singing, even in reference to the king, was accepted as a means of expressing sentiments that were unacceptable as speech. All these aspects of African culture were easily adapted to life in the New World.

J. H. Kwabena Nketia (1974) described these characteristic elements of African music:

- Multipart rhythmic structures
- Repetitive choruses with a lead singer
- The call-response style of alternating phrases, either juxtaposed or overlapping
- Scales of four to seven pitches

These elements reappear in modified form in African American music. The short, repeated phrases that accompanied vigorous dancing upset Europeans accustomed to sedate dances and regular rhythmic patterns. African polyrhythms seemed to them to be noise. Many Europeans could not acknowledge a music that did not conform to their rules of composition or performance.

Many African American instruments and musical styles had roots in African traditions. Richard Jobson, a British trader who visited Africa in 1620-1621, soon after the first Africans were brought to Virginia, described drums and an instrument made from a gourd with a neck fastened to it and up to six strings; surely this was a prototype of the *banjo*. Later travelers reported similar instruments that were to be transported to the New World, sometimes by slaving captains who tried to preserve the health of their cargos by compelling the captives to dance aboard ship. In the New World, the Africans constructed familiar instruments from local materials (Epstein 1977: 49). Besides drums, other instruments frequently described as African included various kinds of rhythm instruments, a xylophone called the *balafo* or *balaphon,* quills (a form of pan pipes), horns, and

Call-response style
A songleader sings a phrase to which the group responds. Also called *call-and-response*

Polyrhythm
More than one rhythmic pattern part played simultaneously

Banjo
African American stringed instrument, usually featuring five strings (one short drone string and four melody ones) and a hoop-shaped resonator covered with a skin head

the banjo. The banjo is found throughout the Caribbean and the North American mainland under various names: *banza, banjah, bandore, banjar,* and others (Epstein 1975:35).

Africans in North America

Although Africans arrived in Virginia in 1619, there are not many descriptions of African musical activity in North America before 1800. This is partially due to the slow growth in the African American population during this period. In the seventeenth and eighteenth centuries, the North America colonies were not nearly as profitable as those in the West Indies, where the population increased rapidly and Africans were brought in vast numbers. As islands became overpopulated, planters and their work forces moved, sometimes to the mainland. In the West Indies, the music brought from Africa was able to survive and flourish for at least a century and a half, but on the mainland, where the black population was relatively smaller, the music became acculturated more rapidly. This was particularly true of the English colonies.

On the mainland, the dances of the Africans were usually confined to Sunday, their only day of rest, but the English clergy was bitterly opposed to this desecration of the Lord's Day and did its best to stop the dancing (Figure 7.1). Dancing was allowed on those holidays

Figure 7.1
"Negro dance" sketched in Lynchburg, Virginia, 18 August 1853, by Lewis Miller of York, Pennsylvania. Courtesy Virginia State Library, Richmond.

Lynchburg—negro dance, August 18th 1853,

that the planters permitted. Traditionally the Christmas holiday lasted until New Year's, and some planters allowed a holiday at Easter. The religious nature of these holidays did not rule out secular music and dancing, which became a central feature of the holiday celebrations.

In 1739 an insurrection by slaves in Stono, South Carolina, was accompanied by singing, dancing, and beating drums, intended to attract more Africans to join the rebellion. As a consequence, the beating of drums was forbidden by law in South Carolina, as it had been earlier in the West Indies. Yet despite this ban, which was rigorously enforced, drumming continued unseen by the authorities. Former slaves in Georgia who were interviewed in the 1930s described how to make drums from hollow trees and recalled dancing to drums, dancing that must have been done in secret.

With drums so central to African music and dancing, substitutes had to be found. Rhythmic support to dancing was provided by hand-clapping, foot-stomping, and a practice apparently unique to the United States, "patting juba." Patting juba was an extension of simple hand-clapping, raising it to the level of a self-contained accompaniment to dancing. It was described as striking the hands on the knees, then striking the hands together, then striking the right shoulder with one hand, the left with the other—all the while keeping time with the feet and singing. The earliest reference to the practice dates from the 1820s. A variation of patting involved the use of two sticks to beat time on the floor, either alone or with other instruments.

Patting juba
Rhythmic clapping of the hands together, on the shoulders, and knees, to accompany dancing

The rate at which this dancing became acculturated is not known and varied from colony to colony. Initially it must have been largely African, but gradually the European influence began to modify the steps. In the northern colonies, some holidays originally observed by whites gradually became associated with the Africans, and African customs—including dancing and drumming—were introduced to these celebrations. "'Lection Day," in Connecticut, Rhode Island, and Massachusetts, involving the election of a king, processions, feasting, and dancing, became known as "Negro Election Day" by the mid-eighteenth century. In these colonies, slaves lived singly or in small groups and had little community life. Gradually they created midyear festivals where they could enjoy their distinctive culture: drumming, dancing, and singing. Banjos, fiddles, and Guinea drums, made from logs covered with sheepskin, provided the music for the Guinea dance. As slaves were caught up in the performance, their behavior was reported as more African.

Although reports of African music and dancing in the southern colonies before 1800 were not common, still rarer were reports of the impact of African culture on European music and dancing. In an era when many people were preoccupied with preserving elements of their European heritage in an alien, often hostile, environment, it is hardly surprising that they recorded very little of an influence that they could not publicly acknowledge. Yet evidence has been found that Europeans performed "Negro dances," not just occasionally but with some regularity. One description of a Virginia dance published in 1776 stated: "Towards the close of an evening, when the company are pretty well tired with country dances, it is usual to dance jigs, . . . borrowed . . . from the 'Negroes'" (Epstein 1977: 121). In Richmond before 1820, the courtly black fiddler Simeon Gilliat performed at balls that began with a reel followed by contra dances, a congo (demonstrably an African term), a hornpipe, and a jig that would wind up the evening.

La Calinda

In Louisiana and contiguous territory, areas that had been settled by the Spanish and the French, developments were quite different. Cultural and governmental ties were not to the other mainland colonies but to Spanish America and to the French West Indies. Louisiana had been settled almost one hundred years after Virginia, with its African population coming directly from Africa between 1719 and 1731. With a relatively homogeneous population, the distinctive character of New Orleans was established early. It is not surprising that African music and dance was observed from the early days of their immigration.

A Frenchman who had worked as a planter wrote in 1758 of the crowds of Africans who danced the *calinda,* widely reported in the French West Indies with its associated instrument, the *banza. La calinda* had been described in Martinique as early as 1694. It was accompanied by two drums of unequal length, each with one open end and one covered with skin. The drummers held them between their legs and played with four fingers of both hands. The larger drum provided the basic beat, and the smaller was played more quickly. The dance was always accompanied by a "guitar" with four strings called *banza.*

> **La calinda**
> African-derived dance performed in the Caribbean and New Orleans area during the seventeenth and eighteenth centuries

Other Popular Dances

Although in the seaboard southern states evangelical religion condemned secular music and dancing, in New Orleans African-style dancing was permitted to flourish. Popular dances included the *chica,* the *bamboula,* the *coonjine* or *counjaille,* and the congo dance. Both the French and Spanish governments had permitted dancing, and after the Louisiana Purchase in 1803, new "Ordinances of Police" specified that the mayor should appoint places for slaves to dance on Sundays. Travelers frequently described these dances at what is now called Congo Square, sometimes giving details of the steps and accompanying instruments.

In 1819, Benjamin Latrobe described what he saw on a Sunday afternoon:

> They were formed in circular groups .... The music consisted of two drums and stringed instrument .... On the top of the finger board was the rude figure of a man in a sitting posture—two pegs behind him to which the strings were fastened. The body was a calabash ....
>
> A man sang an uncouth song ... which I suppose was in some African language, for it was not French. The allowed amusements of Sunday have, it seems, perpetuated here those of Africa. (Epstein 1977:97)

Latrobe accompanied his account with sketches of the instruments, among the very few contemporary drawings of African instruments that have survived from the mainland (Figure 7.2).

FROM AFRICANS TO AFRICAN AMERICANS

The gradual transformation of African culture to something that came to be called "African American" began almost as soon as the Africans landed in the New World. Speaking many different languages, they had to learn to communicate with each other and with their new masters. They had to adjust to new surroundings, new customs, new sounds, smells, and tastes. They observed the music and dances of these strange Europeans and gradually learned to combine them with the music and dance they had brought from Africa. This complex of two cultures, side by side, influencing each other in intangible ways, led gradually to the formation of an African American culture. Acculturation proceeded at different rates in different colonies. African dancing took place in New Orleans in 1819 and later, while as early as 1694 a black fiddler was playing for the dancing of whites in Virginia (Epstein 1977: 80). This same fiddler also might have played for the dancing of his fellow slaves.

There also was considerable variety in the circumstances of slavery in the different colonies. Settled in 1690, Carolina had a black

Figure 7.2
Sketches of African instruments from manuscript journal of Benjamin Henry Latrobe. Entry from February 21, 1819, from New Orleans. Reproduced by permission of the Papers of Benjamin Henry Latrobe, Maryland Historical Society.

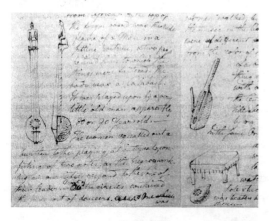

majority by 1708, while the northern states had only a small, scattered black population. Plantations in the southern colonies developed their distinctive society, very different from the more urban society in the North. While slavery flourished in the South with the introduction of the cotton gin after the Revolution, slavery in the northern states declined and gradually disappeared. As more and more blacks were born in the New World, African festivals in the North diminished and were replaced by processions and parades that demonstrated the dignity of the black community. With the passage of time, dancing and singing by African Americans in the northern states tended to be enjoyed in private rather than in public festivals in open fields.

Fiddlers

Although the prejudice against dancing and fiddling was widespread throughout the South, many planters not only permitted the activities but encouraged them. James H. Hammond of South Carolina penciled in his plantation manual: "Church members are privileged to dance on all holyday occasions" (Epstein 1977:212). A Mississippi Planter wrote in 1851, "I have a good fiddler, and keep him well supplied with cat-gut, and I make it his duty to play for the negroes every Saturday night until 12 o'clock" (Epstein 1977:154). Some planters went so far as to provide music teachers for talented servants.

It was customary for a planter to advertise in local newspapers if he had a slave fiddler of a good reputation whom others might wish to hire. Solomon Northup, a free Negro from upstate New York who was kidnapped and sold into slavery in Louisiana, benefited from his ability as a fiddler. His fiddle "introduced me to great houses—relieved me of many days' labor in the field—made me friends . . . gave me an honored seat at the yearly feasts" (Epstein 1977:150). These obscure musicians at times achieved what would have been a professional status if their earnings had remained in their own pockets. Many of them earned a reputation for excellence that extended for miles around.

The dances for which they played often included play-party games and songs that were almost indistinguishable from the songs of white pioneers, but modified with African American rhythm and traditions. These games were also played by children, but few contemporary reports have been found of the play of children before 1900.

Play-party
A celebration for children and young adults featuring games, singing, and dancing

Work Songs

In Africa, singing frequently accompanied group work wherever it took place, in the fields or on the water. This practice was easily transferred to the New World wherever people worked in groups.

Singing coordinated their movements, lifted their spirits, enabled the slower workers to keep up, and warded off fatigue. Singing could accompany hoeing, planting, harvesting, picking cotton, grinding corn, cutting brush, laying railroad tracks, cutting wood, hauling fishing nets, or rowing.

Understandably, planters prized leaders with good, strong voices, commanding personalities, and a strong sense of rhythm. Snapshot 7.1 describes the variety of cries, calls, and hollers that accompanied work.

Snapshot 7.1: African American Cries, Calls, and Hollers

African American cries, calls, and hollers told of the slaves' loves, work, and floggings and expressed the slaves' moods and the reality of their oppression. They sang of the proud defiance of the run-away, the courage of the black rebels, the heartlessness of the slave traders, and the kindness and cruelty of masters (Blassingame 1979 [1972]:115).

Work Songs in African American Culture

In most instances, slaves were required to perform music while working, because slave owners realized the impact that music making had on the work experience. Many masters encouraged slaves to sing as they went about their work, believing that they were more productive when they sang (Bailey 1992:41). An article from 1895 states

> The singing of the slaves at work was regarded by their masters as almost indispensable to the quick and proper performance of the labor, and the leaders of the singings were often excused from work . . . . Wharf laborers were selected and retained largely because of their ability as singers, a good singer being regarded as worth more on the wharves than a laborer . . . . ("Negro Folk Songs" 1976 [1895]:150-151)

Most writers concur that the singing of songs assisted the physical labor and helped arouse and keep up the energy of work. In such situations, it did not matter if the songs were religious or secular. In communal group labor, songs provided a rhythm to coordinate physical activity involved in work (Figure 7.3). Singing thus relieved the tedium and made the time pass more quickly.

Eileen Southern (1997:161) explains that the lone worker performed a different type of song. Because the worker had no need to coordinate work movements with others, songs tended to take on the nature of a deeply personal utterance. Tempo, text, melody—all these things reflected the person's mood of the moment. If the worker was happy, fingers flew and the work song cheered all who might be listening; if the worker was melancholy, the same song

Figure 7.3
Song is used to provide rhythm and coordinate work in groups. This is evident in this photo of "Lightning" and a group of men working at Darrington State Prison Farm, Sandy Point, Texas, Paril 1935. Photo by Alan Lomax, from the Collections of the Library of Congress.

might be sung so mournfully as to slow up the activity and to depress all within hearing.

The Classification of Cries, Calls, and Hollers

Willis Laurence James (1970, 1973) and Harold Courlander (1963) are among the few scholars who have attempted to classify the cry and call systematically. James (1973: 430–444) uses "cry" as a catch-all term to describe musical statements and sounds that have different functions in various contexts:

1. *Call:* the most common; the sound produced by a man who gives orders to a group of men at work; a musical statement which asks something for or from someone else, or pronounces judgment
2. *Street cry:* the most significant, familiar, and self-respecting of all cries; a musical statement used to sell an item or product; can be regarded as a species of the work song
3. *Religious cry:* a subtle, musical use of the voice by a preacher in presenting a sermon
4. *Field cry (corn field whoop):* a brief statement frequently heard in silent, open country; signifies a loneliness of spirit due to isolation of the worker, or serves as a signal to someone nearby, or merely as a bit of self-indulgence
5. *Night cry:* Musical statement that gives a feeling of relaxation and self-expression; may be performed at night while traveling at night as a personal serenade or as a signal in the dark
6. *Dance cry:* the oldest and most vital of all cries; performed when a person naturally gives out a statement of joy while dancing
7. *Water cry:* performed by workers who have served as boatmen, roustabouts, longshoremen, rafthaulers, and fishermen

Courlander (1963) bases his discussion on information obtained from performers in Alabama. Whereas the *call* is used to communicate messages of all kinds—to bring people in from the fields, to summon them to work, to attract the attention of a girl in the distance, to signal hunting dogs, or simply to make one's presence known—the *cry* is simply a form of self-expression, a vocalization of some emotion. It does not have to have a theme or fit into any kind of musical or formal structure. It is short and free and consists of a single music statement or a series of statements that reflect any number of moods: homesickness, loneliness, lovesickness, contentment, exuberance.

A man working under the hot sun might give voice to such a cry on impulse, directing it to the world, or to the fields around him, or perhaps to himself. It might be filled with exuberance or melancholy. It might consist of a long "hoh-hoo," stretched out and embellished with intricate ornamentation of a kind virtually impossible to notate; or it might be a phrase like "I'm hot and hungry," or simply "pickin' cotton, yohhoo." As in the group work songs, hollers drew upon the body of traditional lyrics or were improvised by a singer while working. Some hollers had no words but were just complex combinations of sounds expressing one's state of mind or communicating a particular message to others (Hinson 1978:1).

Worksong
Any song used to accompany work or labor; can be used to help coordinate large groups of laborers or to pass the time for a solo worker
Call
Any form of worksong used to communicate a message
Cry/holler
A free-form vocalization used to express personal feelings

Listen to Musical Example 7.1, "My Little Annie So Sweet." Here, a field holler, sung by Horace Sprott while chopping cotton in Alabama, illustrates the plaintive sound of the lone field worker. Notice the crack of the blade as it comes in contact with the cotton plant, and the tri-partite structure of the song itself—three phrases repeated—a form that would eventually develop into the classic blues.

Although the cry, call, and holler are rarely performed as separate and distinct music types in modern culture, the performance style is still very much a part of the African American musical tradition, found, for example, in the recordings of songs by Alan Lomax (1956). Not only are elements found in various religious forms as well, Evans (1978) believes that field hollers also contributed the basic vocal material to the early blues.

Jacqueline Cogdell DjeDje

Along the coast, boat songs were frequently described by travelers and in memoirs by planters' wives and daughters. Crews of four to eight rowed boats in tidal rivers from one plantation to another or to the nearest city. The leader would sing a line, and the rowers would chime in with a refrain. The words were often improvised and were sometimes compliments to the passengers, sometimes merely unconnected words and phrases. Or they could be more somber: There were songs about separation from loved ones, abuse by one's captain, or longing for freedom. A good leader could speed the boat along, no matter how tired the crew might be. Work and boat songs continued a tradition that had been common in Africa: integrating music into daily life.

Other opportunities for group singing were observed aboard sailing vessels. Hoisting sails, winding the capstan, and loading cargo needed song to coordinate the movements of the men. Mobile, Alabama, for example, became known as a shanty mart where sailors from different countries learned shanties from each other. Sailors from the West Indies were especially known for their prowess at singing shanties. Later when steamboats replaced sailing vessels, especially on inland rivers, firemen worked in a virtual inferno below decks. Fredrika Bremer in 1850 witnessed firemen on the Mississippi. A man standing on a pile of firewood improvised a song, which was punctuated by the sound of wood being tossed to men below. They responded in chorus while hurling firewood into the boat's furnace (Bremer 1853:2:174).

Still another widely reported occasion for song throughout the southern states was corn shucking. As ears of corn were not as perishable as some other crops, the corn was allowed to stay in the field until the other crops were gathered. The ears of corn were then harvested and heaped into two enormous piles, awaiting shucking. The planter would invite workers from neighboring plantations to come on a chosen day. Gangs of workers would march, singing to the appointed place, choose sides, and name their leaders. Each team would strive to outdo the other, spurred on by the magnificent voices of their leaders, to which the crew would respond in chorus. This ceremony had some resemblance to the English harvest home and corn huskings in the North, but the musical competition and the improvised singing were peculiar to the South. When all the corn had been shucked and the winning team acclaimed, the feasting and dancing began. Cotton picking also lent itself to group singing, "some wild, simple melodies" sung in a chorus, "so loud as to be heard from one plantation to another . . . for miles with musical echoes" (Epstein 1977:163). Flailing rice, grinding hominy, and braiding baskets all provided opportunities for singing, with the tempo adjusted to the task at hand.

Work songs, however, did not need large groups. Plentiful reports exist of individuals singing lullabies. Weaving, spinning, shoe shining, and cooking were all accompanied by singing. A self-contained form of song was improvised by street vendors in southern cities. These street cries described what the vendor was selling in terms calculated to attract buyers. Charleston, South Carolina, and New Orleans were especially noted for the skill of their street merchants in improvising attractive cries.

Creole Songs

Quite distinct from the folk songs of the eastern seaboard were the French Creole songs of Louisiana. Many blacks spoke French and enjoyed a Francophile culture. Under the French and Spanish governments, it was relatively easy for slaves to gain their freedom, which created a comparatively large free Afro-Creole population that was relatively prosperous but mingled freely with the slave population. Nowhere else in the United States did circumstances encourage such mingling.

Afro-Creole
People of mixed ancestry, usually having some European or Native American ancestors; in New Orleans, French speaking, fair-skinned people who enjoyed higher social status than the general "colored" population

French-speaking Afro-Creole families enjoyed street parades, dancing, even French opera. Although free blacks were not accepted socially by the white population before the Civil War, their presence in business and trade was familiar and customary. Within their own community, the Creoles of color could move with assurance and pride. Afro-Creole musicians were taught by teachers from the French Opera orchestra, and their folk music was heavily influenced by French music with the addition of African elements, such as rhythm and call-response forms. Traditional Creole songs were known in the French Caribbean as well as on the mainland.

Protest Songs

The African tradition of improvised derisive singing was easily adapted to the American scene. In September 1772 the *South*

Carolina Gazette reported a "cabal of Negroes" near Charleston on a Saturday night, numbering about sixty people. "The entertainment was opened by the men copying (or *taking off*) the manners of their masters, and the women those of their mistresses, and relating some highly curious anecdotes, to the inexpressible diversion of that company" (Epstein 1977:82). When Europeans were present, the entertainment usually involved a more subtle satire, which permitted the expression of ideas that otherwise might have been severely punished.

Improvising satire, sometimes too subtle to be recognized, and making fun of the master and his family in ways that did not provoke offense were specialties of the African American improvisor. Satiric verses could easily be inserted in work songs, whether boat songs or corn songs. However, fewer satirical songs than spirituals have been preserved. Singers may have been reluctant to sing satirical songs, for both religious reasons and self-protection. Even after the end of slavery, it was not wise to sing critical songs in the South.

More explicit comments on the conditions of slavery were sung, sometimes interpolated into religious songs. Harriet Tubman is said to have communicated her intentions to leave the plantation by singing a song of farewell as she walked about the quarters. "Go Down, Moses" was not a safe song to sing in the South, with its refrain of "Let my people go," but a song about the promised land might seem innocuous to the casual listener. The song "Follow the Drinking Gourd" gave instructions on how to use the stars to guide a runaway to the North and freedom. Even corn-shucking songs might include verses of protest like "Grind de meal, gimme de husk; Bake de bread, gimme de crust."

The End of the Nineteenth Century

Despite the influence of the music of the whites by which it was surrounded, African American secular music retained characteristics associated with African music. No matter that most of the Africans had been born in the New World, that they now spoke English in some form, that Africa was known to them only in stories and reminiscences, their music and dancing was immediately recognized by outsiders as non-European. Their skill at improvisation, at making up songs to fit the occasion, to regulate the work at hand, to compliment, or to denigrate—these were remarkable to observers.

In spite of the efforts of some clergymen to disparage secular folk music and dancing, African American secular folk music persisted as a familiar part of everyday work and play, musically very similar to African American sacred music. When the immensely popular minstrel theater caricatured African Americans, their secular music was brought into discredit, leaving the spiritual (also, at times, discredited) as the preeminent form of African American music. Nevertheless, secular music continued to flourish, growing in popularity as the nineteenth century drew to a close. With the development of ragtime, a distinctly American contribution to world music became popular worldwide. As the twentieth century progressed, the blues and jazz were even more influential in demonstrating the power of African American secular music throughout the world.

Dena J. Epstein

Gospel

The dynamic role that music plays in the worship of black Americans has been well documented. From the vivid descriptions of songs shouted out in the invisible church of the black slave, to the music innovations standardized in the newly independent African Methodist Episcopal (AME) congregation founded by Richard Allen, we learn of the repertoire, performance practices, and function of the eighteenth-century genre called the folk spiritual. From twentieth-century accounts by scholars in religion such as Mays and Nicholson (1933) and Drake and Cayton (1970 [1945]) and such respected musicians as the composer John Work (1983 [1949]) of Fisk University renown, we learn of the transference of these musical concepts into the modern black religious context, resulting in the development of gospel music.

Folk Spirituals

Folk spiritual
African American song expressing religious feelings prominent from the late eighteenth century through the Civil War era

The earliest form of black religious music to develop in the United States was what is commonly referred to as the *folk spiritual*. The designation "folk" is necessary to distinguish this late eighteenth century creation from that of the arranged spiritual or concert version that emerged following the Civil War. The folk spiritual was an outgrowth of slavery; it was a uniquely African response to an institution which waged a systematic, though unsuccessful, onslaught onto the cultural legacy of black people in America.

When introduced to Christianity, African slaves reinterpreted their religious instruction through an African cultural lens. From a socio-cultural perspective, the development of the spiritual can actually be considered as an overt act of resistance to the subjugation imposed by Europeans. Consequently, the Negro folk spiritual symbolized Black cultural identity and Black religious expression as it evolved on North American soil (Chase 1987:214; Raboteau 1978; Waterman 1963).

The spiritual emerged in both the North and South as a genre distinctively different from music that characterized European

American musical practice of the period. The critical factor that allowed blacks to articulate and advance a unique musical identity was that of autonomy. In the South, the "invisible church" was the spawning ground. Whether in the ravine, gully, field, or living quarters, African American slaves fiercely guarded their privacy, not merely out of fear of reprisal, but out of their collective desire to express themselves in a way that was uniquely meaningful to them. The character of worship among blacks during slavery was closely related to that of contemporary black worship. There was prayer, communal singing, testifying, and sometimes, but not always, preaching. Prayer was described as extemporaneous, typically moving from speech to song; congregational participation, in the form of verbal affirmations, was not only accepted, but expected, and highly valued. Singing involved everyone present and was accompanied with handclapping, body movement, and if the spirit was particularly high, shouting and religious dance, both peak forms of expressive behavior.

The character of the worship influenced the performance of the songs sung during the worship. In these early spirituals, the African-derived call-response pattern serves in one instance as an agent for stability, with the constant repetition of the chorus, which encourages everyone to participate. But at the same time, this call-response structure serves as an agent for musical change, with constant variation being provided through the solo. Throughout its history, African American music has nurtured this dynamic tension between unity and diversity, individuality and collectivity.

The sequential, staggered entrances highlight the polyrhythmic element of the folk spiritual. Bans on the use of loud musical instruments, especially drums, which could be used as signaling devices did not succeed in eliminating the percussive dimension so highly valued in African music. To quote Bernice Johnson Reagon, "You can take away the drums, but you can't take away the drumming." The hands, feet, or even a stick could be used to keep the spirit of the drum alive.

The Ring Shout

The specific type of folk spiritual variously known as a shout, ring shout or "running spirchil" (Allen, Ware, and Garrison 1867:xv) takes it name from the circle dance that is incorporated into its performance. As one might imagine, the practice of dancing while singing religious songs was not introduced to the slave converts by white missionaries. Because dance had been such an integral part of cultural expression among blacks in their West and Central African homeland, missionaries failed abysmally in their efforts to eradicate this practice in the United States. Instead specific criteria established the ring shout as sacred; when dancing, participants did *not* cross their feet.

Ring shout
A religious song sung while performing a circle dance

Performance Practices

The establishment of the independent African Methodist Episcopal congregation under the leadership of Richard Allen set the stage for the autonomy that fostered the growth of the spiritual in the North. After separating from the white Methodist parent church in Philadelphia in 1787, Allen made a conscious choice to reject its domination and at the same time embrace its doctrines. Allen also rejected the standard Methodist hymnal, choosing instead to compile his own, which included songs he felt had greater appeal for black people. In Allen's hymnal, texts were simplified, and refrain lines and choruses were routinely added. Allen's goal was to generate congregational participation and assure freedom of worship for his members (Maultsby 1975:413; Southern 1983:75).

Nonblack observers of Allen's worship were frequently struck by the high level of congregational involvement in spirited singing. Nonetheless, many commentators did not hesitate to register their displeasure at the AME song style. Both the song texts, and the aesthetic principles that affirmed musical and textual repetition—handclapping, footstomps, and body movement—met with great disapproval from the white Methodist establishment. It was especially disconcerting that blacks were known to use secular melodies in composing sacred songs.

The practices that governed performance by these renegade Methodists were virtually identical to those of the basic folk spiritual or ring shout, illustrating the ability of African Americans to transform genres that they themselves did not create into musical expressions with cultural relevance. People in the local churches viewed the shout as the essence of religion; rings were considered necessary for conversion. Not surprisingly, the white Methodist establishment was appalled by this practice. Unquestionably a perceptual rift between the folk and the educated elite was emerging.

The Arranged Spiritual

The next form of religious music expression to develop among blacks on U.S. soil was the *arranged spiritual*. Prior to the efforts of the Fisk Jubilee Singers in the early 1870s, the Negro spiritual was known and respected almost exclusively by blacks (Southern 1971:249; Dett 1918:173). With the formation of this group, however, the spiritual assumed a character and purpose that differed radically from its folk antecedent. The original group of eleven men and women, mainly ex-slaves, was established under the leadership of George White, the white university treasurer who viewed musical concerts as a viable way of raising much-needed funds for the fledgling institution. According to black composer and Fisk professor John Work:

Mr. White decided on a style of singing the spiritual which eliminated every element that detracted from the pure emotion of the song [. . . .] Finish, precision and sincerity were demanded by this leader. While the program featured Spirituals, variety was given it by the use of numbers of classical standard. Mr. White strove for an art presentation. (Work 1940:15)

Listen to the recording of "Were You There" (Musical Example 7.2), performed by the Fisk Jubilee Singers, directed by John Work, and recorded in 1955. Established in 1871, the Fisk Jubilee Singers were largely responsible for the popularization of the Negro Spiritual in its arranged form. The arrangements of John Work continue to be performed today in concert halls throughout the United States and Europe.

The folk spiritual created as an expression of African American culture and religion was now transferred to the concert stage. This change in function was accompanied by a change in performance practices. The handclapping, footstomping, and individual latitude in interpreting the melodic line that characterized the folk spiritual were replaced by predicability, controlled reserve, and the absence of overt demonstrative behavior. The aesthetic values that characterized George White's own musical culture were now being superimposed onto the Negro spiritual.

> **Arranged spiritual**
> A concert version of the traditional folk spiritual, usually featuring Western-style harmonies and a reserved and polished delivery

University Singers

Early recordings of the Fisk University quartet, one of the first of many university choirs to tour the United States, document the continuing presence of a cappella, syllabic singing and the same use of call-response within the larger verse-chorus form as had characterized the folk spiritual. The melodies of the folk spiritual serve as the point of departure for the arrangements grounded in Western European compositional technique. While the dialect of the earlier spiritual form remains constant, the vocal quality of the singers is generally more reflective of European ideals of timbre. Heterophony is replaced with clearly defined harmony, and the element of dance is eliminated altogether. Whereas folk spirituals could be repeated for indefinite periods of time, performance of the arranged spiritual is bound by the dictates of the printed score.

The Fisk campaign was an overwhelming success, generating the formation of similar groups at other Black colleges. This arranged spiritual tradition has come to symbolize the best in the black college choir tradition, with generations of black composers who established careers developing folk melodies for performance on the concert stage: John Wesley Work, William Dawson, R. Nathaniel Dett, and Undine Smith Moore, to name only a few.

Transitional Gospel Music

By the time gospel music started its slow but steady climb to acceptance and widespread popularity in the 1930s, the folk spiritual had been in existence for well over 100 years. The advent of gospel music was precipitated by the Great Migration of blacks from rural to urban contexts during the years surrounding World Wars I and II (Ricks 1960:10-13; Williams-Jones 1970:205). The one-room folk church of the rural South became the store-front church of the urban North—a key setting for the emergence of gospel music.

During the period from 1900 to 1930, three forms of what I refer to as transitional gospel music emerged:

1. Tindley style, named for the grandfather of gospel music, Charles Albert Tindley (1851-1933)
2. Rural gospel, derived from rural blues
3. Holiness-Pentecostal music, characterized by its broad array of musical instruments and demonstrative delivery closely akin to the Negro spiritual that developed during slavery

Tindley Style

Charles Albert Tindley (1851-1933) was the charismatic minister of Tindley Temple Methodist Church in Philadephia. Some of the services at Tindley Temple were known to continue all night long, filled with spirited congregational singing, extemporaneous prayer, and songs that Tindley himself wrote to complement his sermons. On the other hand, as a devout Methodist, Tindley made sure that the repertoire of the church included European anthems that readily generated congregational response, even shouting.

The first of Tindley's gospel hymns was published in 1901. Among his total output of forty-six songs (Boyer 1992:58, 63) are his enduring compositions "We Will Understand It Better By and By," "Stand By Me," and "The Storm Is Passing Over." Considered representative of the gospel hymn, Tindley's compositions are distinct from the Negro spiritual by the use of instrumental accompaniment. But Tindley further contributes to the evolution of a unique gospel style, as Horace Boyer describes, "allowing space in his melodic line for the interpolation of the so-called blue thirds and sevenths, [. . .] and for the inevitable improvisation of text, melody harmony and rhythm, so characteristic of Black American folk and popular music" (1995:57). Tindley's compositions maintain a link to the spiritual tradition by successfully incorporating call–response into the larger verse-chorus external structure.

Rural Gospel

A second form of transitional gospel music emerged as a counter-part of the rural blues. Often sung by solo blues singers with guitar or harmonica accompaniment, this subgenre is characterized by the minimal chord changes and variable rhythmic structures which typify rural blues around the turn of the century. Performers who represent this style include Blind Willie Johnson and Blind Mamie Forehand, among others.

Holiness-Pentecostal Style

It was in the context of the newly formed Pentecostal denomina-tion that the third form of transitional gospel music evolved. In this setting, the "style and feeling" of the folk spiritual is most evi-dent. Those congregations that evolved from the 1906-1908 Azuza Street Revival in Los Angeles, under the leadership of William J. Seymour, embraced a worship style that was uninhibited and highly demonstrative. Under the anointing of the Holy Spirit con-gregants sang and danced with exuberance to the accompaniment of instruments shunned by the established denominations: trom-bones, trumpets, mandolins, even jugs.

Arizona Dranes is one of the most celebrated pioneers of the Holiness-Pentecostal style.

Although her recording career spanned only two years (1926-1928), her highly rhythmic, percussive ragtime piano style, and her powerful, shouted vocal leads represent the epitome of the high-energy delivery that characterizes Pentecostal worship even today. Dranes also recorded with evangelist F. W. McGee, another pioneer whose work is highly representative of this period and style.

Traditional Gospel Music

During the 1930s, traditional gospel music emerged, spawned by the meshing of the three strands of transitional gospel. The man who figured most prominently in this merger was Thomas A. Dorsey (1899-1993), now referred to as the Father of Gospel Music. Dorsey and two other important gospel music pioneers, Mahalia Jackson (1912-1972) and Roberta Martin (1907-1969), arrived in Chicago as a part of the great migrations of Southern blacks to Northern industrial centers. In the case of Dorsey and Jackson, these pioneering spirits brought with them a musical culture rooted in the sacred and secular traditions of the African American South; the northern context provided the impetus for the growth of something new.

Born in Villa Rica, Georgia (near Atlanta), the son of a traveling Baptist preacher, Dorsey grew up playing organ in church. As a boy, however, he also worked selling soda pop at a vaudeville theater in

Atlanta, where he was regularly exposed to such blues performers as Ma Rainey and Bessie Smith. Before devoting his career to gospel music, Dorsey became a prolific composer of both blues and jazz, and acknowledged that his gospel style was influenced by his background in secular music.

Like Dorsey, Mahalia Jackson (see Figure 7.4) embraced both sacred and secular musics from childhood. A native of New Orleans, Jackson was raised Baptist, finding her place in the church choir at an early age. Her religious exposure also included the Pentecostal church, whose music she loved, located next door to her home. Although her aunt, who raised her, did not expose her to "worldly" music, Jackson seized the opportunity to listen to her older cousin's blues collection whenever her aunt was not at home. Her favorite performer was Bessie Smith, whose vocal quality she greatly admired and admittedly sought to imitate.

As did the folk spiritual, gospel music in its formative years faced staunch opposition and criticism. When Thomas Dorsey began to promote his compositions, he faced serious rejection, in part because the music was viewed as having unacceptable links to secu-

Figure 7.4
Mahalia Jackson performing at the May 17, 1957, Prayer Pilgrimage for Freedom in Washington, D.C. From the Collections of the Library of Congress.

lar music. Dorsey recounts how initially most black preachers and congregations of established Baptist and Methodist churches viewed the music with derision: "Gospel music was new and most people didn't understand. Some of the preachers used to call gospel music 'sin' music. They related it to what they called worldly things—like jazz and blues and show business. Gospel music was different from approved hymns and spirituals. It had a beat" (quoted in Duckett 1974:5).

Joining forces with Mahalia Jackson, Dorsey initiated an "audience development" strategy that bypassed the black religious and musical establishment altogether by taking the music "to the streets" (Goreau 1975:56). In 1932, Dorsey entered into an alliance with other gospel pioneering spirits—Sallie Martin, Theodore Frye, and Magnolia Lewis Butts—in Chicago to form what was to become known as the National Convention of Gospel Choirs and Choruses. With the express purpose of promoting the performance and understanding of gospel music, this organization has grown from its initial nucleus of some 200 members to an international membership of more than 3,000. The Dorsey model has spawned the growth of over a dozen comparable organizations, the largest of which is the James Cleveland Gospel Music Workshop of America, founded in 1969, that boasts annual attendance of more than 20,000.

The music that Thomas Dorsey, Mahalia Jackson, and other gospel pioneers promoted so fervently has now risen to a position of prominence in the worship of African Americans of virtually every denomination across this nation. It is sung by solo and ensemble, choir and quartet, men and women, young and old, black and white. In contrast to the simple accompaniment of piano and organ that characterizes the early years of gospel, there are now no limits to the types of instruments used to complement the voice —from saxophone to synthesizer to symphony.

The gospel quartet has evolved to such an extent that it now garners significant scholarly attention. Research indicates that the evolution of the gospel quartet closely parallels that of gospel music in general. The four-member male quartet first emerged under the sponsorship of such universities as Fisk and Hampton. Their repertoire consisted largely of Negro spirituals sung without instrumental accompaniment. Ethnomusicologist Joyce Marie Jackson indicates that the transition from spirituals to gospel began during the 1930s, when the quartet was expanded to five voices, which allowed the utilization of more than one lead singer while maintaining a full four-part harmonic background. Instrumental accompaniment became a part of the quartet performance style beginning in the 1940s with the guitar (Jackson 1988:125-127). Prominent gospel quartets who pioneered in the development and proliferation of this form include The Golden Gate Quartette, the Soul Stirrers, the Dixie Hummingbirds, the Five Blind Boys of Mississippi, the Swan Silvertones, the Fairfield Four, and the Highway QCs, among others.

Contemporary Gospel

The release of the recording "O Happy Day" by the Edwin Hawkins singers in 1969 ushered in the contemporary gospel era. Initially considered innovative in large part because of its use of the Fender bass, bongos, and horns as accompaniment (which closely paralleled popular musics of the period), and also because of its dynamic rhythms and chord changes, this recording represented the beginning of the development of the crossover market for gospel music. Sales of "O Happy Day" exceeded one million copies, well above the 50,000 to 70,000 units most typical for gospel recording artists, even in the 1990s.

With the advent of the contemporary gospel music era, gospel moved beyond the protective confines of the black church to become a music that knew neither denominational, racial, cultural, nor musical boundaries. Although striking in its distinctiveness when it was first released, "O Happy Day" now falls into the category of traditional gospel music as the musical boundaries of gospel continue to expand. Following the lead of Edwin Hawkins, other artists began to emerge who included contemporary gospel music as a significant part of their repertoire—The Clark Sisters, The Winans, Rance Allen, Andrae Crouch, and the New York Community Choir, among others.

Unlike traditional gospel music, which is embraced by soloist, small ensemble, and mass choir, contemporary gospel music is typically performed by small ensembles. The predictability of traditional gospel music, with its easily memorized melodic lines and parallel motion in the vocal parts, is replaced with more complex forms and harmonies. Both the instrumental accompaniment and the vocal arrangements of contemporary gospel music are virtually indistinguishable from secular musics of the day. For example, the work of contemporary gospel music group Take 6 (Figure 7.5) is rooted primarily in jazz, whereas recordings of Kirk Franklin exemplify the sound of rap, hip-hop, and funk. The music of multi-platinum-selling recording artist Kirk Franklin has crossed over to rhythm and blues charts as well as the Contemporary Christian chart, which reflects a breakthrough into the white Christian market.

The breadth and depth of black religious musical expression in the United States represent the cultural legacy and therefore the cultural *identity* of African-derived people in this nation. Whereas the distinctiveness of African American religious music genres reflects collective adaptation to an ever-changing sociocultural and

Figure 7.5
Contemporary Gospel
Music group, Take 6,
1999. Photo by
Norman Seefe.

political milieu, the continuities between the spiritual and gospel music are equally indicative of the existence of a self-defining core of cultural values among African Americans that have persisted over time.

Gospel music was not created out of the African American's *inability* to satisfactorily reproduce the repertoire characteristic of Euro Americans. On the contrary, African American religious music, from its beginning, must be viewed as both a conscious and willful expression of individual and collective agency, the desire of African Americans to articulate, embrace, and celebrate those beliefs, attitudes, and values that affirm and distinguish them as a people in the United States.

Mellonee V. Burnim

THE BLUES

During the first decade of the twentieth century, the term *blues* began to be applied to a new type of song emerging from black communities in the southern United States. These songs were different both in their formal and musical characteristics and in the topics and attitudes they expressed in their lyrics. The fact that blues songs seem to turn up everywhere in the Deep South more or less simultaneously—in rural areas, small towns, and cities such as New Orleans and Memphis—suggests that the form had been developing for a few years and probably allows us to place its origins in the 1890s.

Throughout their history blues songs have mainly been sung solo, although duet and quartet performances and background vocalizing are not unknown. The singers, especially males, usually play an instrument; in folk blues this has generally been a guitar, piano, or harmonica. Even when other instruments are added, as is the case in most types of popularized blues forms, great emphasis is placed on individual expression and improvisation. Sometimes entire performances of blues—lyrics, melodies, and instrumental work—are improvised, and although some performers are highly creative in this respect, many are also aided by a body of shared and familiar lyric and musical ideas and formulas that they recombine in constantly changing ways.

Early Blues History

Like most forms of black American music created in the nineteenth and twentieth centuries, blues combines elements from both the European and African musical traditions. The European elements occur especially in the areas of form, harmony, and instrumentation. The use of a recurring *multiphrase strophic form* and basic *I-IV-V harmonies* in the instrumental accompaniment are clearly attributable to Western influence.

The major solo and ensemble instruments are all commercially manufactured items well known in Western music, although some secondary instruments used occasionally in blues, such as washboards, jugs, kazoos, and homemade one-stringed zithers, are reinterpretations of originally African instruments. The uses to which the Western instruments are put in the blues, however, would often not be described by European-trained musicians as "proper" or "legitimate," and most of the modifications in playing technique and resultant sound are attributable to the influence of the African musical tradition. Western elements of form and harmony are also frequently altered in ways that can best be explained by reference to African patterns. Beyond this, the African elements in the blues are found chiefly in the area of style, particularly in the music's rhythmic, tonal, and timbral flexibility.

If the Old World sources of the blues are rather far in its historical background, there were other, more recognizable, musical genres in existence at the end of the nineteenth century that can be identified as significant factors in the synthesis that resulted in the creation of the blues. The basic melodic resources of the blues seem to be largely derived from the field holler, a type of solo unaccompanied work song found in the rural South, characterized by great melodic, timbral, and rhythmic freedom and forceful delivery. To this, one could add as influences the more individualized and improvisatory forms of religious vocal expression, such as moaning, chanted prayer, and preaching. Most blues singers throughout the twentieth century were exposed to both farmwork and the church and had plenty of opportunity to listen to and participate in vocal genres characteristic of these contexts.

The harmonic and structural form of blues comes mainly from the folk ballad (see Chapter 6). In the later decades of the nineteenth century, black American singers had adapted this originally European narrative folk song genre. By the 1890s they had begun to create original ballads about characters and subjects of interest within the black community, often about individuals who stood outside the bounds of the law and organized society (for example, "Stagolee," "Frankie and Albert," "Railroad Bill") or whose actions were in some way "bad" and bold (for example, "Casey Jones"). Instrumental accompaniment and the three-line form, which were black American innovations and had not been characteristic of the Euro American ballad tradition, were adapted to the melodic material of the field holler and solo religious expression in the forming of the blues style. The outlaw content of many of the ballads undoubtedly contributed as well to the personal stance adopted by many blues singers. It is one of the great strengths and accomplishments of the blues that it managed to synthesize elements of songs associated with work and religion on the one hand and a carefree, worldly existence on the other.

The geographical heartland of the blues is the plantation country of the Deep South, stretching from the interior of Georgia to eastern Texas; most blues singers were born and raised in this region. Within this large geographical area, certain regions, such as the Mississippi Delta and the river bottomlands of southeastern Texas, proved especially important as places of innovation. The music underwent a less intense, though still significant, development in Virginia and the Carolinas. Over the course of the twentieth century, artists from the "blues heartland" migrated to cities, especially in the Midwest and California, bringing their rural styles with them and contributing to new urban musical syntheses. Over the years, blues has exhibited musical and lyrical traces of its southern rural origins as well as evidence of the desire of many performers and audience members to escape those origins.

Although blues performance sometimes occurs as a solitary activity or in intimate settings such as courtship, it has always been most often found where an audience is present. It exists as music for both listening and dancing, the two often occurring in the same context. In the rural South the most common setting was the house party or outdoor picnic. Another common institution, the juke house or *juke joint*, was a structure, often a residence, temporarily or permanently set up for music, dancing, drinking, eating, and other activities. In the towns blues musicians would gather and perform at cafés and saloons, on sidewalks and street corners, in parks, in railroad and

Juke joint
A rural bar where music, dancing, drinking, eating, and other activities occurred

bus stations, and inside and in front of places of business. In the cities blues were sung in vaudeville theaters, saloons, cabarets, and at house parties, as well as in parks and on streets. Traveling tent and *medicine shows* often hired blues performers, providing opportunities for local and sometimes extended travel. Most of these settings persisted in black American communities until the end of the 1950s, but since then the main locations have been clubs and auditoriums. Concerts and festivals, both within and outside the black community, have provided additional settings for blues music in recent years.

For the first two decades of the twentieth century, blues was generally performed alongside other types of folk and popular music. Most blues performers born in the nineteenth century and the first few years of the twentieth had eclectic repertoires that might also include ragtime pieces, older social dance songs, ballads, versions of popular songs, and even spirituals. Those born after about 1905 increasingly came to identify themselves as blues singers and often concentrated on this genre exclusively. From the beginning, blues were performed as a means of making money. Some of the rural musicians were farmers and sharecroppers, and some urban musicians held weekday jobs, performing blues only on weekends. Often they could make as much in music on a weekend as a person could working all week at another job. Some used this weekend work to enable themselves and their families to live better. Others saw it as a way to make money for good times, and yet others as a way to avoid more onerous types of work. The latter often became itinerant professional performers, working circuits of house parties, juke joints, clubs, or theaters. Blind and other handicapped performers also joined their ranks, often becoming some of the outstanding virtuosos and creative figures in the blues. Because blues performers were often involved in an underworld of gamblers, bootleggers, pimps, and prostitutes, blues music and singers gained an unsavory reputation for much of the music's history. However, this reputation has steadily improved since the 1960s, as many of the older contexts for the music have faded out of existence.

CHARACTERISTICS OF THE BLUES

Although many elements of blues can be traced to older musical forms, this genre was a distinct synthesis that has had an enormous impact on American and world music. Several characteristics of the blues were shocking and challenging to the norms of Western music and American popular music. They entered the larger musical world for the first time through the blues and have come to be associated with blues ever since, although some are now commonplace throughout popular music.

Four characteristics in particular have this special association with the blues:

Medicine show
A traveling show employing entertainers, including musicians and dancers, in order to attract a crowd to sell a "patent" medicine (a cure-all often of dubious usefulness)

1. Frank lyrics expressing a personal worldview: Blues lyrics are almost exclusively concerned with the self. They are not only sung in the first person, but when directed toward another person or about someone else, they deal with the interaction between the other person and the singer.
2. An emphasis on deep emotions and feelings, rather than telling a story: Rather than telling stories in a chronological fashion, blues songs express feelings and emotions or describe actions based on them. These may be the real feelings and activities of the singer or those of a persona created by the singer, an exaggerated or dramatized self.
3. "Realistic," nonsentimental, and serious lyrics: Blues lyrics reflect the real-life experiences of their creators, without glossing over or trivializing them. They may (and often do) contain humor, but this is usually as an expression of irony, cleverness, double or multiple meaning, or social commentary and criticism, not as an illustration of buffoonery or stupidity.
4. Subject matter drawn from "real life," including sex, work, and drugs, that were rarely expressed in popular song before: Blues songs deal with a full range of human feelings and describe the ups and downs of daily life. Many of these topics rarely had been discussed before in American popular song, except in a trivial, sentimental, idealized, or moralistic way.

Musical Example 7.3, "In the Pines" (Black Girl, Where Did You Sleep Last Night?), is performed here by Huddie Ledbetter (Leadbelly 1888–1949), a prolific composer and performer of early blues and ballads, whose music has influenced generations of blues performers. Notice the frank discussion of "real-life" subjects in the text and the use of the "blue" note (a slight bending or flattening of the third note of the scale) in both the vocal part and guitar accompaniment.

The style's realism and seriousness, combined with its concentration on the self and a willingness to delve into sadness, deep feelings, emotions, and confessions, are probably responsible for the music being called "the blues." Although just as many of the songs express optimism, confidence, success, and happiness, it is this melancholy or depressed side of the range of emotions that has given the genre its familiar name.

The blues song's instrumental accompaniment plays a necessary role in the construction and performance of the song itself, rather than serving simply as a more or less optional harmonic and rhythmic background to the vocal part. The instrumental part, especially that of the piano-guitar duo, is, in fact, a second voice (sometimes several voices), punctuating and responding to the vocal lines. It is therefore an integral part of the piece itself. The role of instruments as voices is well known in most forms of African music and their New World derivatives, but seldom has the instrument had such a close conversational dialogue with the singing voice as it has in the blues. This sort of dialogue was certainly not common in nineteenth-century American popular song, but through its use in the blues and the influence of blues on other popular genres it has become commonplace.

As the term itself suggests, blues introduced the concept of the *blue note* into American music. This term essentially means a note, sounded or suggested, that falls between two adjacent notes in the standard Western division of the octave into twelve equal intervals. Blue notes are especially common at the third and seventh degrees of the scale, but they can occur at other points as well, including even such a normally stable place as the fifth. A blue note might be expressed as a *slur*, usually upward from the flat toward the natural, or as a wavering between flat and natural or two other points within the interval. It might also occur as the simultaneous sounding of the flat and natural pitches or simply their use at different times in a piece, suggesting tonal ambivalence or compromise. Finally, it might simply be expressed by the sounding of a flat where a natural would be expected.

Blue notes are easy enough to achieve with the voice, but they can also be played on many instruments by the use of special techniques to "bend" notes, for example, pushing the strings on the neck of the guitar, special tonguing and blowing methods for the harmonica, woodwinds, and horns, glissandos on the slide trombone, and the slide or "bottleneck" technique on the guitar. On fixed-pitched instruments such as the piano, blue notes can only be suggested by rapid alternation of adjacent notes, a flat grace note before a natural, or the simultaneous sounding of flat and natural in a chord or in the separate melodic lines played by the two hands.

The majority of blues utilize the twelve-bar, AAB form or some variant or approximation of it. At its most basic, the stanza consists of a line of verse (A), the same line repeated, and a third line (B) that rhymes with the first two (Figure 7.6). Usually the B line explains, amplifies, comments on, or contrasts with the A line, rather than following from it chronologically. Each line occupies only slightly more than the first half of a four-measure section, the other portion consisting of an instrumental response to the vocal, although the instrumental part is also heard during the singing and interacts with it.

This simple form can be altered in a number of ways. For example, a rhymed couplet can occupy the entire first four bars, which would normally be filled by the A line and its instrumental response. The last eight bars remain the same, occupied by two lines and their

Blue note
A note, sounded or suggested, that falls between two adjacent notes in the standard Western division of the octave into twelve equal intervals

Slur
A vocal glide from one pitch to another
Bent notes
A variety of techniques used by instrumentalists to approximate the vocal slurs and glides commonly heard in the blues
Bottleneck technique
Using a metal slide or neck of a bottle to note the strings on a guitar
Blues scale
A scale that incorporates "blue notes"

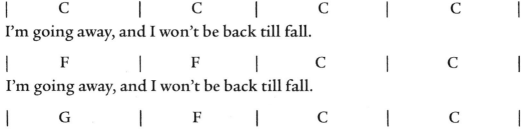

| | C | | C | | C | | C | |

I'm going away, and I won't be back till fall.

| | F | | F | | C | | C | |

I'm going away, and I won't be back till fall.

| | G | | F | | C | | C | |

If my mind don't change, I won't be back at all.

Figure 7.6
A typical twelve-bar blues stanza in the key of C major with measure divisions and implied harmonies.

instrumental responses, but these now become a refrain repeated in every stanza.

The harmonic scheme can also be varied through chord substitutions, the use of *passing harmonies* (all serving to make the piece more harmonically complex), or through simplification to two chords or only one (that is, a strictly modal piece without any suggestion of chord changes). The number of bars can also be shortened or lengthened from the standard twelve. There are, in addition, eight-bar (two-line) and sixteen-bar (four-line) blues with their own typical harmonic patterns as well as variations, and there are some blues that are conceived in a more or less free-form manner without apparent reference to one of these standard patterns. The repetition of the A line, textually and often melodically, is a device typically found in much African music, whereas the use of a repeated multi-phrase form with harmonic changes is more typically European.

Another device that often occurs in the blues and that links it to the African tradition is the use of repeated short melodic-rhythmic phrases or *riffs*. A riff can be used both to extend the instrumental response to vocal lines and as a background behind the vocal lines, serving as an identifying marker for an entire piece. Usually, several different or variant riffs are used in a single blues where this concept occurs. The twelve-bar AAB form and the use of riffs entered the mainstream of American popular music through the blues and have now become so commonplace that they are seldom noticed.

In 1920 vaudeville singer Mamie Smith became the first black vocalist to record blues commercially, having hits with "That Thing Called Love" and "Crazy Blues," both of them compositions of fellow vaudevillian Perry Bradford (Figure 7.7). Her success resulted in the recording of many other vaudeville blues stars during the 1920s, most of them women, accompanied by a small jazz combo. At first the songs were generally the compositions of professional songwriters in the multistrain format of ragtime music, but with blue notes and the occasional twelve-bar AAB strain. Representative singers in this style, besides Mamie Smith, were Lucille Hegamin, Alberta Hunter, and Ethel Waters. By 1923, however, a new wave of singers

Passing harmony or chord
A chord outside of the main harmonic structure of a song, briefly sounded, to link two of the standard chords

Riff
A repeated short melodic-rhythmic phrase

Figure 7.7
Publicity photo of
Mamie Smith, c. 1920,
showing her in a glam-
orous pose. Courtesy
David A. Jasen.

entered the studios, singing songs more often made up of variants of
a single AAB strain and accompanied typically by a pianist, sometimes with one or two added jazz instruments. By this time more of
the songs were composed by the singers themselves. Some of the
more prolific and successful artists in this style were Bessie Smith,
Ma Rainey, and Ida Cox.

Blues musicians also formed larger groups made up of various
combinations of string, wind, and percussion instruments known as
jug bands, skiffle bands, juke bands, washboard bands, string bands,
and hokum bands. Some of the better known recording groups of
this sort were the Memphis Jug Band, Cannon's Jug Stompers,
Whistler's Jug Band, the Mississippi Sheiks, and the Hokum Boys.
All of these duos and small groups were especially prominent in
urban centers of both the South and North, allowing rural migrants
to find common ground in their solo performance styles, explore

new musical directions, and compete with more established urban musicians.

The Great Depression effectively killed the institution of vaudeville and the blues style that was associated with it. As the recording industry began to recover in the early 1930s, Chicago became the primary center of blues recording activity, and the studios concentrated on stables of reliable stars, who could sing, play their own accompaniment, help one another on records, and compose original songs to supply the increasing number of jukeboxes. This was a decade of consolidation and homogenization in the blues. The primary instruments of folk blues were brought into small ensembles (or made to suggest their sounds), as exemplified by the work of guitarists Big Bill Broonzy, pianist Roosevelt Sykes, and harmonica player John Lee "Sonny Boy" Williamson.

Also coming to prominence in the late 1930s and 1940s was a piano blues style known as *boogie-woogie*. Essentially, it is a type of rhythmic barrelhouse piano that features repeated bass figures, or riffs, often transposed to fit the tune's harmonic structure, over which the right hand plays lines that are to some degree improvised and often in a counterrhythm to the bass. Boogie-woogie is attested from the 1910s and was recorded sporadically in the 1920s and more frequently from 1929 following the success of "Pine Top" Smith's "Pine Top's Boogie Woogie." It entered spectacularly into the world of popular music through presentations at Carnegie Hall by Meade Lux Lewis, Albert Ammons, and Pete Johnson in 1938 and 1939. These artists, along with Jimmie Yancey, Camille Howard, and many others, popularized this style through the 1940s. It was often adapted by guitarists as well as swing bands and had a great influence on jazz, country and western, gospel, and the emerging rock and roll.

> **Boogie-woogie**
> A type of rhythmic piano music that features repeated bass figures (or riffs) over which a syncopated melody is performed

The electric guitar was an important factor in new blues sounds that came to prominence in the late 1940s and 1950s. The guitar's role in small combos was enhanced by the louder volume and new timbres of the electric instrument, played alongside the piano and the harmonica, itself now also played through a microphone and amplifier. Such recently arrived southern musicians as Muddy Waters (McKinley Morganfield), Howlin' Wolf, Little Walter, Jimmy Reed, and Elmore James pioneered in these small electric blues combos in Chicago and other cities during this period. At the same time, a new jazz-influenced, hornlike lead style of playing, featuring extensive string bending, was being developed in the cities of the West Coast and South by guitarists Aaron "T-Bone" Walker, Clarence "Gatemouth" Brown, B. B. King, and others, working usually with larger bands containing horn sections. The electric guitar also gave new life to the tradition of solo-guitar-accompanied folk blues, as exemplified in the music of artists Sam "Lightnin'" Hopkins and John Lee Hooker.

In addition to having its own history and stylistic development, blues has played an important role in most other major popular musical genres in the United States. Its intrusion into ragtime in the first two decades of the twentieth century has already been mentioned. The tonal flexibility and improvisational performance style of blues probably hastened the decline of ragtime itself. Blues tunes form a major part of the repertoire of early jazz, and one can hardly imagine jazz music without blue notes, improvisation, and many other qualities doubtless introduced mainly through the blues. The blues has continued to anchor a number of new jazz styles, most notably bebop. Country music had absorbed the blues form by the 1920s, its first major manifestation being the blue yodel as popularized by Jimmie Rodgers.

Blues continued to be a major ingredient in the western swing and honky-tonk styles of the 1930s through the early 1950s and has made a comeback in contemporary country rock styles. Many early rock and roll performers of the 1950s, such as Elvis Presley, Carl Perkins, and Jerry Lee Lewis, had a background in country music, which they fused with newly acquired skills in the blues inspired by contemporary black artists. Many black performers of this time, such as Little Richard, Chuck Berry, Fats Domino, and Bo Diddley, in fact, made important contributions to rock and roll, performing music that was largely blues-based. Many rock styles of the 1960s, such as surf music, British rock, and psychedelic rock, made considerable use of blues repertoire and style, and blues experienced a resurgence within rock in the 1990s. Blues also influenced gospel music through the increased use of blue notes and instrumentation, particularly the guitar. One of the leaders in introducing blues elements to gospel music was Thomas A. Dorsey in the 1930s, himself an ex-blues singer, pianist, and songwriter. Rap artists also have continued to sample blues riffs from earlier recordings. Finally, a number of important twentieth-century composers in the classical tradition, such as George Gershwin and William Grant Still, were greatly influenced by blues. If one also considers the profound influence of blues on the popular musics of Europe, Asia, Latin America, and Africa, blues would have to be a strong candidate for being the most influential music of the twentieth century.

David Evans

Snapshot 7.2: Musical Theater

African Heritage

The essence of African theatricality survived most memorably in the New World in religious rituals. These expressions of shared beliefs, celebrated communally and constructed collectively, placed few boundaries between actors and audiences. The dances, songs, and traditional stories that were recreated on the North American continent and adjacent islands preserved the rich traditions of West Africa in many guises. Whether in search of solace or strength, out of a sense of rebellion, grief, or sheer creative energy, Africans in America have always acted out and sung their sorrows, myths, dreams, and hopes.

Descriptions of festivals such as Pinkster Day document the existence of an African theatrical practice in North America during the eighteenth century. The celebration of this holiday involved the election of a king or governor and featured elaborate costumes, processions, feasting, music, singing, and dance. John Kuner (sometimes called John Canoe or Jonkonnu) Christmas rituals in North Carolina and Jamaica also constitute important theatrical survivals, attested by many accounts from the mid-nineteenth century, which provide details about costumes, makeup (*blackface* and whiteface), musical instruments, parading, and occasionally song texts. "Moorish" dancing and costumes were also recorded in the early Colonial period in the American Southwest, and even modern-day Pueblo dances of New Mexico, called *matachines*, retain masks that suggest African provenance. Other documents, such as the play *High Life Below Stairs* (1759), presented parodies of slaves imitating their white masters' habits of holiday dress, body movement, manner, and attitude. The distinctive character of African American musical theater is evident in all of these precursors: grand gesture, elaborate costumes, spirited music, dance, and parody.

Blackface
Makeup used by white actors (in the early-to-mid-nineteenth century) and later African Americans as well to "darken" their features while portraying stereotypical African American characters

From the Revolution to the Civil War

After 1750, in the English-speaking theater on the Atlantic coast, African Americans were involved in formal, text-defined theatricals only to the degree permitted within a climate generally hostile to all secular forms of theater. It would long remain the dominant American middle-class belief that actors and their business were only barely respectable in the best of venues. Class, occupation, and racial prejudice fenced out all but the most sanitized stage vehicles from public view and record.

Unlike other major American cities, New York, Charleston, and New Orleans took a somewhat more tolerant view by greeting foreign immigrants who brought with them the latest music, dance, and theatrical fashions from Africa, Europe, the West Indies, and South America during the 1700s. Early-nineteenth-century accounts of social dances, pit bands, and community music making in New Orleans document the presence of black entertainers. Other cities evidently supported active coteries of black theatrical musicians from time to time. Eileen Southern (1994) reports the existence of "Negro tunes" or "Negro jigs," which may have been included in the general repertoire of musical theater songs in the early years of the republic.

During the early- to mid-nineteenth century, several shortlived African American theater companies were formed to present "serious" drama and entertainment. In the 1820s, the all-black African Grove theater company in lower Manhattan staged *Othello*, *Hamlet*, and *Richard III*, along with a variety of lighter entertainments and pieces by the African American playwright William Henry Brown. Although short-lived, the African Grove deserves recognition because it not only featured black actors in full productions but trained at least one individual who would later achieve professional status and renown, Ira Aldridge (1807-1867). This theater was active from 1821 until the hostility of the local population—including a nearby white theater—led it to close in 1829. New Orleans featured two early black theatrical companies. In 1838, the Marigny Theater opened for the "free colored population" of the city, so that African Americans of means could enjoy French light comedies and musical shows but be spared the indignity of sitting in segregated theaters. (Both slaves and whites were barred from the Marigny.) The theater remained open for only a few months but revealed potential patrons among the creole citizens of New Orleans for sophisticated theater. The Theatre de la Renaissance, whose orchestra included members of the Negro Philharmonic Society, was opened in 1840 and offered full plays, comic pieces, and variety shows in the years following. Neither of these venues led to the production of new or independently created works, but they represent the passion and persistence with which the black middle class sought cultural participation and validation.

Although African Americans had few opportunities to appear in the mainstream, white theaters, portrayals of African Americans as a part of American culture were common from the early nineteenth century. One of the first to specialize in portraying African Americans on stage was George Washington Dixon (1801-1861), an early blackface (and possibly black) entertainer as well as a political gadfly, athlete, and journalist, was an early star who specialized in portraying African Americans on stage, whose popularity preceded the advent of the minstrel show.

In the 1830s, Dixon sang both with and without blackface makeup and made famous such songs as "Coal-Black Rose" and "Zip Coon." He performed benefit shows for black entertainers, was an ardent advocate of the working class, and may even have held abolitionist sympathies. Further complicating our image of Dixon as a white entertainer who exploited African American music and dance to gain his popularity, Dixon may have been at least partially black himself; he was described in several sources as a mulatto, although allegedly accurate sketches of him in street dress do not suggest African features or complexion.

The Minstrel Show

Individual entertainers such as Dixon were eclipsed when the minstrel show, a more organized kind of four-man team theater event, emerged in the 1840s. Each member in blackface makeup played an African instrument (banjo, fiddle, bones, or tambourine) and performed various songs and dance skits. Although earlier actors working in blackface makeup had conveyed a wide spectrum of ideas, not all necessarily addressing race or the conditions of African Americans, the Virginia Minstrels, the Christie Minstrels, and other white minstrel teams from the 1840s claimed that they were faithfully mirroring the habits and customs of blacks. However, these white minstrel shows—popular in major theaters until the end of the century—say more about the dominant culture's wishes for, and impressions about, the groups they parodied, which included not only African Americans but women, Mormons, rubes, Native Americans, foreigners, and politicians as well.

> **Minstrel show**
> A revue featuring white performers in blackface makeup performing songs, dances, and skits supposedly accurately reflecting African American life

The importance of the minstrel phenomenon cannot be overestimated, because it was so widespread and long-lived. Many groups traveled abroad; large cities and small towns sustained them for decades. Minstrel performers generated huge amounts of music—quick, raucous, and spirited tunes—allied with nonsensical dialect poetry, clearly challenging more elite, genteel products (popular songs) in their general high spirits, explicit politics, and irreverent attitudes. Banjo tunes, with characteristic syncopations, which some whites learned from blacks and presented on the minstrel stage, appeared in printed tutorials beginning in the 1840s. The music of minstrelsy, in such songs as "Turkey in the Straw" (formerly "Zip Coon") and Stephen Foster's "Oh! Susanna" continues to be passed on in the oral tradition.

Musical Example 7.4, "Pea Patch Jig," is a banjo solo often performed in minstrel shows between 1843 and 1853. First published by Dan Emmett, in the mid-nineteenth century, it was probably borrowed from oral tradition. Listen to the syncopation in the banjo—a hint of the form, known as ragtime, to come.

Black Minstrel and Touring Companies of the Late Nineteenth Century

African Americans first entered American popular theater in large numbers via the burgeoning traveling minstrel troupes in the 1850s. They still employed burnt cork makeup, but they also sought to contradict the claim of "authenticity" purveyed by their white counterparts. What could be more authentic than a real black person performing as a black minstrel they asked, and by so doing made a space in which to demonstrate black talent and to reinforce images of independence, intelligence, and black family togetherness. In their skits, they campaigned in favor of Emancipation, the Union, and amicable relations between the races. After the Civil War, more sentimental motifs came to dominate the minstrel song repertoire, as did the message that a new generation of young people not raised in slavery would push aside any misplaced romanticism about "good old Southern life" on the part of their elders.

Prolific black composer and singer James Bland (1854–1911), who wrote "Carry Me Back to Old Virginny" and "Oh Dem Golden Slippers," is probably the most famous of the post–Civil War minstrel men, but many other unsung entertainers made substantial careers in this genre. Usually minstrels were not allowed to address political issues (such as peonage, lynching, or segregation) except by indirection. But many rejected the use of burnt cork and, by clever subversions of well-known jokes, created a stage message with multiple meanings. By 1900, a militant young entertainer such as Robert "Bob" Cole could write an antiminstrel song called "No Coons Allowed!" and get away with performing it in whiteface makeup for a white audience.

With the increasing oppression of the Reconstruction era leading to nearly universal legalized segregation by 1900, the avenues for black expression were narrow indeed. Nevertheless, actors on the stage were often granted a certain license and could pass off social criticism in the guise of a joke, a gesture, or even an unusually inflected word, observed only by those who had ears to hear and eyes to see.

In 1876, a pair of California sisters named Anna and Emma Hyers formed a touring concert company. Subsequently, with the help of supportive playwrights Joseph Bradford and Pauline Hopkins, they presented the first full-fledged musical plays in American history in which African Americans themselves comment on the plight of the slaves and the relief of Emancipation without the disguises of minstrel comedy. Both *Out of Bondage* (sometimes called *Out of the Wilderness*; 1876) and *Peculiar Sam: or, The Underground Railroad* (1879), with various additions, interpolations, and revivals, enjoyed a place in the Hyers touring repertory until the sisters' official retirement in 1893. The Hyers sisters' productions lacked blackface makeup and farcical situations; and their music represented a wide array of popular stage songs of the period, including religious music.

By the late 1870s, the spirituals arranged and sung by the Fisk University students had been widely copied by nonstudent professional groups, henceforth becoming the means by which secular theatricals could be justified and legitimated in the eyes of the white authorities. These spiritual parodies became an influential theatrical product. At the same time, innumerable solo and choral arrangements of the spirituals and jubilee songs constitute the major nineteenth-century American contribution to world musical culture, along with the parlor songs and minstrel show tunes of Stephen Foster.

Opera Theater

In the mid- to late nineteenth century, African Americans made efforts to enter the higher class of entertainments through the creations of full-fledged operas, which attracted an audience within the African American community. Although the commercial impact of these shows was negligible, the landmark works deserve recognition in order to illustrate the full range of black participation long before black performers would be allowed to sing in the New York Academy of Music or the Metropolitan Opera.

Virginia's Ball (1868) by John Thomas Douglass (1847-1886), an accomplished violinist, is generally deemed to be the first opera by an African American composer. Although the music is now lost, a first performance was noted as having taken place in New York in the year of its creation. Bostonian Louisa Melvin Delos Mars was the first African American woman to have an opera produced (in Providence, Rhode Island), *Leoni, the Gypsy Queen* (1889). She eventually composed no fewer than five full-length musical dramas between 1889 and 1896. The participation of educated middle-class women in amateur and church-sponsored operettas was also common by the end of the nineteenth century. Full-fledged African American opera divas such as Marie Selika (ca. 1849-1937) and Sissieretta Jones (1869-1933) had significant careers as touring soloists at the same time.

The Black Musical Comedy: 1897 to 1930

Beginning in the 1890s, African Americans entered into the commercial mainstream of secular nonblackface theatricals with a handful of plays that included "characteristic musical plantation scenes." Most notable among these plays was the perennial favorite *Uncle Tom's Cabin*, George Aiken and George A. Howard's musical play based on Harriet Beecher Stowe's 1852 novel. These productions benefited from expanding urban populations, well-organized road tours, and production syndicates seeking ever-larger audiences. Variety shows—such as Sam Jack's Creole Burlesque Company, John Isham's concert companies, and Sissieretta Jones's ensemble, called the Black Patti Troubadours—also were successful in major cities and on the road.

A sizable coterie of black talent gathered in New York in the 1890s, and out of this vibrant pre-Harlem community, black musical comedy was born. "Bob" Cole and his partner Billy Johnson, veterans of earlier touring companies, put together up-tempo songs, comic dialogue within a modest narrative plot, and several talented young performers to create *A Trip to Coontown* (1897). The simultaneous emergence of ragtime piano pieces and songs—in a style universally recognized as African American—with shows like *A Trip to Coontown* was a fortunate coincidence. By 1896, ragtime had invaded the stage at all levels. Between 1897 and 1930, African Americans made over 300 shows (Peterson 1993) composed of ragtime or novelty tunes (later jazz) and comedic dialogue often embedded in the characteristic revue format (a succession of topical songs and skits using the same actors in different roles).

Without access to the elaborate stage apparatus and expensive trappings of full-blown operettas, the black-cast shows of the early years of the century focused on the talents of individual star players, the powerful energy of the dance with its complexities of movement, the seemingly spontaneous vernacular humor, and the overwhelming vocal power of massed choruses. The black shows used at least two conservatory-trained musicians, Will Marion Cook and J. Rosamond Johnson, whose command of the new syncopated music, together with abundant conducting and arranging skills, glued together their inevitably disparate works. Both men were hit-tune writers in 1900 ("Darktown Is Out Tonight," "Under the Bamboo Tree") and enabled the stars to be presented in well-constructed contemporary vehicles, such as *In Dahomey* (1903).

Both blacks and whites saw and knew these shows—but were seated, of course, in segregated houses. Most of the actors did not don blackface makeup, however, and so although the shows' plots and song lyrics can appear stereotypical (if not downright slanderous) to a modern viewer, they represented an advance in some respects in their own day. Black men and women were placed, through the vehicle of the stage, in a commanding expressive position night after night, all over the country. Consequently, Bert Williams, Aida Overton Walker, and Ernest Hogan (Figure 7.8) were among the most famous African Americans of their day. They were viewed as race leaders, not merely entertainers. The most astute critics of these performers observed their mastery of mime, remarkable comic timing, vital dancing, and a distinctively animated presentation time after time. The overall impression left in the minds of the viewers after an extravaganza like Williams and Walker's *Bandana Land*—with multiple sets, marvelous stage effects, and live animals—must have forcefully contradicted the recollections of tired and tawdry minstrel shows from a bygone era.

After 1912, the first black triumphs on Broadway were pushed aside as Harlem grew and downtown producers feared further competition and the visibility of up-and-coming blacks. The premature deaths of black Broadway business leaders (especially Ernest Hogan

Figure 7.8
Ernest Hogan as Rufus
Rastus, the title charac-
ter of his first full-
length musical comedy
(1906). Billed as "the
unbleached American"
because he did not use
blackface makeup,
Hogan was also a suc-
cessful composer and
business leader in the
black community.

in 1909) led many leading entertainers to opt for traveling vaudeville or neighborhood-based shows in the larger cities. Black ownership of theaters and audiences around the country increased dramatically between 1910 and 1920, and so naturally the places where
a black audience could see black performers grew up in many
urban pockets around the country (Figure 7.9).

In 1921, the black musical returned with a blockbuster, the tune-
ful and energetic hit *Shuffle Along*, featuring the remarkable talents
of singer-lyricist Noble Sissle, pianist-composer Eubie Blake, and
comedians Flournoy Miller and Aubrey Lyles, who wrote the book
on which the musical was based. The cast included a large number
of fresh faces, many of whom later went on to stardom: Josephine
Baker, Caterina Yarboro, Florence Mills, and Paul Robeson on stage
and Hall Johnson, William Grant Still, and Leonard Jeter in the pit.
The show produced a number of memorable hits ("I'm Just Wild
About Harry," "Love Will Find a Way," "Dixie Moon"). The result
was an outstanding success, running for over 500 performances,
touring for two years on the road, and spawning many imitators
through the decade.

As with all great shows, the reasons for *Shuffle Along*'s success

were multiple. The talent was young and dedicated, but the key players drew on considerable experience. The musical material was varied. From the lyrical and romantic to the upbeat and jazzy, it accompanied a veritable kaleidoscope of dances and stage movements. Blake provided flashy piano interludes. The personalities of the stars were alluring. Everything was executed with virtuosity and struck the audience as thoroughly modern. Faced with stringent economies, the production even managed to be credited as sensibly modest. The play was familiar and genuinely funny (although nothing in the way of dramatic substance was ever expected in Broadway comedies of its type). It was produced in a theater that was accessible to regular Broadway theatergoers (at 63rd Street) and to a substantial black neighborhood on the west side of the city, if not quite in the heart of the theater district. Not unimportantly, influential critics loved it.

The stimulus provided by *Shuffle Along* and the boom of the 1920s saw even more black employment in theatricals, especially song-and-dance revues. The new shows combined old-fashioned motifs (plantation scenarios, sentimental Old South clichés, and shuffling characters out of minstrelsy) with novelty updates (urban scenes, themes of black "uplift" and "improvement," glamorous female blues singers, and jazz bands). The show names alone tell much about the high-spirited effervescence of the works, as well as their rather restricted dramatic palette: *Strut Miss Lizzie* (1922), *Runnin' Wild* (1923), *The Chocolate Dandies* (1924), and *Lucky Sambo* (1925).

During the 1920s and 1930s, the black creative component varied among the shows with black casts—arrangers and composers were both black and white—but the financial benefits to African Americans were negligible. Individual black geniuses, such as the eminent Broadway arranger and Gershwin mentor Will Vodery, are almost lost to history. Some chose to work behind the scenes. Others developed alternative careers playing jazz and singing the blues. But the producing dictators of the musical theater stage producers were not yet ready to admit African Americans into full and equal participation on Broadway.

Evolving Images on the Stage, from the Depression to the Civil Rights Era

Desire for heightened realism and more stringent production economies in the 1930s were reflected in the new black shows of that decade. *Brown Buddies* (1930) showed Bill Robinson and Adelaide Hall acting the romantic parts of the loyal soldier and tenderhearted civilian entertainer, respectively. *Sugar Hill* (1931) claimed to be a "sketch of life in Harlem's aristocratic section." Ethel Waters sang four songs (including a plaint about lynching) in Irving Berlin's innovative revue *As Thousands Cheer* (1933). The Federal Theater Project of the Works Progress Administration (1935-1939) also provided work for blacks in musicals as well as straight plays in several American cities. Among the most famous of these Depression-era entries was a jazz version of the Gilbert and Sullivan operetta *The Mikado*, called *The Swing Mikado* (1939), and an opera produced in Seattle, based on the John Henry legend and incorporating black musical idioms, *Natural Man* (1937). Two major musical works featuring black performers but with problematical scripts and contexts, again revealing the divisions and tensions within the entertainment industry of the 1930s, are Marc Connelly's religious pageant *Green Pastures* (1930), which used spirituals sung by the Hall Johnson Choir, and George and Ira Gershwin's opera *Porgy and Bess* (1935). Because creative control was racially restricted in both instances, these works generated and continue to generate controversy.

A gradual trend toward the integration of isolated black stars into white musicals and a growing allowance of more individualized black characters is perceptible in the 1940s, 1950s, and early 1960s, although there were exceptionally few all-black shows, and the amount of black participation in the preproduction process was almost invisible. Despite liberalizing trends favoring racial inclusiveness in the larger post-World War II society, racial barriers still tended to restrict the creative options for black actors while reinforcing the tendency of white producers to rely on minstrel formulas in casting. Black men, women, and children continued to sing, play, and dance on the stage, but they did so largely in the makeup of comic servants, urban vagabonds, and jungle savages.

The Civil Rights movement and the revolutionary ideology of the late 1960s and 1970s seemed inimical to the comic conventions of musical comedy. New independent groups, especially the National Black Theater (NBT) of Harlem (1968-1972), created works using African and West Indian rituals and dances, but longer-lived and less ideologically bound organizations, such as the Negro Ensemble Theater, did not stress musicals in their repertoires at all. The works of Melvin Van Peebles, *Ain't Supposed to Die a Natural Death* (1971) and *Don't Play Us Cheap* (1972), were probably the most artistically serious and invigorating dramatic contributions to this new theater. Their angry confrontational dialogue anticipated by a generation the powerful speech-rhythms of rap artists.

The End of the Twentieth Century

The reintroduction of black folk and religious themes into shows, such as *Black Nativity* (1962), *Tambourines to Glory* (1963), *The Prodigal Son* (1965), *A Hand at the Gate* (1966), *Your Arms Too Short to Box with God* (1976), and *The Gospel at Colonus* (1983) and the revival of older musical styles began to strengthen the black presence once again in the final third of the century. The emergence of rock and roll as the principal style of popular music—with its undeniable African American roots—accompanied the ebbing popularity of the classic productions from earlier decades. The 1970s and 1980s saw more participation of African Americans on Broadway than had occurred since the 1930s, although the musical contents often tended to be retrospective and nostalgic in shows like *Bubblin' Brown Sugar* (1976), *One Mo' Time* (1979), *Sophisticated Ladies* (1982), and *Black and Blue* (1989). In a class apart, *Bring in da Noise/Bring in da Funk* (1996) transcended its dancing show ancestors by creating a tour de force of rhythmic counterpoint realized on suspended pots, pans, and buckets, as well as with the usual tap shoes. The original moves and sustained energy flowing from this show, glossed thinly with a historical veneer, electrified audiences in a lengthy cross-country tour after its New York success. Some black-cast musicals of these same decades began to draw on the proven efforts of black playwrights, in such box office hits as *Purlie* (1970), based on Ossie Davis's *Purlie Victorious*, and *Raisin* (1973), taken from Lorraine Hansberry's *Raisin in the Sun*. Other less successful shows attempted to address the problems of modern black per-formers: *Doctor Jazz* (1975) and *The Tap Dance Kid* (1983).

Three major award-winning shows, *Ain't Misbehavin'* (1978, revived 1988), *Dreamgirls* (1981–1985), and *Jelly's Last Jam* (1992), emphasize that legendary figures from African American popular musical history were more apt than other subjects in this era to inspire dynamic products with substantial box-office appeal. As in the first decades of original African American musicals (1897–1927), the elements that most attracted audiences to the revivalist shows of the 1970s–1990s were syncopated songs, dazzling dance routines, powerful choruses, and distinctive solos. But something had changed.

By the end of the twentieth century, most mainline commercial American popular music was dominated by historically black ele-ments. More important, rock in some form had superseded pre-rock and roll idioms on the Broadway stage itself, not only in the wider market. Tin Pan Alley ballads (typically featuring a chorus of four rhymed text phrases in thirty-two bars of music), the reliable building blocks of musicals since the 1910s, now almost always had to share the bill with songs inspired by the blues, ragtime, jazz, gospel, soul, or rock.

Perhaps the most self-conscious recognition of the dominance of black aesthetics in popular music (coupled with an intuition that Broadway was now ready to accept this fact) was the fantasy-parody *The Wiz* (1975, revived 1984), which took the 1939 film classic *The Wizard of Oz* as a springboard for reinterpreting the black experi-ence in America. Scored by the skillful Charles Smalls, *The Wiz* ran for over 1,500 performances, received numerous Tony and Drama Desk awards, and succeeded with viewers despite the doubts of hos-tile early critics. It was far more than a protest statement, revival, sequel, or imitative revue. Its vibrancy and unapologetic embrace of black vernacular language, matched with a flamboyant visual pro-duction and superb choreography, drew on a variety of sources. Its musical style was modern and rhythmic to the core, and its hit song ("Ease on Down the Road") spoke directly to a wide audience of all races.

Although the financial control of U.S. entertainment, including Broadway, was still firmly held by white corporate interests, the cre-ative and aesthetic impulses that gave life to the stage were strongly African American by the end of the twentieth century. Only time will tell whether just compensation will ever be received by the originators of ragtime, jazz, and rock and roll.

Thomas L. Riis

R&B AND SOUL

Rhythm and blues (R&B) and soul are urban forms of black musical expression that evolved during the World War II era (1938-1945) and the two decades that followed. They are associated with southern blacks who abandoned their jobs as domestics, sharecroppers, tenant farmers, and general laborers and migrated to urban centers throughout the country. More than two million southern blacks left rural areas and small towns in the 1940s, in search of high-paying industrial jobs and to escape racial inequalities sanctioned by Jim Crow laws. R&B and soul, which captured the spirit, pace, and texture of life in the city, are products of this transformation.

The term *rhythm and blues* was first used as a marketing label to identify all types of music recorded by African American artists. Introduced in 1949 to replace the *race music* label (a term in use since 1920), R&B encompassed all black musical traditions, including rural and urban blues, boogie-woogie, black swing, jazz combos, vocal harmony groups, and club lounge trios. It also identified a musical genre that began evolving in the mid-1940s as reinterpretations and hybridizations of vernacular traditions. Although the blues provided the foundation for R&B, other elements came from jazz, spirituals, gospel, and mainstream popular music. By the 1960s, gospel elements began to dominate and transform rhythm and blues into a distinctive genre labeled *soul*.

R&B PIONEERS

The first generation of R&B performers were blues and swing musicians who joined forces to create new musical styles in response to changes taking place in society. When smaller entertainment venues came into vogue in the 1940s, African American musicians adapted by forming new bands with fewer members and developing a new repertoire. Arkansas-born Louis Jordan, a singer and alto saxophonist, ushered in a new musical era in 1938 when he formed Louis Jordan and His Tympany Five. Jordan transformed big band swing into a combo sound by reducing the traditional twelve- to sixteen-member swing band to a seven-piece combo (rhythm section, alto and tenor sax, and trumpet), and creating a jazz-blues hybrid style and contemporary repertoire. While preserving the fundamental components of big band swing, his musical arrangements gave musicians more creative freedom. The sound was polished but had a spontaneous quality characterized by a twelve-bar blues structure, boogie-woogie bass line, shuffle rhythms (triplet quarter note fol-

---

Rhythm and blues (R&B)
African American popular music that developed in the late 1940s and flourished through the mid-1960s, combining elements of various earlier popular music traditions

Soul
Gospel-flavored African American popular music style of the late 1960s and early 1970s

lowed by a triplet eighth note), a syncopated three- and four-note horn riff pattern, a solo saxophone, and group singing on refrain lines.

Jordan's combo style, known as *jump blues,* produced a string of hits on the race/rhythm and blues and pop charts, thereby crossing established racial boundaries. Blacks and whites of various social classes related to all aspects of his performance: the musical aesthetic, novelty lyrics, and engaging showmanship. Working-class blacks especially identified with Jordan's humorous lyrics about urban and rural black life, which connected them to their southern roots and the performance tradition of "down home" or southern blues musicians.

During the early 1940s, Los Angeles clubs became incubators for R&B music. Through jam sessions, blues and jazz musicians pioneered a distinctive West Coast R&B style by adding regional vernacular elements to Jordan's combo model. The combination of guitar and piano stylings from the Texas blues tradition, horn arrangements from southwestern swing bands, rumba rhythms from Cuba via Louisiana, and the "honking" tenor saxophone style (popularized by Illinois Jacquet in Lionel Hampton's 1942 remake of "Flying Home") produced an urban dance music that rocked the nation for nearly three decades (Otis 1984; Shaw 1978:129-225).

A different R&B style from the combo tradition emerged from after-hours clubs in Los Angeles. Labeled *club blues* in black clubs and *cocktail music* in white clubs, this music is distinguished from combo R&B by function and instrumentation. Performers of club blues created an atmosphere for conversation rather than dancing. Chicago-born singer-pianist Nat "King" Cole is credited with originating this tradition in 1937 in Los Angeles, when he formed a trio consisting of piano, guitar, and bass. Cole's songs appealed to both blacks and whites, especially the middle class; they related to the fluid and assimilated sound of his piano and vocal styles. The popularity of Cole's group inspired the formation of similar trios who introduced the blues aesthetic to the tradition. Blues-based trios quickly became favorites in after-hours clubs that attracted the black working class.

By the end of the 1940s, eight independent labels specializing in R&B had been established in Los Angeles. Despite the absence of national distribution networks, this music made its way to other parts of the country and influenced the development of other regional styles. Black Pullman porters on trains served as unofficial distributors for record labels, and the few existing black radio programs broadcast the music. Despite nationwide demand for R&B recordings, major record labels excluded the artists from their rosters. These and other exclusionary practices contributed to the proliferation of independent record labels (Shaw 1978).

Combo R&B
Style pioneered by Louis Jordan that transformed big band swing style into a smaller combo sound; features a swinging rhythm, up-tempo and often humorous songs, and more freedom for individual performers than big band swing

Club blues/ cocktail music
A smoother R&B style pioneered by Nat "King" Cole featuring a mainstream repertoire, relaxed vocal style, and laidback accompaniment

In the late 1940s and early 1950s, the so-called major labels showed little interest in recording the new R&B sounds. In their place, a group of independents began to target the rapidly growing black teenage population, signing teenage performers to attract these consumers. Imperial, Specialty, and Aladdin in Los Angeles and fledgling Atlantic in New York City were among the first labels to search for young black talent. They hired New Orleans jazz bandleader Dave Bartholomew (Figure 7.10) and territory jazz bandleader Jesse Stone as talent scouts and songwriter-arranger-producers.

Bartholomew and Stone created new forms of urban dance music by modifying the rhythms and arrangements of West Coast R&B to conform to the dance styles of southern black teenagers. Bartholomew explains: "I took the bass [pattern] from the rumba and put in my saxophone. Then I had the [string] bass do what we called the walk" (Bartholomew 1985). Fats Domino added triplets and rolling fifth and octave figures from the Texas piano-blues tradition to Bartholomew's formula, producing a distinctive New Orleans rhythm and blues sound. Under Bartholomew's guidance, Domino had numerous hits, including "The Fat Man" (1949) and "Ain't That a Shame" (1955).

Jesse Stone pioneered a slightly different regional sound by modifying the boogie-woogie bass line that he believed "was too busy and didn't fit the dances kids were doing at that particular

Figure 7.10
Dave Bartholomew, bandleader, songwriter, arranger, and producer for Imperial, Specialty and Aladdin Records. Courtesy Archives of African American Music and Culture, Indiana University.

time" (Stone 1982). Stone's formula, which became known as the "Atlantic sound" because he primarily worked for that New York-based label, produced many hits and established Atlantic as a major recording label in the rhythm and blues market.

Paralleling the development of the Atlantic and New Orleans R&B styles was the emergence of new and youthful sounds from street corners, school gyms, and city parks. They were the voices of teenage groups who sang a cappella vocal harmony songs. Initially imitating the jazz-pop styles of the Mills Brothers, the Ink Spots, and the Ravens, these teenage groups (also known as "street corner" groups) developed a musical tradition that represented their values, cultural sensibilities, and lives as city dwellers. The Orioles are credited as being the first R&B vocal harmony group. Singing sentimental ballads in a romantic style, they appealed to teenagers. They became the model for subsequent R&B harmony groups (Five Keys, Swallows, Penguins, and other "bird" groups), many of whom gradually developed their own unique sound.

The romantic-styled harmony groups acquired a new sound when the Spaniels introduced the *doo-wop* concept. James "Pookie" Hudson, lead singer of the Spaniels, explained that the bass voice incorporated the rhythmic phrases "doo-doo-doo-wop" and "doo-doo-doo-doo-doo" to add rhythmic movement to romantic songs (Hudson 1985). These phrases imitated the string bass and became central to the background vocals of harmony groups. The Spaniels popularized this concept in "Baby, It's You" (1953) and "Goodnite Sweetheart, Goodnite" (1954), ushering in the doo-wop era. The Moonglows added yet another dimension to "doo-wop" when they instituted the technique of blowing the phrase "ooh-ooh-wee-ohh-oohwee-oohwee" into the microphone on "Sincerely" (1954) and "Most of All" (1955) to create a different kind of vocal effect, which became known as "blow harmony."

Vocal harmony groups traditionally sang without instrumental accompaniment, but commercial production of their songs led to the use of instruments associated with rhythm and blues trios and combos. The up-tempo and bluesy style produced by combos broadened the spectrum of these groups. The music's aesthetic qualities and danceable character attracted the attention of white teenagers, disc jockeys, and major record labels. The music industry wanted to exploit white teenage consumer markets, and these teenagers wanted to establish their own identity through music, dance, dress, and style. African American music and culture became the foundation for this identity. To obscure the source of the new music embraced by white teenagers, record labels produced cover versions by white artists. Disc jockeys, in turn, substituted the term *rock and roll* for rhythm and blues. But when teenagers discovered the original artists through radio broadcast, they rejected the imitative versions and

Street corner vocal groups Groups usually of teenagers who practiced harmonizing on street corners, at schools, and in community gathering spots

Doo-wop Vocal style of the 1950s featuring a lead vocalist with background vocalists often employing nonsense syllables (such as "doo-doo-doo-wop") to imitate instrumental accompaniment

sought out authentic African American recordings (Garofolo 1990:57-90).

R&B IN TRANSITION

During the era of cover records (approximately 1953-1956), R&B continued to evolve. In 1954, Little Richard introduced a new beat to the tradition that became known as *rock and roll*. Charles Conner, Little Richard's original drummer, explained:

> In rhythm and blues, you had a shuffle with a back-beat, but Little Richard wanted something different . . . with more energy . . . . So Richard brought me down to the train station in Macon, Georgia, in 1954 and he said: "Charles, listen to the choo-choo, choo-choo, choo-choo." I said, you probably want eighth notes or sixteenth notes. We went back to his house couple of days later . . . and we came up with that beat. (Conner 1990)

The *choo choo* beat generated many national and crossover hits for Richard, including "Tutti Frutti" (1955), "Long Tall Sally" (1956), and "Lucille" (1957).

Additional changes occurred when Bo Diddley and Chuck Berry popularized the guitar as the focal instrument. The preference for this instrument among white youth, along with Berry's novelty lyrics, made R&B even more accessible to white teenagers. Diddley's rhythmic guitar style and rumba rhythms ("Bo Diddley" [1955]) and Berry's more melodic approach ("Maybellene" [1955] and "Roll Over Beethoven" [1956]) appealed to the musical tastes and cultural values of all America's youth.

Labeled and promoted as rock and roll performers by the music industry, Bo Diddley, Chuck Berry, Little Richard, and black doo-wop groups generated many hits on R&B and pop charts. They also made appearances on mainstream television shows such as *The Ed Sullivan Show* and *American Bandstand,* and their music landed on jukeboxes and record players in white neighborhoods, causing consternation in mainstream society. Despite lawsuits and various forms of protests to rid the nation of this "licentious jungle" music, R&B remained popular among white youth.

CROSSOVER FORMULAS

Eager to cater to the musical tastes of white youth, record labels pondered new strategies to market R&B recorded by black artists across racial, class, and generational lines. Their solution was to record African American artists singing pop and country and western standards and pop-styled songs. They also applied Tin Pan Alley or pop production concepts to dilute aesthetic qualities associated with black musical performance. In essence, record labels attempted to assimilate black artists into the mainstream of American popular music.

Rock and roll
1950s popular music that features an 8-beat rhythm, small instrumental combo focusing on the guitar as lead instrument, and songs addressing teenage themes

When the pop-oriented vocals and lyrics of the Platters ("Only You" [1955], "The Great Pretender" [1955]) became hits in both the R&B and pop markets, the group demonstrated its cross-cultural and cross-generational appeal. Mercury (the label that released the Platters' records) and Atlantic were among the first to explore crossover production techniques aimed at both teenage and young adult markets. Jerry Leiber and Mike Stoller, the white songwriting and production team that replaced Jesse Stone as Atlantic's primary songwriter-producer, developed crossover formulas for both markets. Their teenage-oriented productions were mainly novelty songs that featured comic lyrics and a playful vocal style accompanied by a rhythm and blues combo (Gillett 1974:156–164). To target an older audience, Leiber and Stoller employed pop production techniques. On ballads, for example, they substituted call-response or blues structures, gospel-blues harmonies, and combo arrangements with sing-along refrains, pop vocal harmonies, and elaborate orchestral arrangements (strings, marimba, tympani, and percussion).

The "uptown" R&B concept, as scholar Charlie Gillett (1983 [1970]) named it, became standard to black music production, and it successfully launched many black female vocal groups. They were produced primarily by young white songwriter-producers, including Carole King and Gerry Goffin, Barry Mann and Cynthia Weil, Luther Dixon, and Phil Spector. The writers centered their song lyrics on the experiences and fantasies of teenagers and incorporated "hook lines" (sing-along repetitive phrases), string arrangements, and Brazilian rhythms. The Shirelles' "Will You Love Me Tomorrow" (1960), Crystals' "He's a Rebel" (1962) and "Da Doo Ron Ron" (1963), Chiffons' "He's So Fine" (1963), and Ronettes' "Be My Baby" (1963) are among the many songs that crossed over into the mainstream and established the commercial viability of "girl groups" in the music industry.

The attempt of record companies and southern whites to prevent the penetration of black musical aesthetics and cultural traditions into the mainstream generated the reverse result. The pop elements introduced into R&B for crossover purposes actually spread black aesthetic qualities further into the arteries of society. When the diluted and toned-down uptown R&B sound recycled back into African American communities, it reentered the mainstream with a different twist. Black artists removed some pop elements and reworked others to conform to the black aesthetic. Through continuous recycling, the full range of African American aesthetic qualities and popular musical expressions gradually became central to American popular music. In the 1960s, for example, the Motown Sound, the Memphis Sound, and soul music were mainstays on the pop, R&B, and soul music charts. Although these traditions can be distinguished from one another and mainstream popular traditions, they share aesthetic features unique to African American cultural expression.

THE MOTOWN SOUND

The Motown record label—named for "Motor Town," the nickname for Detroit—was founded by songwriter Berry Gordy in 1959. Gordy's love for music led him to pursue various business enterprises, including operating a record shop and writing songs. In his autobiography, Gordy admitted that he initially favored bebop and the music of Dinah Washington, Sarah Vaughan, Billie Holiday, the Ink Spots, and the Mills Brothers, and only later came to appreciate the blues and their derivative forms. This eclectic musical taste and Gordy's emphasis on good song lyrics shaped the Motown Sound (Gordy 1994:8-46, 59-77).

Motown's first hit recordings were molded in the traditions of R&B combos (Junior Walker's "Money" [1959] and Marvin Gaye's "Can I Get a Witness" [1963]), vocal groups (the Miracles "Shop Around" [1960] and the Marvelettes "Please Mr. Postman" [1961]), and gospel-pop-styled solo singers (Mary Wells's "You Beat Me to the Punch" [1962]). To these traditions, Gordy added his own innovations: tambourine, hand claps, a metallic ring from the guitar downstroke on beats two and four, jazz-derived bass lines, and a heavy bass drum foundation. This framework, which became the basis for the Motown Sound, appealed to teenagers across class, racial, and regional boundaries (Gordy 1994:110, 122-128).

Most of Motown's vocalists were teenagers who grew up in relatively impoverished neighborhoods in Detroit. Nevertheless, the innocence of their youthful voices resonated through their gospel-pop-flavored song interpretations. The company's songwriters were also young, and their songs dealt with young love, youth experiences, and feelings shared by all teenagers. Following established songwriting principles, they structured their lyrics on catchy and memorable pop- and classical-derived melodies and hook lines, to which were added vocal harmonies and call-response structures from black gospel music. By the mid-1960s, this formula catapulted Motown's artists into national and international prominence. Recordings by Martha and the Vandellas ("Dancing in the Street" [1964]), Mary Wells ("My Guy" [1964]), Marvin Gaye ("How Sweet It Is (To Be Loved by You)" [1964]), the Supremes ("Come See About Me" [1964], "Stop in the Name of Love" [1964], and "You Can't Hurry Love" [1966]), the Temptations ("My Girl" [1964] and "Ain't Too Proud to Beg" [1966]), and the Four Tops ("I Can't Help Myself" [1965]) scored big on the R&B and pop music charts.

In the late 1960s and early 1970s, the Motown Sound began to change, in part influenced by the Black Power movement and the riots in 1967 that devastated a large section of Detroit's ghetto.

Changes in the Motown Sound parallel the social unrest that swept the country from the mid-1960s to the early 1970s as well as internal strife within Motown. During this period, the Motown Sound slowly transformed itself into many distinct sounds that became identified as soul music (Sugrue 1996:105–177).

THE MEMPHIS SOUND

The Stax record label paralleled the development of Motown. James Stewart, a bankteller and country musician, founded the company in Memphis in 1959 along with his sister, Estelle Axton. An amateur recording engineer, Stewart built a recording studio and recorded music as a hobby. Most of Stewart's clients were country musicians, but his stable of artists changed when he relocated the studio from his garage to an abandoned downtown movie theater in the black community. Stax's open-door policy attracted a mixture of black musicians from the neighborhood and white ones who had worked with Stewart in his first location. A core group of these musicians jammed together and became the studio's house band. Known as Booker T. and the MGs (Figure 7.11), they created a unique southern

Figure 7.11
Booker T. and the MGs, house band for Stax Records. Courtesy of BMI Archives.

sound, blending their individual blues, rhythm and blues, and rock-abilly styles. This integrated band, which defied established social policies on race mixing and cultural exchanges, mirrored the goals of the Civil Rights movement (Bowman 1997:3–48).

Like Motown's artists, most of Stax's artists were between the ages of 15 and 22. Although they were from the South, their exposure to both southern and northern popular styles guided the company's first recordings of blues, doo-wop, rhythm and blues combo, and uptown styles. The company's initial success was built on the instrumentals of the Mar-Keys ("Last Night" [1961]) and Booker T. and the MGs ("Green Onions" [1962]), the uptown rhythm and blues tradition of Carla Thomas ("Gee Whiz" [1960]), the gospel-derived styles of William Bell ("You Don't Miss Your Water" [1961]) and Otis Redding ("These Arms of Mine" [1962]), and the R&B combo sounds of Rufus Thomas ("Walking the Dog" [1963]).

The Memphis Sound was spontaneous, bold, gritty, gutsy, and warm, with an urban definition and rural undercurrents. It captured the realities and contradictions of life in the segregated South and the sensibilities of southern black culture. The warm and laid-back rhythm and blues-rockabilly stylings of Booker T. and the MGs, combined with the syncopated horn riffs of the Mar-Keys, gave a southern energy to the rhythm and blues tradition. This instrumental framework provided the foundation for vocalists, who added their individual signatures to the company sound.

Many of Stax's singers wrote their own songs and collaborated with the musicians to create the musical grooves and arrangements (Thomas 1984). This process differed from Motown's creative approach. With the exception of Smokey Robinson, Marvin Gaye, and later Stevie Wonder, most of Motown singers were vehicles through which songwriter-producers, in collaboration with the studio band, presented their creations. Thus, the Motown Sound was more "produced" and less spontaneous than the Memphis Sound. Song lyrics also differed. Whereas Motown focused on teenage issues, Stax's lyrics dealt with all aspects of southern black life—daily experiences, relationships, and social issues. The Memphis Sound was largely unknown outside southern black communities until Al Bell, a black disc jockey in Washington, DC, began promoting the music on the East Coast in 1963 and 1964. He subsequently joined the Stax label in 1965 as its first national director for promotion and, two years later, became vice president and chief operating officer. Under Bell's leadership, Stax became a national and international phenomenon. As demand for the music increased, Stax expanded its roster, signing new artists and adding resident and independent black song writer-producers and arrangers to the staff. The songwriters who perfected and transformed the Memphis Sound into a music labeled *soul* were the team of Isaac Hayes and David Porter.

Soul music is a product of the *Black Power movement* that reflects its ethos and ideology. As the momentum of the 1950s Civil Rights movement continued to build, southern black college students organized under the umbrella of the Student Nonviolent Coordinating Committee (SNCC) in 1960. By the mid-1960s, these students had become increasingly impatient with the disappointingly slow pace of social change and they rejected the nonviolent and inte-grationist approach advocated by Civil Rights leaders. As an alternative, many embraced the black nationalist ideology of Malcolm X in 1966. Under the rubric Black Power, its proponents promoted national black unity, black pride, and self-determination. Thus Black Power became a political movement to which black people assigned social and cultural meanings described as soul (Marable 1991:61-69).

The Black Power movement
Social/political movement of the late 1960s to early 1970s that promoted national black unity, black pride, and self-determination

Soul music was a new style defined by religious overtones and sociopolitical messages. Songwriter-vocalist Curtis Mayfield wrote some of the earliest songs addressing issues of black pride and empowerment, and performed them with the vocal group The Impressions, including "Keep on Pushing" (1964), "People Get Ready" (1965), "We're a Winner" (1967), "This Is My Country" (1968), "Choice of Colors" (1969), and "We People Who Are Darker Than Blue" (1970). Music critic Tom Moon (1990) remembered that "these were the songs that really spoke to what people were feeling. They anticipated and distilled public mood in a way that no one else had ever done before." Mayfield's songs also inspired other musicians and a generation of African Americans to speak out and join the struggle for racial equality.

As Black Power evolved into a national movement, performers promoted its ideology. Themes of black pride and self-respect resonate in the Memphis Sound of Sam and Dave ("Soul Man" [1967]) and the Staple Singers ("Respect Yourself" [1971]). On the King label, James Brown extolled racial pride in "Say It Loud—I'm Black and I'm Proud, Pt. 1" (1968) as well as self-determination in "I Don't Want Nobody to Give Me Nothing (Open up the Door I'll Get It Myself)" (1969) and "Get Up, Get into It and Get Involved" (1970).

Motown also responded to this era of activism. Berry Gordy (1994, 223) explains: "As the new decade was beginning, the changes happening in society inspired changes in our music." Songwriters Norman Whitfield, Barrett Strong, Pam Sawyer, and others introduced themes of social commentary and contemporary sounds to transform the Motown Sound. The Supremes sang about "Love Child" (1968), the Temptations recorded "Ball of Confusion (That's What the World Is Today)" (1970), Gladys Knight and the Pips promoted a "Friendship Train" (1969), Edwin Starr condemned "War" (1970), and Stevie Wonder recorded "Living for the City" (1973) and "Higher Ground" (1973).

The concept of soul also advocated unity and respect in personal relationships. Otis Redding elaborated on these themes in "I've Been Loving You Too Long" (1965), "Respect" (1965), and "Try a Little Tenderness" (1966), as did Sam and Dave in "When Something Is Wrong with My Baby" (1966) and Al Green in "Let's Stay Together" (1971). The "Queen of Soul," Aretha Franklin, provided a female perspective on these themes in "I Never Loved a Man (The Way I Love You)" (1967), "Do Right Woman–Do Right Man" (1967), and "I Can't See Myself Leaving You" (1968).

Soul remained a major form of black popular expression through the first half of the 1970s. During this period, social and political change came at a much slower rate for many innercity residents than for the black middle class. Expressing feelings of the working class and the poor, the Isley Brothers expounded on the need for "Freedom" (1970), and the Chi-Lites and the O'Jays reminded society that the critical mass of African Americans had not yet been empowered in "(For God's Sake) Give More Power to the People" (1971) and "Give the People What They Want" (1975), respectively. Marvin Gaye deplored the social problems that continued to plague innercity residents in "What's Going On" (1971) and "Inner City Blues" (1971). The gospel-flavored interpretation of these lyrics added a unique quality to the sound of soul.

In earlier R&B styles, performers also drew from the gospel tradition by substituting secular for religious lyrics, incorporating call-response structures and vocal harmonies, and imitating the vocal styles of gospel quartets. Ray Charles continued this practice in songs, such as "I've Got a Woman" (1954) and "This Little Girl of Mine" (1955) that are secular versions of "Jesus Is All the World to Me" and "This Little Light of Mine," respectively. Charles also broadened this musical foundation by replacing the R&B combo arrangements with those from gospel music. His original compositions, including "Drown in My Own Tears" (1956), "That's Enough" (1959), and "What'd I Say (Part I)" (1959), for example, employ the $\frac{12}{8}$ meter, formal harmonic and rhythmic structures, and vocal and piano stylings from gospel music (Maultsby 1992:30-31).

James Brown, known as the "Godfather of Soul," also contributed to the transformation of R&B into soul by adding a southern rawness and rhythmic intensity to the tradition. His percussive vocal timbres and repetitive phrases interjected with grunts, screams, and hollers, and his polyrhythmic instrumental structures, further defined the gospel foundation of the soul aesthetic. The recordings "Please, Please, Please" (1956), "Bewildered" (1959), and "Think" (1960) were models for many singers in the 1960s.

The concept of soul encouraged black people to identify with the culture and traditions of the motherland. Responding to this call, performers dressed in African attire accentuated by African adornments and hairstyles. This symbolic connection carried over into album designs, which often featured African-derived art and other images. Soul performers became icons not only as cultural preservers but as economic empowerers. Many soul performers established businesses in the inner city and assisted in building various community programs. James Brown, for example, owned radio stations, restaurants, and other businesses where he employed innercity residents. Both Stax and Motown used their resources to preserve black cultural expressions and to aid community development. For example, they created spoken-word labels to record the speeches of African American political leaders, poets, and comedians, and they organized benefit concerts using their artists to help finance protest demonstrations and to rebuild inner cities. Stax also contributed to the election campaigns of several black politicians and to their organizations. Through political activism and economic and self-empowerment, many black performers and music industry executives inspired African Americans to pursue goals that once seemed unattainable (Bell 1983; Byrd 1984; Gordy 1994:248-252; Maultsby 1983).

Although *soul* had been a household word in African American communities since 1964, the mainstream press resisted using the term. On June 28, 1968, *Time* magazine first acknowledged the institutionalization of the term when it featured Aretha Franklin on the cover and in a lengthy article, "Lady Soul Singing It Like It Is." A year later, *Billboard,* the leading trade music magazine, changed the name of its "R&B" chart to "Soul." These two events signaled a cultural victory for the Black Power movement, because both magazines used a term that was first coined and used by African Americans to describe a new and distinctive black musical genre as well as a cultural style.

Portia K. Maultsby

Over a period of four centuries, the study of African American music advanced from the early descriptive accounts of musical performance by casual observers, the Eurocentric analyses of structure and technique, and subjective interpretations of meaning and significance to a more holistic understanding of music making as a set of black cultural practices associated with specific historical, sociocultural, and political contexts. Approaches to the study of this tradition also changed from nonexistent methodologies to the use of a single research and analytical model and then to the combination of multiple approaches from various disciplinary areas. Although the literature on African American music is uneven in quality, it presents varying interpretations, including those of African Americans, whose views were excluded from the musical canon before the 1970s and 1980s. The last decade of the twentieth century witnessed new trends in black music production as the tradition became appropriated and reinvented in global contexts. These developments generated new research initiatives that will further broaden the study of African American music and culture in the twenty-first century.

REVIEW

Terms and People to Know

Afro-Creole
Arranged spiritual
Banjo
Bent notes
Black Power movement
Blackface
Eubie Blake
James Bland
Blue note
Blues scale
Boogie-woogie
Booker T and the MGs
Bottleneck technique
Call
Call-response style
The Christie Minstrels
Club blues/cocktail music
Nat "King" Cole
Combo R&B
Cry/holler
Fats Domino
Doo-wop
Thomas A. Dorsey
Fisk University Jubilee Singers
Folk spiritual
Aretha Franklin
Berry Gordy
Mahalia Jackson
Louis Jordan
Juke Joint
La calinda
Leadbelly (Ledbetter, Huddeie)
Little Richard (Penniman, Richard)
Curtis Mayfield
Medicine show
Minstrel show
Motown
Passing harmony or chord
Patting juba

Play-party
Polyrhythm
Otis Redding
Rhythm and blues (R&B)
Riff
Ring shout
Rock and roll
Noble Sissle
Slur
Mamie Smith
Soul
Jesse Stone
John Work
Worksong

Review Questions

1. Describe the legacy of African music brought to the United States and the transition to an African American musical culture.
2. From what musical forms did the blues originate? Where did they originate geographically? What are the four main characteristics of the blues as outlined by author David Evans in this chapter?
3. From what musical forms did gospel originate? Who were some of the major composers and performers of early gospel? Contemporary gospel?
4. How did the development of an African American musical theater in the nineteenth and twentieth centuries both parallel and diverge from that of other forms of African American secular music?
5. What were some of the music styles developed by African Americans in the mid-twentieth century as a response to changing social, political, and economic contexts?

Projects

1. Find an African American Baptist church in your area and pay a visit during a Sunday (or weekday) service. Write up your observations of the religious, social, and musical practices in the form of an ethnography.
2. Listen to some early and contemporary blues performances. What characteristics have remained the same and what have changed?
3. Compose a standard blues or gospel song with lyrics based

on events, feelings, or attitudes in your own life, and perform this piece for your friends.

4. Write a research paper comparing two of the forms discussed in this chapter in relation to the social, political, and economic contexts in which they developed.

5. Examine some early scholarship on African American musics. Can you discern a prevailing attitude toward this music and toward African Americans that underlies the text? Discuss how this might have affected the author's perspective.

CHAPTER 8

Latin American Musical Cultures

Daniel Sheehy, Steven Loza, José R. Reyna, and Steven Cornelius

The Spanish were the first Europeans to establish a permanent settlement in what is today the United States, in St. Augustine, Florida,
in the late sixteenth century. From that time, Spanish-speaking
immigrants, as well as Portuguese-speaking Brazilians and mestizos
(people of mixed heritage), have continued to arrive, via Mexico, the
Caribbean, and Central and South America, and they now represent
the second largest and fastest-growing minority population in the
United States. Located primarily in Texas, New Mexico, California,
and New York, Latino musical communities have contributed their
vibrant rhythms, dance forms, instruments, and musicians to the
eclectic American musical landscape. Musical forms, such as the *son*,
conjunto, mambo, rumba, and *cha-cha-chá*, have greatly influenced
popular music—especially African American jazz and dance forms—
in the mid- and late twentieth century, when dance crazes popularized by bandleaders, such as Xavier Cugat and Tito Puente were the
rage. Hispanic/Latino musical elements are so pervasive that they
are, like African and European elements, part and parcel of what we
today define as American music.

Near the close of the twentieth century, an estimated 32 million
Latinos lived in the United States, representing 12 percent of the
total population—nearly one of every eight Americans. Although the
U.S. Bureau of the Census uses the term *Hispanic, Latino* also has
become a widely accepted single label to describe a population of
diverse national origins, cultures, and racial characteristics. More

common terms of self-description, however, are those pointing to national or regional origin—*Mexicano* (Mexican American), *Puertorriqueño* (Puerto Rican), *Cubano* (Cuban), *Guatemalteco* (Guatamalan), *Boliviano* (Bolivian), *Tejano* (Tex-Mex), *Nuevomexicano* (New Mexican), and others—or those that emerged from sociopolitical movements, such as Chicano (Mexican American) or Nuyorican (Puerto Rican New Yorker).

The geographical distribution and internal variation of each of the major Latino population groups—Mexican, Puerto Rican, Cuban, Central American, Dominican, and South American—have been shaped by historical events. When the 1848 Treaty of Guadalupe Hidalgo ended the Mexican War (1846-1848), it ceded half of Mexico's territory—stretching from Texas in the east, California in the west, and southern Colorado in the north—to the United States, and the area's inhabitants became the first significant Latino population under U.S. governance. In the twentieth century, the sporadic need for foreign workers during the two world wars brought legally sanctioned Mexican railroad workers and *braceros* (agricultural workers). Illegal immigration spurred by the lure of greater economic prosperity in the United States occurred throughout the century, particularly during the latter decades.

Along with these "pull" forces, a major "push" force behind immigration was war in various regions of the Americas. The Mexican Revolution (1910-1917) drove many Mexican intellectuals and northern inhabitants across the border into the United States. Fidel Castro's rise to power in 1959 drove many middle- and upper-class Cubans of European descent to Miami and elsewhere in the United States. Continuing hostilities between the United States and communist Cuba brought another influx (this time of less advantaged Cubans of African heritage), most notably during the Mariel boatlift in 1980. Internal warring in El Salvador, Nicaragua, Guatemala, and other areas of Central America pushed those populations northward to the United States in the 1970s and 1980s.

Another important historical factor encouraging Latino immigration was U.S. policy toward the Commonwealth of Puerto Rico, a U.S. jurisdiction since the Spanish American War in 1898. After World War I, Puerto Ricans were granted free entry and citizenship status when coming to the mainland United States. Over the twentieth century, major Puerto Rican communities formed in New York City and other large cities of the Northeast and Midwest. Musicians in particular were attracted by the opportunities for professional musical careers in New York City. A somewhat similar policy existed toward Cuba in the Castro era, as refugees reaching American soil were granted residency.

The persistence of Spanish as the language of preference is a major component of acculturation, a process whereby Latinos adopt "mainstream" North American culture as their own. A 1999 survey showed that while 73 percent of first-generation Latino immigrants spoke Spanish in the home, that figure fell to 1 percent among third-generation Latinos (Goldstein and Curo 2000:A24). On the other hand, many Latinos as a point of pride maintain the ability to speak Spanish. Some other, more private, aspects of Latino cultural heritage are slower to change, such as styles of cuisine, the importance of the family social unit, and religious traditions. While the vast majority of Latinos are at least nominally Roman Catholic, for example, religious traditions and patron saint activities particular to certain nations of origin have carried over into North American life. According to a 1997 Bureau of the Census report, a sizable portion of Latinos live below the poverty level—26.4 percent in 1996—with those of Cuban descent the most affluent of the major groups, and Puerto Ricans the least economically advantaged.

LATINO MUSIC

Latino music in the United States today reflects many of the historical and contemporary trends that we've already mentioned. Regional traditions persist in the Lower Rio Grande Valley and in New Mexico, areas with greater connection to rural life. A high degree of musical continuity exists between certain Latin American nations of origin and their North American counterparts. This has resulted from massive immigration within recent generations, ongoing ties with nations located only hours away by air travel, and the renewal of national identities in urban areas by continued immigration. Close continuity is particularly the case with more commercially successful musical styles, and less so for music with little footing in the popular media. Musical styles identified with a particular ethnic group, especially those popularly thought of as *"música folklórica,"* that is, representative of "old ways," often take on an added dimension of symbolic importance, as cultural minorities employ them as a vehicle to fortify their solidarity and as an emblem to represent themselves to the broader, pluralistic society.

Música folklórica
Folk or traditional musical forms identified with a particular Latino ethnic group

In urban settings, proximity to North American social dance music and jazz, economic opportunities for professional musicians, and a powerful media industry that amplified the voice of commercially successful popular music offered fertile ground for musical innovation. In New York, Caribbean musicians from Puerto Rico, Cuba, and elsewhere parlayed the vogue of Cuban and pseudo-Cuban dance music in the 1930s through 1950s into a niche in the

North American panorama of popular music. Some of these musicians joined Duke Ellington and other leading big bands, adding a vein of Latin Caribbean rhythm to the mix. Tito Puente (and other Latino bandleaders), drawing from both popular non-Latin dance music and Caribbean rhythms, took the lead in creating Latin dance music and Latin jazz with broad appeal.

In the 1930s through the 1950s, Tejano orchestras imitated or incorporated elements of nationally popular swing bands, eventually leading to the emergence of a unique regional popular music style. Los Angeles Chicano musicians, such as the group Los Lobos, drew from African American rhythm and blues in forging a new sound. Gloria Estefan headlined a nationally prominent Cuban-tinged popular musical style. Latino music has made great headway in making its presence known on the national stage. In 2000, for example, the National Academy of Recording Arts and Sciences specifically designated seven of the ninety-eight categories of the Grammy Awards for "Latin" music: Latin Pop Performance; Latin Rock/Alternative Performance; Traditional Tropical Latin Performance; Salsa Performance; Merengue Performance; Mexican American Performance; and Tejano Performance. In addition, that same year, Carlos Santana and Christina Aguilera garnered numerous other major Grammy awards, and a separate Latin Grammys event was inaugurated.

Mexican American Music

Mexican American music includes two major strands:

1. Musics of Mexican origin that are practiced in the United States, including regional traditions of Mexican *Mestizo* folk music, folk-rooted popular Mexican musics, and
2. Internationally popular urban musics created by communities historically associated with Mexico, including regional musical cultures from New Mexico (predating the existence of the Republic of Mexico but strongly influenced by Mexican music), the Lower Rio Grande Valley, and California, as well as hybrid creations spawned by urban life.

The musics most long lived in the United States are those of the Nuevo-Mexicano and Tejano regional groups. *Californios* also developed a regional musical culture, although it has all but faded in the face of intense acculturation and overwhelming immigration from other musical regions in Mexico. More recent Mexican American music creations include the rock and roll originals of Los Lobos and the recordings of the late Tejana vocalist Selena.

Contexts for Musical Performance

While musical distinctions reflect the broader cultural differences among Mexican American subgroups, certain unifying features are shared broadly. Baptisms, birthdays, *quinceañeras* (celebrations for 15-year-old girls), and weddings are universally preferred life-cycle events for music making. *Cinco de Mayo*, commemorating the Battle of Puebla in the 1860s Mexican struggle against the occupying French imperialist forces, emerged as the major annual celebration of Chicano identity, marked by performances of music and dance. Mexican Independence Day on September 16 is of similar importance, especially in communities with more recent roots in the Republic of Mexico. Mother's Day is another day for celebrations accompanied by music.

The Roman Catholic feast day of the Virgin of Guadalupe on December 12 is widely celebrated with a common repertoire of hymns and other songs sung by the congregation and, when possible, live mariachi music performing a post-Vatican Council II version of certain Mass segments, known collectively as the *Misa Panamericana*. Social dances and concerts by touring Mexican superstar vocalists such as Vicente Fernández and Juan Gabriel attract Mexican Americans of all backgrounds.

The custom of the *serenata*—a short serenade to celebrate a birthday, Mother's Day, or a man's devotion to his beloved—also continues to be practiced in the North American context. The Mexican song "Las Mañanitas," sung especially on birthdays, is known widely among Mexican Americans as well as among other Latinos.

The Mexican farmworker movement in the 1960s and 1970s occasioned the performance of *corridos* that recounted strikes, praised leader César Chávez, and aimed to reinforce general commitment to the movement (Figure 8.1). Sparked by the Civil Rights movement beginning in the 1960s, the Chicano movement also inspired greater interest in Mexican roots music as an important cultural symbol. New musical compositions treating important Chicano leaders and events and calling for greater cultural pride came out of the Chicano movement as well.

Styles and Ensembles

Certain popular folk-rooted musical styles are found throughout the United States. *Mariachi* ensembles, typically made up of two trumpets, two or more violins, *guitarrón*, *vihuela*, and six-stringed guitar, arose from regional roots in nineteenth-century west Mexico to become a twentieth-century pan-Mexican musical symbol. It is the principal ensemble for performing *música ranchera*, popular songs often treating matters of unrequited love that evoke sentiment and appeal to pan-Mexican tastes. Songs such as "El Rey" ("The King") and "Volver, Volver" ("Return, Return"), composed and recorded by

Quinceañera
Literally "15-year-old"; coming of age celebration for young girls in Latino cultures

Cinco de Mayo
Literally, "the Fifth of May"; commemorates the Battle of Puebla in the 1860s Mexican struggle against the occupying French imperialist forces

Serenata
A short serenade to celebrate a birthday, Mother's Day, or a man's devotion to his beloved

Corrido
A narrative ballad

Mariachi
Mexican-styled ensemble typically featuring trumpets and stringed instruments (violin, guitar, Mexican guitar-variants)

Guitarrón
Six-stringed,
round-backed
bass
Vihuela
Five-stringed,
round-backed
guitar
Música ranchera
Country music

the late singer/songwriter José Alfredo Jiménez, are staples of the mariachi repertoire and are known by virtually all Mexican Americans. The mariachi is also sought out to perform the Catholic Mass, particularly to celebrate the feast of the Virgin of Guadalupe. The mariachi is also widely known among non-Mexicans in the United States. Mariachi groups are frequently employed to appear at Mexican restaurants, "Mexican theme" events, and celebrations of cultural diversity. Generally speaking, mariachi groups are mobile, musically versatile, professional musical ensembles that are capable of performing a wide range of repertoire, including many non-Mexican songs.

"Los Arrieros" ("The Muleteer"; Musical Example 8.1) is a well-known Mexican song, performed by Nati Cano and his Mariachi Los Camperos, a group based in the Los Angeles area, where mariachi music is especially popular. Notice how the strings and accordion play the accompaniment using the technique of rapidly repeating chords that give life to this performance of an old folk tune.

Conjunto
Mexican popular
ensembles,
usually led by a
button-
accordion player,
normally
performing
dance music and
corridos

The second important style, the accordion-driven *conjunto*, has migrated along with transient Mexican workers to all regions of the United States. These groups may be either of Mexican or Tejano origin. Mexican immigrant *conjuntos* of two or three musicians playing the Hohner or Gabinelli button accordion, the twelve-stringed *bajo sexto,* and, if available, the upright three-stringed *tololoche* are more common outside Texas, reflecting the large number and wide geographic dispersal of Mexican immigrant workers. Amplified *conjuntos* with drum set often provide instrumental music such as Tejano or Mexican polkas for social dances, especially in Texas. Up-tempo, duple-meter songs such as *corridos* on current themes such as *narco-*

traficantes have gained enormous currency, however. The U.S.-based group Los Tigres del Norte (The Tigers of the North) are emblematic of this style of song. Unamplified *conjunto* duos or trios commonly perform for special events in homes, migrant camps, and bars, charging their clients hourly or by the song (see Snapshot 8.1).

Snapshot 8.1: Conjunto Music

The first genre to appear as an independent and identifiable type among Tejanos came to be called *conjunto*. In standard Spanish, the word *conjunto* means "group." In most Spanish-speaking areas of the world it refers to any type of musical group or combo. But in Texas and northern Mexico the term has come to refer to a group in which the accordion plays the lead and the *bajo sexto*, bass, and drums play background and rhythm. This combination of instruments is one that evolved over a period of about a century. Furthermore, the Texas *conjunto* and the northern Mexican *conjunto* (called *conjunto norteño*) have had slightly different histories and characteristics.

The exact origins of *conjunto* music are impossible to determine because it is a folk music and, as such, was not notated; rather, it was and continues to be learned by ear. Perhaps more important is the fact that for many years both the *conjunto norteño* and Texas *conjunto* were considered to be unworthy of formal study or propagation as important cultural forms in their respective countries. In Mexico, for example, the *conjunto norteño* was eclipsed long ago by the mariachi and other regional forms considered to be more representative of Mexican national identity. In Texas, *conjunto* music similarly had been a source of embarrassment to many Chicanos in the mid-twentieth century, especially to those in the emerging middle class eager to disassociate themselves from their Mexican roots and become Americanized. In recent decades, however, interest in all aspects of *conjunto* music has proliferated, and it has enjoyed a great resurgence in popularity among Chicanos as well as among non-Chicanos.

Listen to Musical Example 8.2, "Asi se Baila en Tejas" ("This Is the Way They Dance in Texas"), performed here by Tony de la Rosa, who came to epitomize the second generation of conjunto accordionists. During the 1950s, la Rosa incorporated drum set, electric bass, and amplified bajo sexto into the traditional conjunto ensemble, thus modernizing its style.

In general, this growing interest was due to the larger social, political, and cultural Chicano movement of the 1960s and 1970s, the period to which some scholars refer as the Chicano Renaissance. Entrepreneurs in the Tejano music industry, for example, began to be more conscious of the role of cultural pride in

Bajo sexto
Large guitar-like instrument with six double courses of strings
Tololoche
Three-stringed bass
Narcotraficantes
Drug smugglers; songs associated with their exploits are known as *narcocorridos*

promoting and marketing *conjunto* music. For their part, a new generation of Tejano scholars initiated more formal, scholarly study of Tejano music. Joined by other ethnomusicologists, they have contributed a great deal toward our understanding about its origins and evolution from the nineteenth century to the present.

The beginnings of *conjunto* music can be traced to the arrival in South Texas and Northern Mexico of the accordion. Invented in 1829 by Cyrillys Damian in Vienna, the accordion probably arrived in Texas and Northern Mexico in the mid-nineteenth century. Evidently it was introduced by German immigrants who came to South Texas and Northern Mexico. They also brought the schottische, waltz, polka, and mazurka—all musical and dance forms historically identified with *conjunto* music. Whether *conjunto* music originated in Mexico and expanded into Texas or was created by Texas Mexicans and spread south into Mexico, however, remains a topic of interest. The most plausible *conjunto*-origin theory is that Germans and their music arrived in the Rio Grande Valley (on both sides of the river) in the mid-nineteenth century, after which different traditions emerged on either side of the border.

In the late nineteenth and early twentieth centuries, Tejanos used a number of instrumental combinations, large and small. Perhaps the most popular type was the *banda típica,* which consisted of perhaps eight members, usually local musicians who came together to play for Saturday dances or special occasions such as weddings and *quinceañera* dances. Also, because electricity was not readily available for nighttime illumination, dances were usually afternoon affairs (called *tardeadas*). They were also usually held outdoors, often in wooded areas, where large dance floors (*plataformas*) were erected. Without inventions such as the microphone, electric instruments, and amplifiers, these relatively large "brass bands" were the most appropriate.

There also were smaller gatherings and venues that afforded opportunities for smaller combos. Although a violin and *bajo sexto* combo was popular until the early twentieth century, the accordion evidently replaced the violin and paired up with the *bajo sexto* to form the nucleus of the modern *conjunto*. Acoustics evidently played a part in the emergence of this combo as well. Of the various venues, it was no doubt the *cantina*, ubiquitous in both rural and urban areas, that afforded the accordion and *bajo sexto,* two relatively quiet instruments, the perfect opportunity to coalesce and thrive as a duo.

Completing the instrumentation of the modern *conjunto* were the trap set and the electric bass. The trap set, with its snare drum, bass drum, and cymbal, probably borrowed from the Tejano swing bands of the 1940s, was also added to *conjuntos* during that decade. The electric bass, invented in the 1950s, became

Banda típica
Tejano brass band, usually featuring eight pieces
Tardeada
Dance party held in the afternoon
Plataforma
Large wooden dance floor erected for outdoor parties
Cantina
Honky tonk; bar

the last of the instruments to be added permanently to the ensemble. Prior to the 1940s, accordion and *bajo sexto* duos on occasion would add the upright bass and a *tambora* (a locally made bass drum) to the ensemble.

Conjunto Instruments

Although accordions with piano keyboards were invented soon after the button accordion, folk musicians in Texas (and Mexico) always have preferred the button model, particularly the Vienna- or German-style button accordion. The earliest of these had a single row of ten treble buttons on the right side, on which only one scale could be played in three octaves, and two bass spoon keys on the left. In Texas *conjunto* music, accordionists do not use the bass keys. Instead, the bass line, played by the *bajo sexto* until the 1940s, is now played by the electric bass.

In the late 1920s, a larger, 21-button, double-row model, also manufactured in Germany, was incorporated into Texas Mexican and Northern Mexican *conjunto* music. That model was used until the introduction of the triple-row, 31-button model in the 1940s. Since the mid-1940s, the typical Texas *conjunto* accordion has been the Hohner Corona II model (Figure 8.2) a triple-row, 31-treble-button instrument, although the Italian-made Gabbanelli is also popular. Each button on these accordions plays two notes: one when the bellows are opened, and another when they are closed.

Trap set
Partial drum set, usually including a snare and bass drum and cymbal
Tambora
Bass drum

Figure 8.2
Hohner Corona II button accordion. Standard instrument featured with Texas *conjuntos* since the 1930s. Thirty-one treble buttons on right side; twelve bass buttons on left. Tejano accordionists now play treble board only. Photo by Mary Cavazos-Reyna, February 2000.

Each row of buttons plays only one scale (in three octaves). A three-row instrument, for example, is built to play in three keys. Although accidentals in one key may be found on one of the other two rows, the fingering may be too awkward to reach them. In order to play in a wider variety of keys, professional accordionists must use more than one instrument, with additional keys included. Tonal variety may be achieved by using accordions such as the Gabbanelli, which come equipped with tonal switches. Additional qualities may be added by changing the reeds in any given accordion, by using pickups, or by hooking the instrument up to electronic equipment.

As a lead instrument, the accordion is used not only for the melody line in instrumental pieces such as polkas, but also for introductions, background obbligato, and interludes or solos, especially as accompaniment to singing. Early recordings dating to the 1930s indicate that the typical accordionist of that era relied principally on a simple melody line, which resulted in a very lively sound in faster tempos. By the 1940s, even the average accordionist had mastered two- and three-line harmonies, which contributed to a fuller, more mature sound.

Although in recent decades large chromatic button accordions have been used by a few accordionists, most Tejano accordionists have continued employing the double-row instrument. Innovation has consisted primarily of refinement of traditional introductions and passages and reflects greater mastery of the instrument. A number of riffs are firmly established in the traditional accordion repertoire, that is, they are often "quoted" by modern accordionists and recognized by the public.

Since at least the early part of the twentieth century, the standard guitar used in *conjuntos* has been the *bajo sexto* (Figure 8.3), a twelve-string Mexican guitar almost completely unknown to American musicians. The *bajo*, as it is commonly called, has steel strings and a deeper, more resonant sound than the classical guitar. It also differs from the American twelve-string guitar in the type and size of strings it requires, as well as in the way in which they are arranged and tuned. Pickups used for amplification have enhanced the sound quality as well as technique.

For many years the function of the *bajo* was to provide both a bass line (with the three lower-register string sets) and strummed rhythmic chordal pulses (with the upper-register string sets). When playing waltzes, for instance, the bass would be played on beat one, and the chord accompaniment on beats two and three. On duple-metered pieces such as polkas, it would be bass on one, chord on two. Since the introduction of the electric bass, however, *bajo* lower-register string sets (especially the fifth and sixth) have been rendered practically obsolete. Because the accordion is the lead

Figure 8.3
The *Bajo Sexto* is a twelve-string Mexican guitar used for rhythm and chord accompaniment in Texas *conjunto* music. The bridge (often in the shape of longhorn steer horns) is much larger than on classical guitars. The instrument in this photo (with the thin A or fourth string removed) was hand-crafted in Texas. Photo by Mary Cavazos-Reyna, February 2000.

instrument in *conjuntos,* the *bajo* is rarely foregrounded, although many consider the *bajo* to be the heart of the *conjunto.* Many *bajistas* use a *bajo quinto,* a ten-string *bajo* with five string pairs. It is tuned the same as the *bajo sexto,* without the sixth (lowest pitched) course of strings.

The function of the electric bass is to play the bass line of the accompaniment as well as to provide the beat (on one in $\frac{2}{4}$ or $\frac{3}{4}$ time; on one and four in $\frac{6}{8}$ time; and on one, three, and four in four-beat Latin rhythms such as that underlying the slow *bolero*). An interesting note is that there is no "walking bass" in Tejano music. In fact, the acoustic string bass, with which this style was once associated, is rarely included in contemporary Tejano groups.

The drums, which consist of the same type of trap set used in Anglo American dance bands, became an integral part of Texas *conjuntos* in the 1940s. The style of the drumming itself has evolved from those earlier days, when the bass drum would be pounded loudly on the downbeat, the snare drum struck on the offbeat, and the cymbal hit occasionally, to one in which the bass drum is used

Bajista
Player of the bajo sexton or bajo quinto
Bajo quinto
A ten-string version of the bajo sexton featuring five string pairs

sparingly and muffled, and the snare drum and cymbal are tapped much more lightly.

Modernization of Conjunto

In addition to the incorporation of modern accordions and the addition of the trap set and bass, there have been other important developments in Texas *conjunto* music since the 1950s. In the 1950s, for example, amplification of the *bajo,* bass, and accordion became standard. Another very important development during the 1940s and 1950s was the virtual disappearance of the schottische, Bohemian *redowa,* waltz, and mazurka from the *conjunto* repertoire, although they had been identified with *conjunto* music in Texas for a century. Although *conjunto* accordionists continue to learn these forms as part of their apprenticeship, they are nearly extinct. In fact, even the polka, which continued as a staple in *conjunto* music into the 1960s, is rarely found in recordings from more recent decades, a sign perhaps of its impending demise.

Perhaps the most noteworthy characteristic of *conjuntos* since the 1960s is that the musicians have attained a remarkable degree of proficiency, stylization, and prestige, all of which merit much more attention. While the degree of professionalism, as well as the impact of the recording industry and of broadcasting, reflects an increasing defolklorization of the *conjunto,* the standard ensemble is firmly established as a major genre of Tejano music tradition.

The Tejano Music Industry

A very important part of the success of Tejano music was the emergence, in the 1940s, of a very viable Tejano recording industry in south Texas. Major labels include Bego, Buena Suerte, Freddie, Gaviota, Hacienda, and Ideal. Radio also played an important part in the promotion of Tejano music, which for many years was overshadowed by Mexican music. In recognition of the importance of Tejano music in Texas Chicano culture, the Texas Talent Musicians' Association established the Tejano Music Awards in 1981, with an awards ceremony held every year at the Alamodrome in San Antonio. Performers are nominated in categories similar to those of the Grammy Awards, the Country Music Awards, and the People's Choice Awards.

José R. Reyna

Banda
Brass band
Charcheta
Tenor horn

Other Mexican Folk Musics

Other Mexican regional folk music styles are also present in the United States. The *banda,* with trumpets, trombones, clarinets or saxophones, *charcheta,* sousaphone, bass drum, and snare drum, originated in the states of Sinaloa and Zacatecas, routinely perform in nightclubs and rodeos in California and tour to larger Mexican communities throughout the United States. In the 1990s, the popular media propelled a modified version of the *banda* to enormous popularity in Mexico and among many Mexican Americans. A musical style of rural Michoacán in west Mexico followed *Michoacano* migrants northward to Redwood City, California, Yakima, Washington, and other places where large numbers of *Michoacanos* settled (Figure 8.4). Utilizing a large diatonic harp, one or two violins, *vihuela,* and *jarana,* these groups play fast-paced *sones, canciones rancheras, corridos,* and other pieces appealing to the Michoacán immigrants.

Many Mexican *marimba* ensembles, traditionally identified with the southern Mexican states of Oaxaca and Chiapas but found throughout Mexico, are based in Los Angeles, Houston, and other U.S. cities. Immigrant musicians play the rapid-rhythm *son jarocho* from Veracruz on *arpa,* a "thirty-four-stringed diatonic harp," a regional variant of the *jarana,* featuring eight strings rather than the standard five, and *requinto jarocho.* Many Chicanos, looking to Mexican roots music as a vehicle of cultural/social expression and creativity, have become accomplished performers. The Herrera family of Oxnard, California, and their group, Conjunto Hueyapan, perform the *son jarocho.* Artemio Posadas, a native of the Huastecan region in northeast Mexico and a resident of San Jose, California, and his Chicano disciples perform the *son huasteco* (Figure 8.5).

Figure 8.4
Michoacán ensemble "Los Campesinos de Michoacán," led by Salvador Baldovinos *(far right),* plays in a restaurant in Yakima, Washington. Instrumentation is two violins, *vihuela,* six-stringed guitar and *arpa grande* "big harp." Photo by Daniel Sheehy, October 1992.

Michoacano
A person from the rural, west Mexican province of Michoacán

Jarana
Deep-bodied, five-stringed rhythm guitar

Marimba
Wooden-keyed xylophone played by several musicians, featuring box-shaped resonators under each key

Son jarocho
Rapid dance music from southern, coastal Mexico centering in Veracruz

Arpa
Thirty-four-stringed diatonic harp

Requinto jarocho
Four-stringed melody guitar plucked with a long plastic or bone pick

Son huasteco
Dance music from the Huastecan region in northeast Mexico

Figure 8.5
Artemio Posadas *(left)* of San Jose, California, plays the *son huasteco* on the violin with the accompaniment of an unidentified *jarana huasteca* player *(center)* and *huapanguera* player Russell Rodríguez *(right)*. Photo by Daniel Sheehy, August 1993.

Several of the regional Mexican mestizo musics, along with the mariachi, might also accompany the plethora of Mexican folkloric dance companies found in Mexican American communities throughout the United States.

Three significant North American trends in mariachi music transcend differences found among the various regional styles:

1. Large-scale mariachi festivals
2. School mariachi programs
3. Dinner nightclubs that featured stage-oriented mariachi shows

Large-scale mariachi festivals began in 1979 with the first San Antonio International Mariachi Conference organized by Belle and Juan Ortiz. These festivals built upon two other trends that began in the late 1960s. One was the emergence of school programs of mariachi instruction and performance in a few schools in California, Arizona, and Texas. The other was pioneered in Los Angeles by bandleader Natividad Cano and his Mariachi Los Camperos, who "established the first night club where mariachi music was presented on stage as a dinner show, reaching a new audience of highly assimilated, middle-class, urban immigrants and their offspring" (Fogelquist 1996:20). The San Antonio event combined instruction of youth by master musicians with concerts by Mexico's premier group, Mariachi Vargas de Tecalitlán, and subsequently by leading U.S.-based groups as well. This combination provided a model that was imitated widely by festivals in Tucson, Arizona, Fresno and San Jose, California, Albuquerque and Las Cruces, New Mexico,

Wenatchee, Washington, and elsewhere. By the 1990s, more than 15 of these festivals were scattered throughout the Southwest.

By the late 1990s, hundreds of school mariachi programs existed in Texas, New Mexico, Arizona, Colorado, California, Washington, and Illinois, as well as numerous dinner nightclubs that featured stage-oriented mariachi shows. Following her appearance at the Tucson festival, pop music singer Linda Ronstadt, a Tucson native of Mexican American background, launched a national tour and recording, both entitled *Canciones de Mi Padre* ("Songs of My Father") in the late 1980s. The tour and recording were highly influential in spurring greater interest in mariachi music, especially among young Mexican Americans and in highlighting the music as a focal point for Mexican American cultural/social identity.

Puerto Rican Music

The ceding of Puerto Rico to the United States at the conclusion of the Spanish American war in 1898 began two processes that lasted throughout the twentieth century, especially following the end of World War I in 1918. First, the North American popular music industry, radio, and cinema bombarded the island with current musical vogues. Second, the northward flow to the United States—to New York City in particular—of Puerto Rican professional musicians familiar with these popular styles brought Puerto Rican musical influences to the American musical landscape. Internal economic shifts following the American takeover of the island displaced many workers, including musicians, and the hardships of the Great Depression accelerated the movement of musicians to New York, the hub of the entertainment industry. At the same time, the versatility gained by Puerto Rican musicians through exposure to both Latin and North American musics worked to their advantage.

These events contributed to the prominent place of Puerto Rican musicians in the evolution of New York's musical life and the popular Latin musics it would spawn, especially Latin-Caribbean dance music. The multifaceted musical literacy of Puerto Rican musicians only increased as immigrants and their descendants became integrated into North American cultural life, borrowing from and contributing to important veins of popular music such as jazz and rock and roll. The late Tito Puente, who made over 100 record albums and won many Grammy Awards, was the most prominent example of Puerto Rican centrality to both Cuban-derived popular Latin dance music and Latin jazz. Puerto Ricans such as singer/guitarist José Feliciano and Metropolitan Opera singer Martina Arroyo also achieved national and international prominence.

Several popular forms of Puerto Rican traditional music are actively performed in the United States. The two principal strains of

Figure 8.6
An informal group of Puerto Rican *pleneros* playing different sizes of *pandereta* (round frame drum) performs in a procession in Manhattan for a cultural festival. Photo by Daniel Sheehy, June 1979.

Música jíbara
Puetro Rican folk music style centering on the dance form called the *seis*
Cuatro guitar
A guitar with ten-steel strings; *cuatrista:* cuatro player
Güiro
Gourd scraper
Conjunto jíbaro
Jíbaro ensemble
Aguinaldo
The Puerto Rican Christmastide custom of singing from house to house, asking for small gifts of money or food
Bomba
African-influenced Puerto Rican dance music with multilayered, interlocking rhythmic patterns, performed by a two-headed barrel drum

popular Puerto Rican folk music—*música jíbara* and the more African-derived genres of *bomba* and *plena* (Figure 8.6)—have long been performed in the United States and enjoyed a revival in the 1990s. *Música jíbara* centers on the music and dance form called *seis* and on the ensemble based on the ten-steel-stringed *cuatro* guitar, the six-stringed "standard" Spanish guitar, and the *güiro*. Puerto Rican *cuatrista* Estanislao "Ladí" Martinez was influential in the formation of the modern *conjunto jíbaro*, especially in the 1930s and after. He increased the music's popularity by incorporating a wide range of musical genres into the *cuatro* repertoire and including more instruments: two *cuatros,* bongo drums, and even bass and conga drum in the ensemble. Ladí was closely linked to Puerto Rican musical life in New York City through touring and recordings.

In the 1990s, several *jíbaro*-style ensembles, numerous individual musicians, and a few *jíbaro* instrument makers were active in the United States, especially in larger cities of the Midwest and Northeast such as Chicago, New York, and Hartford, Connecticut. *Cuatrista* Yomo Toro's performances of traditional *seis,* Latin dance music, and Latin jazz gained him significant renown. As in Puerto Rico, *música jíbara* and the musical genre *aguinaldo* are most favored during Christmas season. The music is often associated with an idealized rustic past and the Christmastide custom of singing from house to house, asking for small gifts of money or food, the *aguinaldo*. *Aguinaldo* texts, often improvised, refer to Christmas themes and ask the listener for the *aguinaldo*.

In the 1990s, the number of U.S.-based groups playing *bomba* and *plena* increased several-fold, in great measure the result of the efforts by the group Los Pleneros de la 21 to reestablish the music's prominence in the United States. Led by musician/teacher/bandleader Juan Gutiérrez, the Pleneros elevated the prestige of *bomba* and *plena* music in the United States through innovative instrumentation, frequent performances in the Northeast and upper Midwest, educational presentations, and emphasizing the music's importance to Puerto Rican heritage. To the multilayered interlocking rhythmic core of the *plena*'s three *panderetas* and the *bomba*'s two single-headed barrel drums, the Pleneros added electrified bass, melody instruments such as piano and the *cuatro*, and additional percussion. Many other groups in the region emerged, modeled in various degrees after Los Pleneros de la 21. The popularity of *bomba* also was reinforced by periodic performances by *bomba* groups from Puerto Rico such as those of the Cepeda and Ayala families.

Plena
African-influenced Puerto Rican dance music with multilayered, interlocking rhythmic patterns, performed by the *pandereta*

Pandereta
Round frame drum used in *plena* music

Central American Music

Immigration from Central America increased dramatically in the 1970s, as civil strife drove refugees northward. Large numbers of Salvadorans, Guatemalans, and Nicaraguans established highly visible communities in major cities such as Los Angeles, Houston, Miami, Washington, and New York, bringing with them their regional dialects of Spanish, regional foods such as the Salvadoran *pupusa* (a thick tortilla filled with cheese or meat), and musical tastes. Prior to this time, Panamanians, Costa Ricans, and Hondurans constituted a much larger proportion of Central Americans in the United States. Music in these countries had long been influenced by foreign musics from Mexico, the Caribbean, and the United States disseminated by commercial media. By comparison, Central American countries had fewer means of producing and distributing local music than Mexico, the United States, or other countries. At times, this onslaught of foreign music was a cause for governmental concern, occasionally prompting mandatory broadcasting of domestic music by radio stations. The making and consumption of music by Central Americans in North America reflects both the long-standing acceptance of music from other nations and identification with certain national musical icons.

Perhaps the singlemost distinctive and widely visible Central American musical symbol is the marimba, the Guatemalan marimba in particular (Figure 8.7). The Guatemalan marimba, with minor exceptions, is similar in appearance to the Mexican marimba. Several octaves of tuned wooden slabs, mounted on a frame and resembling a piano keyboard, are played with rubber-tipped mallets by two or more musicians. Below each slab is a wooden box resonator equipped with a vibrating membrane mounted over a small hole, creating a distinctive buzzing sound as the instrument is played. The marimba might be played alone or as the centerpiece of a larger ensemble with electrified bass, percussion, or melody instruments such as saxophone, and singing. Guatemalan marimba groups are

Figure 8.7
Guatemalan marimba group with Jerónimo Camposeco and unidentified musicians resident in the United States rehearses offstage at the Smithsonian Folklife Festival. Photo by Daniel Sheehy, June 1985.

Música tropical
Pan-national, Caribbean-influenced dance music
Cumbia
Livley dance music in duple rhythm developed in Panama and Colombia
Merengue
Lively dance music in duple rhythm, native to the Dominican Republic
Salsa
Literally "sauce"; Afro-Cuban style based on the Cuban *son* that today fuses elements of R&B, jazz, and rock

based in southern California, southern Florida, the mid-Atlantic region, and elsewhere.

Most scholars point to an African origin of the marimba. Slaves imported during colonial times purportedly reconstructed the instruments of their homelands in the New World context, and the word *marimba* has close linguistic cognates in certain regions of Africa. In general, however, Guatemalans and other Central Americans identify the marimba most closely with *mestizo* or American Indian heritage. While other Central American nations are home to marimba ensembles, and while the marimba of Nicaragua's Masaya province is associated with that nation's collective identity, the Guatemalan marimba tradition is most common in the United States.

Pan-national, Caribbean-influenced dance music, often referred to as *música tropical,* maintains an important place among immigrant Central Americans. Under this general rubric, the Panamanian/Colombian-derived *cumbia,* the Dominican-origin *merengue,* and Cuban/Puerto Rican-driven *salsa* music are all staples of their musical life. While this music reaches across borders of national identity, touring bands from individual countries and North American-based groups with names identifying their country of origin attract followings from those communities.

Increasingly in the United States, non-Mexican musicians—Guatemalan and Salvadoran immigrants in particular—have joined the ranks of Mexican professional mariachi musicians. Since the 1930s, Central Americans' exposure to mariachi music through cinema, recordings, and powerful radio stations stimulated their appreciation, consumption, and performance of the music. Many Central Americans, already skilled in performing mariachi music in their homelands, found relatively lucrative employment as mariachi musicians in the United States. Some mariachi ensembles are comprised entirely of Central Americans.

Cuban Music

In addition to Caribbean-derived music, other Cuban musical traditions are also practiced in the United States. In the Cuban community around Miami that resulted from the first wave of refugees (primarily of European background) from Castro-run Cuba, a few musicians continue the rural folk tradition of the *punto guajiro*, singing often improvised poetic texts to the accompaniment of stringed instruments led by the six-stringed *tres*. The *son* is another important genre of this musical style. Practiced much more widely is music of Afro-Cuban origin, predating, but arriving principally in the wake of, the Mariel boatlift of 1980. Several Afro-Cuban religious musical traditions reflect the distinctive strains of African-derived identity in Afro-Cuban culture. Most prominent is the Yoruba-derived *lucumí* tradition popularly known as *santería*. (See also Chapter 4.) Central to the music of *santería* are the three double-conical, two-headed drums of the *batá* ensemble. *Oru* ("songs") sung in the Yoruba-based *lucumí* language praise African deities such as Changó, Ogún, and Obatalá.

Many accomplished musicians and religious leaders in these traditions are based in large cities, particularly in New York, the mid-Atlantic region, southern Florida, and California. A few of these musicians, Francisco Aguabella for example, have been active in the United States since before the Castro era. Some, like Aguabella, who performed with popular Afro-Cuban musician Mongo Santamaría, have been very active in mainstream Latin popular music as well. Others, such as musician/instrument maker Felipe García Villamil, who arrived among the Mariel refugees, have devoted themselves mainly to religious activities. Afro-Cuban religion, ceremony, and music have attracted a growing number of devotees, including participants from outside the Cuban community.

Other than the Cuban-derived music at the core of the diverse, Caribbean-origin popular dance music collectively known as *salsa* from the 1970s forward, the rumba is most central to secular Afro-Cuban music. The rumba emerged in Cuba around the turn of the twentieth century and provided much of the rhythmic grounding for popular dance music that followed. A typical rumba ensemble

Punto guajiro
Cuban, rural folk tradition, consisting of singers who improvise poetic texts accompanied by string-instruments

Tres
Six-string Cuban guitar

Son
Cuban strophnic song with interludes of instrumental improvisation

Santería
Yoruba-derived religious and cultural traditions, representing an Afro-Cuban synthesis

Batá ensemble
Rhythmic ensemble that accompanies Santeria music, consisting of three, double-conical, two-headed drums

Oru
Cuban songs of praise sung in the Yruba-based lucumi language

Rumba
Cuban couple
dance featuring a
distinctive
syncopated
rhythm
Tumbadora
Conga drum
Claves
Two short
resonant sticks
struck together
Cajita musical
guagua
A mounted
hollow wood
block played
with two sticks
Comparsa
Afro-Cuban
percussive
professional
music used in
carnival and other
festivities

might comprise three *tumbadoras*, one of them being the smaller lead *quinto;* the *claves*; and the *cajita musical*, also known as *guagua*. Principal types of rumba are the *guaguancó* and the *columbia*. Rumba music has attracted many other Latinos and non-Latinos as well. In recent decades, instruments and rhythms have been borrowed from the sacred repertoire and incorporated into secular Cuban music. One example is the *batá-rumba*, an amalgam of sacred and secular rhythms and instruments. Carnival music of the *comparsa* is another important secular form of Afro-Cuban music.

In Snapshot 8.2, we take a closer look at some Cuban and Afro-Cuban popular music forms that entered the United States in the mid-twentieth century and forever changed American popular music. Predominantly dance genres, these forms did much to promote the growth and development of big bands and the elaborate dance halls that provided the context for new social and musical interactions to take place.

Snapshot 8.2: Afro-Cuban Popular Musics

Although Cuban influence in New Orleans can be clearly traced back to the 1880s, when the *habanera* first became popular, Cuba's more subtle impact—as heard in *tresillo, cinquillo,* and *clave* patterns, which were embedded in rhythmic and melodic ideas—is much older. This should be expected, for New Orleans was controlled by the Spanish for two generations before the Louisiana Purchase of 1803, and movement between the city and Cuba was commonplace. Ferdinand "Jelly Roll" Morton noted that a "Spanish tinge" was necessary for good jazz. W. C. Handy traveled with his band to Cuba in 1900, where he heard numerous street bands.

Specifically traceable Cuban elements in African American forms, such as jazz, however, go back to Afro-Cuban flutist Alberto Socarras (who came to New York in 1927) and Machito and his Afro-Cubans. Machito's orchestra, which was formed in 1940, combined traditional Cuban elements with jazz. Its rhythm section in the early years was made up of piano, bass, bongo, and *timbale,* played by the young Tito Puente. In 1943, the same year that Mario Bauza wrote "Tanga," conga player Carlos Vidal joined the group.

Afro-Cuban jazz gained a much larger audience in 1946 when Dizzy Gillespie, who had worked alongside Bauza when both were members of the Cab Calloway Orchestra, began a brief collaboration with Cuban drummer, *rumbero,* and Arará initiate Chano Pozo. Although Gillespie and Pozo worked together for just over two years before Pozo's untimely death, Pozo's introduction of the conga drum and the complex Afro-Cuban rhythms associated with it brought a new rhythmic energy to jazz and opened the door for the conga drum to be used in this and other non-Latin styles. Also

Timbale
Metal-shelled,
single-headed
Cuban drum

influenced by the Gillespie-Pozo collaboration and the Machito sound was Stan Kenton, the West Coast pianist-arranger and big band leader, who used some of Machito's percussionists in his 1948 recording of "The Peanut Vendor" and later went on to record Johnny Richards's 1956 work *Cuban Fire Suite* as well as other Latin-influenced arrangements.

Other contributors to Afro-Cuban jazz included Detroit native Les Baxter, who produced a number of LPs for Capitol in the 1940s and 1950s, and the London-born pianist George Shearing, who was strongly influenced by the 1948 Machito orchestra and went on to work with Cuban percussionists Willie Bobo, Armando Peraza, and Mongo Santamaría. Also influenced by Machito was vibist Cal Tjader, who worked with Shearing and eventually recorded some eighty LPs for various labels.

Dance Forms

Rumba, which came to North America by the 1950s, is a noncommercial secular street dance and music style that emerged from the *cabildos* (mutual aid and religious societies) in lower-class black communities of late nineteenth-century Cuba. Primarily a folkloric music today, rumba acts as a powerful social marker supporting traditional Afro-Cuban values and solidarity. Although some Cuban rumba ensembles—such as Los Muñequitos de Matanzas and Los Papines—remain popular, North American rumba, except for folkloric performances, is mostly heard in informal settings within the Latino neighborhoods and parks of large metropolitan areas (Figure 8.8).

While older rumba forms such as the *yuka* or *makuta* may be performed by folkloric ensembles, the most common styles are *yambú, columbia,* and, especially, *guaguanco.* Rumba is generally played on conga drums or, occasionally, wooden boxes called *cajones. Claves* give a timeline that is embellished by a denser rhythm called *cascara.* This rhythm is played with sticks *(palitos)* on a woodblock or bamboo tube (*gua-gua*; Figure 8.9).

The Cuban government's pressure during the 1930s and 1940s to keep African drums out of popular music often diluted the African presence in that country. In North America, commercialization and the desire to reach a mass audience led to softened styles. This was particularly true in the late 1940s and 1950s when, based on Afro-Cuban roots, the *mambo* arrived. It was the first truly North American Latin development.

Probably invented in Cuba by blind percussionist and *tres* player Arsenio Rodriguez or bassist Israel "Cachao" López, the early New York mambo was developed by New York bands led by Marcelino Guerra and José Curbelo (which included Tito Rodríguez, Tito Puente, and Carlos Vidal). In 1947, Tito Rodríguez and Puente left

Cajones
Wooden boxes that are struck with sticks to function as rhythm instruments

Cascara
Dense rhythm that is performed on top of the basic rhythm structure (or *clave*) of an Afro-Cuban dance piece

Palitos
Sticks that are used to strike a woodblock in Cuban music

Gua-gua
Bamboo tube that is struck by sticks

Mambo
Dance style pioneered in the North American Afro-Cuban community in the 1940s and 1950s

Figure 8.8

The folkloric group Patakin, New York City, 1988. Standing, *left to right:* Greg Askew, Louis Bauzá, Frank Malabe, Reynaldo Rivera; Sitting, *left to right:* Lazaro Galarraga, Nydia Ocasio, Ray Romero, Reynaldo Alcantara.

Curbelo to form their own ensembles. Along with Machito and his Afro-Cubans, they led the New York mambo style, which was centered in the Palladium Ballroom (1947–1966) but was also popular at the Savoy Ballroom and Apollo Theater.

The individual most responsible for bringing mambo to a non-Latin audience was Pérez Prado. Born in Matanzas, Cuba, in 1916, Prado worked mostly in Mexico and North America. His music, laced with North American pop sounds, was relatively accessible to non-Latin audiences; with a rhythm section powered at times by Mongo Santamaría and others, he enjoyed immense popularity from the late 1940s through the 1950s. Other important bandleaders were Merced Gallego in San Francisco and, in New York, Alfredo Méndez (born Alfred Mendelsohn).

The roots of the *charanga* go back to the nineteenth-century Cuban form *danzón* and the emergence from that ensemble of the *charanga francesa,* an ensemble made up of wooden flute, strings, double bass, *timbales,* and *güiro.* Although the strings are often replaced by brass, this general combination—with the addition of vocalist, piano, conga, and cowbell—remains a common instrumentation today.

Charanga
Cuban instrumental ensemble, led by wooden flute and strings that accompanies popular dance styles
Danzón
Nineteenth-century Cuban dance form

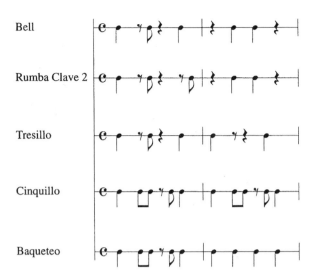

Bell

Rumba Clave 2

Tresillo

Cinquillo

Baqueteo

Figure 8.9
A characteristic rumba rhythm played by the *claves* and *palitos* "sticks."

Perhaps the first North American *charanga* was the short-lived Orquesta Gilberto Valdés, founded in New York in 1952. This ensemble was followed in 1956 by the Chicago-based Orquesta Nuevo Ritmo, founded by Cuban drummer Armando Sánchez and later directed by Mongo Santamaría. The year 1958 brought together the forces of pianist Charlie Palmieri and flutist Johnny Pacheco in the ensemble La Dubonney. Although drummer Ray Barretto's *charanga* enjoyed considerable crossover success with hits like "El Watusi," the 1960s and 1970s belonged to Orquesta Broadway.

Salsa

Salsa (literally, "sauce") is a broad term that generally refers to contemporary popular Latin dance music. Salsa's sound not only encompasses a variety of Cuban styles such as *son*, mambo, and *cha-cha-chá*, but also incorporates ideas from Puerto Rico, the Dominican Republic, and to a lesser extent the rest of the Caribbean, Brazil, and black North American popular music.

Instrumentation reflects this mix. The typical salsa rhythm section consists of piano, bass, congas, bongos, *timbales, güiro*, maracas, and *claves*. The drum set, however, is often used as well. Added to the rhythm section may be any variety of horn arrangements made up of combinations of trumpets, trombones, and saxophones. Finally, the ensemble may also employ flute, violins, electric guitar, and synthesizers.

Perhaps the first use of the term "salsa" in a musical sense goes back to Cuban composer Ignacio Piñeiro's 1933 song "Echale Salsita" (Salazar 1991b:9). Joe Cuba's recording of Jimmy Sabater's

Cha-cha-chá
Popular Cuban dance form that originated in the 1950s

"Salsa y Bembé" (1962), Charlie Palmieri's recording of Víctor Velásquez's "Salsa Na Ma" (1963), and Cal Tjader's "Soul Sauce" are other early examples. The term "salsa" did not come into common usage until the early 1970s, when it appeared in *Latin New York* magazine and was adopted as a category for the 1975 Latin New York Music Awards. From the mid-1970s into the early 1990s, the North American center for salsa was New York City. There, commercially empowered by the marketing of Jerry Masucci and Johnny Pacheco, who founded Fania Records in 1964, salsa became the center of popular Latin music making.

In its early development, salsa was strongly associated with the *barrio* district, working-class issues, the Afro-Cuban religions, and an emerging Latino militancy. The music and lyrics were tough, provocative, and closely aligned to Afro-Cuban culture. Since the late 1980s, commercial considerations, in addition to the increasing Dominican presence in New York City, added a new sensibility to the music. In the 1990s, the most commercially popular Latin music—led by Eddie Santiago, Louis Enrique, Willy Chirino, Jerry Rivera, and others—had a softer feel and was often termed *salsa romántica*.

Many musicians—including vocalist Celia Cruz, Tito Puente, Eddie Palmieri, Ray Barretto, and Israel "Cachao" López, who made their mark in earlier periods—continued to be important leaders in the salsa genre. Leading musicians who came of age in the salsa era include Louis Ramírez, Rubén Blades, Willie Colon, Héctor Lavoe, Gloria Estefan, and Sheila Escovedo. Since the Mariel exodus from Cuba in 1981, the genre has received creative infusions from percussionist Daniel Ponce, drummer Ignacio Berroa, saxophonist Paquito D'Rivera, and trumpet player Arturo Sandoval.

Steven Cornelius

South American Music

South America is an immense region of many nations and hundreds of cultural groups. In North America, South American immigrants and their descendants often maintain social/cultural identities linked to their nations of origin. Large concentrations of specific South American national or cultural groups are few, however, limiting the continuity of South American musical strains in North America. There are notable exceptions to this in musical styles that have achieved sufficient notoriety and commercial success to have a broad following. Pan-Andean ensembles featuring the *quena, zampoña, charango,* six-stringed guitar, *bombo,* and other instruments emerged in many North American cities, especially following their connection with popular resistance to dictatorial regimes such as that of Augusto Pinochet in Chile following the 1973 coup d'état. The popularity of urban folk song in the 1960s and later nightclubs

Barrio
Innercity neighborhood primarily home to Latino immigrants
Salsa romántica
Softer salsa style that became popular in the 1990s, influenced by mainstream pop

Quena
End-blown flute of Peru
Zampoña
Panpipes
Charango
Small, ten-stringed guitar fashioned from the shell of the *quirquincho,* a small armadillo

called *peñas,* the *nueva canción* movement, and the commercial success of groups such as Quilapayún and Inti-Illimani of Chile propelled this instrumental sound and style of music to international popularity throughout Europe and the entire Western Hemisphere. In the 1990s, dozens of these ensembles could be heard regularly in North American nightclubs, on street corners, in subway stations, at public concerts and folk festivals, and in other venues, particularly on the East and West coasts.

Several other South American musics made their presence known on the North American musicscape. Argentine tango music played on the *bandoneón* "large accordion" enjoyed a modest urban revival in the 1990s. Accordion-driven Colombian *música vallenata,* music originating in that country's northern coastal region, attained a degree of widespread popularity as a Latino popular music. In the last decades of the twentieth century, Paraguayan harp music based on the fast triple-meter Paraguayan *polca* and epitomized by the showpiece composition "Pájaro Campana" ("Bell Bird") was played regularly by Paraguayan immigrant musicians in Los Angeles, Las Vegas, New York, Washington, and beyond.

Brazilians, often counted among the ranks of Latinos in the United States, brought the music of their *capoeira',* played on the *berimbao.* In the 1980s and 1990s, *capoeira mestres* (masters) attracted many disciples in urban areas such as New York City and the San Francisco Bay area. In New York, choreographers Loremil Machado and Jelon Vieira established *capoeira* performance ensembles. *Samba* groups emerged in New York, Washington, DC, and other cities.

Dominican Music

Following the political and social upheaval after the death of Dominican Republic dictator Rafael Trujillo in 1961, Dominican immigration to North America, particularly to New York City and other northeastern U.S. urban industrial areas, increased dramatically. Dominicans established their own community identity, such as the Washington Heights neighborhood in New York City popularly called "Quisqueya Heights," *Quisqueya* being the indigenous name for the island shared by the Dominican Republic and Haiti. Dominicans brought their regional musical traditions and, above all, their popular music and dance form the *merengue* to North America. The *merengue cibaeño* (a form of the dance from the Cibao region) played the lead role in the emergence of the internationally popular dance *merengue.* Set in a fast-paced duple meter, the popular *merengue* is associated with a regional musical ensemble including a button-accordion playing a nonstop, dense melodic flow, a metallic rasp called *güira,* a *tambora,* and perhaps a saxophone or marimba. The accordion-driven *merengue,* known as *perico ripiao,* became associated with Dominican national identity and was an important signifier of

Bombo
Two-headed drum struck with two sticks, one of them padded
Peña
Nightclub
Nueva canción
Chilean protest song movement
Bandoneón
Large button accordion
Música vallenata
Accordion-driven music originated in the northern coastal region of Colombia
Polka
Paraguayan dance music in triple meter
Capoeira
Brazilian martial arts/dance
Berimbao
Musical bow
Samba
Brazilian dance form in syncopated, duple rhythm
Tambora
Two-headed drum from the Dominican Republic
Perico ripiao
Accordion-driven *merengue* music

Dominican presence in the multicultural North American environment, as well as a primary link to the Dominican homeland.

A dramatic rise in the popularity of the *merengue* accompanied the major influx of immigration beginning in the 1960s. Accordionist Primitivo Santos was the first *merengue* bandleader to settle in the United States. He and others such as Joseíto Mateo, the "king of *merengue*," who regularly worked in the United States, spread the *merengue* through regular live performances. By the 1970s, Latino dance band *merengue* was highly popular among Latinos in New York City and elsewhere. New York-based bands such as the group Millie, Jocelyn, y los Vecinos established both local and international followings. In the 1990s, another Dominican roots dance music, the guitar-driven *bachata*, was also widely popular.

Other Latino Musics

Spanish immigrants and North Americans of Spanish descent have both been included under the Latino rubric (as in the "Hispanic" category of the U.S. Census Bureau), given their commonalities of language, religion, and values, and excluded because of their origins in Europe, rather than in Latin America. Spanish music—*flamenco* guitar music in particular—and dance music are regularly included in public presentations of Latino culture such as those during National Hispanic Heritage Month. Several accomplished flamenco guitarists and *cantaores*, such as fifth-generation *cante jondo* singer Pepe Culata (José Matallanes) of Chicago, make major North American cities their homes.

Tens of thousands of other non-Spanish flamenco music disciples have taken up this southern Spanish Gypsy tradition. Basques, a linguistically distinct cultural minority from the region embracing a portion of the Spanish-French border, may or may not identify with the Spanish homeland. In the United States, Basque communities in the West might feature Basque accordion music during cultural events or occasionally teach music of the *txistu* and small accompanying drum to instill elements of their unique heritage. Music plays a role in the cultural life of another group marginal to Latino identity, Portuguese Americans. *Fado*—an expressive form of Portuguese popular song—is performed live in the Portuguese immigrant community of Fall River, Massachusetts, and the Portuguese who made their home in the area around the town of Gustine in central California include Portuguese music in public events.

Popular Music

Although the greater volume of Latino music in the United States has largely developed within Latino communities, a significant part of it has become commercially successful and musically highly influential (Roberts 1999). As early as 1930, Cuban bandleader Don

Bachata
Guitar-driven dance music of the Dominican Republic

Flamenco
Song, dance, and guitar style developed in the Andalucia region of southern Spain

Cantaores
Singers

Cante jondo
Literally "deep song"; any of the three types of throaty, impassioned, improvised flamenco song, considered the oldest and most serious

Txistu
Cane vertical flute played in Basque region of the Spanish-French border

Fado
An expressive form of Portuguese popular song

Aspiazu had a major recording hit with the rumba/ habanera "El manicero" (composed by Moises Simon), which was quickly translated into "The Peanut Vendor" and subsequently recorded by many major popular North American artists. During the same period Duke Ellington had a major impact on U.S. musical culture with his recording of "Caravan" (also based on the Afro-Cuban musical style), which he cocomposed with Juan Tizol, his Puerto Rican trombonist, who influenced the bandleader's musical compositions.

In 1940, Machito (Frank Grillo) and Mario Bauza assembled an orchestra, Machito and His Afro-Cubans, and proceeded to experiment in the fusion of Cuban dance music and jazz. By the late 1940s Dizzy Gillespie invited Cuban *conguero* Chano Pozo to become a member of his ensembles, and the fusion of Afro-Cuban music with bebop jazz became known as *Cubop*. By the 1950s dance halls such as the Palladium in New York City represented an intersection of both musical styles and society, as the popular rumba, mambo, and *cha-cha-chá* became personified through the orchestras of Machito, Tito Puente, and Tito Rodríguez. By the 1970s, the use of the word "salsa" would propel the careers of veteran artists including Machito, Puente, Celia Cruz, Eddie Palmieri, Charlie Palmieri, Johnny Pacheco, Ray Barretto, Willie Colón, and Rubén Blades. The latter two, Blades and Colón, would collaborate on a highly successful and historically significant album, *Siembra,* representing salsa's association with sociopolitical themes.

On the West Coast and in the Southwest, different yet related types of Latino music entered the mainstream of popular music in the United States. By the 1930s and 1940s, various Hollywood films were featuring bandleader Xavier Cugat and his Cuban-styled orchestra, and singers such as Miguelito Valdés from Cuba and Pepe Guízar from Mexico were appearing in cameo roles. Also emerging as a major singer in the mainstream recording industry was Mexican American Andy Russell (Andrés Rábago) from Los Angeles. In the 1950s, Cuban singer, bandleader, and actor Desi Arnaz, with his actress/comedian wife Lucille Ball, produced what some consider to be the most successful television sitcom to date, *I Love Lucy.* In 1955 Cuban bandleader Pérez Prado, whose orchestra was based in Mexico City, recorded a *cha-cha-chá,* "Cherry Pink and Apple Blossom White," for a film in Hollywood, which became the year's highest-selling recording in the world. In 1959 Mexican American Ritchie Valens (Richard Valenzuela) had a major hit with "La Bamba," a rock and roll version of a popular, traditional Mexican *huapango.* Valens died the same year in an air crash along with rock stars Buddy Holly and the Big Bopper. Another Los Angeles-based singer to emerge about this time was Vikki Carr (Victoria Cardona), whose first international hits were in English but who also became established as a

Cubop
A fusion of late 1940s jazz (bebop) and Cuban rhythms

Huapango
Popular Mexican musical form with a distinctive rhythm and frequent falsetto vocal embellishments

major popular recording artist in Latin America at the turn of the twenty-first century.

In the late 1960s Carlos Santana, a young Mexican guitarist raised in Tijuana, Mexico, and San Francisco, California, was recorded by Columbia Records and subsequently became the major innovator in what would become known as Latin rock. Santana achieved international popularity with hits such as "Evil Ways," composed by New York Latin jazz percussionist Willie Bobo, and "Oye Como Va," composed by New York-based Tito Puente, who was, like Bobo, of Puerto Rican heritage. Other artists largely inspired by Santana to attain various regional and international recognition included groups such as Malo and Azteca from San Francisco and Tierra and El Chicano from Los Angeles.

REVIEW

Important Terms and People to Know

Bajo sexto
Bomba
Charanga
Chicano movement
Conjunto
Latino
Mambo
Mariachi
Marimba
Merengue
Música Folklórica
Música jíbara
Música tropical
Plena
Tito Puente
Linda Ronstadt
Rumba
Salsa
Carlos Santana
Tejano

Review Questions

1. Define Latino culture. What different ethnic, geographic, and musical peoples have contributed to the growth of Latino culture in the United States since the end of the sixteenth century?
2. What specific musical contributions did Mexican Americans make to the border culture between Mexico and Texas?

3. What is the role of conjunto in maintaining a Mexican American identity in the United States? How has this been viewed by various subgroups within the Mexican American community?
4. How has Afro-Cuban music contributed to the development of popular music in the United States since the mid-twentieth century?
5. Who were/are some of the major musicians and composers who were/are responsible for the growth and popularity of Latino musics in the United States?

Projects

1. Go to a dance instructor or school in your area and watch a few dance classes that feature any of the Latin-derived dances discussed in this chapter. Interview the teacher and some of the students and write up your observations in the form of a small ethnography.
2. Go to a restaurant in your area that features traditional Mexican, Spanish, Cuban, or Caribbean, etc. food (not Taco Bell), and listen to the music that is played there. What kind of music is played? Why? Talk to the owner or manager and perhaps some of the customers and find out what their connection is to Latino music and culture.
3. Write a research paper on the Chicano movement of the 1960s and 1970s and determine the role of music in expressing political, social, and economic beliefs.

CHAPTER 9

Asian American Musics

Terry E. Miller, Susan M. Asai,
and Anne K. Rasmussen

Asians, including people from the Middle East, South and Southeast Asia, and East Asia, are the newest immigrants to arrive in the United States, beginning with the Chinese, and soon after, the Japanese, who were brought to work in the mines during the great Gold Rushes of the mid- to late nineteenth century and to help complete the transcontinental railway. Settling primarily on the West Coast, in California, Oregon, and Washington, many brought with them classical music traditions hundreds of years old, as well as ancient belief systems, religious practices, and popular musics that they, in some cases, sought to replicate in the New World. The Chinese in California, for example, still regularly perform classical Chinese opera for new immigrants as well as third- and fourth-generation Chinese Americans, and instruments such as the Japanese *koto* and *shamisen* are regularly taught in Japanese American communities in California, Hawai'i, and elsewhere. Immigrants from India and Pakistan, as well as late-twentieth-century arrivals, such as the Vietnamese, Cambodians, Lao, and Indonesians, have begun to establish communities large enough to support traditional musical activities in the United States as well as to join other Asian Americans who have ventured into Western popular and classical music activities.

The presence of Asian musics in the United States is a multifaceted subject requiring more than one perspective. Numerous Asian immigrant communities have coalesced throughout this country, in major cities such as San Francisco, New York, Detroit, and Chicago, as well as in many smaller ones such as Rockford, Illinois (Lao),

Arlington, Virginia (Cambodian), Des Moines, Iowa (Thai Dam from Laos), and Fresno, California (Hmong from Laos). Some Asian communities, especially those composed of immigrants from China and the Philippines, have deep roots in the United States. However, most Asian immigrants came after World War II as a result of changes in immigration laws and Southeast Asian wars. As the cultures they represent tend to be quite foreign to those of the mainstream European and British Isles-derived population, they are not easily assimilated, and their musics have usually remained obscure to the mainstream population.

A second facet reflects how the non-Asian-derived population has assimilated Asian musics, often without direct contact. These contacts occur through popular recorded culture, occasional live concerts, the presence of ethnomusicology as an academic discipline, and the "world music" ensembles that have sprung up on college and university campuses. Although many such ensembles are directed by Asian musicians visiting as teachers or students, others are directed by non-Asian Americans who learned the music here or abroad. In a sense, then, Asian musics may be divided into two categories: those that are self-expressions of specific communities and those that have been appropriated by non-Asians.

ASIAN COMMUNITIES IN THE UNITED STATES

People from virtually all parts of Asia have come to the United States for a variety of reasons. Earlier groups, such as the Chinese, were originally brought in as laborers. Many Filipinos migrated to the United States during the period of American colonial rule in the Philippines (1898-1946). A significant number of Asians have come as students and remained, usually in professional positions, after graduation. By far the largest numbers have come seeking asylum from economic and political upheavals in their own countries. The greatest number of refugees has come from mainland Southeast Asia, especially Vietnam, Laos, and Cambodia.

As was true of earlier immigrant groups, people from Asia tended to cluster into communities, especially during the initial stages of settlement here. Some of these ethnic communities have capitalized on their "exotic" appeal by attaining status as tourist attractions. "Chinatowns," most prominent in New York, San Francisco, and Los Angeles, offer more food and souvenirs than music, however. Los Angeles's "Little Tokyo" offers excellent restaurants and shopping. Orange County, California, site of the nation's largest Vietnamese community, offers shopping malls, supermarkets, and a free-standing popular music industry.

Americans have come to associate certain Asian groups with particular economic niches: Chinese and Thai with restaurants; Indians with the medical profession, as well as independent motels; Koreans with greengrocers; and Lao with Chinese and Thai restaurants. Indeed, the most usual form of contact between Asians and non-Asians living in the United States is through ethnic restaurants. While Chinese, Japanese, Middle Eastern, Indian, and Thai restaurants have sprung up throughout North America, more obscure cuisines (for example, Nepalese, Korean, Afghan) are more likely found in university towns.

The nature of each Asian community offers insight into whether or not its music gains significance. Working-class Asians, for example, tend to have less interest in traditional music than do professional-class Asians, but this tendency may not apply if another factor, such as a strong religious center, brings people together to maintain Old Country customs.

Snapshot 9.1 offers a closer look at the Japanese American experience. It details the generational patterns of adjustment since the first Japanese immigrants arrived in America at the end of the nineteenth century by examining the role of music and music making in both preserving a Japanese heritage in America, while also helping this community adapt to or protest new identities and contexts in the United States.

Snapshot 9.1: Japanese Music in America

American musicians of Japanese descent perform and compose mainstream styles of music, such as European classical music, jazz, and assorted popular and fusion styles. In addition, they create music that expresses their cultural heritage and social or political views. This music incorporates elements of traditional Japanese music into Western genres, reinterprets aspects of Japanese music, or employs song texts that make statements about being Japanese American in this country. Third-generation Japanese Americans have been the most active and experimental in creating such music.

Arriving on American Shores

Japanese immigration to the United States before 1890 was insignificant, with the total population of this ethnic group on the American mainland and in Hawai'i barely exceeding 2,000. A dramatic increase in the Japanese population in the United States between 1890 (2,039) and 1900 (24,326) resulted from the legalization of labor emigration after 1884, when Hawaiian sugar planters coerced the Japanese government into changing its policy. Japanese immigrants continued to arrive in great numbers until 1907–1908. During the decade between 1900 and 1910, a total of 132,706 Japanese immigrants were admitted, about 40 percent settling in the mainland, and 60 percent remaining in Hawai'i.

These numbers dwindled when the anti-Asian agitation (first against the Chinese, then the Japanese) of the Pacific Coast states forced President Theodore Roosevelt to forbid Japanese migration from Hawai'i, Canada, and Mexico to the U.S. mainland in 1907. In addition, a gentlemen's agreement between Japan and the United States, which went into effect in 1908, directly stopped further labor immigration from Japan. The 1910 U.S. Census shows a decrease in the number of Japanese immigrants but an increase in the number of U.S.-born Japanese Americans, called *nisei*. The year 1924 marks a clear cutoff point for arriving *issei*, the first genera-

tion of Japanese immigrants. The United States Congress passed the Immigration Act of 1924, an exclusion law that replaced the 1908 gentlemen's agreement and singled out the Japanese.

In 1921, continuing anti-Asian phobia on the West Coast forced the Japanese to end female emigration to the United States ("picture brides" for the many single male laborers) that had been allowable until this time even under the immigration restrictions of 1907 and 1908. This further restriction added to the prejudice many Japanese faced in this country, and the number of immigrants who returned to Japan between 1921 and 1924 increased. The year 1924 marks a clear cutoff point for arriving *issei*. The United States Congress successfully legislated the Immigration Act of 1924, an exclusion law that replaced the 1908 gentlemen's agreement and singled out the Japanese.

It wasn't until the 1950s that Japanese began to arrive on American soil again. The Walter–McCarran Immigration and Naturalization Act of 1952 repealed the Immigration Act of 1924, and an immigration quota was established for Japanese and other Asian immigrants. The act also eradicated the use of race as a criterion for naturalization. The quota numbers were rather insignificant compared to the waves of immigration at the start of the twentieth century. Instead, the second-, third-, and fourth-generation offspring of these early emigrés provide a continuing history of the Japanese on the American mainland.

Issei: Japanese Music in a Foreign Land

The first-generation *issei* retained their language, customs, and cultural traditions as a part of their survival in the United States. Music, art, and poetry cultivated a Japanese sensibility and expressed the beauty and power of the culture they brought with them. Retention of these art forms was particularly valuable and therapeutic in countering the prejudice and inhospitable attitude of many Americans they encountered.

Music making activities of *issei* have been best documented in the urban centers of California. San Francisco and Los Angeles served as cultural hubs for Japanese immigrants, and a range of music

Figure 9.1
Japanese touring ensemble, c. 1910–1920. Touring companies playing "exotic" music were popular throughout the early decades of the twentieth century. Note the players of the shamisen (three-string lute) and taiko drums. From the Collections of the Library of Congress.

Koto
Thirteen-string zither
Shamisen
Three-string plucked lute
Shakuhachi
End-blown bamboo flute
Yøkyoku
Music for *nø* theater
Satsuma *biwa*
Four-string plucked lute
Sankyoku
Chamber music featuring *koto, shamisen,* and *shakuhachi*
Jøruri
Narrative *shamisen* music for puppet theater
Shigin
Chinese poems set to music
Nagauta
Narrative songs for *kabuki* theater
Hauta
Short *shamisen*-accompanied songs
Naniwa-bushi
Popular-style narrative *shamisen* music

taught in San Francisco in 1914 included *koto, shamisen, shakuhachi, yøkyoku,* and Satsuma *biwa* (see Figure 9.1). Also, Japanese pop music bands, such as the Teikoku Band, were active between 1877 and 1910 in San Francisco, where many *issei* first settled. In Los Angeles, the Japanese newspaper *Rafu Shimpo* wrote about musical activities in and around the city from 1926 on. Reports of traditional Japanese music performances mention *sankyoku, jøruri, shigin, nagauta, hauta,* and *naniwa-bushi.*

Little is known about *issei* music-making activities in rural areas, but the labor-intensive nature of agricultural work surely limited these activities. In 1909, about two thirds of all *issei* immigrants worked within the agricultural industry in Hawai'i, California, and the Western states. Music was probably practiced and performed during slack seasons of the agricultural calendar, as was customary in Japan. There is some evidence that traditional Japanese music, both classical and folk, prevailed, serving as a connection for immigrants to their homeland.

Japan's exposure to Western music occurred soon after the country was forced to open its doors to the world by Commodore Matthew Perry and his fleet in 1854 and continued into the Taisho period (1912–1921). A small number of immigrants preferred European classical music and supported community and visiting artist concerts in urban centers featuring violin and piano music, opera, and art songs. John Yamauchi (1994), a *nisei* whose *issei* father was an opera singer, points out that audiences for this music consisted of the more progressive and educated classes of Japanese immigrants.

Fukuinkai
Japanese gospel societies

Japanese gospel societies (*fukuinkai*), as noted by Seizo Oka (1987) of the Japanese History Archives in San Francisco, were other Western-oriented musical groups that were formed at this time. These Christian hymn-singing groups were pro-Western organizations that brought together young intellectuals and encouraged assimilation into American society.

Nisei: The Changing Musical Tide

Members of the second generation of Japanese Americans (*nisei*) were born in the United States between 1910 and 1940. The musical preferences of this generation of American-born citizens began to shift as they attempted to balance Japanese family values and codes of behavior at home with democratic ideals, individualism, and other socially progressive ideas that they learned in school and experienced in American society. *Nisei* led culturally split lives, and their music making increasingly reflected this dual identity.

utai
Nø theater songs

True to their Japanese heritage, many *nisei* continued to pursue traditional music passed on to them by *issei*—music of the *koto*, *shamisen*, and *biwa* as well as *utai*, *shigin*, and music for *kabuki* theater. The anti-Japanese hysteria of World War II and the internment of many Japanese Americans during this period hurried the demise of any interest in traditional Japanese music by many *nisei*, as one's Japanese heritage often became a source of shame rather than pride.

Nisei music making encompassed a variety of musical styles that ranged from hymn singing by choirs, European classical music, Hawaiian music (popular music brought by that portion of the Japanese population that moved to California after being born and raised in Hawai'i), and musical novelties such as musical saw and mouth harp. European classical music was increasingly performed at concerts held by music societies in urban areas and at musical soirées given in the homes of music teachers or classical music lovers. Additional performances featured Boy Scout bands or drum and bugle corps and social club choruses or glee clubs that sang American folk or popular songs. Further, San Francisco was home to the Japanese Harmonica Band, which had a diverse repertoire that ranged from European classical and semiclassical pieces to arrangements of folk and popular Japanese songs (*kayokyoku*). The increased frequency of Western performances is symptomatic of the growing American identity of *nisei*.

Kayokyoku
Popular Japanese songs

American popular music attracted the attention of *nisei* musicians in the 1930s and 1940s. Among Japanese Americans, a growing number of young people wanted to play the big band music of Count Basie, Tommy Dorsey, and Benny Goodman.

Semiprofessional jazz orchestras, such as the Sho-Tokyans ("Lil' Tokyans") in Los Angeles and the Cathayans in San Francisco, performed with a number of *nisei* and other Asian American musicians at dances and talent shows throughout California.

The unwarranted internment of 110,000 Americans of Japanese descent during World War II ironically created unusual opportunities for music making. Music was an important activity for internees as they attempted to normalize their lives in concentration camps located in desolate parts of the United States. Music required for variety and talent shows, Christmas concerts, and other events continued, as well as music lessons, songfests, and dance bands for social dances. In fact, each of the ten concentration camps formed its own dance bands. The Manzanar Jive Bombers band of the Manzanar Relocation Camp, located in northern California, was renowned. Traditional Japanese music was also part of the musical landscape of the camps: folk music for summer O-Bon festivals, *koto, shamisen,* and *shakuhachi* music, Japanese pop songs, *naniwa-bushi,* and music for Japanese dramas. It was primarily *issei* who retained these traditions as a way to pass the time and seek comfort in their difficult living circumstances as internees.

Sansei: The Emergence of a Transculturated Music

Sansei, members of the third generation of Japanese immigrants, who by the 1960s were entering high school and college, are diverse in their musical tastes and activities. Overall, their music making has few boundaries; many are classically trained musicians and composers in the European tradition, whereas others play rock, pop, Latin, jazz, and even traditional Irish music. However, a small number play traditional Japanese music, mostly *koto, shamisen,* and *shakuhachi,* as a way to explore or maintain their cultural connection to Japan. Of primary interest here, however, is the creation of a Japanese American sound and the musical genres that best express this transculturated music.

Sansei are the creative force in shaping Japanese American music today. Japanese American music refers to music that is for the most part composed and performed by Japanese Americans who synthesize Japanese music with Western music by incorporating Japanese instruments and their playing styles, scales, melodies, rhythms, timbres, or aesthetic concepts borrowed from or suggestive of traditional Japanese music. *Sansei* create this new transcultural music by reconciling and giving credence to their Japanese heritage; it is part of their search for self, particularly in a society where many of this ethnicity still feel marginalized.

Sansei
Third generation of Japanese immigrants to the United States

The *sansei*'s musical quest to experiment with and create music that fulfills their ethnic well-being initially began with the Asian

American movement of the 1970s. This movement, inspired by the civil rights and Black Power movements, formed as Asian Americans united in building and expressing their sociopolitical views concerning education and issues of identity and empowerment. Asian American artists involved in the movement turned toward their own history and experience, and in the late 1960s and 1970s, folk music in the social-commentary style of Bob Dylan served to express the struggles and prejudices faced by Asians in the United States. Two groups that traveled to college campuses and communities to express such views were Joanne, Chris, and Charlie (New York City) and Yokohama California (San Francisco).

 "Something About Me Today" (Musical example 9.1) is the kind of popular music that developed in the 1970s that commented upon the experience of Japanese Americans in the United States. It is a song of protest about the role of the media—seen here as a tool of the white ruling class—in forming "American" images and values.

The most pervasive Japanese American music genre to emerge in the late twentieth century was *taiko* drumming (Figure 9.2). The foundation for this music was initially based on o-Suwa *daiko,* Chichibu *yataibayashi,* and Buddhist *uchiwa daiko,* representing various drumming traditions found in Japan. Kinnara Taiko, an ensemble affiliated with the Senshin Buddhist Church in Los Angeles, inaugurated this style of group drumming more than 25 years ago as a way to attract *sansei* and now *yonsei* to the Buddhist faith. *Taiko* drumming exemplifies the integration of Japanese and American musics, with the folk *taiko* tradition representing Japan and various compositional and rhythmic innovations representing America. Currently more than 100 *taiko* groups exist throughout the United States in locations as diverse as New York, Seattle,

Figure 9.2
Side view of a *taiko* ensemble at the Santa Barbara Japanese O-Bon Festival, August 1981. The body stance and stylized drumming movements are an important feature of the *taiko* tradition. Photo by Susan M. Asai.

Denver, Chicago, Ogden (Utah), White River (Washington), Boston, and Bennington (Vermont). Performance contexts for *taiko* drumming include weddings, Asian cultural festivals, Japanese festivals, anniversary celebrations of Japanese American organizations, and diversity programming in public schools and on college campuses.

Jazz-based music is a rich avenue for many *sansei* composer-musicians in expressing their ethnic identity or sociopolitical views. Jazz appeals to those who take their cue from African American culture and music. According to Paul Yamazaki, a *sansei* formerly active in the Asian American Creative Music scene in San Francisco, composers choose to write in a jazz-based idiom because African American music is an "almost perfectly balanced dialectic between the individual and the collective. There is a very unique tension there, where neither the individual is subsumed underneath the collective, nor is it a totally individual act" (Auerbach 1985:37). This dialectic reinforces the social purpose and strong communal ties that certain *sansei* musicians assert. Jazz is considered to be America's greatest cultural contribution, a musical style indigenous to this country and thus an expression of being an American. Yamazaki continues, "[T]he structure and spirit of jazz allows a great deal of openness. All of the open elements of the music [jazz] make it conducive for other people taking their own indigenous experiences into this music and creating more particular forms."

A number of jazz-based compositions by *sansei* composers are an important part of the Japanese American music repertoire. The compositions address the conflict many *sansei* feel about the internment of members of their families and of all Japanese Americans and the race and war hysteria that created the need for such drastic measures. This music serves as a form of reconciliation for those embittered by the injustice of the internment that caused so much suffering and humiliation.

Glenn Horiuchi, a pianist and Japanese *shamisen* player, wrote *Poston Sonata* in response to his father's and other family members' testimony about the hardships they endured in the camps. Inclusion of the *shamisen* as a solo instrument, Japanese scales in slightly modified form, and *taiko* drum rhythms give Horiuchi's modern jazz-based composition a unique quality. *Poston Sonata*, named after the internment camp in Arizona where Japanese American residents of San Diego were interned (including Horiuchi's family), is written for *shamisen*, alto sax, tenor sax, bass clarinet, bass, percussion, and piano.

Another important piece is New York-based jazz pianist and composer Sumi Tonooka's *Out from the Silence*, inspired by her mother's own internment experience. The National Japanese American Citizens League commissioned Tonooka to write this piece. *Out from the Silence* is a suite for *koto, shakuhachi*, violin,

Taiko drumming
A style of Japanese group drumming using large, barrel-shaped, two-headed drums

Yonsei
Fourth-generation Japanese Americans

clarinet, trumpet, tenor sax, trombone, vibes, rhythm section, and voice. The progression of the three movements musically represents the sociocultural evolution of each succeeding generation of Japanese Americans: *issei, nisei,* and *sansei.*

Percussionist and composer Anthony Brown has also written a piece, *E.O. 9066* (*Truth Be Told*), commemorating the indomitable spirit of Japanese Americans imprisoned during World War II. The first movement, dedicated to the *issei,* employs an arrangement of an eleventh-century *gagaku* composition, *Ichikotsu-cho,* as well as the use of *taiko, koto, shakuhachi, takebue,* and an assortment of Japanese folk percussion.

San Francisco is an important center for a circle of musician-composers who collectively form the Asian American Creative Music scene. Major composers in this scene include Mark Izu (bass), Vijay Iyer (piano and violin), Jon Jang (piano), Miya Masaoka (piano and *koto*), and Francis Wong (saxophone, clarinet, flute). These composers write jazz-based, contemporary, or avant-garde music. AsianImprov Arts, an umbrella organization that supports and promotes the experimental efforts of Asian American musician-composers, includes an independent recording company (AsianImprov Records) that produces recordings of Asian American musicians throughout the United States. The Los Angeles-based group Hiroshima, which formed in the 1970s in tandem with the Asian American movement, is notable within the jazz/rhythm and blues/pop fusion style. One of the first bands to incorporate the *koto, taiko,* and *shakuhachi,* Hiroshima provided the impetus for many bands looking for ways to give voice to their Asian heritage in an innovative and appealing style.

Rap music is also an effective political voice for *sansei* in commenting on the internment camps of World War II. Key Kool and his deejay, Rhettmatic, are part of the underground rap scene in Los Angeles, and their song "Reconcentrated" is a pointed commentary on the treatment of Japanese Americans who endured the concentration camps euphemistically referred to as internment camps. This song vents *sansei* anger concerning the humiliation and hardship of their families and to question the legality of the American government in imprisoning its own citizens without just cause.

On the East Coast, the Japanese American population is thin and spread out. *Taiko* drumming groups in New York (Soh Daiko) and Boston (Odaiko New England) stand out as particularly Japanese American, although many of the members of these ensembles are increasingly non-Japanese. Sumi Tonooka's big band jazz compositions *Out from the Silence* and *Taiko Jazz Project* also distinguish themselves as distinctly Japanese American. Another band that incorporates aspects of traditional Japanese music is the Far East

Gagaku
Music of the Imperial Japanese court
Takebue
Bamboo transverse flute

Side Band, which seamlessly fuses jazz, ambient, and traditional Chinese, Japanese, and Korean music. Other than this, music is heard as one component of multimedia productions such as *Testimony: Japanese American Voices of Liberation,* stories of Japanese Americans interned during World War II through music, poetry, and movement; *In Their Shoes,* which uses music, dance, words, and images to speak of Japanese American families' World War II experiences; and *Bamboo and Barbed Wire,* a piece by Killer Geishas A Go-Go, an all-Asian women's writing and performing arts group. It is clear by these pieces and many others that *sansei* have a desire to reconcile the Japanese American past.

New York City is the center for Japanese American and, in general, Asian American music on the East Coast. In addition to performances in concert halls and schools and at community events, the annual Asian Pacific American Heritage Festival (presented by the City of New York), and the annual O-Bon Dance Festival, sponsored by the New York Buddhist Church, provide continuing and stable contexts for Japanese American music groups.

Susan M. Asai

Economic Communities

North America's Chinatowns were founded primarily by Cantonese-speaking immigrants from the Guangdong province (including Hong Kong) during the nineteenth and early twentieth centuries. Sharing a common language, the residents engaged in business, including both the familiar restaurants and souvenir shops as well as export-import companies, making these communities cohesive beehives of activity.

Because of the language barrier, few outsiders could appreciate locally produced or itinerant musical performances, such as opera troupes performing Cantonese opera, or performances by most silk and bamboo instrumental groups, which were provided by private organizations of amateurs. Later, Chinese immigrants from both Taiwan (the Republic of China) and the People's Republic of China tended not to become part of the Chinatown community, because they spoke different languages and often came for professional reasons. *Jing xi* (Beijing opera) in New York and Washington, DC, for example, is not a Chinatown phenomenon. Therefore, Chinese communities have provided a context for traditional performances, but these have attracted little notice from outsiders.

Jing xi
Beijing opera

However, in the case of Orange County's Little Saigon, a thriving music industry has developed. Because so many of the Republic of Vietnam's prominent popular singers and musicians escaped to the United States (and many settled in California), it is no surprise that they have been able to reestablish their careers within the large and increasingly prosperous Vietnamese communities. The Vietnamese music industry produces great numbers of audiotapes, music videos, and compact discs of popular songs, and artists are able to perform live in concerts that attract large audiences. Traditional music, however, attracts little interest, although locally made videos of the popularized South Vietnamese theatrical genre called *cai luong* are widely available. Live performances are few.

Religious Communities

Where religion unifies a community, its center may provide a context for traditional music. The religions of Asia represented through organized centers in North America include Hinduism, Islam, and Buddhism. Of these, Hindu temples have provided the most hospitable context for traditional music, almost exclusively that of southern India (the Karnatic tradition). Such music includes both *bhajan*, "lay devotional songs," and classical vocal genres. Temples also provide a venue for teaching. Festivals celebrating the sacred, vocal compositions of St. Thyagaraja (1767-1847), southern India's greatest composer, often become successful by featuring both local and visiting performing artists (Figure 9.3). Because the people of northern India are of various religious systems, the impetus for Hindustani music has tended to come from Indian professionals or

Bhajan
Lay devotional songs of the Karnatic (southern Indian) tradition

Figure 9.3
Held at Cleveland State University every spring for more than twenty years, the St. Thyagaraja Festival celebrates the works of Karnatic India's most famous composer, St. Thyagaraja (1767-1847), using both local and imported talent, all supported by the local Indian community, 1984. Photo by Terry E. Miller.

community organizations (such as the cultural Indian Sunday schools) rather than religious centers.

Although Chinese, Japanese, and Vietnamese Buddhist temples, all part of the Mahayana tradition, may maintain some forms of chant, they have not been significant contexts for other kinds of traditional music. The same is largely true of the Theravada Buddhist temples established by the Lao and Cambodian communities, but the Thai Buddhist temples in Chicago, Los Angeles, and New York have brought in Thai music teachers and developed traditional ensembles. Islamic mosques have not figured prominently in encouraging the traditional musics of immigrant groups from West and Central Asia.

A number of Asian immigrant groups have also founded Christian churches. Most prominent are Koreans, Japanese, Chinese, and Filipinos. As the practices of most Asian Christian churches are heavily, if not entirely, Westernized, and many traditional musics are associated with non-Christian cultural beliefs and activities, these churches are rarely associated with such musics.

Other Institutions

Some first-generation Asian immigrants were skilled musicians, but few were able to continue their professional lives in the United States. The question remains, will these musics take root and be passed to younger generations, or will they simply cease upon the passing of the carrier? Arts councils in a number of states have established apprenticeships in the traditional arts that encourage traditional masters, through modest financial incentives and public recognition, to find apprentices within the community. Reviews of this process suggest mixed levels of success. Few wish to devote the time, energy, and money needed to learn traditional music if there is neither financial reward nor ready context for its performance.

Classical Indian music and dance are likely the most systematically organized Asian traditions in the United States. A small number of masters work nearly full time teaching classical Bharata Natyam dance, *sitar* and *sarod*, *vina*, and both *tabla* and *mridangam*. These activities take place in private studios, under the auspices of Hindu temples, and in at least one fully established educational institution, the Ali Akbar College of Music in San Rafael, California. In addition, this training is available to both Indian and non-Indian students.

Media

Many major cities have public access television and radio stations that allow various ethnic groups to broadcast music and programs. Most often, popular music videos or popular songs are featured, rather than traditional music. Music videos and movies, audiotapes,

Sitar
Long-necked plucked lute of North India
Sarod
Short, unfretted Hindustani plucked lute with a deep-waisted, skin-covered body that narrows into a metal-plated neck
Vina
Struck zither with seven strings (four melody strings, three drones) of Indian classical music
Tabla
Paired, Indian kettle-shaped drums played with the hands
Mridangam
Indian, two-headed, barrel-shaped drum

Bollywood
The name given to the large Indian film industry, featuring epic-length films with elaborate musical scores

compact discs, and epic-length Chinese or Indian films from *Bollywood*, the name given to India's gigantic film industry, are often available for rental or purchase at Asian grocery stores. A number of small companies, started by immigrant Asians, manufacture and market tapes, videos, and compact discs of both material brought from Asia and newly recorded releases. Little of this material is known to the non-Asian community.

THE ROLE OF MUSIC IN MAINTAINING UNITY AND PRESERVING IDENTITY

Although popular genres (songs, film music, rock bands) outweigh traditional Asian musics in North America, both play roles in maintaining unity and identity within immigrant communities. For example, to non-Indians, all people from India may be assumed to be of the same culture, but for Indians, the distinction between Karnatic (southern) and Hindustani (northern) usually remains clear. This is especially true with regard to music performances. St. Thyagaraja Festivals only occur where there are large populations of Karnatic Indians, and a *sarod* concert will attract a large audience only where there are many Hindustani Indians. Similarly, Cantonese opera attracts Cantonese speakers, who tend to maintain an identity separate from Mandarin-speaking Chinese, who would more likely support Beijing opera. Concerts and other events offering music from the homeland not only reinforce the audience's identification with its native countries, but they often serve to subdivide audiences according to geographical, linguistic, or religious origin.

When refugees from Vietnam and Laos began arriving in North America in 1975, all were subsumed in one group, either Vietnamese or Lao. Before their arrival, however, all had clear notions of where they belonged in their homeland. Chinese-derived Vietnamese did not consider themselves to be "Vietnamese" in the same way that ethnic Vietnamese did, and few realized that many of the people from central Vietnam were in fact Cham, not Vietnamese. The Cham, who in Vietnam had to mute their ethnic identity, have reasserted it in the New World. Besides costume and language, a main ingredient used to invoke Cham identity is dance and music. People who had never paid much attention to these modes of expression in Vietnam now find them important in asserting a Cham identity as distinct from both Vietnamese and American identities. Other so-called Vietnamese were in fact upland Mon-Khmer speakers unrelated to the lowland ethnic Vietnamese.

For North Americans, Lao constituted a single, if obscure, ethnic identity, but within Laos distinctions are made between lowland, mid-upland, and high-upland groups, with most of the latter speaking non-Lao languages. The lowland Lao-speaking immigrants

demonstrate their musical identity through (rarely heard) performances of *lam* singing accompanied by *khene*.

Musical Example 9.2, "Lam khon savane," illustrates a rare musical genre of traditional repartee singing known as *lam*. It is performed here by Lao Americans, Khamvong Insixiengmai (male) and
Thongkhio Manivong (female), accompanied on the *khene*. The
singing consists of memorized and extemporized poetry that may
continue for hours, often taking the form of an imaginary love
affair.

Today, especially among Lao youth, one is more likely to hear
performances featuring rock bands that alternate traditionally
derived dances and melodies with American line dances and whatever else is currently popular. Upland Lao, especially the Hmong,
declare their distinctiveness in unaccompanied chanting of poetry
and its realization on instruments, especially the *qeej* (*gaeng*).

In Snapshot 9.2, the author chronicles the arrival and growth of
diverse cultural and musical Middle Eastern communities in the
United States, stressing the subtle interplay between westernized
notions of exoticism, orientalism, and "pan-ethnic" Middle Eastern
identity and the need for individual communities and peoples to
express their own uniqueness through specific musical practices.

> **Lam singing**
> Traditional Lao
> singing in
> repartee form
> **Khene**
> Lowland Lao
> free-reed mouth
> organ; also
> spelled *khaen*
> **qeej (gaeng)**
> Upland Lao
> (Hmong) free-
> reed mouth
> organ

Snapshot 9.2: Middle Eastern Musics

There has been a Middle Eastern musical presence in North
America for over 100 years. At the end of the nineteenth century,
Americans first experienced Middle Eastern culture when the "oriental" dancer "Little Egypt" and her ensemble of Egyptian musicians entertained at the Chicago World's Fair of 1893. Some 20 to
30 years later, Middle Easterners were conspicuous enough in
urban America to attract accounts in the popular press of Turkish-
style coffeehouses in Boston and New York where men smoked
water pipes and conversed in strange tongues to the background
wail of a singer accompanied by his "ood." Following World War II,
immigrant musicians and dancers from Arab, Turkish, Armenian,
and Greek communities captured the imagination of American
audiences performing in "Middle Eastern" nightclubs. At the end
of the twentieth century, music of the Middle East is one of several
deterritorialized musics of the world that can be heard in prestigious concert halls, at ever-popular ethnic festivals, in universities,
and in the context of myriad ritual events and celebrations.

Middle Eastern Immigration to North America

Middle Eastern immigrants are likely to represent one of four
broad linguistic-cultural-regional groups: Arabs, Armenians,
Iranians, and Turks. They come to North America from many

regions, including Turkey, Iran, the Caucasus, and countries in the Arab world. Ethnic populations, for example, Assyrians and Kurds who come from Iran, Iraq, Syria, Lebanon, and Turkey, are also represented in smaller numbers in North America. Although often lumped together by the American mainstream, each group has a distinct history of immigration and a unique cultural life in which the role of music is paramount.

With a population of around two million in the United States, Arab Americans are the largest subgroup of people of Middle Eastern origin in North America. Since the arrival of the first Syrian in Brooklyn, supposedly in 1854, Arab Americans have settled primarily in the large urban areas of California, New York, Michigan, and elsewhere. The majority of early Arab immigrants were Christians of Maronite, Melkite, and Greek and Syrian Orthodox faith from the Ottoman province of Syria, which until the 1940s included Mount Lebanon, Syria, and Palestine. First-wave immigrants who originally came with few resources are now well established both economically and socially. Groups of immigrants who came in subsequent waves of immigration include significant populations of Egyptians, Palestinians, students from the Gulf, Assyrians, Yemenis, and North Africans, as well as many Sunni Muslims and thousands of people of limited economic means who have come to work as laborers in the automotive industry in Detroit or on the farms in the central valley of California.

First-wave populations were relatively homogeneous, but today's immigrants are divided along national, regional, religious, and political lines. Because music events are supercharged with notions of ethnicity and origin as well as regional, national, and religious affiliation, reasons for migration and resettlement are central to music making in Arab American communities.

 Musical Example, 9.3, "Sabá Melody," opens with an improvisation (*taqasim*) followed by a medley of Arab folksongs in the mode of Sabá, played on the Arab reed flute (*nay*), by performer, composer, and professor of ethnomusicology, Ali Jihad Racy. Percussion accompaniment on the ceramic, case-shaped drum, *tablah* or *darabukka,* is provided by Souhail Kaspar.

Armenian Americans have maintained a musical culture in exile that dates to the turn of the twentieth century. With community members emanating from Turkish, Russian, Arab, Persian, and East European cultures, national identity, as expressed in musical style, song lyrics, and repertoire, is a dynamic source of both creativity and tension among Armenian Americans.

Immigrants from Turkey constitute the smallest national group of Middle Easterners in North America. Turkish culture (especially Turkish music), however, which spread throughout the Middle East during the nearly 500 years of Ottoman rule, has been an

Figure 9.4
Detroit musicians
Nadim Dlaikan, playing
mizmar, Mustapha Ata,
playing tabl baladi, and
singer Ameed perform
at the Arab World
Festival in Detroit, June
1988. Photo: Anne K.
Rasmussen.

important component of the cultural heritage brought by the first
wave of Arab and Armenian immigrants. Few Turks, however, emigrated to America prior to the 1960s, when the relaxed immigration laws promoted Turkish immigration. Today the Turkish community numbers over 100,000. Turkish Americans are concentrated
in New York, Chicago, Detroit, Los Angeles, Philadelphia, and San
Francisco (see Figure 9.4)

The Turkish musical culture transplanted and perpetuated by
early immigrant groups include the instruments of the classical
repertoire, and the system of melodic modes and rhythmic patterns
cultivated in the elite artistic circles of the court and Sufi brother-
hoods of the Ottoman world. Later, Turkish semiclassical and popular styles and repertoire were part of the eclectic polyethnic nightclub sound of the 1950s and 1960s in America. Immigrants who
today bring with them a post-Attatürk (Kemal Attatürk [1881–
1938], the founder and first president of the Turkish Republic)
cultural orientation are likely to identify not with the elite cultural
traditions of the Ottoman past but rather with the nationalized,
urbanized folk music that is actively promoted by the Turkish government. On the other hand, American tours by Turkish musicians
of classical Ottoman and Sufi music promote anew the cultural
artifacts of the Ottoman past for both people of Turkish heritage
and mainstream Americans.

Iranian immigration became significant only during the last
three or four decades of the twentieth century. A first wave of
Iranians arrived before the Islamic revolution of 1978–1979, when
economic and political conditions were favorable for extranational
exploration and education. A second wave of emigration from Iran
occurred after the revolution, when many Iranians became

estranged from the strict Islamic regime in the country. Today, the United States hosts an Iranian community of about 250,000. The majority of Iranians in North America are Shi'i Muslims, but there are also groups of Armenian Christians, Jews, Baha'is, and Zoroastrians from Iran living here. The largest communities of Iranian Americans live in California, New York and New Jersey, Washington, DC, Illinois, and Texas.

Iranian Americans' wealth has given them immediate access to most of the practices and material goods of their new host culture, and as a result many Iranians have assimilated easily into North American society. The Islamic revolution from which they fled presented not only a repressive regime but one that was especially hostile and prohibitive, if not lethal, especially for modern artists. Unlike most immigrant communities, which include only a small subpopulation of artists who are responsible for the maintenance and production of the immigrant culture's music, the Iranian immigrant community is unique in that it includes the majority of the popular musicians of Iran. The lion's share of these emigré entertainers came to Los Angeles, which is now thought to be the center for Persian popular music not only for North America but for the world. Traditional musicians, who continue to be endorsed by the postrevolutionary Iranian government, have not emigrated in such overwhelming numbers.

While there are certain connoisseurs and practitioners of Persian traditional music, much music created and consumed in Los Angeles and other North American cities reflects an enthusiastic adaptation of the styles and techniques of Western popular culture. Popular Iranian music is not simply a scaled-down reproduction of that which occurs in the more "authentic" and "traditional" homeland; it is rather a thriving musical culture-in-exile, in which creative artists set trends that are followed by musicians and audiences in other diaspora communities and even, with the exchange of audio and video recordings, in Iran itself.

Modernization, Americanization, and the Nightclub

Following the difficult years of the Great Depression and World War II, immigrant communities, which included by that time second- and even third-generation American-born offspring, were relatively stabilized. Contexts for musical performance and the performing artists were well established. Experimentation and innovation naturally superseded the imitation and reproduction that characterized musical performance of the 1920s and 1930s. A gradual erosion of Arabic, Turkish, and Armenian languages took place, especially among the American born, and musicians of various ethnic backgrounds began playing together. To complement their mélange of Middle Eastern genres, the instruments, styles, and techniques of American popular music and big band jazz began to permeate their authentic Old World sounds.

The Turkish-Armenian ensembles that performed in the *hantes* and at *kef-time* celebrations began to feature a jazzier style, with more improvisation, faster tempos, more percussion, and the addition of American instruments such as saxophones and electric keyboards and guitars. Arab American musicians consistently reported that in contrast to the *haflah,* which was for serious music or "the heavy stuff," the outdoor *mahrajan* was the appropriate place for light music and popular songs (*taqatiq*), which were likely to be sung in colloquial, not classical, Arabic and were to please the young folks and, according to one prominent musician, the women. In fact, musicians who emphasized their love and promotion of authentic classical music also identified the landmarks in their careers in terms of their composition and recording of humorous and popular songs.

The Nightclub

Popular music evolved and thrived within the community, but the performance arena that best nurtured the modernization and Americanization of this music was the Middle Eastern nightclub. The *surjaran* and the phenomenon of *café aman* were certainly prototypes for the myriad clubs that sprang up on and around Eighth Avenue in New York City.

The nightclubs that were established in cities across the United States were patronized not only by families from various ethnic communities but also by cosmopolitan-minded Americans who fancied an exotic evening out on the town. For the American of European heritage, the nightclub was a temporary mecca of orientalism complete with the stereotypic decor, cuisine, music, and dance of the alluring Middle East. Belly dancing, practiced primarily by American women, was integral to this performative reinterpretation of the oriental world. Within the context of the nightclub, the Middle East was presented in a general way, as a caricature that captured all the images and stereotypes that made the region, history, and culture so captivating to the American public. Because of the eclectic audience they entertained, musicians were careful to present only a selection of the indigenous elements of their native music as well as to exaggerate the most exotic (and thus the most alluring) elements of their cultural product. Eventually, nightclub musicians deemphasized the languages spoken by their parents, complicated vocal genres, and traditional musical forms and styles and replaced them with simpler strophic songs enhanced by Western instrumentation and a jazzier, faster, and louder beat.

Hante
Armenian American all-day religious celebration

Kef-time celebration
Armenian American weekend-long music retreat featuring multiple bands

Haflah
Arba American party featuring "serious" music, food, drink, and dance

Mahrajan
Arab American weekend-long festival featuring popular music and food

Taqatiq
Turkish-Armenian light music and popular songs

Surjaran
Armenian American coffeehouse featuring music, conversation, and refreshment

Café aman
Arab American coffeehouse

With the addition of electric keyboard, guitar, and bass, they dia-tonicized the scales of Middle Eastern music and harmonized a heretofore monophonic musical idiom.

With the influx of thousands of new immigrants from the Middle East following the relaxation of immigration quotas in 1965, the stylistic fusion that occurred in the nightclub has become largely a phenomenon of the past. Although there are still venues and ensembles that feature mixed groups, most Middle Eastern communities have been bolstered with new blood from the Old World. Ironically, while these new populations bring with them the cultural and linguistic tradition and authenticity of the homeland, the musical practices they have brought and continue to develop are modern and popular. Although many musicians in North America still play the traditional instruments of the Middle East, it is not at all uncommon to find ensembles or bands composed solely of American Western electronic instruments. *'Uds, qanuns,* and *neys* are difficult to find and keep in good repair, and a synthe-sizer can take the place of all three of these instruments. Furthermore, a certain prestige is associated with the creative adap-tation of Western instruments, techniques, and technology. As they neglect tradition and adopt contemporary ideas and techniques, musicians do not seem to perceive themselves as impoverished but rather as empowered.

The Implications of Musical Style and Repertoire

Musicians underscore elements of ethnicity, nationality, and even regional, religious, and political affiliation with their musical style and repertoire. In the Arab American community, musicians of the 1930s and 1940s played classical music to a primarily Syrian-Lebanese Christian audience, but their task during the 1960s and 1970s in the nightclub was to perform popular Arab, Turkish, Armenian, and Greek music and even to throw in an occasional Italian or Irish tune for their eclectic, polyethnic audience. Today musicians have to keep up with the latest hits from home as well as know tunes from many Arab world countries and when to play them. In addition to the mention of countries, cities, or regions in song lyrics, musical styles and genres may be suggestive of national sentiment.

In the culture of exile, traditional, popular, regional, and religious musical genres carry evocative messages about social class and political stance. In the Iranian American context, for example, popular music and its supporting institutions threaten some, while the traditional music network bothers others. Classical musicians who have come from Iran to perform in American cities are upheld as symbols of traditional art by the intelligentsia, but they may be

'Ud
Plucked Arab lute, featuring a fretless neck and a pear-shaped body with a round belly
Qanun
Trapezoidal plucked zither or psaltery found throughout the Arab world
Ney
End-blown flute or reed pipe found throughout the Arab world

Music Cultures in the United States

seen by the broader community as puppets of the regime and as representative of the repressive government that forced the musical community into exile. In the Armenian context, the musical representation of nationalism is even more complex. Older generations of Armenian Americans were brought up singing Turkish songs and playing Turkish-style music; younger generations, however, as a result of a renewed awareness of the Turkish massacres of their ancestors, tend to boycott anything Turkish.

Sosi Setian's research among Armenian Americans on the East Coast shows the suggestive power of Turkish-style music among Armenian Americans. Even though musicians have for generations been playing Turkish-style music (also referred to as *à la Turka*) in nightclubs, and especially at *kef-time* events, they are now subject to complaints and even threats of violence from newer, second-wave community members. Ironically, although the power of Turkish song lyrics is potentially destructive, the same audience that insists that Turkish music is unacceptable will often let a Turkish song sung in Armenian or played as a dance tune go by unnoticed.

Armenians have long been recognized for their ability to master diverse styles. Today, however, the performance of a particular style may be more a matter of survival than choice. One young musician of Lebanese-Armenian heritage explained that he has had to learn to sing in Armenian, Turkish, Arabic, and Farsi in order to cater to the multinational Armenian American clientele of Southern California for whom he plays. In public venues when the audience is mixed, his choice of repertoire can be problematic, engendering impolite criticism and audible disapproval.

During these events, communities divided by ethnic politics can become united by musical styles and gestures. Sometimes conflict is voluntarily sparked by one faction or another from within a group; sometimes, however, a Middle Eastern American community and the musical aspects of their culture are involuntarily affected by the turbulent news from the Middle East. During the Gulf War of January 1991, for example, musical events in Arab American communities came to a virtual standstill. Not only were community members themselves reluctant to engage in happy music parties, but the patronage of Arab-American-owned restaurants and nightclubs was sluggish due to the general American population's reluctance to associate with anything Middle Eastern.

Music Patronage and Education

Among Middle Eastern Americans, individual musicians and their patrons have been their community's managers of musical knowledge. In producing musical events, their role has not been simply to perpetuate some given age-old indigenous musical tradition imported from the homeland but rather to define a musical tradition for their community. Although musicians ultimately have the power, through their performances, to reconfirm and reinforce the traditional or modern repertoires they value as individuals, their strategies on the stage are greatly influenced by the audiences for whom they play and the patrons from whom they receive their money. Outside the commercial nightclub or restaurant, community-specific societies, clubs, associations, newspapers, religious institutions, dance groups, political committees, and charitable organizations have been the backbone of musical patronage for Middle Eastern musicians in the United States.

In the final decades of the twentieth century, American institutions have become important patrons of and participants in Middle Eastern music, and Middle Eastern musical projects have received the financial support of major granting agencies: Major universities have sponsored performance and scholarship of various types of Middle Eastern music and also have started their own ensembles to perform it. Although university ensembles may be composed primarily of newcomers to Middle Eastern music, the ensembles, which tend to specialize in traditional acoustic music and often host guest artists, have become well known among people of Middle Eastern heritage in the surrounding communities. Community members—who may find an American band playing Middle Eastern music a curious phenomenon—may nevertheless hear the music as an alternative to the synthesizer-driven popular music of community events or the expensive concerts of big stars from overseas. These groups may also serve to introduce or reintroduce Middle Eastern music to people of Middle Eastern heritage.

Since the beginning of the twentieth century, Middle Eastern music in America has been operating as a music culture in exile. While musicians emigrating from the Middle East may bring with them to the United States the experience of conservatory or other professional music training, those who emigrated during their childhood or are American born tend to be self-taught, a method combining listening to records and cassettes, attending music events, an occasional lesson from someone more knowledgeable, and a great deal of experience sitting in, either during informal gatherings or on stage at community events. Because of the sometimes haphazard nature of this system of musical education, complicated by the traditional low status attributed to the musical profession in general, the quality and depth of the musical culture may suffer. Developing new contexts and institutions for music learning appropriate for people living in North America is the biggest challenge faced by Middle Eastern American music cultures today.

Anne K. Rasmussen

Various Asian musics have had a strong appeal in the non-Asian community. Although by no means exhaustive, two groups dominate this area: ethnomusicology or world music programs in academia, and a counterculture of freelance composers, world music performers, and improvisers. Preceding the latter were a number of internationally known composers, some of whose works show influences from Asian musics.

Academia

Until the 1960s, ethnomusicology in the United States was primarily part of anthropology and folklore and focused on native traditions. Two institutions at opposite ends of the nation changed that. Connecticut's Wesleyan University's world music program brought in significant numbers of professional performer-teachers who trained American students to perform Asian traditions, particularly those of Indonesia and India. Mantle Hood of the University of California, Los Angeles (UCLA), espoused the concept of bimusicality as a means of learning non-Western musics. A number of his students—many of whom went on to found ethnomusicology programs—were originally composers seeking alternative ideas for their works. Hood founded a large Javanese *gamelan*, the Venerable Dark Cloud, and other ethnomusicology faculty and students offered performance training in Thai, Chinese, Arabic, and other musics. Under Hood's influence, both Javanese and Balinese gamelan were founded at institutions throughout the country, becoming so ubiquitous that having a program in ethnomusicology today virtually assumes you also have a gamelan.

Gamelan
Indonesian orchestra, especially of percussion instruments

With the proliferation of ethnomusicology programs and the offering of courses on Asian musics to a broad range of students, an increasing number of Americans have become aware of and been attracted to various Asian musics. During the 1960s and 1970s, Asian musics were sometimes associated with the youth counterculture. Partly because of the Beatles' use of Indian instruments and musicians, and George Harrison's study of the *sitar* with Ravi Shankar, Indian music remained popular until African and African-inspired drumming rose to prominence in the 1980s. Javanese and Balinese gamelan attracted many students both to play and to attend concerts. Musics from Asia took on importance for many in North America, but their meanings were often changed to fit the interests and agendas of Westerners.

Today, numerous academic institutions offer Asian performance studies. Few of these ensembles, however, have permanent status and depend on the continuous presence of individual faculty members or the availability of graduate assistants from specific countries. To use Thai-specialist David Morton's expression, these ensembles are mostly "hot-house plants" (Morton 1970:1). In 1976, several experienced players in New York founded the (Javanese) gamelan Son of Lion ensemble, under the direction of Barbara Benary, using instruments built locally of steel and aluminum, and have commissioned new works (see **Snapshot 4.3** for more about Benary and gamelan Son of Lion). A number of organizations have been founded to promote various Asian musics, some organized by Asian Americans, some by non-Asian Americans. These include New York's Music from China, which performs both traditional and new compositions. In Chicago, the Chinese Music Society of North America publishes a semischolarly magazine, *Chinese Music*, and provides performances by a modern-style Chinese orchestra staffed by a mixture of Chinese and non-Chinese musicians. The International Association for Research in Vietnamese Music, founded by Phong Nguyen and Terry E. Miller, encourages the performance of traditional Vietnamese music and, until 1999, published a scholarly journal, *Nhac Viet*. The Cambodian Network Council in Washington, DC, has organized conferences on both music and art, as well as performances. The American Gamelan Institute, based in Hanover, New Hampshire, publishes *Balungan*, an occasional journal devoted primarily to Indonesian music. Other organizations offer concerts and lectures devoted to Asian musics.

Composition

Western classical composers have dabbled in Asian musics at least since the late nineteenth century, when Asian exoticism became attractive (see also Chapter 4). But Europeans such as Gustav Mahler (*Das Lied von der Erde*), Giacomo Puccini (*Madama Butterfly* and *Turandot*), and Nikolai Rimsky-Korsakov ("Song of India") paid little attention to matters of authenticity. During the twentieth century, both European and American composers continued their interests in Asian musics but with increasing knowledge and firsthand experience. Lou Harrison (1917-2003) and John Cage (1912-1992) imitated the sounds of the Indonesian gamelan as early as 1941 in their *Double Music* (see **Snapshot 3.4**). Colin McPhee (1901-1964) lived in Bali, Indonesia, during the 1930s and wrote not only a scholarly book on Balinese music but also compositions that suggest Balinese influence. Most prominent is *Tabuh-Tabuhan* (1936) for orchestra. Henry Cowell (1897-1965) also traveled extensively in both Eastern and Western Asia from the 1930s through the 1950s and produced numerous early recordings of Asian music for Folkways Records. Having spent 1956-1957 in Iran, Cowell wrote, among other works, *Homage to Iran* in 1957 for violin, piano, and *dombak*. Between 1962 and 1965, he also wrote two concertos for Japanese *koto*, "zither." Halim El-Dabh, born in Egypt in 1921, has written two works for

Dombak
Persian double-headed drum
Koto
Japanese raft zither

Arabic *darabukka*, timpani, and strings, a concerto for *darabukka*, and *Fantasia-Tahmeel* for Middle Eastern percussion.

Darabukka
Arab single-headed, ceramic-bodied cylindrical drum

Composers active in the minimalist movement, which dates to the 1960s but continues to be a major stream in today's composition, were stimulated in part by their early participation in non-Western ensembles, particularly those of Africa and Indonesia. Philip Glass, like Beatle George Harrison, studied Indian music directly from *sitar* artist and film composer Ravi Shankar and internationally acclaimed *tabla* player Alla Rahka from 1964. The music of Glass, Steve Reich, Terry Riley, La Monte Young, and others often invokes a generalized atmosphere of suspension, cyclical structure, and contemplations created through repeated, but slowly changing, patterns. Whereas gamelan music is in fact progressive in structure, the minimalist works that suggest it only conserve its apparent monotony and the perception of suspension in time. This is clearly heard in Steve Reich's *Music for Mallet Instruments, Voices and Organ*, and *Six Pianos*.

Other composers have departed entirely from Western instruments and built their own instrumentaria. As early as the 1940s, John Cage's prepared pianos imitated non-Western (including Asian) instruments, and both Cage and Harrison imitated the gamelan by using brake drums, cans, pots, animal bells, etc. American composer and sometime hobo Harry Partch (1901-1976) composed all of his music for instruments of his own creation, many derived from Asia. In addition, Partch explored alternative tunings derived from Arabic and Chinese sources.

Composition for Asian ensembles, with or without added Western instruments, has become prominent both in the West and in Asia. Lou Harrison, who spent the years 1961-1963 traveling in East Asia, with instrument builder William Colvig, built Asian-derived instruments, including two Javanese gamelan, for use in his compositions. Harrison's works for actual Asian instruments, with added chorus, cello, violin, or horn, began in 1963 and continued to his death in 2003. Other composers who have followed this stream include David Loeb, Bruce Gaston (an American composer living and working in Thailand), and Ingram Marshall.

Michael Tenzer, an American-born composer, who has spent years performing, studying, and composing music in Bali, has recently written a piece, "Unstable Center/Puser Belah" (2003), (Musical Example 9.4) part of which is presented here. Combining two gamelans that both cooperate and conflict with each other throughout the piece—with conflict dominating at the end—Tenzer raises the profound question of whether two different cultures are able to live together peacefully.

Also inhabiting this musical twilight zone between East and West are numerous composers and improvisers who occupy the space between classical and popular cultures. Because this music invokes other times, other cultures, and other universes, much of it has been labeled New Age. Although the Windham Hill record label has been long associated with New Age music, most composer-performers publish on obscure or self-owned labels. Jaron Lanier, for example, composes and improvises music involving diverse Asian instruments, including Chinese *zheng*, Lao *khaen*, and Balinese *angklung*, "shaken bamboo rattles." Robert Bassara's work involves great numbers of Asian percussion instruments, especially the Burmese *kyi-zi*, "metal chime."

Few of these composer-performers using Asian instruments, alone or as part of world music ensembles, give heed to the original, authentic styles, but instead create their own styles for their own purposes. For example, No World Improvisations, consisting of Korean *kayageum* player Jin Hi Kim and American oboist Joseph Celli, improvises new music that is neither Western nor Eastern but blends elements borrowed from each. Although using world instruments, especially those associated with the apparently mystical cultures of Asia (for example, Zen Buddhism and Sufism), has come to symbolize openness, freedom, creativity, and spirituality, it has also required a process in which Westerners assign new meanings to adopted foreign instruments and forms.

Zheng
Chinese half-tube zither, related to the Japanese *koto*
Angklung
Balinese shaken bamboo rattles
Kyi-zi
Burmese metal chimes
Kayageum
Korean zither, related to both the Chinese *zheng* and Japanese *koto*

Popular Culture

The worlds of serious and formalized composition and of improvisation and popular forms, such as world beat, have no clear boundary. The combining of East and West within the latter's popular music began in England with the Beatles' use of Indian instruments and musicians in the albums *Revolver* (1966) and *Sgt. Pepper's Lonely Hearts Club Band* (1967) and continued with English-born John McLaughlin, who emigrated to the United States in 1968 and founded the Mahavishnu Orchestra in 1971, blending jazz, rock, and Indian music. Although Indian music waned as African influences waxed, it was India that had inspired the generation of popular musicians active in the 1960s and 1970s. Slightly later, Ancient Future, a band organized in California around 1980, invoked a variety of Asian sounds, including Balinese frogs. In addition to using Balinese instruments, Ancient Future used a number of northern Indian instruments. Jade Warrior's creations included invoking the sounds of Balinese *ketjak* (from *kecak*, "monkey chant"). Wendy Carlos (formerly Walter Carlos) synthesized numerous Asian musics, including those of Tibet and Bali, in her 1986 album *Beauty and the Beast*. Womad Productions/Realworld has produced concert tours blending Asian and American musicians and has issued recordings of both traditional and newly blended musics.

Asian martial arts have attracted the attention of numerous North Americans, including both Euro- and African Americans. Both the Chinese Lion Dance organizations that have proliferated in the larger cities, and the martial arts groups usually associated with them often include a percussion ensemble to accompany performances. Although Lion Dance is performed by Chinese within the Chinese community in places such as New York City, and Cleveland, Ohio, all Lion Dance organizations are Asian American.

A MULTITUDE OF MUSICS

The existence of Asian-derived musics within the United States can thus be explained from several viewpoints. Clearly, these musics exist outside their original contexts, although immigrant communities often provide authentic but new contexts. This raises questions as to whether these musics should be heard as artifacts or as part of an evolving process that not only changes the musics but assigns them new meanings. These musics, then, can be seen along a continuum from so-called pure survivals brought from places where the original music has been changed or lost, to newly fused musics created by stripping parts from world musical traditions and reuniting them in new ways. Those engaged in these processes include first-generation Asian Americans who wish to identify themselves musically with both Asia and the West, as well as non-Asians who adopt and adapt Asian musics and musical instruments in pursuit of multifarious and often conflicting agendas.

Asian musics have come to the United States through proliferating media—records, compact discs, audiocassettes, films, videos, CD-ROM, VCDs, television and radio shows, live concerts, performance courses—but most of these are experienced in new and often personal contexts (for example, the privacy of headphones or viewing rooms). As such, they usually come in objectified form, stripped of their original meaning and awaiting the assignment of new functions and meanings. Asian musics, therefore, may be given meanings connected to novelty, liberalness, liberation, spirituality and the New Age, originality, exoticism, multiculturalism, cultural diversity, environmentalism, and a host of other thoughts, agendas, and desires. The users may know but care little (or nothing) about the musics' original intentions, functions, or meanings, but harness them to express a contemporary American music here and now.

REVIEW

Important Terms and People to Know
Asian American Movement
Café Aman

Culture of exile
E.O. 9066 (Truth Be Told)
Ethnomusicology
Mantle Hood
Immigration Act of 1924
Issei
Koto
Minimalism
Nisei
Oud
Out from the Silence
Poston Sonatai
Quota System
Simon Shaheen
Shakuhachi
Shamisen
Taiko
Yonsei

Review Questions

1. What are some of the strategies Asian American communities use to both preserve traditional musical values while at the same time respond to changing social and musical contexts in the United States?
2. How have certain musical instruments or contexts, especially within the Japanese and Middle Eastern American communities, become iconic of a pan-ethnic identity in the United States? What instruments/contexts have been used especially?
3. How have third- and fourth-generation Japanese Americans responded musically to the internment of members of their community during World War II?
4. What kinds of institutions have supported music and music making of Asian Americans in the United States?
5. How have traditional cultural identities from Asia changed as a result of interaction within a highly heterogeneous population in the United States? What has been the role of music in this negotiation?

Projects

1. Go to an Asian restaurant or market/store in your area and interview the owners and perhaps customers. Find out about their immigrant experience (or that of their parents or

grandparents) and the role of both Asian and Western musics in this experience.

2. Research some of the influences of Asian, especially Indian, Indonesian, and Japanese musics on Western popular and/or classical musics during the twentieth century.

3. Go to a temple or mosque in your area (check the phonebook) and observe the ritual/religious activities. What kinds of music are used? How do the people respond to the music? Interview a few of them to discover their relationship to this music and to the religious practices celebrated here.

Part III
Global Musics in the
United States

CHAPTER 10

Contemporary Concert Musics

William Kearns, Rob Haskins, Steven Loza, Josephine R.B. Wright, and Ingrid Monson

In this chapter we explore two large, yet interrelated, genres of music that have, in the late twentieth and early twenty-first centuries, become associated with the concert hall: classical musics and jazz. Neither of these genres, though, began there. What we generally call "classical music" today began as an outgrowth of church and court practices of medieval and Renaissance Europe, only becoming a middle-class form of concert entertainment and social interaction in the nineteenth century. Jazz began in the juke joints and dance clubs of the rural, then urban South of the early twentieth century, and has only recently become associated with concert hall performance.

Furthermore, unlike much of the music discussed in the previous chapters, Western classical music and African American jazz (along with popular music, discussed more fully in Chapter 11) have become truly global musics, associated with concert halls everywhere. Japan, Korea, and to some extent, China, for example, have adopted Western classical musical forms, instruments, and ensembles, as well as schools and concert spaces, modeled primarily on the French conservatory and performance environments of the nineteenth century. Jazz has become widely popular in Europe and India among many other places, where it has become part of the local/global soundscape of these areas.

Finding an American Voice

European art music overwhelmed the United States during the nineteenth century, just as it continues to be virtually synonymous with classical music today. Although acquiring compositional skill was a first priority for our early composers, some drew on the American environment for inspiration. Toward the end of the nineteenth century, younger European composers drew on the folk music of their countries as an antidote to the Germanic style then dominating classical music. Among them was Antonín Dvořák, who had come to America in 1892 to become the director of the National Conservatory of Music in New York. His most famous piece using "native" materials was the *Symphony from the New World*, premiered by the New York Philharmonic in December 1893. Dvořák urged American composers to draw on their own folk sources, particularly African American and Indian, as he had apparently done in his American compositions.

A younger generation of composers hastened to Dvořák's call and, for a brief time, the so-called Indianist composers flourished. Among the better known are Arthur Farwell and Charles Wakefield Cadman. Cadman made an intense study of American Indian music, visited the Omaha and Winnebago reservations, and gave lecture-recitals with a Native American singer, Princess Tsianina Redfeather. His "Land of the Sky-blue Water," from a set of Indian Songs, op. 45 (1909), crossed over into popular music and became a best-seller. In addition to writing music on Indian themes, Farwell organized the Wa-Wan Press (1901-1912), which became the principal voice of composers using indigenous music.

William Kearns

The Twentieth Century

At the turn of the twentieth century, American musical institutions, such as orchestras, chamber groups, and opera companies, reflected a primary commitment to the Western European concert music tradition. The few American composers who held academic posts—for example, John Knowles Paine (1839-1906) and Horatio Parker (1863-1919), who taught at Harvard and Yale, respectively—had themselves studied in Europe and were meticulous but thoroughly conservative craftsmen. Younger Americans who wanted to devote themselves to composition studied with them or with similar pedagogues. Many also studied in Europe, either in Germany with such composers as Engelbert Humperdinck (1854-1921) and Joseph Rheinberger (1839-1901) or in France with Vincent d'Indy (1851-1931). Some younger composers took this solid training as a base from which they could absorb more current European concerns.

Charles Tomlinson Griffes (1884–1920), for instance, was influenced by impressionism and knew some music by both Schoenberg and Stravinsky; the Boston Symphony premiered his tone poem *The Pleasure Dome of Kubla Khan* (1919) in the last year of his short and financially troubled life.

Other young American composers from the early twentieth century rejected their conservative training. In the symphonic and chamber music of Charles Ives (1874–1954), nearly all of which was completed by 1921, we find such modern traits as polyrhythm, extreme dissonance, and the use of earlier music that ranged from simple quotation to allusion (with or without subtle transformation)—despite the fact that Ives was practically unaware of European contemporary music. Ives's appropriation of other musics within his own remains a powerful evocation of America's heterogeneous culture. Carl Ruggles (1876–1971) developed a painstaking and completely intuitive method of composing in a small handful of works he allowed to be released (he destroyed any pieces he felt to be unsatisfactory). His orchestral *Sun-Treader* (1926–1931) is his best-known work. Nevertheless, it is important to remember that neither composer had much impact until the 1930s or even later, because the then-existing musical institutions were unable and probably unwilling to perform such works. Ives made his living selling insurance; Ruggles struggled with various odd jobs and the support of patrons until he found a more lucrative career as a painter.

In the 1920s and 1930s composers attempted to establish an American identity through ever more diverse stylistic choices; more important, support from institutions both old and new gave their work increased visibility. George Gershwin (1898–1937) was essentially self-taught as a composer and began his successful career writing popular songs and a string of hit Broadway musicals. His *Rhapsody in Blue* (1924) was probably the most successful work in the movement to bring jazz into the concert hall, but, ironically, it is better known today through lush arrangements for full symphony orchestra that have smoothed out the vernacular idiosyncrasies of its original performance style.

Henry Cowell (1897–1965), born in California, was one of the so-called ultramodernists; he was already writing piano music that exploited *tone clusters* (played with the fist or forearm) when he came under the enlightened tutelage of Charles Seeger (1886–1979). In 1917–1918, during his time with Seeger, Cowell wrote an important compositional and theoretical primer, *New Musical Resources* (although not published until 1930; Cowell 1996). Cowell's concert tours to Europe and Russia inspired him to help American composers organize performances and publications of their music; this he did through the quarterly *New Music* (1927–1957) and through his leadership, from 1929 to 1933, of the Pan American Association of

Ultramodernist
Term coined in the 1930s to describe younger composers who employed a variety of then-radical composition techniques

Tone clusters
Blocks of notes played on the piano by using either the fist or forearm

Composers (1928–1934) founded by French immigrant composer Edgard Varèse (1883–1965).

Finally, a large number of composers who had trained under the great French pedagogue Nadia Boulanger (1887–1979) worked to establish a more populist, but distinctly symphonic, American idiom. Of a number of symphonies produced by these composers, perhaps the best known is the *Third Symphony* (1938) by Roy Harris (1898–1979). In this work, a number of traits appear that mark an American symphonic sound later taken up by many composers: massive but spacious textures; a new emphasis on vital, syncopated rhythms (sometimes referring to popular music traditions); and a rich harmonic palette based on compounds of simple major and minor chords in different keys and inversions. This great flowering of the American symphony found favor in concert halls across the country.

Rob Haskins

Snapshot 10.1 highlights some of the contributions to western classical music from the Latin American community living in the United States at mid-century. Mexican American composers and performers, living primarily in Los Angeles, were especially productive, contributing a different voice to American classical music practice.

Snapshot 10.1: Latin American Music in Mid-Century Los Angeles

As World War II came to an end, musical life in the Mexican community of Los Angeles thrived. Performances by local musicians and other entertainers, films, and theatrical presentations from various Latin American countries were an integral part of the musical scene, with interest in the contemporary music of the period often focusing on Latin American composers such as Heitor Villa-Lobos.

Mexican composer Carlos Chávez (1899–1978) conducted a concert devoted exclusively to his own music and performed by the Los Angeles Philharmonic Orchestra on January 11, 1945. The concert was well received by the public and was favorably reviewed in the January 14 issue of *La Opinión* by Samuel Martí, the Mexican violinist and musicologist. Martí was also founder of "Conciertos Martí," chamber recitals that increased recognition of Mexican artistic values in the United States and transmitted American artistic endeavors to Mexico.

Juan Aguilar (Juan Aguilar y Adame) (1893–1953) taught at Mt. Saint Mary's College in 1949 and also served as organist at St. Vibiana Cathedral in downtown Los Angeles. Born at Pueblo de Cosío near Aguascalientes, Mexico, Aguilar studied piano and composition in Mexico City and eventually settled in Guadalajara. To escape the ravages of the revolution, he took his young family to Chihuahua in 1916, then to El Paso, Texas, in 1917. The next year he emigrated to Los Angeles, where he found immediate employment as pianist in the nine-member Pryor Moore instrumental ensemble that played popular music nightly at Boos Brothers Cafeteria until the outbreak of World War II. Aguilar composed prolifically throughout his entire career and was recognized as a virtuoso organist as early as June 30, 1920, when he played for the dedication of the new organ in San Gabriel Church, Los Angeles.

Steve Loza

Destructions and Rebirths: 1945 to 2000

An important site of activity for symphonic and chamber music in mid-century was in the universities and conservatories, whose music departments were coming of age just after World War II. The exodus of European Jews escaping the brutal Nazi regimes brought many composers, scholars, and their families to this country. Among composers, Paul Hindemith (1895-1963), whose wife was Jewish, was at Yale, and Arnold Schoenberg (1874-1951) was at the University of Southern California and the University of California at Los Angeles. More than a few composers from Nadia Boulanger's tutelage, including Harris and Walter Piston (1894-1976), found a haven in academia as well.

John Cage and His Influence

The growing prominence of John Cage (1912-1992; Figure 10.1) in the 1960s had a profound impact on music making within the uni-

Figure 10.1
John Cage, in Los Angeles, 1987. Photographer: Russ Widstrand. Courtesy of the John Cage Trust.

versity system and on a new generation of younger, "independent" composers as well. Cage himself held no extensive academic appointment; however, many of Cage's works were eagerly performed in universities and colleges. Cage is best known for developing *chance* and *indeterminate music*. He designed questions concerning all aspects of a composition from the most general to the most specific, determined possible answers for each question, and answered them through "chance operations." Coin tosses (or, later, a computer program) generated one of the hexagrams from the Chinese book of philosophy the *I Ching*; the number of the hexagram corresponded to one of the several possible answers for each compositional question. For example, in *Europeras 1 & 2* (1987), Cage allowed singers to perform the arias of their choice, but used chance operations to create the orchestra parts (a collage from various operas); chance also determined the times in which each musician performed, the sets, lighting design, and other elements. In this way, Cage removed much of his own taste from the act of composition and created combinations of sounds and images that he could never imagine on his own.

Cage's long personal and professional partnership with the choreographer Merce Cunningham (b. 1919) led him and others naturally toward theater; many other composers were inspired to create rarefied music-theater pieces, notably George Crumb (b. 1929), in his chamber music with voice. Cage's continuing support from New York visual artists (such as Robert Rauschenberg and Jaspar Johns) frequently led to performances of his music that were often outside traditional venues for concert music. Indeed, like Babbitt, he had unsatisfactory and even unhappy experiences with symphony orchestras earlier in his career, as in the New York Philharmonic's miserable performances of *Atlas Eclipticalis* (1961). In the final years of his life, however, Cage fulfilled many commissions with over forty instrumental works collectively known as the Number Pieces; these works—one example is *Fourteen* (1990), a work for bowed piano and thirteen instruments—represent his final thoughts on chamber and orchestral composition.

Around the same time, a rich experimental tradition on the West Coast resulted in some unusual chamber music that explored simple collections of pitches at great length. The *Trio for Strings* (1958) by La Monte Young (b. 1935) was an extremely early work, one that began the musical style known as *Minimalism*; a work that achieved even greater fame was a chamber work for variable ensemble, *In C* (1964) by Terry Riley (b. 1935). By this time, Young had already moved to New York, where in 1961 he and Richard Maxfield (1927-1969) produced a famous series of concerts in the downtown New York loft of Cage's friend Yoko Ono (b. 1933). These concerts are said to have begun the so-called Downtown tradition, a large and fairly loose-knit community of composers and performers whose work did not fit in

Aleatoric/chance music
A theory of composition developed by John Cage that used "chance methods"—such as tossing a coin—to determine the basic elements of a composition

Minimalism
A style of mid-century classical composition that explored simple collections of pitches, utilizing repetitive structures and rhythms

Downtown tradition
A large and loose-knit community of composers and performers centered in downtown New York City whose work did not fit in academic settings or in the traditional venues for concert music

academic settings or in the traditional venues for concert music. Certainly many others composers followed in the tradition of Cage and his students (for example, the conceptual performance art of the *Fluxus* group).

Minimalism

Of all the various styles of music that emerged from the Downtown tradition, however, the most conspicuous was that by the younger minimalist composers. The most prominent of these were Steve Reich (b. 1936), who had participated in the *In C* premiere, and Philip Glass (b. 1937). New York's art community had strong ties with both men. After Reich and Glass established their own ensembles to play their own music, many of their early performances were in artists' lofts or galleries (for instance, a notable pair of concerts at the Whitney Museum's *Anti Illusion* exhibit in 1969). Glass's ensemble in particular, with its relatively stable instrumentation of electric keyboards, winds, and soprano voice, became the prototype of a new kind of amplified chamber music.

Around the same time, several composers with strong academic backgrounds and pedigrees turned away from their earlier, more complex music and began exploring new possibilities for tonality. George Rochberg's (b. 1918) "Concord" String Quartets (Nos. 4-5, 1977-1979) juxtapose tonal and atonal styles within a movement. Some, like String Quartet No. 5, are almost entirely tonal. The trend hit younger composers as well, as in the famous series of pieces based on Lewis Carroll's *Alice's Adventures in Wonderland,* written between 1969 and 1986 by David Del Tredici (b. 1937). After some resistance, the *Neoromantic movement* gained considerably more visibility, most obviously in the series of New York Philharmonic concerts produced by Jacob Druckman (1928-1996) during the 1982-1983 season; these concerts were advertised with the description "Since 1968: A New Romanticism?"

Rob Haskins

Serialism

The serialists saw themselves as a part of the internationalist way of thinking. Austrian composer Arnold Schoenberg, for example, saw his own evolution from late-romantic music through *atonality* to *serialism* as an inevitable progression in the Grand Western Tradition. Serialism is a technique of composing based on a logical organization of tones rather than adherence to key feeling and traditional melodic-harmonic principles. A refugee in the United States during the World War II period, Schoenberg reached out to a generation of American composers from the 1940s through the 1960s, many of whom also wrote serial music. The resulting musical textures were startling to most classical music lovers, who felt aban-

Fluxus
An art and music movement of the 1960s that inspired "Happenings," multimedia presentations that called for audience participation

Neoromantic movement
A return to more complex, lush, tonal musical forms in the 1970s, as a reaction to the more sparse Minmalism composers

Atonality
Literally music with no tonal basis; atonal music has no fixed key and does not follow traditional harmonic rules

Serialism
A technique of composing based on a logical organization of the 12 scale tones; also called *twelve-tone music*

doned by the rapid evolution music was undergoing. Leading post-World War II composers Roger Sessions and Elliott Carter, although not strictly serialists, wrote compositions with melodic-harmonic textures akin to serialism.

William Kearns

Another group of composers, especially Milton Babbitt (b. 1916), who taught both at Princeton and Juilliard, came to even greater prominence in the 1950s and 1960s. Through his activities as theorist, composer, and pedagogue, Babbitt explored the limits of the twelve-tone system and indeed extended those limits in fascinating and exciting directions. The extreme complexity and precision that his music required led him to turn away, for a time, from large orchestral pieces—the disastrous Cleveland Symphony Orchestra performance of his *Relata I* (1965) is the most famous example of the problems musicians faced in playing his music—to electronic music and also to smaller chamber ensembles (especially the string quartet). Such complex music challenged some musicians, who created their own ensembles (many of which were affiliated with colleges or universities) to tackle their difficulties and to commission new works.

Rob Haskins

Musical Example 10.1, "Raudra," written by composer Robert Morris in 1978, uses serial techniques of inversion, retrograde, and retrograde inversion on a set of pitches that forms the core of this solo flute composition. The title refers to one of the nine Indian *rasas* (affects) that give emotional flavor to Indian classical music and is an excellent example of a piece that combines Western techniques with Asian sensibilities.

At the same time Babbitt also became a leading proponent of *electronic music* (see Snapshot 10.2), which resulted in astonishing innovations in melody, harmony, rhythm, form, and particularly tone color. Whether in its *musique concrète* form (tape manipulation of natural sounds) or as a music produced synthetically, electronic music offered the composer a means of making music unfettered by the limitations of the human performer or traditional instruments. But electronic composition has not become a major classical music style. Ironically, electronic techniques are more prevalent in today's popular and commercial music. Thus, electronic music appears to be finding its place as a tool in many types of music, but it is a master in none.

William Kearns

Musique concrète
Composing directly on magnetic tape; sounds are often assembled by taking short sections of tape and splicing them together to form new, unexpected combinations

---

Snapshot 10.2: Electronic Music in the Twentieth Century

Certainly nothing affected the composition, performance, production, and dissemination of music in the twentieth century more

Music Cultures in the United States

than electronic technology. Part of our everyday lives, electronic media such as radio, television, synthesizers, and computers have forever changed the ways we make and receive music. Here are two examples showing the profound effects of electronics on two very different musics.

To American composers trained in the literature and traditions of concert music, electronic music was an exciting new terrain with unimagined possibilities. Indeed, experimental composers such as John Cage (1912–1992) believed that electronic technology would not only inspire a new music unique to its possibilities but would also make a permanent impact on composition for conventional acoustic instruments (Cage 1961:7–12). But the medium proved even more flexible in its appeal to the American entertainment industry (especially film, television, and popular music). In turn, these media have had some measure of influence on both the composition and performance of American concert music, thus revealing a fascinating blurring of cultural boundaries.

The earliest American activity with electronic music began with composition that involved the tape recorder, following the French techniques of *musique concrète* in which composers used natural sounds that they altered and/or superimposed with the device. At first there was no institutional support for such work, and composers shared resources, often with individuals in the commercial sector. Hundreds of prerecorded sounds in Cage's *Williams Mix* (1952), for example, came from the library in the studio of Louis (1920–1989) and Bebe (b. 1927) Barron. (The Barrons are best known for the soundtrack they produced for the 1956 science fiction film *Forbidden Planet*.) Around the same time, Vladimir Ussachevsky (1911–1990) began his famous experiments with tape music composition. Unlike Cage, whose *Williams Mix* is a dense collage of sound assembled entirely by chance-determined splices, Ussachevsky favored a combination of traditional and nontraditional sounds. Pieces like his *Sonic Contours* (1952) include elaborate piano textures built up with tape delay as well as the rerecorded sounds of a piano and human speech at different speeds; nevertheless, the overall shape and character of the work are quite conventional.

In part, Ussachevsky's academic affiliation with Columbia University helped him and his colleague Otto Luening (1900–1996) to gain increased visibility for the new electronic music. In the early 1950s, Ussachevsky and Luening helped to establish the Columbia-Princeton Electronic Music Center, which became a model for many other American universities and music conservatories. One of the Columbia-Princeton Center's major pieces of equipment was a large device originally developed at the RCA laboratories in Princeton for the purpose of reproducing traditional instrumental

Electronic music
Music created electronically, through the use of computers and synthesizers or through tape recorders (or, more recently, digital recorders [such as samplers])

sounds for popular music. This device, which became known as the RCA Synthesizer, was used in the electronic music of Luening, Ussachevsky, and, quite importantly, Babbitt. Babbitt found in the RCA Synthesizer the ideal medium for realizing his desire to extend the principles of twelve-tone composition into the domains of timbre, duration, and volume. His completed works for synthesizer were always on tape in their final form; they ranged from compositions for synthesizer alone (*Composition for Synthesizer,* 1961) to later works that combined a live performer with tape (*Reflections,* for piano and tape, 1975).

Babbitt, of course, was an important music scholar as well as a composer; in his electronic music he attempted to make a profound break with conventional musical patterns in the spirit of humanistic research that the university environment fostered. And although both his works and his attitudes have been much criticized (the latter generally distorted), he has always hoped that listeners will attempt to find meaningful pathways of understanding through his music; for the electronic works, most of which are not completely notated, that process is difficult, though it has begun (Morris 1997).

Other composers in the 1960s of even more radical bent found in electronic technology a surprising variety of possibilities for live performance. On the West Coast, Pauline Oliveros (b. 1932) codirected the San Francisco Tape Music Center, a locus for many experimental projects. She and Richard Maxfield (1927-1969) pioneered techniques of live performance with electronics; one example, Oliveros's *I of IV* (1966), uses tape delay and mixer feedback systems. In the Midwest, the interdisciplinary ONCE group (based in Ann Arbor, Michigan, although not officially affiliated with the university there) involved architects, dancers, theater performers, and filmmakers, as well as such composers as Robert Ashley (b. 1930) and Roger Reynolds (b. 1934). Ashley's *Wolfman* (1964), a shocking piece that uses extreme amplification and feedback to change both live speaking and tape, is a notorious example of his theatrical work.

Cage's own forays into live electronics covered a typical range of possibilities that mirrored the frenzied pluralism of the 1960s. In *Cartridge Music* (1960), the performers insert small objects into phonograph cartridges; they then strike or rub the objects, and the amplified sounds that those actions produce constitute the piece. Many of the works in the *Variations* series (1958-1967) similarly involve amplification, sometimes of everyday actions. In a more elegant use of technology, the piece *Reunion* (1968) involves a chessboard rigged with photoresistors; moves in an actual chess game (between Cage and Marcel Duchamp at the premiere) trigger live electronic music composed by David Tudor (1926-1996), Gordon

Mumma (b. 1935), David Behrman (b. 1937), and Lowell Cross (b. 1938) (Cross 1999).

Throughout the 1960s, designers labored to produce commercial music *synthesizers* for use in professional and academic studio settings; one of the best-known was Robert Moog (b. 1934). In 1968, Moog's name became a household word with the release of the Columbia record *Switched-On Bach,* and a great number of people became powerfully aware of the musical potentials of Moog's synthesizer. This album, a collection of imaginative Bach transcriptions conceived and performed by Wendy Carlos (b. 1939), brought to the fore fascinating issues of electronic "orchestration." Carlos, herself a student of Ussachevsky's, explored a combination of imaginative programming and recording techniques in subsequent albums, especially *The Well-Tempered Synthesizer* (1969). The variety of sound combinations and textures that she achieved through all these techniques served her well in her own music; her important work *Timesteps* (1971) demonstrated how the electronic medium could serve a composer who wanted to explore electronic sounds within the context of a more accessible concert music.

As the technology continued to develop, designers made synthesizers ever more portable in an attempt to interest popular musicians in them. And while many certainly took advantage of the new synthesizers, some younger concert music composers took on the technology for their own performances. The most famous examples from the 1970s are the minimalists Philip Glass (b. 1937) and David Borden (b. 1938). Glass used Farfisa organs (an early portable electronic keyboard instrument) in the early years of his own Philip Glass Ensemble, a group of amplified keyboards and winds with voice. Later, after the composer-performer Michael Riesman (b. 1943) joined the ensemble, a variety of new synthesizers came on board as well. Borden's Mother Mallard Portable Masterpiece Co. was the first all-Moog ensemble.

The repetitive rhythms and modal textures of such works as Glass's *Music in Twelve Parts* (1971–1974) and Borden's *The Continuing Story of Counterpoint* (1976–1987) have much in common with the art rock of the period. Indeed, as minimalism became more pervasive in the late 1970s and 1980s the style could be found frequently in contemporary rock music; its spirit stills finds a home in the dance music known generally (and somewhat imprecisely) as *Electronica*. John Adams (b. 1947) has used the synthesizer in almost every one of his major orchestral works and operas; the synthesizer part in his *Chamber Symphony* (1994) is just as important as the parts for the remaining members of the ensemble.

An important chapter in the history of American electronic music concerns work done with mainframe and microcomputers. Max Mathews (b. 1926) pioneered techniques using computers to

Synthesizer
An electronic instrument that allows the user to create sounds through shaping wave forms, thus influencing timbre, attack, duration, intensity, and other elements of a sound

Moog synthesizer
First commercial synthesizer, made by Robert Moog

Electronica
Popular dance music relying on synthesizers to create its basic audio tracks

Mainframe computer
The large centralized computers used in the 1950s and 1960s mostly located in universities or major science labs

Microcomputer
Smaller computers that brought the power of mainframes to the average user; commonly called personal computers (PCs)

Hyper-
instruments
Instruments
developed by
composer Tod
Machover that
use sensors to
send musical
signals to
computers for
additional
processing

generate sound in the late 1950s during his work at Bell
Laboratories. Lejaren Hiller (1924–1994) used mainframe computers
both to construct algorithms (which would make compositional
decisions) and to make sound. Charles Dodge (b. 1942) and Paul
Lansky (b. 1944) have done extensive work with the creation of user-
friendly software for computer sound synthesis, and some of their
important work has involved the synthesis of human speech.
Lansky's *Six Fantasies on a Poem by Thomas Campion* (1978–1979) is
one of the most important such works. Another composer, Tod
Machover (b. 1953), has developed *hyperinstruments,* conventional
musical instruments equipped with sensors that send musical signals to computers for additional processing and even real-time elaboration. His *Begin Again Again . . .* (1993) was written for the cellist Yo
Yo Ma (b. 1955).

Hiller, Dodge, Lansky, and Machover all held or hold university
appointments, but similar computer-based technology has also
been championed by composers who prefer to work outside the
academy. Of these, the best-known and most promising is Scott
Johnson (b. 1952); Johnson's "Soliloquy" from *How It Happens*
(1991) combines the recorded voice of the left-wing journalist I. F.
Stone (1907–1989) with string quartet. Johnson bases the rhythms
and pitch material of the music on Stone's voice (which he sometimes repeats or otherwise modifies) in subtle and extremely moving ways.

Electronic and computer technology is increasingly pervasive in
the United States. It has allowed people from a wide variety of cultural backgrounds to make their own music; and it will continue
to allow the production of musics both avant-garde and conventional, but always with sounds largely unimagined and otherwise
unavailable.

Rob Haskins

The Development of New Styles

Certainly the majority of twentieth-century American composers
can be classed as neither radical innovators nor vernacularists. Some
followed a more conservative cast, using ideas, textures, and forms
closer to the ones of the past. Others used avant-garde and vernacular (taken from popular music) techniques, but rarely to the extent
of alienating the listening public. Composers such as Howard
Hanson, Peter Mennin, William Schuman, Samuel Barber, Ned
Rorem, Leonard Bernstein, and Morton Gould appeared to place
emphasis on traditional craft and its gradual evolution.

The new romantic movement began with a number of composers whose purpose was to recapture the communicative power
that music of the nineteenth century had held for audiences. It has

now evolved into many different approaches. Sometimes it deals very directly with neohistoricism by means of nostalgia, embracing large portions of tunes, styles, and literary sources from the past, such as David Del Tredici's Alice orchestral pieces (1968-1985), which use Lewis Carroll's famous stories as inspiration, or William Bolcom's *Symphony No. 3* (1979), which juxtaposes pointillistic writing with the lushness of past popular music. Some composers wrestle with traditional compositional procedures, such as are found in John Harbison's cantata "The Flight into Egypt" (1987), subtitled "A Sacred Ricercar," in which imitative points gradually draw together and spread out again. Orchestral virtuosity can be found in Joan Tower's *Silver Ladders* (1986) featuring extended solos for clarinet, oboe, marimba, and trumpet, as well as in Ellen Taaffe Zwilich's "Cello" Symphony (No. 2, 1985), which features the entire cello section.

William Kearns

Composer-Performers Today

The model of the composer-performer popularized by Reich and Glass continues to hold sway with younger composers today. Some, who no longer feel that they need be bound to any particular style or ideology, eagerly embrace a wide variety of styles and manner in their work. This group, which Kyle Gann has dubbed *Totalists* (1997), includes such composers as Michael Gordon (b. 1956), whose string orchestra, electronics, and video "opera" *Weather* (1997) shows a typical range of utterance and traceable influences. These individuals have more often than not formed their own collectives to produce concerts largely devoted to their own work. Most famous, perhaps, is the Bang on a Can All-Stars, a group under the artistic leadership of Gordon, David Lang (b. 1957), and Julia Wolfe (b. 1958). In the face of ever more dire predictions for symphony orchestras in the twenty-first century, the growing number of such ensembles suggests that their influence may become even more pervasive in the foreseeable future.

Rob Haskins

Composers today are also increasingly embracing the music of non-Western cultures, and nowhere has the search for inspiration been more apparent than in the Pacific rim. One of the most dedicated was Lou Harrison (1917-2003), who directed a company producing Chinese music and used many Asian instruments in his works. He both constructed and wrote for gamelan (Indonesian orchestra). Chinese American composer Chou Wen-chung (b. 1923) has made an impressive fusion of Chinese and Western idioms in his compositions. Our growing awareness of the past and our increasing knowledge of many cultures have ushered in what might be called a time of extended eclecticism. Today's composers are shaping these historical and multicultural resources according to their individual creative inclinations.

William Kearns

African American composers also began to contribute to the growing classical music traditions in the United States (see Snapshot 10.3). Often denied entrance into major music schools and departments, especially during the late nineteenth and early twentieth centuries, many African American composers found their own paths by attending historically black colleges and universities.

Snapshot 10.3: African American Concert Music in the Twentieth Century

By the early twentieth century, several prominent composers taught at traditional black colleges and universities, and a few earned critical acclaim at home and abroad for their music, which ran the gamut of contemporary forms and styles. Their legacy was passed on to composers active during the 1960s and beyond, whose impact has been felt throughout the academy and music industry.

William Grant Still

William Grant Still (Figure 10.2), the "dean of African American composers," opened new vistas for black musicians between the 1930s and 1960s. Drawing upon prior experiences in theater orchestras, with the recording studio of the Black Swan label, and in jazz, he brought an intimate knowledge of vernacular traditions of African American music to the craft of composition and was, as Eileen Southern (1982) observed, the first African American composer to apply blues and jazz to symphonic music. His watershed

Figure 10.2
William Grant Still.
Photo courtesy William
Grant Still Music,
Flagstaff, Arizona. All
rights reserved.

work, the *Afro American Symphony* (1930), was premiered in 1931 by the Rochester Philharmonic. A versatile composer, Still wrote four additional symphonies, several symphonic essays, extended pieces for orchestra, chorus, or soloists (for example, *And They Lynched Him on a Tree*, *Plain-Chant for America*, and *Lenox Avenue*), art songs, solo instrumental music, chamber music, and seven operas. His *Troubled Island*, which had its debut performance in 1949 with the New York City Opera, was the first full-length opera by a black composer mounted by a major American company. Still also pioneered as a black composer in the media, creating sound tracks for the films *Lost Horizon* (1935), *Pennies from Heaven* (1936), and *Stormy Weather* (1943), and incidental music for the original *Perry Mason* television show (1954). His awards included fellowships from the Harmon (1928), Guggenheim (1934, 1935, 1938), and Rosenwald Foundations (1939-1940), as well as commissions from CBS, the New York World's Fair, the League of Composers, and leading orchestras.

Musical Example 10.2 is a movement of Still's "Danzas de Panama: Tamborito," written for string quartet and percussion in 1953. Based on West African folk music, first brought to Panama in the seventeenth century by slaves, the work combines the lively Panamanian dance melodies with percussive taps representing the dancer's footsteps. This is another good example of a piece of music that combines aspects of two separate musical cultures into a satisfying whole.

Dramatic social and political changes took place in the United States during the twentieth century: the two great wars; the Depression; the landmark decision in *Brown v. Board of Education of Topeka* (1954), which struck down judicial segregation of public schools; and the Civil Rights movement of the 1960s, which prompted passage of new legislation to protect African American citizens. Composers who grew up in the mid-twentieth century reaped benefits from many of these transitions, particularly greater accessibility to higher education and expanded vistas within which to work. By the 1950s, membership of African Americans in such music-licensing organizations as ASCAP and BMI increased significantly, which ensured them greater protection of their intellectual property. Selected black composers enjoyed commissions and expanded venues for the performance, publication, and recording of their music. With a few notable exceptions, most of the well-established composers obtained professorships at major American universities or schools of music by the 1970s, 1980s, and 1990s.

By the mid-century, Ulysses Kay, Howard Swanson, Julia Perry, and George Walker began to achieve prominence. Each embraced neoclassic concepts from a slightly different perspective. Kay, who had studied with Bernard Rogers and Howard Hanson at the

Eastman School of Music (M. Mus. 1940), and later with Paul Hindemith (1941-1942) and Otto Luening (1942-1946), composed music characterized by an elegant lyricism of melody, dissonant polyphony, rich orchestration, and pulsating rhythms, with no overt hint of African American folk or vernacular music. Although his extensive works lists comprised symphonic music, chamber works, art songs, and choral music, as well as operas, he excelled as a composer of orchestral music. *Markings* (1966), a symphonic essay dedicated to the memory of Dag Hammarskjöld, Secretary-General of the United Nations, and the film score for James Agee's documentary *The Quiet One* (1948) are among his masterpieces.

Howard Swanson, a graduate of the Cleveland Institute of Music (B. Mus. 1937) and a student of Nadia Boulanger in France (1938), consciously integrated African American musical idioms into the neoclassical forms he created. He attracted national attention in 1949 when Marian Anderson sang "The Negro Speaks of Rivers" (text by Langston Hughes) at Carnegie Hall, and he gained further publicity in 1951 when Dmitri Mitropoulos and the New York Philharmonic Orchestra performed his *Short Symphony*. Although not a prolific composer, Swanson produced three symphonies, a concerto for orchestra, miscellaneous chamber pieces, two piano sonatas, and several art songs that remain staples in the modern repertoire of American recitalists.

Julia Perry, an alumna of Westminster Choir College in Princeton, New Jersey (B. Mus. 1947; M. Mus. 1948), studied with Boulanger and privately with Luigi Dallapiccola in Florence, Italy, during the 1950s and was highly regarded during this period as one of the foremost female composers, black or white. She worked effectively in large forms, composing ten symphonies, a string quartet, a viola concerto, and assorted pieces for chamber instruments. In addition to the *Stabat Mater* for contralto and string orchestra (1951) that launched her career, her best-known offerings include *Homage to Vivaldi* for symphony orchestra (1959, rev. 1964), *Homunculus C.F.* for piano, harp, and percussion (1960), and *The Cask of Amontillado* (1953), a one-act opera.

George Walker (Figure 10.3), an alumnus of the Oberlin Conservatory (B. Mus. 1941) and Curtis Institute (1941-1945), and of study with Boulanger and Robert Casadesus (1947), holds the distinction of being the first African American to earn the D.M.A. degree at the Eastman School of Music (1957), as well as the first of his race to receive the Pulitzer Prize in music (1996). Over the years he has developed a distinctive style that fuses modern compositional techniques with jazz as well as African American sacred and vernacular music, and he has composed for full orchestra, chamber ensemble, chorus, solo instrument, and solo voice. His *Sonata for Cello and Piano* (1957), *Piano Concerto* (1976), *Concerto for Cello and*

Figure 10.3
George Walker. Photo
courtesy George
Walker. Photography
by Wonderland
Studios, 1990s.

Orchestra (1981), and four sonatas for piano (1953–1984) are among his most frequently performed compositions.

In recent years Alvin Singleton has emerged as a new star among the avant-garde. After spending much of the 1970s in Europe, he returned to the States in the mid-1980s. Singleton's experimentations range from the use of tonal and post-tonal pitch classifications and sound-space structures to minimalist techniques. He has concentrated since the 1980s on writing orchestral music, including *After Fallen Crumbs* and *Shadows* (1987) for the Atlanta Symphony, *Sinfonia Diaspora* (1991) for the Oregon Symphony, and *Durch Alles* (1992) for the Cleveland Orchestra.

Classical and jazz/vernacular music found a synthesis in *Third Stream music* (a term coined in 1957 by Gunther Schuller), which has come to dominate the work of David Baker, professor and chairman of the jazz department at Indiana University (1966–2000), and Frederick Tillis, professor emeritus of the University of Massachusetts, Amherst, both of whom bring extensive experience as jazz performers to the craft of writing art music.

Third Stream music
Compositions that combine elements of classical instrumentation and structure with jazz stylings

Baker has composed in a variety of Western forms (cantatas, oratorios, art songs, choral music, symphonies, solo sonatas, chamber music, symphonic essays) and experimented with mixed media, often combining traditional musical instruments with jazz combos, gospel choirs, or electronic instruments. Among his important works are the cantata *Le Chat Qui Pêche* (1974), the *Concerto for Cello and Chamber Orchestra* (1975), *Singers of Songs/Weavers of Dreams* for cello and percussions (1980), and *Roots II* for piano trio (1992).

Tillis has drawn eclectically from traditional African, African American, and Southeast Asian music as well as contemporary Western forms and compositional techniques. Among his representative works are *Ring Shout Concerto* for percussion and orchestra

(1974), *Niger Symphony* for chamber orchestra (1975), *Concerto for Pro Vivo* and chamber orchestra (1980), a series of eighteen *Spiritual Fantasies* for various instruments (1980-1998), and *Kabuki Scenes* for brass quintet and timpani (1991).

Employing black folk and vernacular idioms in Western art forms remained a fairly consistent theme among many classically trained African American composers in the twentieth century. Tania León (b. 1943) has added to this tradition the sounds of her native Cuba, where Afro-Cuban, Yoruban, Congolese, and creole Spanish cultures commingle. Emigrating from Havana to the United States in 1967, she has established a solid reputation as a composer, conductor, and musical director. Through her visibility as a composer-conductor, León has promoted cultural exchanges between musicians within the Americas as the artistic advisor of Sonidos de las Américas. Recent examples of Afro-Caribbean influences in her music are found in *Kabiosile* for piano and orchestra (1988), *Indígena* for chamber orchestra (1991), and the symphonic essay *Carabalí* (1991).

The late twentieth century witnessed the rise of a new generation of promising composers with James Kimo Williams (b. 1950), whose *Symphony for the Sons of Nam* (1986, rev. 1990) has been programmed by National Public Radio; Anthony Davis (b. 1951), whose *X: The Life and Times of Malcolm X* was premiered in 1986 by the New York City Opera; Lettie Beckon Alston (b. 1953), a finalist in the 1993 Detroit Symphony Orchestra's Unisys African American Composers Forum competition; Julius P. Williams (b. 1954), who directed the Bohuslav Martinů Philharmonic in a 1993 recording of his *Meditation: From Easter Celebration*; Jeffrey Mumford (b. 1955), first-prize winner of the 1994 National Black Arts Festival/Atlanta Symphony Orchestra competition; William C. Banfield (b. 1961), winner of the 1995 Detroit Symphony Orchestra's Unisys African American Composers Forum competition for *Essay for Orchestra*; and Gregory Walker (b. 1961), son of the composer George Walker and author of *Dream N. the Hood*, a rap-symphonic essay.

Josephine R. B. Wright

JAZZ

Jazz is widely regarded as the pinnacle of African American music in the twentieth century, distinguished by the originality of its improvisation, the virtuosity and erudition of its performers and composers, and its professionalism and artistry. Many of its practitioners regard jazz as America's classical music, or African American classical music, although this definition is sometimes contested. The respectability acquired by jazz in the late twentieth century stands in stark contrast to the denigrated status of the music and its practitioners earlier in the century.

Several broader social forces have shaped the history of jazz and its changing cultural meaning in the twentieth century, including urbanization, racism, the advent of recording and broadcasting technology, modernism as an aesthetic ideology, two world wars, and the Civil Rights movement. The musical hallmarks of jazz are improvisation, syncopation, a rhythmic propulsiveness known as swing, a blues feeling, and harmonic complexity. Unlike most other African American musical genres, instrumental rather than vocal performance has been most prestigious and influential.

Early History

Historians place the origins of the jazz in New Orleans during the first years of the twentieth century, concurrent with the heyday of *ragtime*. Cornetist Buddy Bolden's band, which established a distinctive sound between 1897 and 1907, is often considered the first jazz band. Bolden (1877-1931) was known for his improvisational elaboration of melodies, an ability to play very loudly, and his deep feeling for the blues. Bolden's competition in New Orleans included both bands and dance bands that featured a variety of repertoire, including marches, ragtime, and waltzes. Around 1900, brass bands, which generally had featured the careful execution of written arrangements, began admitting "ear" musicians or "routiners," who created *head arrangements* and brought a more improvisational and blues-inflected style to the music. Brass bands were particularly important in transforming a straight march beat into the *slow drag* and *up-tempo strut*, the two basic feels of New Orleans jazz style.

Hardening racial relations in New Orleans at the end of the nineteenth century shaped the emergence of jazz as a distinctive genre. Increased contact between French-speaking Creole musicians and English-speaking African Americans was a byproduct of the emergence of Jim Crow laws in the 1890s and the use of the "one drop" rule of racial classification that enforced them. Under this criterion persons of as little as $\frac{1}{32}$ black ancestry (sometimes even less) were considered black regardless of appearance. The traditionally three-tiered New Orleans racial hierarchy that recognized white, Creole, and black hardened into a two-tiered structure recognizing only black and white, especially after the *Plessy v. Ferguson* decision in 1896 (the Supreme Court decision that established the doctrine of "separate but equal").

Creoles of color *(gens de couleur),* who were predominantly Catholic, of French-speaking heritage, and generally of light complexion, resided "downtown" and had long cultivated an instrumental virtuosity, musical literacy, and training in classical music. They considered themselves superior to their English-speaking and less

Ragtime
An instrumental style featuring a steady bass beat against which a syncopated melody is performed

Ear musician/ "Routiner"
A musician who doesn't read music notation but rather plays "by ear"

Head arrangement
An unwritten arrangement created "on the spot" by the band members

Slow drag
A slow, syncopated dance rhythm

Up-tempo strut
An adaptation of the up-tempo syncopation of ragtime to a band setting

musically literate black neighbors, who resided predominantly "uptown." Uptown musicians were noted for the blues, their improvisational abilities, and their abilities as ear musicians. The emergence of jazz as an instrumentally virtuosic, improvisational tradition that also valued musical literacy emerged from a meeting of uptown and downtown. Among the Creole musicians most important to the development of jazz are pianist and composer Jelly Roll Morton (Ferdinand LeMothe, 1890-1941), clarinetist Barney Bigard (1906-1980), trombonist Kid Ory (1890-1973), and clarinetist and saxophonist Sidney Bechet (1897-1959). The most pathbreaking early soloists were uptown musicians, among them cornetist Joe "King" Oliver (1885-1938) and trumpeter Louis Armstrong (1901-1971; see Figure 10.4).

Despite the longstanding notion that jazz traveled up the Mississippi to Chicago (a legend that overlooks the fact the river does not pass through Chicago), California (Los Angeles and San Francisco) was an equally important market for jazz before 1917. The bands of Freddie Keppard and Kid Ory were among the many that brought jazz to California between 1914 and 1922. Chicago, nevertheless, holds a special place in the history of 1920s jazz, because it was there that Louis Armstrong's bold and virtuosic

Figure 10.4
King Oliver's Jazz Band with Louis Armstrong. L to r: Johnny Dodds, Baby Dodds, Kid Ory, Louis Armstrong, King Oliver, Lil Hardin [Armstrong], and Johnny St. Cyr, c. 1924. Courtesy David A. Jasen.

Music Cultures in the United States

improvisational style became the talk of the town and ultimately set the direction for jazz.

In the summer of 1922 King Oliver asked Louis Armstrong to join his band in Chicago. Oliver's band played along "The Stroll," a thriving nightlife district on South State Street featuring several African-American-owned clubs: the Deluxe Café, the Pekin, and the Dreamland Café. These and other clubs became sites of racial boundary crossing as interested young whites came to enjoy the music, among them saxophonist Bud Freeman (1906-1991), cornetist Jimmy McPartland (1907-1991), clarinetist Frank Teschemacher (1906-1932), and drummer Dave Tough (1908-1948). Many of Chicago's south side clubs were "blacks-and-tans," cabarets that presented African American performers and catered to both black and white audiences. Chicago in the early 1920s tolerated greater racial mixing in these venues than New York did. Nevertheless, racial boundary crossing in Chicago was not reciprocal, because black musicians and audience members could not patronize north-side white clubs. Despite the reputation of jazz as a cultural arena where there was greater interracial contact during the Jim Crow years than in other arenas of American cultural life, it is important to remember that whites had far greater mobility in crossing the color line.

Between 1925 and 1928 Louis Armstrong made a series of recordings for OKeh (arranged by his wife and pianist Lil Hardin [1898-1971]) with groups known as the Hot Five and the Hot Seven. These are among Armstrong's most celebrated recordings, and they virtually defined the expansive improvisational style that was to become the hallmark of early jazz. Armstrong moved away from melodic paraphrase to a more elaborate improvisation guided by the underlying harmonies rather than the melody alone. Despite the fact that these recordings were made in Chicago and that there are many earlier recordings by other bands that include improvised solos, Armstrong's style set the standard for New Orleans jazz. The Hot Five and Hot Seven recordings also established Armstrong as a cultural hero, especially in African American communities, where his tremendous success contributed to a communal sense of pride.

Composers, Ensembles, and Big Bands

Although the emergence of the improvising soloist is the hallmark of jazz, it is important to note that the development of the jazz ensemble (large and small) was also key. Indeed, a particular sound produced through distinctive rhythmic, harmonic, melodic, and timbral vocabularies of the ensemble are just as crucial to defining jazz as a genre as improvisation is. Among the early jazz composers and arrangers who contributed to this emerging sound were Jelly Roll Morton, Duke Ellington (1899-1974), Fletcher Henderson (1897-1952), and Don Redman (1900-1964).

Jelly Roll Morton's 1926 recordings for Victor provide examples of the creative use of the ensemble in early jazz. Among the most highly regarded compositions from these sessions are "Black Bottom Stomp," "Grandpa's Spells," "The Chant," and "Smokehouse Blues." Unlike the Hot Five recordings, which omitted bass and drums, these recordings feature one of the best rhythm sections in early jazz. In "Black Bottom Stomp," Morton and his band deploy a full range of early jazz time-feels to provide contrast and excitement to the well-planned architectural shape of the performance.

In New York of the 1920s Fletcher Henderson and Don Redman developed a big band sound by incorporating jazz soloists such as Louis Armstrong and Coleman Hawkins (1904–1969) into a dance band of larger instrumentation than that of the typical New Orleans jazz ensemble. Henderson's band featured three trumpets, a trombone, three reeds, and a rhythm section. Henderson and Don Redman worked as a team, developing an arranging style that featured *call and response* between the brass and reed sections and the use of one instrumental choir as an accompanimental background (often featuring a *riff*) for the other. Redman also wrote ensemble sections in the style of improvised jazz solos. All these devices and techniques became staples of big band arranging in the 1930s.

The composer who developed the most unique style for jazz ensemble in the 1920s was undoubtedly Duke Ellington (see Figure 10.5). Ellington's singular style combined the "sweet" (that is, not blues inflected) dance band style with the exuberant New Orleans and blues-inspired trumpet style of New Yorker Bubber Miley (1903–1932) and Ellington's own stride- and ragtime-based piano style. Miley pioneered the growling trumpet sound that became a trademark of Ellington's so-called jungle sound. There were several keys to producing this sound: the use of a straight mute, an ordinary bathroom plunger to produce the wah-wah sound, a literal growl in the throat of the trumpeter, and the simultaneous humming of a pitch into the horn. Ellington's recordings of "East St. Louis Toodle-Oo" and *Black and Tan Fantasy* from 1926 to 1927 provide excellent examples of Miley's "talking" brass effect. Tricky Sam Nanton (1904–1946) adapted this sound to the trombone, and thereafter mastery of the growl sound was an essential for brass players in the Ellington band. These new brass sounds were only one aspect of Ellington's interest in timbral variety and unusual orchestration. "Mood Indigo," one of the composer's most famous ballads, features an opening trio of muted trumpet, muted trombone, and clarinet that is as easily identifiable by timbre as by thematic content.

In 1927 Duke Ellington got his first major break when he was hired at the Cotton Club, a Harlem nightclub catering to a whites-only clientele and decorated in plantation motif. The Cotton Club featured shows combining music, exotic dancing (some performed

Call and response
In big-band jazz, the alternation of short melodic phrases played first by the brass section and then "answered" by the reeds
Riff
A short melodic idea that is usually repeated
Sweet band/style
Dance bands that play more straightforward arrangements of popular tunes, with little blues influence

Figure 10.5
Duke Ellington in a
publicity collage from
the late 1930s.
Courtesy David A.
Jasen.

in pseudo-African garb), and theatrical presentation. The Ellington orchestra, now expanded from six to eleven members, provided to the wealthy white clientele the "primitive" ambience they were looking for, often through sophisticated musical means beyond their imagination. The club's regular radio broadcasts during Ellington's tenure (1927-1932) brought the "Ellington Effect" into America's living rooms and made him a national figure.

Broadcasting and the Swing Era

Radio broadcasts from major hotels, clubs, and dance halls were crucial in establishing and maintaining the reputations of the bands headed by Benny Goodman (1909-1986), Tommy Dorsey (1905-1956), Count Basie (1906-1984), and Duke Ellington, among others. There were two types of radio broadcasts: *sustaining programs* originating late at night from hotels and clubs and featuring a variety of bands, and *sponsored programs*, for which a company such as Coca-Cola or Lucky Strike hired particular bands for long-term contracts. Access to radio broadcast opportunities was racially structured, with white bands at an advantage. White bands were more likely to be booked at hotels and clubs with radio broadcast capability, because most such venues had segregated booking policies. Even so, many black bands were able to make radio appearances from locations such as the Cotton Club, the Savoy Ballroom, or Chicago's Grand Terrace. Sponsored programs were out of the question for black bands. Not until 1946 was there an all-black sponsored radio program—NBC's *Nat King Cole Trio Time*—and even guest appearances on white programs by prominent black musicians were rare.

Sustaining program
A radio program broadcast late at night from hotels and clubs and featuring a variety of bands
Sponsored program
A radio program sponsored by a company such as Coca Cola or Lucky Strike, which hired particular bands for long-term contracts

Segregation in the public arena caused interracial collaborations of various kinds to occur in less visible ways. Hiring arrangers from across the color line was one way; recording (but not appearing) with a mixed ensemble was another. Fletcher Henderson's compositions and arrangements, which white clarinetist Benny Goodman bought in 1934, served as the principal component of the Goodman band's repertoire as it established its national profile. Goodman later hired African Americans Henderson and Jimmy Mundy (1907-1983) as staff arrangers for the band and defied the performance color line by hiring vibes player Lionel Hampton (1908-2002) and guitarist Charlie Christian (1916-1942) as musicians. African American pianist Teddy Wilson (1912-1986) recorded with the Benny Goodman trio a year prior to his famous 1936 appearance with the bandleader at Chicago's Congress Hotel. Although a considerable amount of interracial mixing had taken place in black venues from the very beginning, the mixing in a predominantly white setting was what was newsworthy about this event.

The ambivalent reception of Benny Goodman's title "King of Swing," especially later in the twentieth century, stems from the racially structured aspects of his rise to prominence. Goodman's story serves to illustrate several themes in ongoing debates over the relationship between black and white jazz. In late 1934 Goodman was offered a regular slot on NBC's *Let's Dance,* a radio program sponsored by the National Biscuit Company. In choosing Goodman, NBC overlooked many prominent black bands including those of Duke Ellington, Earl Hines, and Jimmie Lunceford (1902-1947). Goodman's success on the show was fueled by Fletcher Henderson's compositions and arrangements, and thus many white audience members came to know the swing music of an African American composer through the medium of white performance. Goodman was crowned the "King of Swing" even though he was not its origi-nator; consequently, swing did not appear to be black music to the broader white public. This perception was reinforced by Jim Crow barriers that kept African American bands from being heard through the same high-visibility broadcast channels. That Goodman as an individual took actions facilitating the employment of African Americans in mainstream white dance bands (generally in advance of other white bandleaders) cannot be denied, yet he was also a ben-eficiary of the racial status quo in the music industry.

Swing music
Big band jazz style of the 1930s that incorporated short, repeated riffs and a lightly syncopated beat

Swing Music

The major big bands of the swing era served as important training grounds for younger musicians. Many improved their music-reading skills, understanding of harmony, ensemble skills, and (for some) composing and arranging skills under the tutelage of more experi-enced musicians. One hallmark of *swing music* is the extensive use of riffs as ensemble textures. Riffs were used in many ways: (1) as melodies; (2) in call and response with another riff or an improvised passage; (3) as a continuous supporting texture underneath a soloist or written passage; and (4) in layers. Shout choruses were often used at the very end of a piece as a climax. The artful use of repetition, which served as a solid anchor for dancers, was another hallmark of swing style.

Many virtuosic soloists emerged in the 1930s, from small groups as well as big bands. Expanding on Armstrong's lead, musicians strove to extend the scope of solo improvisation. Among the most prominent soloists were Roy Eldridge (1911-1989), trumpet; Lester Young (1909-1959) and Coleman Hawkins, tenor saxophone; and Art Tatum (1909-1956), piano. Vocalist Billie Holiday (1915-1959), whose inventive paraphrases of melody and timing inspired many, including Lester Young, also became prominent in the late 1930s, recording with many members of the Count Basie orchestra.

Bebop

With World War II came not only a new aesthetic in jazz but a new attitude in African American communities as well. The Double V campaign (which called for victory over racism at home as well as victory for democracy in Europe) perhaps symbolized the transition best, as African Americans deemed fit to risk their lives in battle chafed at the glaring racial injustices at home. As Scott DeVeaux (1997) has noted, professional jazz musicians were a relatively privileged elite who worked in an industry that accorded greater personal freedom, mobility, and prosperity than did most occupations available to black Americans. The symbolic value of that hard-won success and freedom to the broader African American community was enormous.

During the war years, musicians who had become frustrated with the limited possibilities for extended improvisation in big bands and dismayed by the dominance of white bands in the popular music market forged an ambitious improvisational style that came to be known as *bebop* (musicians first called it "modern music"). No longer content to be entertainers, the younger jazz musicians demanded to be taken seriously as artists. The heroes of this movement were Charlie Parker (1920-1955; see Figure 10.6), alto sax; Thelonious Monk (1917-1982), piano; Dizzy Gillespie (1917-1993), trumpet; Kenny Clarke (1914-1985), drums; Max Roach (b. 1924), drums; and Bud Powell (1924-1966), piano. The series of legendary jam sessions that are said to have created the style took place in Harlem at Minton's and Monroe's Uptown House.

The musical innovations of bebop affected several dimensions of the music: instrumental virtuosity, harmony, phrasing, rhythmic feel, timbre, and tempo. Charlie Parker and Dizzy Gillespie reharmonized

Bebop
Black jazz style pioneered in the 1940s that featured accelerated tempos, more complex rhythms, and virtuosic soloing

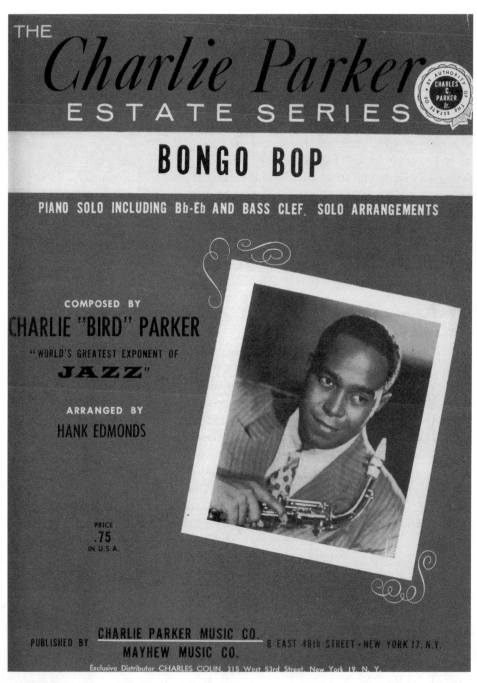

Figure 10.6
Charlie Parker pictured on the sheet music cover for "Bongo Bop" released shortly after his death. Courtesy David A. Jasen.

and/or wrote new melodies for standard jazz tunes such as "Cherokee," "I Got Rhythm," and "What Is This Thing Called Love?" increasing the harmonic rhythm (the pace at which harmonies change) and the tempo and improvising highly subdivided phrases that set a new standard for instrumental virtuosity in the music.

Gillespie's trademark goatee and beret were widely emulated by fans of the new music, and by the late 1940s bebop had acquired a subcultural quality that shunned mainstream "squares." Bebop style included the use of "bop talk" (drawn from African American vernacular speech), a critique of the racial status quo, and the unfortunate fashionability of heroin use. Charlie Parker's well-known addiction set the example, as many young musicians seemed to conclude that Parker achieved his genius because of, rather than in spite of, the drug. Many musicians suffered arrest, loss of their New York cabaret cards, jail time, or death in pursuit of a habit that was rumored to intensify one's hearing. Although the drug addictions of several prominent African American musicians (Charlie Parker, Miles Davis [1926-1990], Sonny Rollins [b. 1930]) are more widely known, several prominent white musicians (Stan Getz [1927-1991], Chet Baker [1929-1988], Art Pepper [1925-1982]) share similar stories.

In contrast to Parker and Gillespie, Thelonious Monk is recognized more for the originality of his compositions than for his virtuosity as a soloist. In 1947 Monk made a series of recordings for the Blue Note label that included many of his most famous compositions, "Thelonious," "Ruby My Dear," "'Round Midnight," "Well You Needn't," and "In Walked Bud" among them. Although greatly admired within the jazz world of the late 1940s (pianist Mary Lou Williams [1910-1981] was among his earliest champions), Monk did not achieve broader prominence until the late 1950s and early 1960s.

Monk's loss of his cabaret card in 1951 certainly contributed to his marginality, but perhaps a more important factor was the great difference between his aesthetic and that of mainstream bebop. If Parker and Gillespie's music emphasized dazzling virtuosity, Monk's own soloing seemed to argue that less is more. A celebrated example of Monk's ability to say more with less is his 1954 recording of "Bags' Groove" with Miles Davis. Over nine choruses of the blues Monk uses spare means to build a compelling larger shape for the solo. The openings of the first three choruses illustrate one way in which Monk accomplishes this. Each chorus begins with a riff that is developed over twelve bars (see Figure 10.7). Notice that the riff for the first chorus begins with eighth notes, the second with triplets, and the third with sixteenth notes. Monk's use of rhythmic displacement (shifting a figure's position within a bar) as a means of variation are apparent in the triplet and sixteenth-note passages in choruses two and three.

The Civil Rights Movement

By the mid-1950s the burgeoning Civil Rights movement exerted pressure on musicians to do their part in supporting efforts to end Jim Crow. The black community expected musicians to demonstrate

Figure 10.7
Openings of the first three choruses of "Bags' Groove," 1954 (Monson, pg. 659; score).

their commitment to the larger cause of racial justice and publicly shamed those artists (such as Nat King Cole [1919-1965] and Louis Armstrong) who continued to accept engagements in performance venues that segregated audiences. The issue of audience segregation was far more important to Civil Rights organizations than whether or not a particular band had mixed personnel. Southern white audiences, after all, had long been comfortable with black and mixed entertainment as long as segregated seating remained. The activist climate emerging from the principal events of the Civil Rights movement had important consequences for jazz of the 1950s and 1960s.

The jazz community reacted in various ways to civil rights events by performing benefit concerts, recording albums with political themes, attributing political meaning to particular jazz aesthetics, exploring African and other non-Western musical and religious ideas, and engaging in highly charged dialogues about race and racism in the jazz industry. The emergence of several of the most revered figures in jazz and the aesthetics they represent—among them Miles Davis, John Coltrane (1926-1967), Charles Mingus (1922-1979), and Ornette Coleman (b. 1930)—took place against this volatile historical backdrop.

Modal Jazz

Modal jazz
Compositions that reduced the number of harmonic changes, allowing soloists to improvise for an extended period of time over one or two chords

Among the most important musical innovations in this period was the development of *modal jazz*. Exemplified by Miles Davis's album *Kind of Blue* (1959), modal compositions reduced the number of harmonic changes, allowing soloists to improvise for an extended period of time over one or two chords.

The conceptual father of a modal approach to harmony in jazz is George Russell, whose *Lydian Concept of Tonal Organization* (1953) and *Lydian Chromatic Concept of Tonal Organization* (1959) offered the improviser and composer a complex system of associating chords with scales organized by their degree of consonance or dissonance. Russell emphasized the multiple choices available to performers and was widely known in the jazz community for his expertise in modes and scales. Both Miles Davis and pianist Bill Evans (1929-1980), who appeared on *Kind of Blue,* were familiar with Russell's ideas. The Lydian Concept, however, was intended as a more general approach to harmony that could be applied to harmonically dense as well as harmonically sparse musical settings.

Modal jazz also came to imply a more open-ended approach to form and harmonic voicings. Instead of observing a chorus structure, jazz musicians explored pieces that allowed a soloist to play indefinitely over a recurring chord pattern or rhythmic vamp. The vamp to John Coltrane's "My Favorite Things" (1960) is a good example. Charles Mingus's "Pithecanthropus Erectus" (1956) and Art Blakey's extended percussion solos on "Orgy in Rhythm" (1957) and "Holiday for Skins" (1958) provide additional examples of a more open-ended conception of form. Blakey's collaborations with Afro-Cuban musicians on these albums—including Sabu Martinez (1930-1979), Patato Valdez (b. 1926), and Ubaldo Nieto—took place at the time of Ghana's independence, when there was much discussion of Africa in the African American press.

In the early 1960s John Coltrane shifted from a well-developed modern bebop style featuring harmonically dense compositions such as "Giant Steps" (1959) to an open-ended modal conception that actively explored not only African but Indian sources of musical and spiritual inspiration. Coltrane's legendary ensembles developed the rhythmic as well as harmonic implications of open-ended modal approaches to improvisation, something that Miles Davis's quintet of 1963-1968 did also. Freed from the necessity of delineating frequently changing harmonies, bassists expanded their use of *pedal points*, pianists accompanied long sections with intricate vamps and riffs, and drummers played with greater rhythmic density and *cross-rhythms* than had been customary in earlier styles. Among the recordings exemplifying this sound include Coltrane's *My Favorite Things* (1960), *Africa Brass* (1961), *India* (1961), *Crescent* (1964), and *A Love Supreme* (1965) and Miles Davis's *My Funny Valentine* (1964), *Miles in Berlin* (1964), and *Live at the Plugged Nickel* (1965).

Free Jazz

A major aesthetic controversy erupted in the jazz world in early 1960 when alto saxophonist Ornette Coleman emerged on the New York scene. Coleman's dissonant harmonic style and abandonment of chorus structures and fixed harmonic changes as means of organizing improvisational flow were claimed by some as *The Shape of Jazz to Come* (1959) (the title of Coleman's first release after his arrival in New York), decried by others as the destruction of jazz, and championed by still others as a music of social critique. Over the next seven years an aesthetic community of jazz musicians committed to what was variously termed *free jazz*, the New Thing, or avant-garde jazz

Pedal point
The root note of a chord played to suggest a more complete harmony
Cross-rhythms
Two or more rhythms played simultaneously

emerged on the New York scene. Among them were Coleman, Cecil Taylor (b. 1933), Albert Ayler (1936–1970), Archie Shepp (b. 1937), Sun Ra (1914–1993), and John Coltrane. Coltrane's turn toward free jazz gave considerable prestige to the burgeoning free jazz movement. The new approach also fostered the creation of collective musical organizations such as Chicago's Association for the Advancement of Creative Musicians (AACM) (1965) and later St. Louis's Black Artists Group (BAG) (1968).

Free jazz was claimed by its advocates as the left wing of jazz expression, its musically adventurous means taken as a sign of revolutionary social critique, spiritual awareness, and freedom. The political meanings attached to the genre must be viewed in dialogue with the riveting events of the Civil Rights movement that took place during its emergence. Shortly after Ornette Coleman's New York debut in late 1959, the Greensboro lunch counter sit-ins occurred (February 1960), launching the most activist phase of the Civil Rights movement. For many the dissonance of the music was taken as a sign of social dissidence. On the other hand, for modernist-oriented jazz critics, such as Gunther Schuller (b. 1925) and Martin Williams (1924–1992), the appeal of free jazz lay in its parallel with the historical development of Western classical music. These critics stressed that musical logic determined the organic evolution of music from simple to complex, from tonal music to avant-garde. Here free jazz was of interest for its modernist aesthetic, rather than its political radicalism.

Among the greatest champions of free jazz as a political music was playwright, poet, and critic Amiri Baraka (LeRoi Jones; b. 1934), whose *Blues People* (1963) viewed free jazz as the logical outcome of the black musician's centuries of struggle with racism in America. *Blues People* was the first major book by an African American author to advocate a sociological and culturally contextualized view of black musical history. Among musicians, Archie Shepp publicly raised the issue of racism in the jazz industry, in outspoken published pieces such as "An Artist Speaks Bluntly" (1965). Max Roach raised comparable issues and shifted toward free jazz in the 1960s as well. Later, Frank Kofsky's *Black Nationalism and the Revolution in Music* (1970) took a political view of avant-garde jazz.

For many artists, however, the politics of free jazz expression was a byproduct of its spiritual implications. For Albert Ayler, John Coltrane, and Sun Ra, spiritual communion (a different sort of liberation) through avant-garde expression was a primary motivation for their expressive choices. Ayler's work drew heavily upon the African American gospel and folk traditions, turning familiar hymn melodies into abstract wails and pleas of deep emotional intensity. Both Coltrane and Sun Ra were drawn to non-Western modes of spirituality. Both men were widely read in spiritual traditions from

Africa, India, China, and West Asia (the Middle East). Sun Ra's aesthetic embraced both ancient Egypt and outer space as metaphors for liberation and spiritual depth.

Critics of free jazz failed to see progress in the atonality and indefinite time feels of the music. They viewed the avant-garde as a decline, brought on by young musicians who didn't do their homework or pay their dues in the tradition. An observer for *Muhammad Speaks,* the organ of the Nation of Islam, even suggested that avant-gardists like Coltrane were pandering to white critics. Observers from the mid-1960s confirm that as the music became increasingly atonal, many black audience members defected to the immensely popular Motown and soul sound, or to soul jazz—the classic organ trio or quartet sound popularized by Jimmy Smith (b. 1925), Stanley Turrentine (1934-2000), and Shirley Scott (b. 1934)—leaving a disproportionately white audience for free jazz. During the Black Power years of 1966-1970, a tense dialogue between a militant African American radical intelligentsia and radical white audience members and musicians often took place through free jazz performances.

The 1970s

The release of Miles Davis's *Bitches Brew* in 1969 augured a new direction for jazz in the 1970s, one that embraced rather than rejected popular musical styles. Widely heralded for its creative synthesis of jazz improvisation and rock and roll, *Bitches Brew* used electrified rock and roll time feels, as well as many of the post-production techniques of popular music, including overdubbing and looping. Davis was particularly inspired by guitarist Jimi Hendrix (1942-1970), who was able to reach a broad audience with his creative guitar pyrotechnics. Later Davis's fusion interests turned toward soul and funk in an effort to reach a younger African American audience. His albums *A Tribute to Jack Johnson* (1970) and *On the Corner* (1972) illustrate this trend. Several other bands offering various mixes among jazz, rock and roll, soul, rhythm and blues, and non-Western musics emerged in the 1970s, including, most prominently, Weather Report, John McLaughlin (b. 1942) and the Mahavishnu Orchestra, Herbie Hancock (b. 1940) and the Headhunters, and Chick Corea (b. 1941) and Return to Forever.

The 1970s also witnessed an expansion and internationalization of avant-garde jazz. Major figures and ensembles of the decade include multireedist and composer Anthony Braxton (b. 1945), the Art Ensemble of Chicago, Cecil Taylor, David Murray (b. 1955), Steve Lacy (b. 1934), and several individual members of Chicago's AACM, including Lester Bowie (1941-1999), Roscoe Mitchell (b. 1940), and Joseph Jarman (b. 1937). European audiences proved to be especially receptive to free jazz, and an indigenous European avant-garde inspired by American jazz emerged including such figures as Albert

Mangelsdorff (b. 1928), Willem Breuker (b. 1944), and the Global Unity Orchestra.

Another artist to emerge as leading jazz composer and performer at this time was pianist Mary Lou Williams (1910–1981). Born in Atlanta, she became a chile performer and eventually began arranging and composing for jazz artists, such as Duke Ellington, Louis Armstrong, Dizzy Gillespie, and others. Here is a recording of her "Gloria" (Musical Example 10.3) taken from one of three masses she composed in the 1970's, "Mary Lou's Mass." Notice the strong connection with the earlier blues form in this recording.

Lincoln Center

By the early 1980s many young jazz musicians found greater inspiration in the "golden age" of modern jazz (from 1945 to 1965) than in much of the contemporary offerings of *fusion* or avant-garde styles. Trumpeter Wynton Marsalis (b. 1961) made no secret of his disappointment in the jazz of the early 1980s, passionately advocating a return to basic jazz values (particularly the chord changes and swinging rhythms) through studying the classic recordings of such masters as Art Blakey, Miles Davis, John Coltrane, Thelonious Monk, and Duke Ellington. Marsalis's outspoken criticism of the jazz avant-garde and the most recent fusion efforts of Miles Davis polarized older jazz listeners, who cast Marsalis as an aesthetic conservative and latter-day "moldy fig." Marsalis nevertheless inspired and nurtured a group of young musicians who later became known as the Young Lions, among them trumpeters Roy Hargrove (b. 1969) and Terence Blanchard (b. 1962), drummer Jeff "Tain" Watts (b. 1960), bassist Christian McBride (b. 1972), and pianists Marcus Roberts (b. 1963) and Cyrus Chestnut (b. 1963).

Wynton Marsalis's prominent success in both jazz and classical music (he was the first artist to win Grammy Awards in both jazz and classical performance) made him the ideal figure to actualize a long-standing dream: that someday jazz would be treated as equal in stature to classical music and accorded an institutional home. In 1988 New York City's Jazz at Lincoln Center program, dedicated to advancing jazz through performance, education, and preservation, was launched with Marsalis as its artistic director. Marsalis organized the Lincoln Center Jazz Orchestra, and in the 1990s Lincoln Center offered a highly acclaimed series of jazz concerts and educational events, often devoted to the repertoire of particular jazz figures such as Duke Ellington.

Critics of Lincoln Center have often decried the narrowness of Marsalis's programming decisions, objecting to his neglect of the avant-garde in jazz, his failure to commission more adventurous jazz compositions, and his tendency to feature his own works over those of others. This left wing of critical opinion, which aims to retain the

Fusion
Artists combining jazz with one or more other popular music styles, including rock and roll, soul, rhythm and blues, and non-Western musics

Moldy fig
A conservative jazz fan, who prefers older styles to more modern trends. First used to describe those listeners who rejected bebop in the 1940s

Young Lions
The group of musicians centering on Wynton Marsalis in the mid-1980s and 1990s who revived earlier jazz styles

tradition of social criticism and musical experimentation in jazz, has found a leader in clarinetist Don Byron (b. 1958). Byron's more eclectic jazz series at the Brooklyn Academy of Music has often been viewed as an alternative to Lincoln Center.

A more conservative criticism of Lincoln Center has come from white musicians who claim that white artists have been overlooked by Lincoln Center's prioritization of the African American heritage in jazz. This is the latest chapter in a long history of the charge of "reverse racism," which has generally emerged at moments of black political activism and black advancement. Historical antecedents include the 1940s, when mixed bands became possible, and the Civil Rights period, when many white musicians claimed that black band-leaders failed to hire them because of their color. Although jazz has historically been associated with having greater racial tolerance than the rest of American society, there has also been a significant history of white backlash in response to African American visibility and influence in the music.

The turn of the new century has amplified debates over both the legacy and the future of jazz. Lincoln Center is accused of dwelling on the past rather than creating a vision of the future, even though it has attracted a new generation of musicians into its fold. Younger musicians shaped by funk and hip-hop (Steve Coleman [b. 1956], Russell Gunn [b. 1971], Don Byron, and Kenny Garrett [b. 1960]) have incorporated beats and performance conventions of contemporary urban popular music into more traditional jazz offerings, generating in the process a new wave of jazz fusion. Some musicians and critics argue that jazz is dead, having been murdered by corporate influence, mainstream marketing, lack of creativity, and the loss of responsiveness to social movements. Advocates of this perspective perceive a loss of individualism and originality among musicians associated with Wynton Marsalis. The classicization and institution-alization of jazz have, from this perspective, been a mixed blessing. Others celebrate the entry of jazz into institutional prominence and mainstream visibility. As always, debates over the legacy and future of jazz have generated a variety of aesthetic and political perspectives among musicians, audiences, and critics. As the music enters the new century the great tradition of jazz as a virtuosic improvised tradition is likely to continue to evolve in multifaceted directions.

Ingrid Monson

Important Terms and People to Know

Juan Aquilar
Louis Armstrong
Milton Babbit
Bebop
Nadia Boulanger
John Cage
John Coltrane
DukeEllington
Free jazz
Dizzy Gillespie
Benny Goodman
Lincoln Center
Winton Marsalis
Minimalism
Modal jazz
Thelonious Monk
Jelly Roll Morton
Musique concrète
New romanticism
Arnold Schoenberg
Serialism
William Grant Still
Swing
Synthesizer
Vladimir Ussachevsky

Review Questions

1. How did American composers of the early twentieth century attempt to find an "American voice" for their music? Who are some of the composers that were successful in this venture? Why were they successful?
2. What were some of the contributions made by Latin and African American composers and performers to Western classical music in the twentieth century? How did such composers respond (or not respond) to their own ethnicities in their musics?
3. What are some of the new directions that music composition took after 1950 in the United States? What composers do you associate with Minimalism? Serialism? New Romanticism? Electronic music? Non-Western music?

4. Who were some of the great instrumentalists, composers, and arrangers of early jazz? How did black/white relations promote or prohibit the development of early jazz?
5. What are the major musical and formal characteristics of jazz? How have these traits persisted throughout jazz's history to the present day?
6. What was the role of the Civil Rights movement in the development of new jazz forms? What composers/performers are especially associated with newer forms, such as modal and free jazz?
7. How has the recent controversy surrounding the performance of jazz at Lincoln Center polarized the jazz community?

Projects

1. Go to a classical music concert in your local area. What music was performed? Could you place it in one of the categories described in the section on classical music in this chapter? If not, why not? What is the role of classical music performance in your city or town today?
2. Listen to and transcribe a portion of three different jazz performances of the same song. Compare the way each musician plays or sings his or her solos. What are some of the improvisational choices each made? How and where do the basic musical and formal characteristics of the song remain the same?
3. What do classical musics and jazz have in common and how are they interrelated? Did composers borrow or adapt musical ideas from one another? How? And who?

CHAPTER 11

Popular Musics

Charles K. Wolfe, Rob Bowman, Sara Nicholson, Dawn M. Norfleet, and Jeremy Wallach

Since our European beginnings in the eighteenth century, German band music, operatic arias from Italy, songs by Stephen Foster, and later by Tin Pan Alley composers were widely published, eventually broadcast on the radio and other media, and made instantly available to everyone. Today, popular music is so widespread that it accounts for the vast majority of sales in this country and abroad, and most radio stations and record stores vie for their niche with specialized formats.

This chapter presents four consecutive Snapshots highlighting four contemporary popular musics, each with its own history and development within the past few decades: country, rock and roll and rock; rap; and, most recently, world beat. Although interrelated, these forms are also distinct in terms of their own aesthetics and primary audiences. And, although they are all homegrown, that is, they had their beginnings in the United States, they are, like classical musics and jazz, known and enjoyed throughout the world.

Snapshot 11.1: Country Music

Country music is a vernacular form of American popular music that traditionally has been associated with the Southeast and with the rural Midwest. It is generally characterized by an emotive and highly ornamented singing style, an instrumental accompaniment that relies heavily on small ensembles of stringed instruments, and a repertoire that has been derived from and influenced by older folk balladry and nineteenth-century popular song. Although the actual term "country music" did not gain widespread acceptance until the 1940s, the music itself emerged as a commercial art form in the years from 1922 to 1927. From its earliest days, country music has been promoted through the mass media—especially radio and phonograph records—and many scholars feel that this involvement is one of the essential, distinctive features of the genre. The first center for the music was Atlanta, Georgia, but in later years locations like Chicago; Los Angeles; Cincinnati; Charlotte, North Carolina; and, finally, Nashville served as hubs. At various times, starting in the 1940s, country music has had significant impact on mainstream popular music, but it routinely became self-conscious about its own identity and retrenched to reaffirm its traditional roots. The music has been generally conservative in a number of ways: politically, musically, socially, philosophically, and even technically. It has frequently served in many ways as the rear guard in the parade of American music.

The Roots of Country Music

The roots of country music singing are found in the oral tradition of balladry that accompanied Scottish and Irish immigrants into the Southeast in the nineteenth century. (See also Chapter 6.) In this tradition, the old songs of love and death were performed unaccompanied, often in a free-meter style, using *gapped scales*, and often sung at full volume and at the very top of the singer's range. This "high lonesome sound" became an element of later country singing that gave it a soulful, strident quality that one heard in major singers like Hank Williams, Roy Acuff, Bill Monroe, and Dolly Parton. Most of these modern singers experienced at least some firsthand contact with older, precommercial ballad singing.

Another key stylistic element is what older singers called "snaking the melody," in which an individual word or syllable may be stretched over a number of notes, as is heard in recordings by the Texas singer Lefty Frizzell and the California singer Merle Haggard. Country vocal ornamentation includes the use of scoops and slurs; the use of "feathering" at the ends of lines (a short glissando up to a *glottal stop*); the deliberate dropping of a beat or measure between lines; the use of *falsetto*, either as a high keening or as some sort of yodel; and an emphasis on nasality and head tones.

Notions of vocal harmony were derived from southern gospel music singing schools and song books, although often sung a full octave above the printed sources. At various points in country music's development, major singers broke with this older style and eschewed newer, smoother styles that were derived from mainstream pop singers like Bing Crosby; such smooth singers included

Gapped scale
A scale with fewer than the standard seven notes of the common Western scales; thus there are "gaps" where certain intervals are omitted

High lonesome sound
The characteristic sound of country singing, characterized by a nasal, high-pitched vocal style

Snaking the melody
A singing technique in which an individual word or syllable is stretched over a number of notes; compare melisma

Feathering
A vocal technique used at the end of a melodic line, consisting of a short glissando (slide) to a glottal stop

Red Foley (in the 1940s), Jim Reeves (in the 1950s), and Eddy Arnold (1950s-1960s).

The Instruments of Country Music

The three main instruments associated with country music are the fiddle, the banjo, and the guitar. The *fiddle* was a staple in the Scots-Irish culture, and Americans were staging fiddling contests as early as the 1760s. Light and easily portable, the fiddle soon found its way into the rural Southeast, along with a battery of tunes carried across the water. Dozens of new tunes emerged as fiddlers plied their solitary wares at country dances, barnwarmings, county fairs, auctions, and political rallies. A variety of unorthodox tunings emerged, such as what many called "cross tuning" (A-E-A-E) to get a harmonic drone effect. By the turn of the twentieth century, the fiddle had become the anchor for string bands and was being used less and less as a solo instrument.

For years it has been accepted that the banjo was an African instrument first brought to this country by slaves; we now know that its roots reach far into the culture of sub-Saharan Africa, with some references to a banjo-like instrument dating as far back as thirteenth-century Mali. Through its use in minstrel shows in the 1840s, the banjo made its way into Anglo American musical circles and into the hands of rural southerners. Here it also was subjected to unorthodox, un-European tuning systems (especially complicated by the addition of a fifth drone string in the 1840s) and to a rich variety of tonal textures brought about by home-made skin heads and handcarved fingerboards. Although the instrument was a favorite of many pioneer performers, such as Tennessee's Uncle Dave Macon, the banjo fell out of favor in the 1940s as the music became smoother, only to reemerge in the 1950s as the centerpiece of a new subgenre, bluegrass, at the hands of innovator Earl Scruggs.

The central icon for country music, however, was the third and most recent addition to this trio of instruments: the guitar. The guitar had been a part of the American musical landscape for most of the nineteenth century, but it wasn't until the turn of the twentieth century that the instrument came into its own. Improvements in the instrument's design, and the adoption of steel strings (previous instruments were strung with animal gut), gave the guitar much more volume and brightness and allowed it to take its place in the string bands of the day. Guitars were further popularized by the giant mail-order firms of Sears, Roebuck and Montgomery Ward, which began selling inexpensive guitars by mail. Unlike other folk instruments such as the banjo or dulcimer, the guitar was not easy for amateurs to make, and the cheap Sears Silvertones and

Glottal stop
The interruption of the breath by the abrupt closing of the glottis (the space between the vocal chords)

Falsetto
A high vocal register created by restricting the vocal cords

Fiddle
Structurally identical to the Western violin, although with many modifications in playing technique

Cross tuning
Special tuning of the fiddle so that the two lower strings are identical to the two upper (A-E-A-E), allowing for the playing of a harmonic drone

Banjo
African American stringed instrument, usually with four melody strings and a shorter, fifth "drone" string, and a circular rim covered with a skin head

Supertones went all over the South. As musicians became more proficient, they aspired to a better guitar, the best being the flat-topped Martin (originated in Pennsylvania before the Civil War) or the arch-top Gibson (dating from the 1890s); these two models are still considered the standards for country music today. By the 1920s, the guitar had made its way into rural southern string bands; many veteran country performers can even remember the first time they saw the guitar and how it changed the nature of both singing and instrumental music.

Major Figures

The commercialization of what would become country music began in 1922 and 1923, with the first recordings by Texas fiddler Eck Robertson ("Sallie Gooden," 1922) and Georgian Fiddlin' John Carson ("The Little Old Log Cabin in the Lane," 1923). With these releases, the big commercial record companies from the Northeast realized that there was an untapped market among southern audiences for this kind of "hill country" or "old time" music, and they wasted no time in sending talent scouts into the area to set up temporary studios. One such studio, set up by A&R man Ralph Peer in Bristol, Tennessee, struck paydirt almost immediately. It yielded a singing trio from nearby Maces Spring, Virginia, named the Carter Family (Figure 11.1), who had a knack for taking old mountain songs, putting harmony to them, and arranging them for guitar and autoharp accompaniment. Their recordings of songs like "Bury Me Under the Weeping Willow Tree" (1928) and "Wildwood Flower" (1929) became standards. The Carter singing style and harmony is still heard today, as is the "thumbstroke" guitar style perfected by Maybelle Carter.

A day after the Carters were discovered, Jimmie Rodgers, a young singer from Mississippi, auditioned for Peer. Rodgers offered a unique singing style heavily influenced by blues and cowboy songs; the Rodgers forte was a pliant, expressive voice and an ability to break into falsetto phrasing on refrains, a technique that became forever associated with his career song "Blue Yodel" (or "Blue Yodel No. 1," 1928). Rodgers and the Carter Family dominated early country music; they sold more records than any other acts and had more influence. Although Rodgers died prematurely in 1933, the Carters continued to work on records and radio until their breakup in 1943. Other important first-generation performers included the banjoist and songster Uncle Dave Macon, the singer Charlie Poole, the Georgia string band the Skillet Lickers, and the ballad singer Bradley Kincaid.

During country music's second decade, the 1930s, performers quickly found they could use income from radio shows and personal appearances to become full-time professionals. This led to a

Figure 11.1
An early photograph of
the Carter Family on
their family farm; l to r:
Maybelle, Sara, and
A.P. Courtesy Southern
Folklife Collection,
University of North
Carolina at Chapel Hill.

dramatic increase in technical proficiency as well as an increase in original songs and styles. Innovations during this time often led to new subgenres within the music. One was the soft, plaintive close-harmony duet singing exemplified by groups such as the Blue Sky Boys (Bill and Earl Bolick) and the Delmore Brothers (Alton and Rabon). When Texas yodeler Gene Autry left his spot on WLS Chicago radio to go to Hollywood to try his hand at films, he started another subgenre built on the image of the singing cowboy. Soon hundreds of singers, including many in the Southeast, were adapting a cowboy image and repertoire. The third major innovation, *western swing*, also came from the Southwest. Popularized, though not invented, by Texas-born Bob Wills, the music merged old-time fiddle breakdowns, blues, and *norteño* (Tex-Mex) music with the uptempo swing style of bands such as Benny Goodman's and Jimmie Lunceford's. During World War II, Wills transplanted his music to California, where it flourished and led to an entire musical scene in the southern part of the state.

By the 1940s, radio had become even more important, and powerful shows like WSM Nashville's *Grand Ole Opry*, WLS Chicago's *National Barn Dance*, and WWVA's *Wheeling Jamboree* were attracting

Western swing
A style popularized by Bob Wills and his band, Western swing incorporated elements of old-time fiddle breakdowns, blues, Tex-Mex, and jazz music

national attention for the music. During and after the war, the Armed Forces Radio Network recorded a number of country programs and sent them around the world to various GI outposts, further spreading the music. Smooth-singing Bing Crosby imitators dominated country radio for a while, and the music seemed about to lose its identity. But then country was rejuvenated by two rough-hewn but powerful singing stylists, Texan Ernest Tubb and Alabaman Hank Williams. These singers addressed the problems of the modern-day working class: drinking, divorce, lost love, and money. Tubb's "Walking the Floor over You" (1941) and Williams's "Lovesick Blues" (1949) became emblematic of the new style and defined a direction that still continues today. Other stylists of note during the late 1940s and early 1950s included Roy Acuff, Lefty Frizzell, Red Foley, and Faron Young.

Women, who had been generally discouraged from professional country by public opinion, had found an early role model in singing cowgirl Patsy Montana, who had a huge hit in 1936 with "I Want to Be a Cowboy's Sweetheart" (ARC). In 1952, women found an even stronger model in Tennessean Kitty Wells, whose "It Wasn't God Who Made Honkytonk Angels" (Decca) showed that a song from a woman's point of view could become a best-seller.

By now new instruments were helping define what was being called "country and Western music." The electric amplified guitar was featured on many of Ernest Tubb's recordings in the 1940s, as well as in many western swing bands; it soon became the lead instrument in the country band. In the 1920s numerous musicians had also adapted the acoustic Hawaiian guitar to country music, eventually resulting in the manufacture in the 1930s of the *Dobro*, or resonator guitar, that was also played with a metal slide. Emerging in the 1940s was a solid-body amplified steel guitar called a "lap steel," and in the late 1940s many players began to experiment with a "pedal steel," a flat steel guitar on a stand attached to a series of rods and pedals that allowed the performer to alter the string pitches and modulate chords. The pedal steel soon became country's most distinctive instrument: No other popular music genre utilized it. Webb Pierce's hit recording of "Slowly" (1954), featuring Nashville session man Bud Isaac's pedal steel guitar work, inspired hundreds of guitarists around the country and helped make the pedal steel a key part of the country music sound.

By the early 1950s Nashville had emerged as the geographical center for country music. One reason for this was that the city's WSM's radio show *Grand Ole Opry* had emerged after the war as the nation's most popular country radio show, and many leading performers had moved to Nashville to be near it. The city was also becoming a center for country music publishing, with the formation of the first nationally successful firm, Acuff-Rose, in 1942.

Dobro
A guitar featuring a metal resonator in the middle of its body; usually played with a metal slide

Lap steel
A solid-body amplified guitar played with a metal slide

Pedal steel
A flat steel guitar on a stand attached to a series of rods and pedals that allow the performer to alter the string pitches and modulate chords

Music Cultures in the United States

Nashville also was home to a cadre of superior studio engineers, and by 1946 two of them had set up the first permanent studio in town. This led major record companies to come to town to record and to open branch offices in the 1950s.

All of this eventually evolved into a phenomenon called "the Nashville studio system," which nurtured a new generation of specialized musicians who did little but play in recording studios. Producers like Chet Atkins and Owen Bradley, both musicians themselves, set up an assembly-line type of system in which performers would come into a studio without a band and would be given a studio band of crack technicians for backing on the record. While the music was clean and competent, the system left little room for innovation, and by the 1960s it was being blamed for a blandness that was infecting the music. Newer generations of session musicians have remedied that to some extent, and the session system was still in place in the first decade of the twenty-first century.

Country's predictable musical settings of the 1950s were especially vulnerable to the rise of rock and roll. As youth stars like Elvis Presley and Carl Perkins began to add a drum kit to their stage shows and added a heavy beat to the loud electric guitars, country bookings plummeted. Although Presley, from Memphis, began his career touring with country package shows, the new teenaged record-buying fans had little interest in the established Opry stars. Some country stars, such as Marty Robbins, tried to accommodate the new sound by exploring the hybrid genre called "rockabilly," a country sound with a strong beat. It did help weather the storm, and by the 1960s a new generation of singers and songwriters was arriving in Nashville to rejuvenate the music. Writers like Willie Nelson, Tom T. Hall, Harlan Howard, and Kris Kristofferson dropped the commonplace clichés of country lyrics and experimenting with new song forms and subject matter. Kentuckian Loretta Lynn, a protegé of Patsy Cline's, gave women fans a new voice in the country repertoire, addressing issues including spousal abuse ("Don't Come Home A-Drinkin' with Lovin' On Your Mind," 1966) and birth control ("The Pill," 1975). From the Bakersfield area in California came two of the most popular singer-songwriters of the 1960-1980 era, Buck Owens and Merle Haggard. It was Haggard's songs like "Working Man Blues" and "Okie from Muskogee" that helped restore a social sensibility in the music.

In 1980, with the release of the film *Urban Cowboy,* country music found itself threatening once again to "go pop." New artists like Mickey Gilley and Johnny Lee, as well as light rock acts like the Eagles and Linda Ronstadt, soon married the dance hall beat to new, hip lyrics like Lee's "Lookin' for Love in All the Wrong Places" (1980). During this time a number of veteran rock musi-

> **Rockabilly**
> A 1950s hybrid that combined country music with a rock beat

cians from the 1960s and 1970s moved to Nashville and made their presence felt in the studios. But by the mid-1980s a countertrend emerged in the person of North Carolinian Randy Travis, who revived the themes and styles of Hank Williams and Lefty Frizzell. The so-called new traditionalism also won new respect for established performers like George Jones and Tammy Wynette and helped pave the way for a new generation of singers like Alan Jackson and George Strait.

Women, who had been a crucial part of the music since the Carter Family, came totally into their own in the mid-1980s. Suddenly the bestselling *Billboard* charts were full of new hits by K.T. Oslin, Reba McEntire, Tanya Tucker, Emmylou Harris, Dolly Parton, and The Judds, among others. By the 1990s dynamic performers such as Shania Twain were openly exploiting a provocative sexual image in the new video medium and were outselling almost all of their male counterparts.

In the 1990s, the various independent record and publishing companies that defined Nashville and country music were being purchased by larger corporations, and much of the artistic control over the music was passing out of Nashville, or into the hands of executives who cared little for music at all. The spectacular success of Oklahoman Garth Brooks in the 1990s showed that aggressive corporate marketing could increase profit margins far beyond any Nashville expectations. Within a span of 70 years, country had expanded far beyond a niche music for a specific audience to a nationwide phenomenon and a major international commercial success. Although still largely centered in Nashville, country music of today can boast of fans, media outlets, and concert venues all over the country.

Charles K. Wolfe

Snapshot 11.2: Rock and Roll and Rock Music

The history of rock music can be seen as a confluence of intersecting streams of musical styles and social interactions. Clearly divided into an early "rock and roll" period, heavily influenced by rhythm and blues, and later into a plethora of "rock" styles influenced by new technology and media, rock is the quintessential music of youth.

Early Rock and Roll

Various commentators over the years have argued over what should be considered the first rock and roll record. Three candidates are commonly nominated for this honor:

1. "Rocket 88," released in 1951 by Jackie Brenston and his Delta Cats
2. "It's Too Soon to Know" by the Orioles, first issued in 1948
3. "Cry" by Johnny Ray, released in 1951

Taken together, these three recordings include qualities common to most of the music of this period that was described by contemporaries as "rock and roll":

1. The consumption on a large scale of black popular culture by white youth
2. The use of distortion, fast tempos, and teen-oriented lyrics
3. The production of music by white artists that, to one degree or another, manifests a substantial debt to black music, especially in terms of the articulation of overt emotional catharsis

The first black records to begin to show up with regularity on the (white-oriented) pop charts were by black vocal groups (the Ravens in 1947, the Deep River Boys and the Orioles in 1948, Billy Ward and the Dominoes in 1951). In 1952 and 1953 New Orleans rhythm and blues star Fats Domino had two minor pop hits, as did New York-based singer Ruth Brown and vocal groups the Four Tunes and the Orioles. But it was not until 1954 that a sizable number of black artists achieved hits on the pop charts, including the Crows ("Gee"), the Drifters ("Honey Love"), Hank Ballard and the Midnighters ("Work with Me Annie"), and the Chords ("Sh-Boom"). It is significant that Fats Domino was the only solo black male artist associated with rock and roll to achieve crossover success prior to 1955. Black vocal groups and female vocalists were less sexually threatening to white males and thereby more easily garnered white radio play as it proved easier on psychological levels for white youth to consume.

Covers

With the advent of black artists on independent labels beginning to penetrate the pop charts, the major labels, which had previously controlled the pop market, began to routinely "cover" with white artists any black recording that exhibited the potential to cross over. The most famous example of this was the Crew Cuts's cover of the Chords' "Sh-Boom." The Chords released "Sh-Boom" on June 19, 1954. Two weeks later, on July 3, their record entered the rhythm and blues charts, immediately charting pop as well. That same week Mercury rushed the Crew Cuts into the studio to cover the song. On July 10 the cover version entered the pop charts. Eventually the Chords reached the No. 2 spot on the rhythm and blues charts while peaking at No. 5 on the pop charts. The Crew Cuts's version vaulted to the No. 1 spot on the pop charts, where it stayed for nine weeks, making their record far and away the best-selling disc of the year.

For the next few years, the covering of black rhythm and blues records originally released on independent labels by white artists on major labels proliferated. It is important to note, though, that in this period, cover versions were a routine part of the business, so much so that between 1946 and 1950, 70 percent of the records that entered the Pop Top Ten appeared in more than one version. It is also worth noting that at the same time major labels were covering rhythm and blues/rock and roll records originally released on independent labels, they were also covering the odd country tune that showed signs of potential pop success. Finally, it was not uncommon for black rhythm and blues artists recording for independent labels to cover white pop tunes originally issued on major labels. The cover syndrome, then, was not necessarily based on racism, as is often asserted. Instead, it was a standard practice within the business to garner and control market share practiced by both major and independent labels with white and black artists.

In the early and mid-1950s, though, the specific nature of the practice developed both racial implications and ramifications. By 1956 the cover syndrome abated, as the black originals began routinely to outsell the white covers, and the major labels had begun to sign the first young white rock and roll artists such as Elvis Presley (RCA; see Figure 11.2), Gene Vincent (Capitol), and Johnny Burnette and the Rock 'n' Roll Trio (Decca) in their attempt to meet the demand of white youth for this new style of music.

In the 1950s rock and roll substantially changed the political economy of the record industry. Between 1954 and 1959 gross sales in the industry grew from $213 million a year to $603 million. At the same time, independent labels with new, often black artists began to acquire a significant share of the pie, resulting in a drop in the concentration of Top Ten pop hits controlled by the four largest firms from 74 to 34 percent. The most telling fact, however, was that independent labels issued 69 percent of all rock and roll hits that charted pop between 1955 and 1959, representing 30 percent of all hits on the pop charts.

The year 1955 clearly marked the watershed as black rock and rollers Little Richard, Chuck Berry, and Bo Diddley all enjoyed their first hits (for Specialty and Chess), Fats Domino enjoyed his first Top Ten pop hit (after twelve Top Ten rhythm and blues hits between 1950 and early 1955, all released on Imperial), and white rock artist Bill Haley and the Comets reached the No. 1 spot for eight weeks straight with the rerelease of "(We're Gonna) Rock Around the Clock," which was also featured in the film *Blackboard*

Cover version
A new recording that substantially copies the sound and styles of a previous release; often used in association with white artists "covering" songs previously recorded by R&B acts

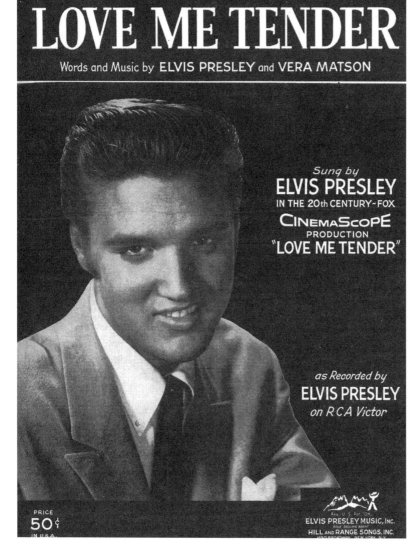

Figure 11.2
Elvis Presley pictured
on the sheet music
cover for "Love Me
Tender," the theme for
his first film, 1956.
Courtesy David A.
Jasen.

Jungle. By March 1956 Elvis Presley would begin to chart nationally. Equally telling is the fact that in 1954 major labels released forty-two of the fifty top-selling singles, while in 1955 that number had dropped to seventeen of the fifty top-selling singles as the pop charts became inundated with rock and roll records released on independent labels.

Early White Rock and Roll Artists

It is not surprising that the first examples of music made by white artists that was called rock and roll combined elements of country and pop music with rhythm and blues. Elvis Presley's first five releases on Sun Records in 1954 and 1955 all combined one rhythm and blues song with one country song. In all cases Presley modified the songs, adding substantial rhythm and blues elements to his recordings of country material and, similarly, adding country and pop elements to his versions of rhythm and blues songs. Subsequent white rock and roll artists including Carl Perkins and Buddy Holly stated that it was hearing Presley's unique fusion of rhythm and blues, country, and pop that made them realize that they could combine the black music they had been hearing for several years on black appeal stations on the radio with the country and occasional pop material they had begun to play as professional musicians. This new style was called rockabilly, the name itself being a hybrid of the terms for black rock and roll and white hillbilly music.

Presley was not the only artist experimenting with the cross-pollination of black and white styles. Many aspects of Chuck Berry's multistring guitar style can be traced to country guitarists such as Chet Atkins, while his predilection for text-heavy extended linear narratives also resonates with long-standing country practices. For example, Berry's first single and first hit, "Maybelline," was a rewrite of a public domain country fiddle tune known as "Ida Red." By the mid-1950s Tin Pan Alley songwriters clearly recognized that rock and roll was a combination of the two main tributaries of vernacular white and black musics.

Early Reactions to Rock and Roll

From the broadcasts of black-appeal radio stations in the late 1940s to white deejay Alan Freed's first rock and roll dance concerts in Cleveland in the early 1950s to the large-scale package tours of the mid- and late 1950s, rock and roll presented the United States with a music that was being consumed by both black and white youth and, beginning in the mid-1950s, that was being produced by black and white artists. In essence, rock and roll represented the first public phenomenon since the Great Awakening at the beginning of the nineteenth century that was integrated on this scale. As such, it threatened the segregated status quo that was at the time the norm throughout the country, albeit more overtly in the South.

Although it seems that no one was disturbed enough to comment in 1951 when Billy Ward and the Dominoes entered the pop charts with "Sixty Minute Man," a song that, although humorous, sonically portrays ejaculation. By the mid-1950s, church groups, local governments, police authorities, and white citizens' councils began actively to denounce rock and roll, connecting it in an unholy alliance to race, sex, and delinquency.

Three significant developments provided the context for the antirock and roll sentiment of the mid-1950s:

1. The Civil Rights struggle, manifest in the 1954 *Brown v. Board of Education* judgment, the May 1955 admonishment of the Supreme Court to move with "all deliberate speed" toward integrating public education and the beginning of the Montgomery bus boycott in December 1955, all of which threatened substantial change to the American system of apartheid.
2. Black rhythm and blues recordings began regularly to outsell white covers, meaning the black presence on the pop charts became much more significant.
3. Elvis Presley's sexualized movements on stage, broadcast to one and all on national television, suggested what could happen if white youth immersed themselves in African American musical culture.

Rock and roll's critics quickly connected it to issues of morality, including juvenile delinquency and premarital sex, racial miscegenation, anti-Christian practice, and communism. Much of the antirock and roll sentiment was fueled by Asa Carter, the head of the North Alabama Citizens' Council (NACC) and a member of the Ku Klux Klan. In April 1956, members of the statewide coordinating Alabama Citizens' Council assaulted Nat King Cole on stage in Birmingham when Cole sang a duet with white pop singer June Christy. The NACC's magazine, *The Southerner,* subsequently published pictures of Cole and June Christy with inflammatory captions such as "Cole and Your Daughter" and "Cole and His White Women." *The Southerner* also accused the NAACP of deliberately trying to corrupt white teenagers with rock and roll.

The widespread press coverage that followed the attack on Cole provided Carter and his group with a national stage. In *Newsweek* Carter was quoted as saying that "[rock and roll] is the basic heavy beat of Negroes. It appeals to the very base of man, brings out the animalism and vulgarity (*Newsweek,* April 23, 1956, 32). Carter subsequently wrote to the mayor of Birmingham protesting the use of the Municipal Auditorium "for indecent and vulgar performances by Africans before our white children." By December 1956 the Municipal Auditorium was instructed not to book any type of event with an interracial cast of performers.

Fueled by the publicity accorded Carter, antirock and roll sentiment spread throughout the South and eventually the rest of the country. In the summer of 1956 Louisiana passed a law that prohibited interracial dancing, social functions, and entertainment. In July the San Antonio Parks Department banned rock and roll from jukeboxes at the city's swimming pools. Throughout the rest of the summer and into the fall numerous city councils across the country simply banned rock and roll performances. Even President

Eisenhower saw fit to state publicly that "[rock and roll] represents some kind of change in our standards. What has happened to our concepts of beauty, decency and morality?"

Although their politics were clearly spurious, the antirock and roll forces were in a sense quite right. Rock and roll in the 1950s *did* promise to transform American society. Many of the white teens who consumed this new exciting music made by black artists and found themselves dancing at public concerts, oftentimes alongside black kids, began to question the racist status quo that governed America. A number of those white teenagers would grow up, go to college, and participate actively in the Civil Rights movement of the early 1960s.

The Early Splintering of Rock and Roll

By the early 1960s, the major labels, aided by the tightening of radio playlists due to the payola scandal and the rise of the Top 40 format, regained control of the pop market and began to promote and distribute a safer, softer, more pop-oriented version of the music, now performed by white teen idols such as Paul Anka, Ricky Nelson, and Johnny Burnette. A small number of American artists and producers, including Phil Spector, Link Wray, and the Beach Boys, pioneered new variants of rock and roll music in this period, but it would not be until the British Invasion in 1964, led by the Beatles (see Figure 11.3), the Rolling Stones, and others, that rock and roll would return full force for a couple of years before mutating into various new styles subsumed under the term *rock*.

Rock itself would mutate in a myriad number of directions over the next three-and-a-half decades, at various points incorporating influences from folk, jazz, renaissance, baroque, classical, romantic, avant-garde, "new music," blues, *norteno, tejano,* Celtic, reggae, Native, and various so-called world musics. While rock would continue to be primarily produced and consumed by white youth, the age range of the audience would expand upward as the original fans of the music in the 1950s and 1960s grew older. This expanded demographic produced a number of tensions as rock became heavily stratified in the late 1970s, many newer styles such as punk, new wave, various forms of heavy metal, grunge, rap, and dance musics being actively positioned in opposition to the music of the late 1960s and early 1970s, the latter now renamed "classic rock."

Rob Bowman

Rock/Classic rock
The music produced after the "British Invasion" of the mid-1960s through about the mid-1970s, featuring a standard guitar-bass-drum lineup and an eight-beat rhythm, primarily produced by and aimed at a white, teenage audience

Rock Since the 1970s

Although popular music is by definition a commercial art form, rock artists through the latter half of the twentieth and into the

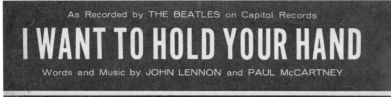

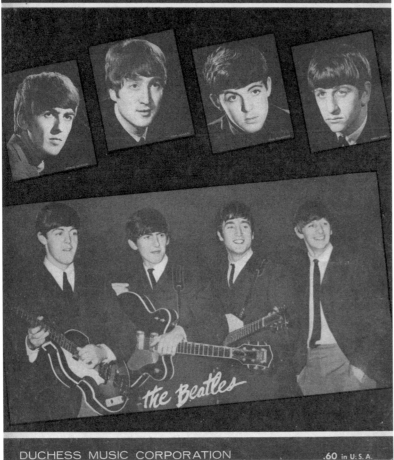

Figure 11.3
Sheet music cover for
the Beatles' "I Want to
Hold Your Hand,"
1964. Courtesy David
A. Jasen.

twenty-first century have consistently rebelled against the establishment of which they are a part. The consciously constructed image of the rock artist as the outsider, a marginalized member of society, resonated with a large audience and challenged the comfortable image and music of more mainstream groups, specifically rock's more commercially acceptable counterpart, Top 40. In the last three decades of the twentieth century, the gulf between rock and Top 40 widened further as the rock genre fragmented into myriad subgenres. No longer attracting the homogenous audience of the 1950s, rock music of the late 1960s and beyond captivated a similarly fragmented and expanding audience of teens and baby boomers. As these audiences grew, so too did record sales, topping one billion dollars for the first time in 1967 and quadrupling over the next decade. Often the gulf between rock and Top 40 was exploited by artists who maintained the attitude and appearance of outsiders while achieving great success on the pop charts; this tendency can be traced throughout this period, from Led Zeppelin to Guns n' Roses.

Early Fusions

Led Zeppelin achieved its pinnacle of popularity during the 1970s. Heavily blues-influenced, Led Zeppelin routinely performed medleys of songs by Elvis Presley and blues guitarist Robert Johnson in concert. Zeppelin's recordings are an amalgamation of this prominent blues influence, fantasy-based lyrics, and a loud, distorted sound similar to hard rock forerunner Cream. Zeppelin's music strongly contrasted the softer sound of 1970s pop that appealed to a more conservative audience. Although Zeppelin achieved great musical success, the band's on- and offstage behavior, along with Jimmy Page's preoccupation with the occult figure Aleister Crowley, lent the band a mysterious and dangerous image.

Groups including Yes, Pink Floyd, King Crimson, Genesis, and Emerson Lake and Palmer (ELP) began to incorporate increasingly sophisticated formal, harmonic, and rhythmic structures into their music, referred to as progressive rock ("prog rock"), art rock, or classical rock, in the late 1960s and into the 1970s. Influenced by the technical virtuosity of Eric Clapton and Jimi Hendrix, the complexity of classical music, and the experimental nature of later Beatles recordings, many of these groups appealed to a particular subculture comprising young musicians themselves, searching for more intricate and contemplative music. Such groups maintained this small but consistent fan base through the 1980s and 1990s. Meanwhile, bands such as Blood, Sweat, and Tears, The Mahavishnu Orchestra, Weather Report, and Return to Forever were influenced by Miles Davis's recordings of the late 1960s and combined jazz-based elements within a rock format to create the art-rock subgenre of jazz rock or jazz-rock fusion.

As Led Zeppelin's popularity rose and progressive rock found its niche audience, fellow Englishman Ozzy Osbourne joined another blues-based rock group, Earth, later known as Black Sabbath. The band's eponymous debut album in 1970, followed by *Paranoid* (1970), codified the heavy metal sound. The blues influence played a subtler role in Black Sabbath's music, which Osbourne and band mates imbued with slower tempos, darker lyrics filled with references to the occult, and an ominous stage presence. Often cited as the seminal heavy metal band, Black Sabbath inspired—at least in part—the heavy metal music popular throughout the 1980s.

Hard rock
Rock characterized by a loud, distorted sound, heavy rhythm, and blues-influenced songs

Progressive ("Prog") rock
An attempt to combine classical music sensibilities within the rock style

Jazz-rock
Rock that combined elements of jazz instrumentation and improvisation with the basic rock style

Heavy metal
Harder than hard rock, heavy metal combined slower tempos, darker lyrics filled with references to the occult, and an ominous stage presence

"Glam" and Punk Rock

Between 1970 and 1975, Lou Reed (former Velvet Underground singer), David Bowie (see Figure 11.4), and others created a music that departed from the hard rock of Led Zeppelin and Black Sabbath and foreshadowed the punk rock movement soon to follow. Variously termed glamour ("glam") rock, glimmer rock, or glitter rock, the music of Bowie and his contemporaries shared much of punk rock's minimalistic sound but contained relatively more harmonic variety, a polished musical production, and a manicured stage dress. Androgyny was integral to the stage personae of these performers, achieved by their donning women's clothing along with heavily applied makeup.

The Sex Pistols, the Clash, the Damned, and other British groups spearheaded the punk rock movement of the late 1970s, which was—as were all previous rock movements—decidedly anti-establishment. In contrast to previous movements, punk rockers rebelled not just against society's mores but also against current trends in both pop and rock music as well as the seemingly monolithic recording industry. Punk groups dispensed with guitar solos and any other displays of technical prowess in favor of a simple chordal texture

Glam rock
A stripped-down, but highly produced, version of rock, focusing on elaborate stage sets and androgynous makeup and costumes

Punk
A reaction to the highly polished commercial rock of the 1970s, punk groups favored fast tempos, simple song structures, harmonies, and rhythms, along with an aggressive stage image and anti-establishment lyrics

Figure 11.4
David Bowie in his Glam phase.

and standard $\frac{4}{4}$ drum beats—both reminiscent of 1950s rock and roll—played at breakneck tempos. The use of fast tempos and heavy distortion, coupled with politically charged lyrics that the singer more often screamed than sang, created a stark contrast to the polished, heavily produced sound of disco as well as to the sounds of progressive and mainstream rock. American punk rock groups, including The Ramones and Iggy Pop, were also forming at this time. The shunning of such groups by radio station executives on both sides of the Atlantic only reinforced their authenticity and cult status. The Ramones rebelled against the glitzy, polished appearance of glimmer rock. In contrast, performers displayed ripped clothing, dyed hair, and safety pins as jewelry, mimicking in appearance the "do-it-yourself" punk sound.

The intentionally extreme dress and notorious behavior of punk rock groups, particularly The Sex Pistols, rendered them virtually unmarketable. Thus, some groups lessened their rebellious look and sound to create a cleaner, more marketable music dubbed New Wave. Groups including Blondie and the Go Go's began their careers in the New York City punk scene but then reworked their sounds and later achieved great commercial success. Similarly, bands like the Police and Generation X (with Billy Idol) attempted to create a style that offered a compromise between punk and pop. Many punk rock groups viewed New Wave and hybrid styles as sanitized versions of punk, manufactured by artists who had "sold out."

The notoriety of early punk bands spawned punk chic, a mode of dress adopted by Top 40 artists as well as the general public. The ripped clothes and spiked hair that were once shocking were now commonplace and mass-marketable-punk had lost its edge. Although punk rock groups seemingly vanished, numerous bands remained active in the underground scene through the 1980s and resurfaced in the early 1990s.

New Wave
Rock groups influenced by the punk movement, but with a more commercial, accessible look and sound

Heavy (and Other) Metal Groups

The heavy metal genre of the 1980s synthesized the sound of predecessors Black Sabbath, Deep Purple, and Led Zeppelin with the look of 1970s glamour rock. Glam rockers including Mötley Crüe, Poison, and Cinderella paradoxically combined Bowie's androgynous look with overtly sexual lyrics that, along with the band's cover art and videos, consistently objectified women. Female artists constructed a curious subgenre of this trend, exemplified by Vixen and Lita Ford, who adopted the musical style, stage persona, and lyrical sexual aggressiveness of 1980s heavy metal. Other heavy metal and hard rock bands of the 1980s recaptured the guitar virtuosity of the late 1960s and early 1970s dormant during the punk rock craze. Metallica, Anthrax, and Judas Priest played *speed metal,* or thrash, identified by the use of fast tempos and rapid double bass drum attacks. *Death metal* bands including Slayer, Death, and Obituary combined speed metal and satanic, often violent lyrics sung with vocal distortion. The negative reaction to misogynist themes in heavy metal prompted Tipper Gore to found the Parents' Music Resource Center (PMRC) in 1985, an organization that targeted this music she termed "porn rock" (Gore 1987).

In the last years of the 1980s, and briefly into the 1990s, Guns n' Roses commanded the radio and marketplace. Selling over 15 million copies, the band's debut album, *Appetite for Destruction* (1987), was the second-biggest-selling debut album in rock history. With a guitar-based sound, Axl Rose's unique vocal delivery, and the band's intriguing stage presence, Guns n' Roses managed to make a subcultural phenomenon mainstream. The band, however, quickly unraveled after the somewhat disappointing release of its fifth album, *The Spaghetti Incident* (1993).

Grunge

The rapid decline of audience interest in heavy metal has been attributed to the burgeoning Seattle grunge scene of the early 1990s. Led by Nirvana and other bands signed to the independent label Sub Pop, *grunge* musicians combined a gritty punk rock sound with less politically charged lyrics and other pop elements. With Nirvana's release of its major label debut album *Nevermind* (1991), grunge and punk found a mass audience. Similar to the punk movement of the late 1970s, grunge eschewed the visual excesses of 1980s rock and spawned its own mode of dress, including flannel shirts, often worn over long underwear, paired with tattered jeans and combat boots. The product of Generation X malaise, grunge lyrics reflect a sense of disillusionment and uselessness.

Grunge
A do-it-yourself music of the early 1990s, centered in Seattle, that took punk's simplicity and married it with less aggressive lyrics and dress

Like 1970s punk and 1980s heavy metal music, grunge, too, splintered into a variety of subgenres. The year 1991 saw the emergence of a group of female rock artists collectively known as Riot Grrrls who explored issues of feminine sexuality and celebrated anger through their music. These latter-day punks, led by Bikini Kill, Hole, and Babes in Toyland, adopted punk and grunge elements and co-opted previously derogatory terms targeted at women to further empower themselves and their music. In the mid-1990s, bands including Green Day and the Offspring created a new punk-pop hybrid with faster tempos, more melodic lines, and a less downtrodden sentiment. Seattle groups including Soundgarden, Pearl Jam, and Alice in Chains injected Nirvana's formula with decidedly heavy metal riffs.

Rap-Influenced Rock

Rap music, popular since the late 1970s, heavily influenced a group of hard rock bands, now referred to as rap rock groups, beginning with the Red Hot Chili Peppers. In the mid- to late 1990s, however, bands including Korn, Limp Bizkit, and the Kottonmouth Kings added a heavy metal element to rap rock and have garnered recent success. These bands not only frequently employ rap lyrics but also incorporate samples into the fiber of their music.

The consistent, weblike proliferation of rock subgenres renders a linear, evolutionary history of rock music of the past three decades both impossible and undesirable. A certain theme or trope can, however, be traced through the years—something one could call the "paradox of rock": the tendency of rock artists to achieve popularity by consciously and aggressively resisting popularizing mechanisms. The disjunction between pop and rock continues to evolve as rock fractures into more and more subgenres. Furthermore, aided by different recording media technology and new innovations in the transmission of rock—specifically file sharing and other Web-based distribution systems—the future of rock is unclear. Although rock as a musical genre is no longer the monolith it was in its early years, the profusion of artists and music assures its longevity.

Sara Nicholson

Hip-hop culture
A collection of artistic forms centering on rap music, including graffiti art, break dancing, DJ-ing, and rapping
Rap music
An African American popular musical expression that emphasizes stylized verbal delivery of rhymed couplets, typically to prerecorded accompaniment, or "tracks"

Snapshot 11.3: Hip-Hop and Rap

Hip-hop (hiphop or hip hop), also called hip-hop culture, is a creative expression, aesthetic, and sensibility that developed in African American, Afro-Caribbean, and Latino communities of the Bronx and Harlem, New York City, by the mid-1970s. Hip-hop, now an internationally recognized cultural phenomenon largely due to the popularity of rap music, encompasses a wide range of competitive performance expressions that often go unnoticed by the mainstream public. These four elements are aerosol art (graffiti); b-boying/girling (break dancing); DJ-ing, or the art of using turntables, vinyl records, and mixing units as musical instruments; and MC-ing (rapping), the art of verbal musical expression (rap music). Those who consider their primary aesthetic to be shaped by hip-hop culture and/or claim a personal stake in its development form what is known as the hip-hop community. Community insiders are sometimes referred to as hip-hoppers. Rap music, which is the most popularized manifestation of hip-hop, is an African American popular musical expression that emphasizes stylized verbal delivery of rhymed couplets, typically to prerecorded accompaniment, or "tracks."

Early History

Rap music is rooted in cultural and verbal traditions from the Caribbean as well as the United States. Mainland traditions that remain visible in hip-hop include "jive-talking" radio personalities of the 1940s and 1950s and oral traditions of storytelling, toasting, and "playing the dozens," a competitive and recreational exchange of verbal insults. Jamaican traditions include toasting and mobile disk jockeys. Many of the hip-hop pioneers were Caribbean immigrants, who brought some of the musical practices from their native countries and adapted them for their new situation.

The mingling of Caribbean immigrant and native-born African American and Latino communities in the United States set the stage for the development of the new art form. A large Caribbean community had developed in the boroughs of New York, where the first rap musical dance events were said to have begun as early as 1972 in the Bronx. The native-born African American inhabitants of New York had a strong and vibrant verbal culture as well. Toasting also took place in the United States, albeit in the form of long, rhymed stories, often memorized and passed on orally. "The Signifying Monkey" is one such popular toast. Another, "Hustlers' Convention," was commercially recorded by The Last Poets, a spoken-word trio based in New York.

Rapping as a distinct musical form developed in New York in the early 1970s as only one of the cultural expressions encompassed by hip-hop. Socioeconomic conditions in the Bronx and Harlem in the 1960s and 1970s profoundly shaped the aesthetics and activities of hip-hop culture. The 1959 construction of the Cross-Bronx Expressway escalated the deterioration of buildings and the displacement of people in south Bronx communities in particular (Rose 1989, 1994). Youth gangs and gang violence escalated in these economically poor neighborhoods during this time. Despite the turbulence of the 1960s and 1970s, Bronx youths developed and/or popularized a wealth of diverse creative expressions that eventually came to be associated with hip-hop culture, then primarily consisting of graffiti and highly competitive dance. Hip-hop became a powerful cultural symbol of urban youth that within a few years spread beyond the immediate environs of the Bronx.

1970s: The Era of the Hip-hop DJs

Although hip-hop began in the south and west Bronx, the accessibility of rap music was aided by several factors: residents who moved or traveled beyond the New York area; the local dissemination of the art form through the sale of home-produced cassette tapes of rap shows; and the non-Bronx residents who came to see the live performances and reported on or imitated the events in their respective neighborhoods. At this time the primary mode of rap musical expression was through live performance, held in parks, community centers, school gymnasiums, neighborhood clubs, private basements, and the like. Similarly, the dominant means of establishing one's reputation as a rap artist was through performing at these events, as well as through privately taped performances of the shows and locally pressed records. Taped rap music was sold from the trunks of cars and briefcases for as much as $15 per cassette. These tapes, which were duplicated even further and passed on, contributed to the popularity of such acts as the Cold Crush Brothers, the Funky Four Plus One, and Kool Moe Dee and the Treacherous Three several years before the advent of music videos.

The Bronx DJs, Kool DJ Herc, Afrika Bambaataa, and Grandmaster Flash are most frequently credited with the development of hip-hop and rap music. The DJ is acknowledged among New York hip-hoppers as the foundation of hip-hop culture, and in rap music the DJ is a crucial defining element that distinguishes rapping from poetry recitation and other types of oral performance. The DJ was also the central focal point in the early stages of hip-hop, providing the music as the backdrop for the other forms of hip-hop expression. Although the DJ provided music from prerecorded discs, taking the place of a live band, the DJ makes the musical practice equivalent to a live event through techniques of spinning, cutting, mixing, and scratching, the production of percussive sounds by moving a record back and forth rhythmically under a phonographic needle. Thus DJs recontextualized the phonographs, turntables, and mixing units as musical instruments.

Hip-hoppers acknowledge Kool DJ Herc as the "Father of Hip-hop." Having arrived in the west Bronx from Jamaica in 1967 as an adolescent, Herc brought with him the practice of the mobile DJ, the Jamaican tradition of toasting, and competitive musical display. By 1973 he began providing music at social events in homes (house parties), public spaces (block parties), and community centers. By the disco era of the 1970s, he became known not only for his selections of records, ranging from funk and rhythm and blues to Latin, but also for the manner in which he played the music. Using two turntables with identical records, he would select the most percussive or rhythmically appealing sections ("the breakdown"), which often featured Latin instruments such as congas, timbales, and cowbells. Then he would switch back and forth between the two turntables, finding the approximate spot where the section began. This resulted in an extended "break" section,

Breakdown
The most percussive or rhythmical section of a track, selected by a DJ, and played several times in sequence on two different turntables

Breakdancing
Dancing performed to the breakdown by b-boys/girls, including stylized and athletic movements

which was highly appealing to dancing patrons. The popular term for hip-hop dancing, or b-boying/girling, became popularized as break dancing.

Afrika Bambaataa began as an informal student of Kool Herc's style and by 1976 emerged as his former mentor's competitor. He established his reputation as a DJ by mixing obscure and unusual records for his Bronx audiences, including rock, cartoon theme songs, and even excerpts from Western art music in his mix. Bambaataa, also of West Indian origin, promoted hip-hop expression into the late 1990s through an organization known as the Zulu Nation. This organization began as a notorious Bronx gang in the early 1970s known as the Black Spades. Bambaataa is credited with redirecting the activities of the gang toward creative competition rather than violence, through b-boying/girling and graffiti writing.

DJs Kool Herc and Bambaataa were known primarily for their musical choices and blending of one song into another, rather than for the complex turntable maneuverings, techniques, and tricks that marked later DJs. The Barbados-born, south Bronx resident Grandmaster Flash was one of several Bronx DJs who further developed the act of turntable manipulations into a distinct musical practice. Flash combined his background in electronics with his musical interests to become one of the most influential figures in hip-hop. His technological innovations with mixing units and the electronic percussion system came to characterize the hip-hop sound, particularly in the 1980s, of the electronic "beat-box."

1979–1985: Rap Music Enters the Mainstream

The year 1979 marks rap music's first commercial release: "Rappers Delight," recorded by the New Jersey-based Sugar Hill Gang on an independent label owned by former R&B vocalist Sylvia Robinson. Although the song "King Tim III," recorded by the funk group Fatback Band, actually preceded Sugar Hill Gang's release as the first song featuring a hip-hop-style rapped section, "Rappers Delight" became the more popular.

The earliest recordings of rap music often featured a rap artist rhyming over an instrumental version of a popular song played by a live band or a combination of simple synthesized percussion and live instruments. As was done in the Jamaican dub tracks, the rapper would add his or her voice to the layer of live instruments. In 1982, however, recordings by Bambaataa's group, the Soul Sonic Force, defined the hip-hop sound of the 1980s by introducing synthesizers and electronic musical devices to rap music. Bambaataa and, later, Boogie Down Productions employed the technique of

Sampling
Using snippets of previously recorded music as the basis for new material

Figure 11.5
Grandmixer D. St.,
1984. Photo courtesy
DXT.

"sampling," or using snippets from previously recorded music as a basis for new material, as part of a polyphonic layer, or as a thematic reference. A popular Bronx DJ, Grandmixer D. St., was featured on versatile jazz pianist Herbie Hancock's "Rockit" (1983; Figure 11.5). This recording was the first recorded jazz/hip-hop collaboration and the first hip-hop-influenced record to win a Grammy Award, thus extending the hip-hop audience beyond its local beginnings.

MTV

The advent of MTV (Music Television) in 1981 and use of the music video as a widespread marketing tool for music have been cited by a number of hip-hoppers as having adversely affected the live performance of rap music, although the visual format potentially permits unknown and emerging groups greater public exposure. Some rap artists have complained that attention record companies pay to developing artists as live performers has been greatly diminished, as the companies substitute the tightly controlled performance environment of a video for the troublesome unpredictability of staged performances. Whereas the establishment of a rap artist's reputation through live performance was a mark of what came to be known in the later 1980s as "old school," the new school artists heavily utilized technological innovations such as samplers and synthesizers. This phenomenon can arguably be seen as a representation of the American fascination with the computer-based technological boom in the 1980s, which had reached into the realm of hip-hop aesthetics; as a result, synthesized sounds became preferable to those produced by live instruments. Live performance, however, was further deemphasized particularly with the concurrent growth of hardcore hip-hop and the fear of violence at rap music concerts, which many owners of performance venues cited as reasons for not booking rap artists.

Once the cable station expanded beyond its initial "rock only" format, MTV came to be the prime means of popularizing emerging and existent rap artists with its video program, *Yo! MTV Raps,* in 1989. During the mid-1980s hip-hop became a popular symbol of black life to the wider American society, embodied by the young black male, seen as exotic, dangerous, and feared, yet appealing and marketable. Negative events associated with hip-hop performances were greatly publicized, while peaceful rap music concerts, philanthropic activities of rap artists such as the Stop the Violence movement, and violence at white rock concerts were underrepresented by the media. Despite the growing controversy surrounding rap music lyrics toward the end of the decade, acts such as Eric B. and Rakim were known for their powerful imagery, delivery, and high lyrical quality rather than violent and misogynist themes.

The Late 1980s

In the late 1980s, largely African American and Latino communities of northern and southern California emerged as important new bases of hip-hop culture. In the West Coast style, the hip-hop traditions of hyperbole, self-grandeur, and storytelling stemming from the African American popular toasts such as "The Signifying Monkey" and "Hustlers' Convention" blended in with themes influenced by popular black gangster movie characters such as Superfly and Dolemite. The result was a distinctive brand of hardcore known as "gangster" or "gangsta rap," exemplified in the music of Oakland's Too Short and Compton's Niggaz with Attitude (NWA). The often violent and drug-related activities of rival youth gangs such as the Bloods and the Crips, which had become highly organized by the mid-1980s, were familiar themes in West Coast street culture. Many West Coast acts claimed hip-hop authenticity because their lyrics reflected a California innercity lifestyle—albeit often idealized, exaggerated, or conjectured—depicting guns, violence, peer allegiance, sex, drugs, and the exploitation of women. The popularity and record sales of West Coast acts such as Ice-T, Compton's Most Wanted, and, in the early 1990s after the break-up of NWA, Dr. Dre and Snoop Doggy Dogg surpassed sales of the New York artists. The hip-hop subgenre of gangsta rap was considered by many West Coast hip-hoppers to represent the authentic, ignored voices of urban California youth, some of whom considered the term *reality rap* more accurate than gangsta rap.

Gangsta/reality rap
Rap style that originated on the West Coast that addresses intercity issues, including violence, gang life, sex, drugs, and the exploitation of women

Many New York-area hip-hoppers considered these West Coast artists to be inauthentic "studio gangsters," that is, leading a life close to mainstream society, yet creating a gangsta persona in the recording studio for the sake of commercial appeal. The East Coast/West Coast rivalry emerged at this time and was later blamed at least in part for the murders of two prominent artists, The West Coast's Tupac Shakur (1996) and the East Coast's Biggie Smalls/Notorious B.I.G. (1997).

By 1991 rap music consumers recognized distinct subgenres of hip-hop: *hardcore*; *R&B rap* (which utilized sung choruses and was exemplified by Heavy D and the Boys, and CC Music Factory); and *pop or commercial rap* (Vanilla Ice, MC Hammer, and Jazzy Jeff and the Fresh Prince), which usually had the broadest popular appeal. Hardcore rap music itself could be broken down into subcategories, such as gangsta (NWA, Geto Boys); sexually explicit (2 Live Crew, Lil' Kim, Foxy Brown); political (Public Enemy, Boogie Down Productions/KRS-One, Paris); and entertainment, which combined powerful urban imagery with aggressively percussive musical accompaniment (Naughty By Nature, Eric B., and Rakim). Listeners could choose among the hard, aggressive sounds that emphasized strong electronic or sampled drum, found in the style of KRS-One; the smooth, jazz-influenced styles of A Tribe Called Quest and Digable Planets; and the funky styles that emphasized bass and/or live instruments, exemplified by the music of EPMD and Ice Cube. Producers of rap music began to use jazz samples, jazz tunes, and even live jazz musicians as source material for their new songs (Guru and Jazzmatazz, US 3) as a change from what had come to be traditional source material from James Brown and funk music of the 1960s and 1970s. The impact of rap music as an influential American expression reached into the realm of law by the early 1990s, with publicized cases involving censorship due to some rap music's sexually and violently explicit subject matter (NWA's "F–Tha Police"; Paris's "Bush Killa"); gang violence and verbal/physical abuse of women (NWA, Ice-T, Geto Boys); and copyright infringement rulings involving common sampling practices in rap music (Biz Markie).

Women and Rap

Women have been part of hip-hop expression from its early days, primarily as part of MC crews such as the Funky Four Plus One and Sugar Hill's female group, Sequence. For most of hip-hop's recorded history, however, women MCs were mostly seen as novelty acts, with a few exceptions. In the mid-1980s, some female artists were popularized momentarily through "answer" songs, which ridiculed popular songs by male acts. These answer songs included Roxanne Shante's "Roxanne's Revenge" (responding to UTFO's

1984 song "Roxanne, Roxanne") and Peblee Poo's "Fly Guy" (responding to the Boogie Boys' 1985 song "A Fly Girl"). Some of the most enduring female hip-hop acts released premiere albums in 1986. Salt-N-Pepa (Cheryl "Salt" James, Sandi "Pepa" Denton, and DJ Dee Dee "Spinderella" Roper) was the most successful hip-hop group with its first album, *Hot, Cool and Vicious.* Queen Latifah emphasized strong social messages and female empowerment in her first album, *All Hail the Queen.* MC Lyte recorded her first album, *Lyte as a Feather,* at this time. Many female artists who appeared or recorded during the early 1990s adopted the extant masculine-oriented hip-hop images prevalent in hardcore rap music. MC Lyte, for example, recorded a hardcore album in 1993 entitled *Ain't No Other.* This album's first hit single, "Ruffneck," was MC Lyte's first "gold"-selling single. After the decline of gangsta hardcore rap music in the mid- to late 1990s, women remained on the periphery of hip-hop, with the exception of the occasional pop hit, such as the platinum-selling Atlanta-based artist DaBrat's *Funkdafied* (1994).

By the late 1990s, artists such as Lil' Kim and Foxy Brown publicly celebrated—or exploited—female sexuality through explicit lyrics and widespread publicity campaigns that presented these scantily clad artists as sex symbols. For the most part, however, female artists failed to receive respect within the hip-hop community as competent MCs and recording artists in their own right, although achieving mainstream success. Most of the writers and producers for the female groups were male, particularly through the late 1990s.

The year 1998, however, was pivotal for women in hip-hop. Rapper-producer-songwriter Missy Elliot began gaining notoriety with her debut album, *Supa Dupa Fly* (1997). Lauryn Hill (Figure 11.6) had already established herself as a respected MC and vocalist in the mid-1990s as the frontwoman from the popular and eclectic hip-hop band The Fugees. However, Hill's first solo effort, *The Miseducation of Lauryn Hill,* was a phenomenal success; it was nominated for ten 1998 Grammy Awards and won five. For the first time, women in hip-hop achieved major success as respected artists, producers, and stars in the forefront, in the hip-hop community, and in the mainstream media. Elliot's and Hill's success in diversified realms of hip-hop may indicate the beginning steps of the normalization of female voices in the male-dominated genre of rap music.

Stylistic Features

Old and New Schools
The history of rap music and hip-hop is popularly divided into old and new schools. These descriptions, which appeared by the late

Figure 11.6
Rapper Lauryn Hill.
© Ruffhouse/Columbia
Records 1998. Photo
by Warren du Preez.
Courtesy DXT.

1980s, were coined by professional promoters of the emerging style of rap music who sought to distinguish this new style, considered to be more street-oriented, harder, and more aggressive, from that of their dance party-based predecessors.

Generally, *old school* is

> **Old School Rap**
> Original rap styles of the late 1970s to about 1985, that emphasized a party atmosphere

1. A temporal reference to hip-hop's early days, the 1970s to about 1985
2. A stylistic description of the rhythmic pattern characteristic of hip-hop's early days, that is, a literal interpretation of the AABB rhyme structure, where each couplet was performed by a leader answered by a group in a rhythmic call and response
3. A thematic description of the lyrical content, consisting mainly of braggadocio and dance party-oriented subject matter

The early old school recordings often featured live bands and/or congas and other Latin percussion accompanying the rap artists, reflecting the Latino presence and influence in early hip-hop (examples are Sugar Hill Gang's "Rappers Delight," and Spoonie Gee and the Treacherous Three's "Love Rap" [1980]).

The *new school* is

> **New School Rap**
> Harder-edged rap style appearing in the mid-1980s, with more street-oriented lyrics and more aggressive presentation and rhythms

1. A temporal reference to the prominent rap musical styles starting at approximately 1986
2. A stylistic description of the loose interpretation of the AABB rhyme scheme, in which rhythms are normally highly syncopated and the rhymed syllables appear at varied, irregular, or unpredictable places

3. A thematic reference, of which the artist and his or her over-all style may be described as hardcore, smooth, gangsta, pop, and so on

Early new school artists (1986–1990) preferred synthesized per-cussion, such as the electronic beat-box and other synthesized instruments, refraining from live instruments nearly altogether. Later new school artists preferred to use sampled material from popular and obscure rhythm and blues, jazz, and rock recordings from the 1970s. Sampled material used to form the basis of new songs ranged from a highly disguised snippet as short as a single chord or percussion strike to an entire section of a previously recorded popular song, literally re-presented with new lyrics or rere-corded to avoid or circumvent expensive licensing fees. In spite of the reemergence of live musical instruments in the later 1990s, new school recordings have nevertheless deemphasized live percussion, so that the Latin influence is not nearly as visible as in older recordings.

The application of the old or new school label to rap music or its artists is by no means precise, and there is much stylistic overlap-ping. A mid-1980s act such as Run-D.M.C. may have the visual and musical markings of the new school acts, but its rhyming tenden-cies reflect the relatively simple syncopations of the old school. Furthermore, many of the new school artists who emerged in the 1980s, such as Boogie Down Productions, Run-D.M.C., and Kool Moe Dee, were marketed as old school artists in the late 1990s to promote radio and concert programming that featured hip-hop "classics." Nevertheless, the labels are useful as a means to identify stylistic, lyrical, and thematic differences in rap music of the 1970s to the mid-1980s and the mid-1980s to the late 1990s.

Rap artists began to vary the rhyming patterns in the late 1980s, often by introducing the first rhymed word of the couplet at the beginning of the A line, rather than at the end. The matching rhyme would occur at the beginning of the second A line. By 1991 the prevailing hip-hop aesthetic preferred more intricate and com-plex rhyming styles and unpredictable or highly syncopated rhyth-mic placement. By the 1990s rap music that presented a literal interpretation of the AABB rhyme scheme with relatively pre-dictable syncopations and regular beats was considered outdated and old school by emerging artists and their fans.

Compared with live presentations of rap music in the 1990s, per-formances of the 1970s tended to feature "dressing up" for such shows, from the space fantasy outfits of Bambaataa typical of African American and disco groups of the 1970s to displays of exaggerated wealth by the wearing of heavy gold jewelry and other expensive accessories symbolizing "the good life" of the early 1980s.

In both cases, clothes were used to heighten the distinction between onstage performers and offstage audience members. With the emergence of hardcore hip-hop and the concern of rap artists of the 1990s to "keep it real"—that is, to publicly assert one's allegiance to community and peers—"dressing down," or in a manner similar to that of the peer audience members, became the norm of live acts. With stage effects such as lighting, costumes, and jewelry kept to a minimum (compared to rock shows), the artists of the 1990s symbolically maintained their peer connection by wearing clothing similar to that of the audience members: name-brand sneakers or hiking boots, very baggy pants, and oversized sweatshirts and headgear with the names of famous European and American designers prominently displayed. Female artists who emerged during the hardcore era tended to take on dress, themes, and rhyming styles similar to those of the males. Toward the late 1990s, as the "ghetto fabulous" style (a glamourized combination of "street"-inspired designer wear and 1970s black film costuming popularized by Sean "Puffy" Combs, Mary J. Blige, and Lil' Kim) became widespread, popular female acts came to have a more distinctly feminine style that included dyed blonde hair fixtures, revealing clothes, and heavy makeup.

In the 1990s stylistic distinctions became recognized in rap music, developing what can be considered cultural areas associated with regional modes of informal communication (slang), manners of speech, tempo, and thematic emphasis. Five such areas and the general characteristics with which they are associated are the East Coast, West Coast, Miami/Southwest, South, and Midwest.

Hip-hop is a multifaceted mode of creative expression, of which rap music is its most visible and exploited element. Rap music, the music of hip-hop culture, has roots in both the United States and the Caribbean, particularly Jamaica. Since its start as youthful entertainment in the 1970s, hip-hop came to be considered the single most important voice and vehicle for the expression of contemporary African American urban youth in the last quarter of the twentieth century, and at the beginning of the twenty-first it has become one of the most influential cultural expressions worldwide.

Dawn M. Norfleet

World beat
A hybrid musical form that combines European American popular music with selected elements from Latin American, African, Asian, Caribbean, Australian, European, and/or North American vernacular musics

Snapshot 11.4: World Beat

World beat refers to a hybrid musical form that combines European American popular music with selected elements from Latin American, African, Asian, Caribbean, Australian, European, and/or North American vernacular musics. The term is often contrasted with "world music," a label that describes non-Western folk

Music Cultures in the United States

and traditional art musics marketed to Western audiences—musics that lack obvious Western pop influences.

World beat recordings usually contain musical features typical of world popular musics: standard chord changes, danceable rhythm, verse-chorus pop song structure, electronic and electrified instruments, and Western equal-temperament tuning. In addition, the "beat" that forms an underlying rhythmic framework for the exotic timbres of world beat's stylistic fusions is often an African American-derived backbeat, similar to that used in rock music.

Common world music ingredients in the world beat musical mixture include Indian classical instruments, Afro-Brazilian percussion, the Australian aboriginal *didgeridu,* Indonesian gamelan music, Andalusian flamenco guitars, and Eastern European folk melodies; by far the most frequent sources of inspiration for world beat artists today are sub-Saharan African drumming traditions and Celtic folk music. Popular mass-mediated genres that have crossed over into the world beat market include Algerian *rai,* Congolese *soukous,* South African *mbaqanga* and *iscathamiya,* South Asian *qawwali,* Ghanaian *highlife,* Nigerian *juju,* Jamaican *reggae,* and Trinidadian *soca.*

Creating a Market for World Beat

Although the sounds of world beat come from all over the globe, as a marketing category it is primarily a British import. The phrase *world music* was coined in 1987 at a meeting of British music business figures as a way to promote musics of non-Western peoples as popular music genres in their own right, instead of as mere curiosities stuck in the back corners of record stores (Spencer 1992). Many music retailers agreed to use the category, and the formerly impoverished section in the back devoted to "international" music was expanded and diversified. In the 1980s, because of the popularity of albums by Paul Simon, David Byrne, Peter Gabriel, and others, many commentators predicted that world beat, recognized as the most accessible variety of world music, would become a major popular music genre in North America, rivaling rock itself. This claim, which arose during one of the periodic "crises" in the commercial and artistic viability of mainstream rock music, was overly optimistic (or perhaps premature). At the close of the 1990s, world music/world beat remains a marginal but stable genre in the North American music market, akin to jazz and folk (that is, less than 3 percent of total annual sales). In fact, many record store chains still use the antiquated "international" label to classify their world beat recordings, although these sections are certainly larger and more diverse than ever before. *Billboard* magazine introduced its world music album chart in 1990, and the first Best World Music

Album Grammy was awarded a year later (to Grateful Dead percussionist Mickey Hart's *Planet Drum* album).

World beat aficionados often possess a highly sophisticated knowledge of their favorite genres, and their expertise is often beyond that of professional ethnomusicologists. The most comprehensive reference work for this type of music, *World Music: The Rough Guide* (Broughton et al. 1994), contains thirteen lengthy chapters covering exhaustively all the major musical regions of the world. Not surprisingly, the continent of Africa is covered in five different chapters, whereas East and Southeast Asia are combined in a single chapter entitled "The Far East." Nevertheless, the guide does cover the careers of such Asian musical megastars as Rhoma Irama, Lata Mangeshkar, and Oum Kalthoum, who are hugely popular in their own countries but are virtually unknown to European American audiences.

Graceland *and Its Critics*

The greatest boost to world beat's commercial visibility was a 1986 album by the popular American singer-songwriter Paul Simon, whose *Graceland* almost singlehandedly carved out a space for African musicians in the European American mainstream. The album's phenomenal success inspired countless other musicians. The album is indeed a masterpiece, an effective combination of quirky songwriting and striking musical eclecticism. The Zulu a capella group Ladysmith Black Mambazo is the best known of Simon's *Graceland* collaborators, but the album also contains contributions from (among others) Senegalese pop star Youssou N'Dour, Nigerian pedal steel guitarist Demola Adepoju, the Boyoyo Boys (an mbaqanga group from Soweto), Angeleno roots-rock band Los Lobos, and a zydeco group, Good Rockin' Dopsie and the Twisters. According to the album's liner notes, Simon chose to work with the latter two North American groups because their accordion-and-saxophone-driven compositions reminded him of the music of South Africa.

Graceland remains a highly controversial work. Indeed, a veritable cottage industry has grown up around debating the ethics, politics, and aesthetics of this seminal album. Portions of the album were recorded in South Africa (at Ovation Studios in Johannesburg) in direct violation of the United Nations-sponsored cultural boycott of South Africa. Critics have also voiced concerns about ownership; the songs on the album are copyrighted by Paul Simon alone. Without proper writing credits, the other musicians who contributed to *Graceland* cannot collect royalties.

Despite the problematic conditions of its production, even *Graceland*'s detractors admit that the songs on the record are musically compelling. Nonetheless, while Paul Simon's album provides an attractive blueprint for subsequent world beat collaborations, the difficult ethical issues regarding artistic control, ownership, and global politics raised by *Graceland* continue to haunt such endeavors.

Other Collaborations

Ethical considerations aside, the most artistically successful world beat recordings capitalize on musical affinities between different styles. Ry Cooder, the American slide guitarist, has won two world music Grammy awards for his collaborations with V. M. Bhatt, an Indian musician who plays Hindustani classical music on a modified Western guitar, and Ali Farka Toure, a Malian *griot* and *kora* virtuoso. Cooder has also displayed his uncanny ability to blend stylistically with different musics and musicians on albums recorded with Okinawan folksinger Shoukichi Kina and Hawaiian guitarist Gabby Pahinui. Mickey Hart's *Planet Drum* project features a number of very accomplished percussionists from different world traditions, including the Hindustani *tabla* virtuoso Zakir Hussein. Like many American world beat musicians, Hart is also an active producer of world music recordings, and he has used his fame as percussionist for the Grateful Dead to promote both his world music and world beat projects.

A dramatic example of cross-cultural musical fusion can be found on Kongar-ol Ondar's album *Back Tuva Future* (1999). The title indexes a typical preoccupation with juxtaposing "ancient" and "modern" musical styles found among North American world beat fans and promoters. Ondar, a Tuvan throat singer who is so popular in his home region that he has been compared to Elvis Presley, has produced an extraordinary recording with his American collaborators that combines Tuvan folk melodies and throat-singing techniques with slickly produced rap, funk, country, and even Native American chanting. The album features contributions from American country music star Willie Nelson, and, more strangely, some posthumous percussion and vocal recordings by the renowned American physicist Richard Feynman are also added to the mix. The resulting rustic hybrid was dubbed "country and eastern" by one concert promoter.

Technological Appropriations

While world beat collaborations between American and non-Western musicians can raise difficult ethical questions, more controversial still is the related practice of technologically plundering the sounds and grooves of world music to be reused in new compositions. The orientation of U.S. music producers toward the cultivation of original and exotic sounds, a quest frequently aided by digital audio technologies (Théberge 1997), has led to the increasing incorporation of the sounds of the *didgeridu,* sitar, gamelan, North Indian *tabla* drums, the Japanese *shakuhachi,* and other "ethnic" instruments into American pop, rock, rap, and jazz recordings (not to mention the soundtracks to countless television commercials and movies).

Vocal samples of Bulgarian choirs, Tibetan monks, and Tuvan throat singers are also mixed into new compositions. The highly distinctive sounds of African Pygmy chants have been sampled by artists including Herbie Hancock and Madonna (who actually sampled the Hancock track). Steven Feld, one of world beat's most outspoken critics, claims that such appropriation is yet another form of colonial exploitation, in which the music of non-Western primitives become "raw material" for further processing and refinement in the metropole by bourgeois artists (1996). Feld's objection is powerful, but the appropriative practices enabled by new musical technologies will no doubt continue to make the "exotic" sounds of world music ever more ubiquitous in the North American music scene.

Producing World Beat

Recording a world beat album "involves more than adding rock instruments to traditional music, or superimposing different musical styles; it is also a question of imposing sophisticated sound ideals and recording techniques typical for rock music" (Van Peer 1999:383). While world music purists continue to stress the authenticity of unadulterated field recordings, state-of-the-art multitrack recording studios define the sound of world beat. Most major releases are the product of hundreds of hours of overdubbing, editing, and mixing. In many cases traditional instruments are recorded with various electronic effects, such as chorus and reverberation, that alter the instrumental timbre. Sometimes the sounds of these instruments are sampled and approximated on an electronic keyboard.

Studio technologies have begun to erode the distinction between world music and world beat. With the more recent technical advances in portable recording, particularly the invention of digital audio tape, coupled with the now common practice of rerecording and remixing field recordings in a multitrack recording studio prior to their commercial release, the line between sophisticated studio productions and "raw" aural documentation has blurred. Feld (1994a) has argued that record companies intentionally try to collapse the distinction between world beat and world music, part of a strategy to lend the aura of authenticity to the former and pop trendiness to the latter. If this is indeed the case, their attempt has been remarkably successful.

The Impact of World Beat on American Music

Beginning in the late 1980s, world beat became a significant influence on popular music as a whole. Tracy Chapman's debut album (1988) features an electric *sitar* and Afro-Latin percussion performed by Paulinho Da Costa. More recently, the soundtrack to the film *Dead Man Walking* (1995) includes two stunning collaborations between Pearl Jam frontman Eddie Vedder and the late *qawwali* master Nusrat Fateh Ali Khan. But does the true impact of world beat extend beyond these instances of crossover?

It is difficult to predict the commercial and artistic future of world music/world beat in North America. Many commentators predict that an overall increase in global awareness will characterize North America in the twenty-first century, and they see world music as part of that emerging consciousness. In truth the appearance of world music/world beat is typical of the period of post-1960s genre fragmentation in the North American popular music market, which gathered speed in the 1980s and 1990s. This same period saw the invention of numerous new genres of varying degrees of commercial viability, including rap, techno, New Age, dance hall, "smooth jazz," and house music.

In the United States, of course, ignorance of even basic world geography is widespread, and any step toward greater understanding of other countries would certainly be welcome. However, many academic critics of world beat point out the lack of explicit political commentary in the music of the most popular artists. (Again, Paul Simon's solipsistic "Me Decade" lyrics on *Graceland,* which made no mention of apartheid, were a cause of some concern to critics.) Cultural critic Timothy Taylor derides world music as "music for grown-ups, music as wallpaper, music that does not, on its reasonably attractive and accessible surface, raise sticky problems about misogyny, racism, colonialism, what have you" (1997:6). It is certainly possible to relate the popularity of world beat among middle-aged, middle-class baby boomers to their embrace of New Age, adult acoustic, alternative, and even country music as more pleasant choices than discordant 1980s and 1990s youth musics like metal, rap, and hard-core. Certainly neocolonialism, poverty, exploitation, human rights violations, and other assorted miseries of the contemporary globalized world do not figure prominently in the music of Youssou N'Dour or the Gipsy Kings. But it is also true that world beat is often linked to progressive causes, especially environmental conservation and protecting the rights of indigenous people.

In fact, world beat may ultimately owe its existence to the so-called charity-rock phenomenon, which raised awareness about international human rights issues, famine in Ethiopia, and South African apartheid in the 1980s, and also had the effect of exposing Western pop stars to the popular musics of other countries, particularly sub-Saharan Africa (Garofalo 1997:387–389). Among these artists was Paul Simon, who participated in the USA for Africa project.

Another important, if unintended, consequence of world beat's popularity is the discipline of ethnomusicology's increased visibility and importance in American universities. Throughout the 1990s, introduction to world music classes were among the most popular offerings in college music departments, guaranteeing the usefulness of ethnomusicologists in an era of academic downsizing. Although many ethnomusicologists continue to denounce world beat, it is clear that this genre has contributed to the relevance of their research in the eyes of the general public and widened that research's potential audience.

World Beat in Historical Perspective

The historical development of twentieth-century American popular music has been characterized by the emergence of new hybrid genres that combine diverse nonelite vernacular styles with elements from commercial pop. Often these new styles are introduced to the mainstream public via musical popularizers who present a watered-down, familiarized version, which then leaves consumers hungry for the "real thing." These cycles of appropriation, commercialization, and the pursuit of authenticity have played a central role in the historical development of ragtime, jazz, swing, blues, country, rock, and rap music. Despite the exotic origins of much world beat music, the aesthetic and political debates that surround it appear to be the result of similar cultural dynamics. It is therefore not surprising that debates about authenticity and "selling out" that characterize rock music discourse have now been carried over to discussions of world beat artists.

The attraction of novel timbres and musical techniques, a cosmopolitan but unchallenging sense of global citizenship, and fantasies of community and premodern wholeness all undoubtably play a role in world music/world beat's (modest) commercial success in the United States, as does a genuine interest in the creative musical endeavors of other peoples. There can be no doubt, however, that the production, marketing, and promotion of these musics are part of a recurring process of musical popularization that has long been a feature of the North American musical landscape.

Finally, the possibility exists that world beat will become a genuine grassroots music among young people in North America. The increasing number of non-Western performing ensembles on North

American college campuses (usually Javanese or Balinese gamelan, West African drumming groups, or Arab music ensembles) have exposed America's youth to non-Western sounds, playing techniques, and repertoires and may encourage some world beat consumers to become producers of new, unforeseen musical hybrids.

Jeremy Wallach

REVIEW

Important Terms and People to Know

B-boying/girling
Carter family
Classic rock
Covers
Steven Feld
Gangsta Rap
Glam rock
Graceland
Grand Ole Opry
Grunge
Heavy metal
Hip-hop
Kool DJ Herc
Pedal steel guitar
Elvis Presley
Rap
Riot Grrrls
Jimmie Rodgers
Sampling
World beat
World music

Review Questions

1. What changes, especially in instrumentation, account for renewed interest in and popularity of country and Western music at the beginning of the twentieth century? At the beginning of the twenty-first?
2. Describe some of the social and musical changes of the 1960s that changed "rock and roll" into "rock." Who are some of the great artists associated with pre- and post-1960s rock?
3. Distinguish between the many different forms of rock that are available today. What are some of the differences in lyrics, music, and costuming between these forms?

4. What are the basic values of hip-hop culture, and how does rap represent these through its musical forms?
5. Distinguish between old and new schools of rap. What has been the role of technology in the history of rap?
6. Consider the ethical issues in "sampling" and adapting various world music cultures for sale as world beat. What are some of the arguments for and against this practice?
7. Discuss the role of women in these popular music forms. What has enabled or prohibited women from achieving success as performers, producers, and/or promoters?

Projects

1. Spend a few days listening to the radio stations in your area. What kinds of music are presented on the various stations? Make a chart that shows the relative air time for country and Western, rock, rap, and world beat musics.
2. Compare the lyrics of two or three of the forms presented in this chapter. What are the major differences in topic? Attitude? Delivery? How do these relate to the aesthetic values and audiences for these musics?
3. Choose one of the genres of music presented here and talk with someone who is older than you. Try to determine what this music was like 20 years or more ago. Do some research in the library on this music, using what you've collected in the interview to illustrate your research.

Bibliography

A Celebration of Gongs. Gamelan Lake of the Silver Bear. Directed by Michael Zinn. Instruments built by Michael Zinn. Comsitions by William Naylor, Christopher Venaccio, and Zinn; also pieces from Sunda and Central Java. Independently produced cassette.

Abraham, Sameer Y. and Nabeel Abraham. 1983. *Arabs in the New World: Studies on Arab-American Communities.* Detroit, MI: Wayne State University Press.

Abrahams, Roger D. 1992. *Singing the Master: The Emergence of African American Folk Culture in the Plantation South.* New York: Pantheon Books.

Abrahams, Roger D., and George Foss. 1968. *Anglo-American Folksong Style.* Englewood Cliffs, NJ: Prentice-Hall.

Acosta, Leonardo. 1991. "The Rumba, the Guaguancó, and Tío Tom." In *Essays on Cuban Music: North American and Cuban Perspectives,* ed. Peter Manuel, 51-73. Lanham, MD: University Press of America.

Adams, Robert H. 1991 [1977]. *Songs of Our Grandfathers: Music of the Unami Delaware Indians.* Dewey, OK: Touching Leaves Indian Crafts.

Adorno, Theodor. 1988. *Introduction to the Sociology of Music.* Trans. E. B. Ashton. New York: Continuum.

Adorno, Theodore. 1991 [1944]. "The Culture Industry: Enlightenment as Mass Deception." In *Dialectic of Enlightenment,* ed. Theodore Adorno and Max Horkheimer. New York: Continuum.

Ahlquist, Karen. 1997. *Democracy at the Opera: Music, Theater, and Culture in New York City, 1815-60.* Chicago: University of Illinois Press.

Alba, Richard D. 1990. *Ethnic Identity: The Transformation of White America.* New Haven, CT: Yale University Press.

Albrecht, Theodore. 1975. "German Singing Societies in Texas." Ph.D. dissertation, North Texas State University.

Allen, James Paul. 1988. *We the People: An Atlas of America's Ethnic Diversity.* New York: Macmillan.

Allen, William Francis, ed. 1867. *Slave Songs of the United States.* New York: A. Simpson.

Allen, William Francis. 1983 [1867]. "General Characteristics of Slave Music." In *Readings in Black American Music,* 2nd ed., ed. Eileen Southern, 149-174. New York: Norton.

"Americanism in Music." 1899. *The American Monthly Review of Reviews.* January.

Amira, John, and Steven Cornelius. 1991. *The Music of Santería: Traditional Rhythms for the Batá Drums.* Tempe, AZ: White Cliffs Media, Inc.

Ammer, Christine. 1980. *Unsung: A History of Women in American Music.* Westport, CT: Greenwood Press.

Aoki, Tatsu. 1994. *Kioto.* Asianimprov Records Air 0017. Compact Disc.

Armenians on 8th Avenue. 1996. Produced by Harold G. Hagopian. With 22-page booklet of notes, photographs, and song lyrics. Traditional Crossroads CD 4279. Compact disc.

Arts in America 1990: The Bridge between Creativity and Community. 1990. Washington, DC: National Endowment for the Arts.

Asai, Susan. 1985. "*Itøraku:* A Buddhist Tradition of Performing Arts and the Development of *Taiko* Drumming in the United States." In *Asian Music in North America,* ed. Nazir A. Jairazbhoy and Sue Carole DaVale, 163-172. *Selected Reports in Ethnomusicology* 6. Los Angeles: University of California.

Asai, Susan. 1991. "The Jazz Connection in Asian American Music." *Coda* 238 (July-August).

Asai, Susan. 1995. "Transformations of Tradition: Three Generations of Japanese American Music Making." *The Musical Quarterly* 79(1).

Asai, Susan. 1997. "*Sansei* Voices in the Community: Japanese American Musicians in California." In *Musics of Multicultural America,* 257-285. New York: Schirmer Books.

Asian American Arts Dialogue. 1995. New York: Asian American Arts Alliance.

Attali, Jacques. 1985. *Noise: The Political Economy of Music.* Trans. Brian Massumi. Minneapolis: University of Minnesota Press.

Auerbach, Brian. 1985. "Asian American Jazz: An Oral History with Paul Yamazaki." *Options* (March-April).

Auerbach, Susan. 1994. *Encyclopedia of Multiculturalism.* New York: Marshall Cavendish.

Austerlitz, Paul. 1997. *Merengue: Dominican Music and Dominican Identity.* Philadelphia: Temple University Press.

B.A.N.G. (Bay Area New Gamelan). 1986. Directed by Jody Diamond and Daniel Schmidt. Instruments built by Daniel Schmidt. Compositions by Schmidt, Diamond and Ingram Marshall. Lebanon, NH: American Gamelan Institute. AGI01. Cassette.

Babbit, Milton. 1970. "On *Relata I.*" *Perspectives of New Music* 9(1):1-22.

Babbit, Milton. 1987. *Words About Music.* Ed. Stephen Dembski and Joseph N. Straus. Madison: University of Wisconsin Press.

Babbit, Milton. 1962. "Twelve-Tone Rhythmic Structure and the Electronic Medium." *Perspectives of New Music* 1(1):49-79.

Bach for Dummies. 1996. EMI 7243 5 66270 0 0. Compact disc.

Bailey, Ben E. 1992. "Music in Slave Era Mississippi." *The Journal of Mississippi History* 54(1):29-58.

Baker, David N., Linda M. Belt, and H. C. Hudson, eds. 1978. *The Black Composer Speaks.* Metuchen, NJ: Scarecrow Press.

Balinese Music in America. Gamelan Sekar Jaya. Directed by Wayne Vitale (*gong keb- yar*) and Carla Fabrizio (*angklung*). Notes by Marc Perlman. Compositions by I Wayan Beratha, I Nyoman Windha, I Ketut Partha, Dewa Putu, Berata, and Wayne Vitale. GSJ-011. Compact disc.

Baraka, Amiri. 1991. "The 'Blues Aesthetic' and the 'Black Aesthetic': Aesthetics as the Continuing Political History of a Culture." *Black Music Research Journal* 11(2):101–109.

Barlow, William. 1999. *Voice Over: The Making of Black Radio.* Philadelphia: Temple University Press.

Barrand, Anthony G. 1991. *Six Fools and a Dancer: The Timeless Way of the Morris.* Plainfield, VT: Northern Harmony.

Barrow, David C. 1882. "A Georgia Corn-Shucking." *The Century Magazine* 24(n.s.2):873–878.

Barth, Fredrik. 1969. *Introduction to Ethnic Groups and Boundaries: The SocialOrganization of Difference*, ed. Fredrik Barth, 9–38. Boston: Little, Brown.

Bartholomew, Dave. 1985. Personal interview. 14 May.

Bartis, Peter. 1982. "A History of the Archive of Folk Song at the Library of Congress: The First Fifty Years." Ph.D. dissertation, University of Pennsylvania.

Bartlett, David W. 1993. "Housing the Underclass." In *The Underclass: Views from History,* ed. Michael B. Katz, 118–157. Princeton, NJ: Princeton University Press.

Baudrillard, Jean. 1970. *La Societé de la Consommation.* Paris: Gallimard.

Baudrillard, Jean. 1996 [1968]. *The System of Objects.* Trans. James Benedict. London: Verso.

Bayard, Samuel P. 1950. "Prolegomena to a Study of the Principal Melodic Families of British-American Folk Song." *Journal of American Folklore* (63):1–44.

Bayard, Samuel P. 1951. "Principal Versions of an International Folk Tune." *Journal of the International Folk Music Council* (3):44–50.

Bayard, Samuel P. 1982. *Dance to the Fiddle, March to the Fife.* University Park: Pennsylvania State University Press.

Beethoven for Dummies. EMI 7243 5 66264 0 9. Compact disc.

Belevich, Alexander. 1988. "History of the Balalaika." *Balalaika and Domra Association of America Newsletter* 11(1):8,11.

Bell, Al. 1983. Personal interview. 26 May.

Beloff, Jim. 1997. *The Ukulele: A Visual History.* San Francisco: Miller Freeman.

Benary, Barbara, ed. 1983. "North American Gamelan Directory." *Ear Magazine,* 7(4).

Benary, Barbara. 1983. "One Perspective on Gamelan in America." *Asian Music* 15(1):82–101.

Benary, Barbara. 1993a. *Gamelan Works Vol. 1: The Braid Pieces.* Lebanon, NH: American Gamelan Institute.

Benary, Barbara. 1993b. *Gamelan Works Vol. 2: Satires.* Lebanon, NH: American Gamelan Institute.

Benary, Barbara. 1993c. *Gamelan Works Vol. 3: Pieces in a Single Tuning.* Lebanon, NH: American Gamelan Institute.

Benary, Barbara. 1995. *Gamelan Works Vol. 4: Seven Pieces in Mixed Tuning: Slendro and Pelog.* Lebanon, NH: American Gamelan Institute.

Berendt, Joachim. 1975. *The Jazz Book: From New Orleans to Rock and Free Jazz.* Trans. Dan Morgenstern and Helmut and Barbara Bredigkeit. Westport, CT: Lawrence Hill and Co.

Berlin, Edward A. 1980. *Ragtime: A Musical and Cultural History.* Berkeley: University of California Press.

Berry, Venise. 1994. "Feminine or Masculine: The Conflicting Nature of Female Images in Rap Music." In *Cecilia Reclaimed,* ed. Susan C. Cook and Judy S. Tsou, 183–201. Urbana: University of Illinois Press.

Bindas, Kenneth J. 1995. *All of This Music Belongs to the Nation: The WPA's Federal Music Project and American Society.* Knoxville: University of Tennessee Press.

Blassingame, John W. 1979 [1972]. *The Slave Community: Plantation Life in the Antebellum South.* Rev. and enl. ed. New York: Oxford University Press.

Blesh, Rudi. 1985. *Shining Trumpets: A History of Jazz.* 2nd ed. New York: Knopf.

Block, Adrienne Fried. 1998. *Amy Beach, Passionate Victorian.* New York: Oxford University Press.

Blum, Joseph. 1978. "Problems of Salsa Research." *Ethnomusicology* 22(1):137-149.

Boggs, Vernon, ed. 1992. *Salsiology: Afro-Cuban Music and the Evolution of Salsa in New York City.* New York: Greenwood Press.

Bohlman, Philip V. 1979. "Music in the Culture of German Americans in North-Central Wisconsin." Master's thesis, University of Illinois.

Bohlman, Philip V. 1985. "Prolegomena to the Classification of German American Music." *Yearbook of German American Studies* 20:33-48.

Bohlman, Philip V. 1988. *The Study of Folk Music in the Modern World.* Bloomington: Indiana University Press.

Botkin, Benjamin Albert. 1959 [1942]. Notes to *Negro Work Songs and Calls.* Library of Congress, Division of Music, Recording Laboratory AAFS L8. LP disk.

Bowers, Jane, and Judith Tick, eds. 1986. *Women Making Music: The Western Art Tradition, 1150-1950.* Urbana: University of Illinois Press.

Bowman, Rob. 1997. *Soulsville U.S.A.: The Story of Stax Records.* New York: Schirmer Books.

Boyer, Horace C., comp. 1976. "A Portfolio of Music: The New England Afro-American School." *Black Perspective in Music* 4(2):213-237.

Brackett, David. 1993. "Economics and Aesthetics in Contemporary Art Music." *Stanford Humanities Review* 3(2):49-59.

Brahms for Dummies. 1996. EMI 7243 5 66272 0 8. Compact disc.

Bremer, Fredrika. 1853. *The Homes of the New World: Impressions of America.* Trans. Mary Howitt. New York: Harper & Brothers.

Brett, Philip, Elizabeth Wood, and Gary C. Thomas, eds. 1994. *Queering the Pitch: The New Gay and Lesbian Musicology.* New York: Routledge.

Bronson, Bertrand. 1950. "Some Observations About Melodic Variation in British-American Folk Tunes." *Journal of the American Musicological Society* 3:120-134.

Bronson, Bertrand. 1959-1972. *The Traditional Tunes of the Child Ballads.* 4 vols. Princeton, NJ: Princeton University Press.

Bronson, Bertrand.1976. *The Singing Tradition of Child's Popular Ballads.* Princeton, NJ: Princeton University Press.

Broughton, Simon, et al. eds. 1994. *World Music: The Rough Guide.* London: Rough Guides.

Brown, Charles T. 1983. *The Rock and Roll Story: From the Sounds of Rebellion to an American Art Form.* Englewood Cliffs, NJ: Prentice-Hall.

Brown, Rae Linda. 1990. "William Grant Still, Florence Price, and William Dawson: Echoes of the Harlem Renaissance." In *Black Music in the Harlem Renaissance: A Collection of Essays,* ed. Samuel A. Floyd Jr., 71-86. Westport, CT: Greenwood Press.

Browne, Ray B. 1954. "Some Notes on the Southern Holler." *Journal of American Folklore* (67):73-77.

Budds, Michael J. 1990. *Jazz in the Sixties: The Expansion of Musical Resources and Techniques.* Iowa City: The University of Iowa.

Buertle, Jack V. and Danny Barker. 1973. *Bourbon Street Black: The New Orleans Black Jazzman.* New York: Oxford University Press.

Bufwack, Mary A. and Robert K. Oermann. 1993. *Finding Her Voice: The Saga of Women in Country Music.* New York: Crown.

Burkhart, Charles. 1952. "Music of the Old Order Amish and the Old Colony Mennonites: A Contemporary Monodic Practice." Master's thesis, Colorado College.

Burnett, Robert. 1996. *The Global Jukebox.* London: Routledge.

Burr, Ramiro. 1999. *The Billboard Guide to Tejano and Regional Mexican Music*. New York: Billboard Books.

Byrd, Bobby. 1984. Personal interview. 8 September.

Cage, John. 1961. *Silence: Lectures and Writings*. Middletown, CT: Wesleyan University Press.

Cage, John. 1987. *Haikai for gamelan degung*. Musical score. New York: C. F. Peters.

Cantwell, Robert. 1993. "When We Were Good: Class and Culture in the Folk Revival." In *Transforming Tradition*, ed. Neil V. Rosenberg, 35-60. Urbana: University of Illinois Press.

Cantwell, Robert. 1996. *When We Were Good: The Folk Revival*. Cambridge: Harvard University Press.

Carby, Hazel. 1990 [1986]. "It Jus Be's Dat Way Sometimes: The Sexual Politics of Women's Blues." In *Unequal Sisters: A Multicultural Reader in U.S. Women's History*, ed. Ellen Carol DuBois and Vicki L. Ruiz, 238-249. New York: Routledge.

Carby, Hazel. 1998. *Race Men*. Cambridge: Harvard University Press.

Carter, Madison H. 1986. *An Annotated Catalog of Composers of African Ancestry*. New York: Vantage Press.

Chadabe, Joel. 1997. *Electric Sound: The Past and Promise of Electronic Music*. Englewood Cliffs, NJ: Prentice Hall.

Chanan, Michael. 1994. *Musica Pratica: The Social Practice of Western Music from Gregorian Chant to Postmodernism*. London: Verso.

Chanan, Michael. 1995. *Repeated Takes: A Short History of Recording and Its Effects on Music*. London: Verso.

Charlton, Katherine. 1994. *Rock Music Styles: A History*. Boston: McGraw-Hill.

Chase, Gilbert. 1987. *America's Music: From the Pilgrims to the Present*. Urbana: University of Illinois Press.

Check-List of Recorded Songs in the English Language in the Archive of American Folk Song to July, 1940. 1942. Washington, DC: Library of Congress.

Child, Francis James. [1882-1898]. *The English and Scottish Popular Ballads*. New York: Dover.

Chiswick, Barry R., ed. 1992. *Immigration, Language and Ethnicity: Canada and the United States*. Washington, DC: AEI Press.

Clinton, George. 1995. Personal interview. 5 March.

Cockrell, Dale. 1997. *Demons of Disorder: Early Blackface Minstrels and Their World*. Cambridge: Cambridge University Press.

Coffin, Tristram P. 1963. *The British Traditional Ballad in North America*. Philadelphia: American Folklore Society.

Cole, Bill. 1993 [1976]. *John Coltrane*. New York: Da Capo.

Collier, James Lincoln. 1978. *The Making of Jazz: A Comprehensive History*. Boston: Houghton Mifflin.

Collier, James Lincoln. 1983. *Louis Armstrong: An American Genius*. New York: Oxford University Press.

Coltrane, John. 1960. "Coltrane on Coltrane." *Down Beat* 29:26-27.

Coltrane, John. 1968. *Om*. Impulse A-9140. LP disk.

Conjunto! Texas-Mexican Border Music. (1988-94) Vol. 1-6. Rounder Records 6023. Compact disc.

Conner, Charles. 1990. Personal interview. 10 November.

Cook, Susan C. 1992. "Listening to Billie Holiday: Intersections of Race and Gender." *Sonneck Society Bulletin* 18(3):94-97.

Cook, Susan C. and Judy S. Tsou, eds. 1994. *Cecilia Reclaimed: Feminist Perspectives on Gender and Music*. Urbana: University of Illinois Press.

Cook, Will Marion. 1947. "Clorindy, the Origin of the Cakewalk." *Theater Arts* 31(9):61-65.

Cooper, Sarah, ed. 1996. *Girls, Girls, Girls: Essays on Women and Music.* New York: New York University Press.

Cornelius, Steven. 1991. "Drumming for the Orishas: Reconstruction of Tradition in New York City." In *Essays on Cuban Music: North American and Cuban Perspectives,* ed. Peter Manuel, 139-155. Lanham, MD.: University Press of America.

Courlander, Harold. 1956. *Negro Folk Music of Alabama.* Folkways Records FE 4417.

Courlander, Harold. 1963. *Negro Folk Music U.S.A.* New York: Columbia University Press.

Covach, John and Graeme M. Boone, eds. 1997. *Understanding Rock: Essays in Musical Analysis.* New York: Oxford University Press.

Cowell, Henry. 1996 [1930]. *New Musical Resources.* New York and Cambridge: Cambridge University Press.

Crawford, Richard. 1993. *The American Musical Landscape.* Berkeley: University of California Press.

Cross, Brian. 1993. *It's Not About a Salary: Rap, Race and Resistance in Los Angeles.* New York: Verso.

Crystal, David. 1999. *The Cambridge Factfinder.* 3rd ed. Cambridge: Cambridge University Press.

Cummins, Tony. 1975. *The Sound of Philadelphia.* London: Methuen.

Cureau, Rebecca. 1980. "Black Folklore, Musicology and Willis Laurence James." *Negro History Bulletin* 43(1):16-20.

Curtis, Natalis. 1907. *The Indians' Book: An Offering by the American Indians of Indian Lore, Musical and Narrative, to Form a Record of the Songs and Legends of Their Race.* New York: Harper.

Dahl, Linda. 1984. *Stormy Weather: The Music and Lives of a Century of Jazzwomen.* New York: Pantheon.

Dankworth, Avril. 1968. *Jazz: An Introduction to Its Musical Basis.* London: Oxford University Press.

Das Efx. 1992. *Dead Serious.* EastWest Records America 7 91627-4. Compact disc.

Davis, Miles, with Quincy Troupe. 1989. *Miles: The Autobiography.* New York: Simon and Schuster.

Davis, Miles. 1954. *Bags' Groove.* Prestige OJCCD-242-2 (P7109). Compact disc.

De Curtis, Anthony, ed. 1992. *Present Tense: Rock & Roll and Culture.* Durham, NC: Duke University Press.

De Lerma, Dominique-René. 1981-1984. "Bibliography of Black Music." In *Greenwood Encyclopedia of Black Music.* 4 vols. Westport, CT: Greenwood Press.

DeLio, Thomas. 1984. *Circumscribing the Open Universe.* Lanham, MD: University Press of America.

Denisoff, R. Serge. 1971. *Great Day Coming: Folk Music and the American Left.* Chicago: University of Illinois Press.

Denisoff, R. Serge. 1983. *Sing a Song of Social Significance.* 2nd ed. Bowling Green, OH: Bowling Green State University Press.

Denny, Martin. 1957. *Exotica.* Liberty Records, LRP-3034. LP disk.

Densmore, Frances. 1942. "The Study of Indian Music." From the Annual Report of the Smithsonian Institution for 1941. Publication 3671. Washington, DC: U.S. Government Printing Office.

Densmore, Frances. 1909. "Scale Formation in Primitive Music." *American Anthropologist* 11(1):1-12.

Densmore, Frances. 1926. *The American Indians and Their Music.* New York: The Woman's Press.

DeVeaux, Scott. 1997. *The Birth of Bebop: A Social and Musical History.* Berkeley: University of California Press.

Diamond, Beverley, M. Sam Cronk, and Franziska von Rosen. 1994. *Visions of Sound: Musical Instruments of First Nations Communities in Northeastern America*. Chicago: University of Chicago Press.

Diamond, Jody. 1992. "Making Choices: American Gamelan in Composition and Education (From the Java Jive to Eine Kleine Gamelan Music)." In *Essays on Southeast Asian Performing Arts: Local Manifestations and Cross-Cultural Implications*, ed. Kathy Foley. Berkeley, CA: Centers for South and Southeast Asian Studies.

DiMaggio, Paul. 1972. "Country Music: Ballad of the Silent Majority." In *The Sounds of Social Change*, ed. R. Denisoff and R. Peterson, 31-56. Chicago: Rand McNally.

DjeDje, Jacqueline Cogdell, and Eddie S. Meadows, eds. 1998. *California Soul: Music of African Americans in the West*. Berkeley: University of California Press.

Dornish, Margaret H. 1986. "Wisdom and Means: D. T. Suzuki's Theology of Culture." Unpublished paper, delivered to the Pacific Coast Theological Society. Berkeley, California. February.

Douglass, Frederick. 1845. *The Narrative of the Life of Frederick Douglass, an American Slave, Written by Himself*. Boston: The Anti-Slavery Office.

Dr. Dre. 1991. *The Chronic*. Priority Records P257129. Compact disc.

Dr. Licks. 1989. *Standing in the Shadows of Motown: The Life and Music of Legendary Bassist James Jamerson*. Wynnewood, PA: Dr. Licks Publishing.

DuBois, W. E. B. 1992 [1903]. *The Souls of Black Folk*. Ed. Henry Louis Gates Jr. New York: Bantam.

Duckworth, William. 1995. *Talking Music. Conversations with John Cage, Philip Glass, Laurie Anderson, and Five Generations of American Experimental Composers*. New York: Schirmer Books.

Dunn, David. 1996. "A History of Electronic Music Pioneers." In *Classic Essays on Twentieth- Century Music: A Continuing Symposium*, ed. Richard Kostelanetz et al. 87-123. New York: Schirmer Books.

Dyen, Doris and Philip V. Bohlman. 1985. "Becoming Ethnic in Western Pennsylvania: Processes of Ethnic Identification in Pittsburgh and Its Environs." Paper presented at the American Folklore Society Annual Meeting, Cincinnati, Ohio.

Ellington, Duke. 1930. *Mood Indigo*. RCA ADL 20152(e). LP disk.

Emery, Lynne Fauley. 1972. *Black Dance in the United States from 1619 to 1970*. Palo Alto, CA: National Press Books.

Encyclopédie, or Dictionnaire Raisonné des Sciences, des Arts et des Métiers. Paris: Briasson, 1751-1765.

Endo, Kenny. *Taiko* Ensemble. 1994. *Eternal Energy*. AsianImprov Records AIR 0021. Compact disc.

Epstein, Dena J. 1975. "The Folk Banjo: A Documentary History." *Ethnomusicology* 19(3):347-371.

Epstein, Dena J. 1977. *Sinful Tunes and Spirituals: Black Folk Music to the Civil War*. Urbana: University of Illinois Press.

Epstein, Dena. 1963. "Slave Music in the United States before 1860: A Survey of Sources, pts. I-II." *Notes of the Music Library Association* 20(Spring):195-212; (Summer):377-390.

Erdely, Stephen. 1979. "Ethnic Music in the United States: An Overview." *Yearbook of the International Folk Music Council* 11:114-135.

Ethnic Recordings in America: A Neglected Heritage. 1982. Washington, DC: Library of Congress American Folklife Center.

Evans, David. 1978. Notes to *Let's Get Loose: Folk and Popular Blues Styles from the Beginnings to the Early 1940s*. New World Records NW 290. LP disk.

Faris, James C. 1990. *The Nightway: A History and a History of Documentation of a Navajo Ceremonial*. Albuquerque: University of New Mexico Press.

Feagin, Joe R. and Melvin P. Sikes. 1994. *Living with Racism: The Black Middle-Class Experience.* Boston: Beacon Press.

Feather, Leonard. 1959. *Jazz.* Los Angeles: Trend Books.

Feld, Steven. 1994a. "From Schizophonia to Schismogenesis: Notes of the Discourses of World Music and World Beat." In *Music Grooves: Essays and Dialogues,* ed. Charles Keil and Steven Feld, 257–289. Chicago: University of Chicago Press.

Feld, Steven.1994b. "Notes on World Beat." In *Music Grooves: Essays and Dialogues,* ed. Charles Keil and Steven Feld, 238–246. Chicago: University of Chicago Press.

Feld, Steven.1996. "Pygmy POP: A Genealogy of Schizophrenic Mimesis." *Yearbook for Traditional Music* 28:1-35.

Feldman, Walter. 1975. "Middle Eastern Music Among Immigrant Communities in New York City." In *Balkan-Arts Traditions,* ed. Martin Koenig, 19-25. New York: Balkan Arts Center.

Fenton, William N. 1940. Masked Medicine Societies of the Iroquois. Annual Report of the Smithsonian Institution for 1940. Washington, DC: Government Printing Office, 397–429.

Fenton, William N. 1942. Songs from the Iroquois Longhouse. Library of Congress AFS L6. LP disk.

Fenton, William N.1978. Iroquois Social Dance Songs. 3 vols. Iroqrafts, Ontario: Ohsweken.

Fernando, S. H., Jr. 1994. *The New Beats: Exploring the Music, Culture, and Attitudes of Hip-Hop.* New York: Doubleday.

Ferris, William and Mary L. Hart, eds. 1982. *Folk Music and Modern Sound.* Jackson: University Press of Mississippi.

Fewkes, Jesse Walter. 1890. "A Contribution to Passamaquoddy Folklore." *Journal of American Folklore* 3:257-280.

Fikentscher, Kai. 1995. "'You Better Work!' Music, Dance, and Marginality in Underground Dance Clubs of New York City." Ph.D. dissertation, Columbia University.

Fikentscher, Kai. 2000. *"You Better Work!" Underground Dance Music in New York City.* Hanover, NH: Wesleyan University Press/University Press of New England.

Flanagan, Hallie. 1940. *Arena: The History of the Federal Theater.* New York: B. Blom.

Fletcher, Tom. 1984 [1954]. *The Tom Fletcher Story: 100 Years of the Negro in Show Business.* New York: Da Capo Press.

Floyd, Samuel A. Jr. and Marsha J. Reisser. 1983. *Black Music in the United States: An Annotated Bibliography of Selected Reference and Research Materials.* Millwood, NY: Krau International.

Floyd, Samuel A. Jr., ed. 1999. *International Dictionary of Black Composers.* Chicago: Fitzroy Dearborn.

Fogelquist, Mark. 1996. "Mariachi Conferences and Festivals in the United States." In *The Changing Faces of Tradition: A Report on the Folk and Traditional Arts in the United States,* ed. Elizabeth Peterson, 18–23. Research Division Report no. 38. Washington, DC: National Endowment for the Arts.

Fox, Stephen. 1984. *The Mirror Makers: A History of American Advertising.* New York: Morrow.

Franklin, John Hope. 1994. *From Slavery to Freedom: A History of African Americans.* 7th ed. New York: Knopf.

Frey, J. William. 1949. "Amish Hymns as Folk Music." In *Pennsylvania Songs and Legends,* ed. George Korson, 129-162. Philadelphia: University of Pennsylvania Press.

Friedlander, Paul. 1996. *Rock and Roll: A Social History.* Boulder, CO: Westview Press.

Friend, Robyn and Neil Siegel. 1986. "Contemporary Contexts for Iranian Professional Musical Performance." In *Cultural Parameters of Iranian Musical*

Expression, ed. Margaret Caton and Neil Siegel, 10-17. Redondo Beach, CA: The Institute of Persian Performing Arts.

Frisbie, Charlotte J. 1987. *Navajo Medicine Bundles or* Jish: *Acquisition, Transmission, and Disposition in the Past and Present.* Albuquerque: University of New Mexico Press.

Frisbie, Charlotte J. 1993. "NAGPRA and the Repatriation of *Jish.*" In *Papers from the Third, Fourth, and Sixth Navajo Studies Conferences,* ed. June-el Piper, 119-128. Window Rock, AZ: Navajo Nation Historic Preservation Department.

Frith, Simon and Andrew Goodwin, eds. 1990. *On Record: Rock, Pop, and the Written Word.* New York: Pantheon.

Frith, Simon and Angela McRobbie. 1990. "Rock and Sexuality." In *On Record: Rock, Pop and the Written Word,* ed. Simon Frith and Andrew Goodwin, 277-292. New York: Routledge.

Frith, Simon. 1978. *The Sociology of Rock.* London: Constable.

Frith, Simon. 1996. *Performing Rites: On the Value of Popular Music.* Cambridge: Harvard University Press.

Gabree, John. 1968. *The World of Rock.* Greenwich, CT: Fawcett Publications.

Gagne, Cole and Tracy Caras. 1982. *Soundpieces: Interviews with American Composers.* Metuchen, NJ: Scarecrow Press.

Gann, Kyle. 1997. *American Music in the Twentieth Century.* New York: Schirmer Books.

Garland, Phil. 1969. *The Sound of Soul.* Chicago: Henry Regnery.

Garofalo, Reebee and Steve Chapple. 1977. *Rock & Roll Is Here to Pay: The History and Politics of the Music Industry.* Chicago: Nelson Hall.

Garofalo, Reebee. 1988. *The Death of Rhythm and Blues.* New York: Penguin Books.

Garofalo, Reebee. 1990. "Crossing Over: 1939." In *Split Image: African Americans in the Mass Media,* ed. Jannette L. Dates and William Barlow, 57-121. Washington, DC: Howard University Press.

Garofalo, Reebee. 1997. *Rockin' Out: Popular Music in the U.S.A.* Boston: Allyn and Bacon.

Gaunt, Kyra. 1995. "African-American Women between Hopscotch and Hip-hop: 'Must Be the Music (That's Turnin' Me On).'" In *Feminism, Multiculturalism and the Media: Global Diversities,* ed. Angharad Valdivia, 277-308. Thousand Oaks, CA: Sage Publications.

Genovese, Eugene D. 1974 [1972]. *Roll, Jordan, Roll: The World Slaves Made.* New York: Pantheon Books.

George, Nelson. 1985. *Where Did Our Love Go?* New York: St. Martin's Press.

George, Nelson. 1998. *Hip Hop America.* New York: Penguin Books.

Gillespie, Dizzy, with Al Fraser. 1979 [1970]. *To Be or Not to Bop: Memoirs of Dizzy Gillespie.* New York: Da Capo.

Gillet, Charlie. 1983 [1970]. *The Sound of the City.* Rev. and expanded ed. New York: Pantheon Books.

Gillett, Charlie. 1974. *Making Tracks: Atlantic Records and the Growth of a Multi-Billion-Dollar Industry.* New York: E. P. Dutton.

Gitler, Ira. 1985. *Swing to Bop: An Oral History of the Transition in Jazz in the 1940s.* New York: Oxford University Press.

Glass, Philip. 1987. *Music by Philip Glass.* New York: Harper and Row.

Glasser, Ruth. 1995. *My Music Is My Flag: Puerto Rican Musicians and Their New York Communities, 1917-1940.* Berkeley: University of California Press.

Glazer, Nathan and Daniel P. Moynihan, eds. 1975. *Ethnicity: Theory and Experience.* Cambridge, MA: Harvard University Press.

Gleason, Philip. 1980. "American Identity and Americanization." In *Harvard Encyclopedia for American Ethnic Groups,* ed. Stephan Thernstrom, Ann Orlov, and Oscar Handlin, 31-58. Cambridge, MA: Harvard University Press.

Goertzen, Chris. 1985. "American Fiddle Tunes and the Historic-Geographic Method." *Ethnomusicology* 29(3):448–473.

Goldman, Albert. 1978. *Disco.* New York: Hawthorn.

Goldstein, Amy and Roberto Suro. 2000. "La Nueva Vida/Latinos in America: A Journey in Stages." *The Washington Post,* 16 January, A1, A24.

Gombert, Greg. 1994. A Guide to Native American Music Recordings. Fort Collins, CO: MultiCultural Publishing.

Gordy, Berry. 1994. *To Be Loved.* New York: Warner Books.

Gore, Tipper. 1987. *Raising PG Kids in an X-Rated Society.* Nashville, TN: Abingdon Press.

Gourse, Leslie. 1996. *Madame Jazz: Contemporary Women Instrumentalists.* New York: Oxford University Press.

Grame, Theodore C. 1976. *America's Ethnic Music.* Tarpon Springs, FL: Cultural Maintenance Associates.

Gray, John, comp. 1988. *Blacks in Classical Music: A Bibliographical Guide to Composers, Performers, and Ensembles.* Westport, CT: Greenwood Press.

Graziano, John. 1990. "Black Musical Theater and the Harlem Renaissance Movement." In *Black Music in the Harlem Renaissance*, ed. Samuel A. Floyd, Jr., 87–110. Westport, CT: Garland Press.

Green, Archie. 1972. *Only a Miner: Studies in Recorded Coal-Mining Songs.* Urbana: University of Illinois Press.

Green, Mildred Denby. 1983. *Black Women Composers: A Genesis.* Boston: Twayne.

Greene, Victor R. 1992. *A Passion for Polka.* Berkeley: University of California Press.

Guillory, Monique and Richard C. Green, eds. 1998. *Soul.* New York: New York University Press.

Guralnick, Peter. 1986. *Sweet Soul Music.* New York: Harper and Row.

Hadley, Peter. 1993. "New Music for Gamelan by North American Composers." Master's thesis, Wesleyan University. Distributed by the American Gamelan Institute.

Hakala, Joyce. 1997. *Memento of Finland: A Musical Legacy.* St. Paul, MN: Pikebone Music.

Hamm, Charles. 1979. *Yesterdays: Popular Song in America.* New York: Norton.

Hamm, Charles. 1983. *Music in the New World.* New York: Norton.

Handy, D. Antoinette. 1981. *Black Women in American Bands and Orchestras.* Metuchen, NJ: Scarecrow.

Handy, D. Antoinette. 1995. *Black Conductors.* Lanham, MD: Scarecrow Press.

Hannerz, Ulf. 1969. *Soulside: Inquiries into Ghetto Culture and Community.* New York: Columbia University Press.

Haralambos, Michael. 1985 [1974]. *Soul Music: The Birth of a Sound in Black America.* New York: Da Capo.

Haralambos, Michael. 1975. *Right On: From Blues to Soul in Black America.* New York: Da Capo.

Hare, Maude Cuney. 1936. *Negro Musicians and Their Music.* Washington, DC: Associated Publishers.

Harrison, Lou. 1988. *Music for Gamelan with Western Instruments.* Scores and parts. Lebanon, NH: American Gamelan Institute.

Harvey, Steven. 1983. "Behind the Groove: New York City's Disco Underground." *Collusion* 9:26–33.

Hatch, James V. 1970. *Black Image on the American Stage: A Bibliography of Plays and Musicals, 1770–1970.* New York: DBS Publications.

Hay, Samuel A. 1994. *African American Theater: A Historical and Critical Analysis.* Cambridge: Cambridge University Press.

Hebdige, Dick. 1987. *Cut'n' Mix: Culture, Identity and Caribbean Music.* New York: Methuen.

Hentoff, Nat. 1968. Liner notes for John Coltrane, *Om.* Impulse A-9140. LP disk.

Hill, Lauryn. 1998. *The Miseducation of Lauryn Hill.* Ruffhouse/Columbia CK 69035. Compact disc.

Hill, Trent. 1992. "The Enemy Within: Censorship in Rock Music in the 1950s." In *Present Tense: Rock & Roll and Culture,* ed. Anthony DeCurtis. Durham, NC: Duke University Press.

Hinson, Glenn. 1978. Notes to *Eight-Hand Sets and Holy Steps: Traditional Black Music of North Carolina.* North Carolina Department of Cultural Resources Crossroad C-101. Cassette.

Hiroshima. 1979. *Hiroshima.* Arista Records AB 4252. LP disk.

Hiroshima. 1979/1980 . *Ongaku.* Arista Records ARCD 8437. Compact disc.

Hiroshima. 1980. *Odori.* Arista Records AL 9541. LP.

Hitchcock, H. Wiley and Kyle Gann. 2000. *Music in the United States: A Historical Introduction.* 4th ed. Englewood Cliffs, NJ: Prentice-Hall.

Hohmann, Rupert K. 1959. "The Church Music of the Old Order Amish of the United States." Ph.D. dissertation, Northwestern University.

Holland, Brian and Eddie Holland. 1983. Personal interview.

Hoogland, Eric, ed. 1987. *Crossing the Waters: Arabic-Speaking Immigrants to the United States Before 1940.* Washington, DC: Smithsonian Institution Press.

Horiuchi, Glenn. 1989a. *Issei Spirit.* AsianImprov Records. LP disk.

Horiuchi, Glenn. 1989b. *Manzanar Voices.* AsianImprov Records AIR 006. LP disk.

Horn, David. 1977. *The Literature of American Music in Books and Folk Music Collections.* Metuchen, NJ: Scarecrow Press.

Horowitz, Joseph. 1987. *Understanding Toscanini.* New York: Knopf.

Horsman, Reginald. 1981. *Race and Manifest Destiny: The Origins of American Racial Anglo-Saxonism.* Cambridge: Harvard University Press.

Horstman, Dorothy. 1975. *Sing Your Heart Out, Country Boy.* Rev. ed. Nashville, TN: Country Music Foundation Press.

Hosokawa, Bill. 1969. *Nisei: The Quiet Americans.* New York: William Morrow.

Howard, James Henri and Victoria Lindsay Levine. 1990. *Choctaw Music and Dance.* Foreword by Bruno Nettl. Norman: University of Oklahoma Press.

Howard, James Henri. 1968. The Southeastern Ceremonial Complex and Its Interpretation. Columbia: Missouri Archaeological Society.

Howard, John Tasker. 1941. *Our Contemporary Composers: American Music in the Twentieth Century.* New York: Thomas Y. Crowell.

Hudson, James "Pookie." 1985. Telephone interview. 28 March.

Hughes, Langston and Milton Meltzer. 1967. *Black Magic: A Pictorial History of the Negro in American Entertainment.* Englewood Cliffs, NJ: Prentice-Hall.

Hughes, Walter. 1994. "In the Empire of the Beat: Discipline and Disco." In *Microphone Fiends: Youth Music and Youth Culture,* ed. Andrew Ross and Tricia Rose, 147-157. New York: Routledge.

Hurston, Zora Neale. 1983. *The Sanctified Church.* Berkeley, CA: Turtle Island.

Huyssen, Andreas. 1986. "Mass Culture as Woman: Modernism's Other." In *Studies in Entertainment,* ed. Tania Modleski, 188-207. Bloomington: Indiana University Press.

Ichihashi, Yamato. 1932. *Japanese in the United States: A Critical Study of the Problems and the Japanese Immigrants and Their Children.* Stanford, CA: Stanford University Press.

Indian Chipmunks, vol. 2-. 1983. Indian Sounds IS 3031. Cassette.

Isaacs, Tony. 1969. Kiowa 49: *War Expedition Songs.* Indian House IH 2505.

Izu, Mark. 1992. *Circle of Fire.* AsianImprov Records AIR 0009. Compact disc.

Jabbour, Alan. 1996. "The American Folklife Center: A Twenty-Year Retrospective (Part 2)." *Folklife Center News* 18(3, 4):3-23.

Jackson, George Pullen. 1965 [1933]. *White Spirituals in the Southern Uplands.* New York: Dover.

Jackson, John A. 1991. *Big Beat: Alan Freed and the Early Years of Rock & Roll.* New York: Schirmer Books.

Jairazbhoy, Nazir A. and Sue Carole DeVale, eds. 1985. *Selected Reports in Ethnomusicology: Vol. VI: Asian Music in North America.* Los Angeles: UCLA Department of Music.

James, Willis Laurence. 1970. *Afro-American Music: A Demonstration Recording by Dr. Willis James.* ASCH Records AA702. LP disk.

James, Willis Laurence. 1973 [1955]. "The Romance of the Negro Folk Cry in America." In *Mother Wit from the Laughing Barrel,* ed. Alan Dundes, 430–444. Englewood Cliffs, NJ: Prentice-Hall.

Jhally, Sut. 1987. *The Codes of Advertising.* New York: St. Martin's Press.

Joe, Radcliffe A. 1980. *This Business of Disco.* New York: Billboard Books.

Johnson, James Weldon. 1968 [1930]. *Black Manhattan.* New York: Arno Press.

Jones, Jafran. 1991. "Women in Non-Western Music." In *Women and Music: A History,* ed. Karin Pendle, 314–330. Bloomington: Indiana University Press.

Jones, LeRoi (Amiri Baraka). 1963. *Blues People: Negro Music in White America.* New York: Morrow.

Jones, Maldwyn A. 1960. *American Immigration.* Chicago: University of Chicago Press.

Junker, Jay. 1998. "Steel Guitars." In *Garland Encyclopedia of World Music,* Vol. 9: *Australia and the Pacific Islands,* 389–390. New York: Garland.

Katkin, Wendy F., Ned Landsman, and Andrea Tyree, eds. 1998. *Beyond Pluralism: The Conception of Groups and Group Identities in America.* Urbana: University of Illinois Press.

Katz, Michael, ed. 1993. *The Underclass: Views from History.* Princeton, NJ: Princeton University Press.

Keeling, Richard, ed. 1989. *Women in North American Indian Music: Six Essays.* Special Series, no. 6. Bloomington, IN: The Society for Ethnomusicology.

Kef Time: Exciting Sounds of the Middle East. 1994 [1986]. Produced by Harold G. Hagopian. With 6-page booklet of notes and song lyrics. Traditional Crossroads CD 4269. Compact disc.

Keil, Charles and Steven Feld, eds. 1994. *Music Grooves.* Chicago: University of Chicago Press.

Keil, Charles, Angeliki Keil, and Dick Blau. 1992. *Polka Happiness.* Philadelphia: Temple University Press.

Keil, Charles. 1994. "On Civilization, Cultural Studies, and Copyright." In *Music Grooves,* ed. Charles Keil and Steven Feld, 227–231. Chicago: University of Chicago Press.

Kenney, William H. 1993. *Chicago Jazz: A Cultural History, 1904–1930.* New York: Oxford University Press.

Kernfeld, Barry. 1988. *The New Grove Dictionary of Jazz.* London: Macmillan.

Key Kool and Rhettmatic. 1995. *Kozmonautz.* Up Above Records AC-1001. Compact disc.

Keyes, Cheryl L. 1993. "We're More Than a Novelty, Boys: Strategies of Female Rappers in the Rap Music Tradition." In *Feminist Messages: Coding in Women's Folk Culture,* ed. Joan N. Radner, 203–220. Urbana: University of Illinois Press.

Keyes, Cheryl. 1991. "Rappin to the Beat: Rap Music as Street Culture Among African Americans." Ph.D. dissertation, Indiana University.

Keyes, Cheryl. 1993. "We're More than a Novelty, Boys: Strategies of Female Rappers in the Rap Music Tradition." In *Feminist Messages: Coding in Women's Folk Culture,* ed. Joan Newlon Radner, 203–220. Chicago: University of Illinois Press.

Kimball, Robert and William Bolcom. 1973. *Reminiscing with Sissle and Blake.* New York: Viking Press.

Kingman, Daniel. 1998. *American Music: A Panorama.* Concise 3rd ed. New York: Schirmer Books.

Kingsbury, Paul, ed. 1998. *The Encyclopedia of Country Music.* New York: Oxford University Press.

Kingsbury, Paul, ed. 1996. *The Country Reader.* Nashville, TN: Vanderbilt University Press and Country Music Foundation Press.

Kitwana, Bakari. 1994. *The Rap on Gangsta Rap.* Chicago: Third World Press.

Knott, Sarah Gertrude. 1953. "The Folk Festival Movement in America." *Southern Folklore Quarterly* 17 (June):143-155.

Kochman, Thomas, ed. 1972. *Rappin' and Stylin' Out: Communication in Urban Black America.* Urbana: University of Illinois Press.

Kofsky, Frank. 1970. *Black Nationalism and the Revolution in Music.* New York: Pathfinder.

Korb, Ken. 1993. *Japanese Mysteries.* Toronto: Oasis Productions.

Korb, Ken. 1994. *Flute Traveller.* Toronto: Oasis Productions. Compact disc.

Korb, Ken. 1995. *Behind the Mask.* Toronto: Oasis Productions. Compact disc.

Koskoff, Ellen, ed. 1989. *Women and Music in Cross-Cultural Perspective.* Urbana: University of Illinois Press.

Koskoff, Ellen. 1980. *The Musical Self.* Pittsburgh: University of Pittsburgh, External Studies Program.

Kostelanetz, Richard, ed. 1990 [1970]. *John Cage: An Anthology.* New York: Da Capo.

Kurath, Gertrude Prokosch. 1968. Dance and Song Rituals of Six Nations Reserve, Ontario. National Museum of Canada Bulletin 220.

Kurath, Gertrude Prokosch.1977. *Iroquois Music and Dance: Ceremonial Arts of Two Seneca Longhouses.* St. Clair Shores, MI: Scholarly Press.

LaFrance, Ron. 1992. "Inside the Longhouse: Dances of the Haudenosaunee." In *Native American Dance: Ceremonies and Social Traditions,* ed. Charlotte Heth, 19-32. Washington, DC: Smithsonian Institution.

Laing, Dave. 1985. *One Chord Wonders: Power and Meaning in Punk Rock.* Philadelphia: Open University Press.

Landry, Bart. 1987. *The New Black Middle Class.* Berkeley: University of California Press.

Laws, George Malcolm. 1957. *American Balladry from British Broadsides: A Guide for Students and Collectors of Traditional Song.* Philadelphia: American Folklore Society.

Lears, Jackson. 1994. *Fables of Abundance.* New York: Basic Books.

Lebrecht, Norman. 1997. *Who Killed Classical Music? Maestros, Managers, and Corporate Politics.* Secaucus, NJ: Birch Lane Press.

Levine, Lawrence W. 1977. *Black Culture and Black Consciousness: Afro-American Folk Thought from Slavery to Freedom.* New York: Oxford University Press.

Levine, Lawrence. 1988. *Highbrow/Lowbrow: The Emergence of Cultural Hierarchy in America.* Cambridge, MA: Harvard University Press.

Lewis, Lisa A. 1990. *Gender Politics and MTV.* Philadelphia: Temple University Press.

Locke, Ralph P. 1993. "Music Lovers, Patrons, and the 'Sacralization' of Culture in America." *Nineteenth Century Music* 17(2):149-173.

Lockwood, Normand. 1996. Letter to author, 29 June.

Lomax, Alan. 1956 [1942]. *Afro-American Spirituals, Work Songs and Ballads,* record notes. Library of Congress, Division of Music, Recording Laboratory AAFS L3. LP disk.

Lomax, Alan. 1960. *The Folk Songs of North America in the English Language.* New York: Doubleday.

Lomax, Alan. 1968. *Folk Song Style and Culture.* Washington, DC: American Association for the Advancement of Science.

Lomax, John and Alan Lomax. 1934. *American Ballads and Folk Songs.* New York: Macmillan.

Lomax, John. 1910. *Cowboy Songs and Other Frontier Ballads.* New York: Sturgis and Walton.

Lomax, John. 1947. *Adventures of a Ballad Hunter.* New York: Macmillan.

Loomis, Ormond, ed. 1983. *Cultural Conservation: The Preservation of Cultural Heritage in the United States.* Washington, DC: Library of Congress.

Lornell, Christopher "Kip" 1978. *Non-Blues Secular Black Music,* record notes. BRI Records BRI 001. LP disk.

Lornell, Kip and Anne K. Rasmussen, eds. 1997. *Musics of Multicultural America: A Study of Twelve Musical Communities.* New York: Schirmer Books.

Lou Harrison: Gamelan Music. 1992. Gamelan Si Betty. Directed by Trish Neilsen and Jody Diamond. Instruments by Lou Harrison and William Colvig. Compositions by Lou Harrison. Music Masters 01612-67091-2. Compact disc.

Loza, Steven J. 1993. *Barrio Rhythm: Mexican American Music in Los Angeles.* Urbana: University of Illinois Press.

Lumer, Robert. 1991. "Peter Seeger and the Attempt to Revive the Folk Music Process." *Popular Music and Society* 15(1):45–58.

Lydon, Michael. 1998. *Ray Charles: Man and Music.* New York: Riverhead Books.

Malm, Krister and Roger Wallace. 1992. *Media Policy and Music Activity.* London: Routledge.

Malone, Bill C. 1990. "Classic Country Music." Notes to *Classic Country Music: A Smithsonian Collection.*

Malone, Bill C. 1985. *Country Music U.S.A.*, rev ed. Austin: University of Texas Press.

Mankin, Lawrence David. 1976. "The National Government and the Arts: From the Great Depression to 1973." Ph.D. dissertation, University of Illinois.

Manning, Peter. 1993. *Electronic and Computer Music.* Oxford: Clarendon Press.

Manuel, Peter L. 1988. *Popular Musics of the Non-Western World: An Introductory Survey.* New York: Oxford University Press.

Manuel, Peter, ed. 1991. *Essays on Cuban Music: North American and Cuban Perspectives.* Lanham, MD: University Press of America.

Manuel, Peter. 1993. *Cassette Culture: Popular Music and Technology in North India.* Chicago: University of Chicago Press.

Marable, Manning. 1991. *Race, Reform, and Rebellion.* Rev. 2nd ed. Jackson: University Press of Mississippi.

March, Richard. 1998. *Deep Polka: Dance Music from the Midwest.* Washington, DC: Smithsonian Folkways SF CD 40088. Compact disc and 28-page booklet.

Markoff, Irene. 1991. "The Ideology of Musical Practice and the Professional Turkish Folk Musician: Tempering the Creative Impulse." *Asian Music* 22(1): 129-246.

Marks, J. 1968. *Rock and Other Four Letter Words.* New York: Bantam Books.

Marrocco, W. Thomas and Harold Gleason. 1964. *Music in America.* New York: Norton.

Masaokam, Miya. 1993. *Compositions/Improvisations.* AsianImprov Records AIR 00014. Compact disc.

Mason, John. 1992. *Orin Orisa: Songs for Selected Heads.* New York: Yoruba Theological Archministry.

Mauleón, Rebeca. 1993. *Salsa: Guidebook for Piano and Ensemble.* Petaluma, CA: Sher Music Co.

Maultsby, Portia K. 1979. "Contemporary Pop: A Healthy Diversity Evolves from Creative Freedom." *Billboard,* June 9, BM10, BM22, BM28 [Black Music Section].

Maultsby, Portia K. 1982 and 1983. Unpublished field study on the "Musical Preferences of African American College Students."

Maultsby, Portia K. 1983. "Soul Music: Its Sociological and Political Significance in American Popular Culture." *Journal of Popular Culture* 17(2):51-60.

Maultsby, Portia K. 1986. *Rhythm and Blues (1945-1955): A Survey of Styles.* In *Black American Popular Music,* ed. Bernice Johnson Reagon. Washington, DC: Program in Black American Culture, Museum of American History, Smithsonian Institution.

Maultsby, Portia K. 1992. "The Influence of Gospel Music on the Secular Music Industry." In *We'll Understand It Better By and By: African American Pioneering Gospel Composers,* ed. Bernice Johnson Reagon, 19-33. Washington, DC: Smithsonian Institution Press.

Maultsby, Portia K. 1984 and 1985. Informal discussions with black faculty. Ford Foundation Postdoctoral Minority Fellows conference. Washington, DC.

McAllester, David P. 1964. *Peyote Music.* New York: Johnson Reprint Corporation.

McAllester, David P. 1973. *Enemy Way Music: A Study of Social and Esthetic Values as Seen in Navaho Music.* Milwood, NY: Kraus Reprint Co.

McCallum, Brenda. 1988. "Songs of Work and Songs of Worship: Sanctifying Black Unionism in the Southern City of Steel." *New York Folklore* 14(12):9-33.

McClary, Susan. 1991. *Feminine Endings: Music, Gender, Sexuality.* Minneapolis: University of Minnesota Press.

McLuhan, Marshall. 1964. *Understanding Media: The Extensions of Man.* New York: McGraw-Hill.

Meadows, Eddie S. 1981. *Jazz Reference and Research Materials: A Bibliography.* New York: Garland Publishers.

Meintjes, Louise. 1990. "Paul Simon's *Graceland,* South Africa, and the Mediation of Musical Meaning." *Ethnomusicology* 34(1):37-73.

Melton, J. Gordon. 1989. *The Encyclopedia of American Religions.* 3rd ed. Detroit, MI : Gale Research.

Merriam, Alan P. 1967. *Ethnomusicology of the Flathead Indians.* Chicago: Aldine.

Middleton, Richard. 1990. *Studying Popular Music.* Milton Keynes, England: Open University Press.

Miezitis, Vita. 1980. *Night Dancin'.* New York: Ballantine.

Miles, Elizabeth. 1997. *Tune Your Brain: Using Music to Manage Your Mind, Body, and Mood.* New York: Berkley Books.

Miller, Rebecca. 1996. "Irish Traditional and Popular Music in New York City: Identity and Social Change, 1930-1975." In *The New York Irish,* ed. Ronald H. Bayor and Timothy J. Meagher, 481-507. Baltimore, MD: Johns Hopkins University Press.

Miller, Terry. 1986. *Folk Music in America: A Reference Guide.* New York: Garland.

Mina, Niloofar. n.d. *"Musiqi-ye Pope Irani* and Iranian Immigrants in New York: Cultural Orientation and Identity." Ph.D. dissertation, Columbia University. Forthcoming.

Mingus, Charles. 1971. *Beneath the Underdog.* New York: Knopf.

Miyamoto, Nobuko. 1997. *Nobuko. To All Relations.* Bindu Music BIN 9602-2. Compact disc.

Mockus, Martha. 1999. "Sounding Out: Lesbian Feminism and the Music of Pauline Oliveros." Ph.D. dissertation, University of Minnesota.

Monson, Ingrid. 1995. "The Problem with White Hipness: Race, Gender, and Cultural Conceptions in Jazz Historical Discourse." *Journal of the American Musicological Society* 48(3):396–422.

Monson, Ingrid. n.d. *Freedom Sounds: Jazz, Civil Rights, and Africa, 1950-1967.* New York: Oxford University Press. Forthcoming.

Moon, Tom. 1999. Radio interview. On Talk of the Nation: "The Death of Musician Curtis Mayfield and the Impact of His Music on Today's Musicians." National Public Radio. 28 December.

Mooney, James. 1973 [1896]. *The Ghost-Dance Religion and Wounded Knee.* Reprint of the Fourteenth Annual Report (Part 2) of the Bureau of Ethnology to the Smithsonian Institution, 1892-93: The Ghost-Dance Religion and the Sioux Outbreak of 1890.

Moreau de Saint-Méry, Médéric. 1797. *Déscription Topographique, Physique, Civile, Politique et Historique de . . . l'Isle Saint-Dominique . . .* Philadelphia: Chez l'Auteur.

Morgan, Lewis Henry. 1962 [1851]. *League of the Ho-dé-no-sau-nee or Iroquois.* Secaucus, NJ: Citadel Press.

Morgan, Robert P. 1992. *Twentieth-Century Music.* New York: Norton.

Morris, Robert. 1997. "Milton Babbitt's Electronic Music: The Medium and the Message." *Perspectives of New Music* 35(2):85-99.

Morton, David. 1970. "Thai Traditional Music: Hot-House Plant or Sturdy Stock." *Journal of the Siam Society* 58(2):1-44.

Murasaki Ensemble. 1994. *Niji.* A Murasaki Production. TME 8994. Compact disc.

Murphy, John. 1991. "The Charanga in New York and the Persistence of the Típico Style." In *Essays on Cuban Music: North American and Cuban Perspectives,* ed. Peter Manuel, 117-135. Lanham, MD: University Press of America.

[n.a.]. 1968. "Lady Soul Singing It Like It Is" *Time,* 28 June, 62-66.

Naficy, Hamid. 1996. "Identity Politics and Iranian Exile Music Videos." In *Middle Eastern Diaspora Communities in America,* ed. Mehdi Bozorgmehr and Alison Feldman, 105-123. New York: The Hagop Kevorkian Center for Near Eastern Studies of New York University.

Naficy, Hamid. 1993. *The Making of Exile Cultures: Iranian Television in Los Angeles.* Minneapolis: University of Minnesota Press.

National Standards for Arts Education: What Every Young American Should Know and Be Able to Do in the Arts. 1994. Reston, VA: Music Educators National Conference.

Needleman, Jacob. 1970. *The New Religions.* Garden City, NY: Doubleday.

"Negro Folk Songs." 1976 [1895]. *The Black Perspective in Music* 4(2):145-151.

Negus, Keith. 1992. *Producing Pop: Culture and Conflict in the Pop Music Industry.* London: Edward Arnold.

Nettl, Bruno. 1949; 2nd ed. 1960. *An Introduction to Folk Music in the United States.* 3d ed., rev. and expanded by Helen Myers (1972), under the title *Folk Music in the United States: An Introduction.* Detroit, MI: Wayne State University Press.

Nettl, Bruno. 1954. North American Indian Musical Styles. Memoirs of the American Folklore Society, vol. 45. Philadelphia: American Folklore Society.

Nettl, Bruno. 1957a. "The Hymns of the Amish: An Example of Marginal Survival." *Journal of American Folklore* 70:323-328.

Nettl, Bruno. 1973. *Folk and Traditional Music of Western Continents.* 2nd ed. Englewood Cliffs, NJ: Prentice-Hall.

Nettl, Bruno. 1981. Shawnee!: The Ceremonialism of a Native Indian Tribe and Its Cultural Background. Athens: Ohio University Press.

Nettl, Bruno. 1983. *The Study of Ethnomusicology: Twenty-Nine Issues and Concepts.* Urbana: University of Illinois Press.

Nettl, Bruno. 1989. *Blackfoot Musical Thought: Comparative Perspectives.* Kent, OH: Kent State University Press.

Nettl, Bruno. 1990a. *War Dance: Plains Indian Musical Performance.* Tucson: University of Arizona Press.

Nettl, Bruno. 1990b. *Voices from the Spirit World: Lakota Ghost Dance Songs.* Kendall Park, NJ: Lakota Books.

Nettl, Bruno. 1998. *Lakota Cosmos: Religion and the Reinvention of Culture.* Kendall Park, NJ: Lakota Books.

Neuls-Bates, Carol. 1996 [1982]. *Women in Music: An Anthology of Source Readings from the Middle Ages to the Present.* 2nd ed. Boston: Northeastern University Press.

Nguyen, Phong, with Adelaida Reyes Schramm and Patricia Shehan Campbell. 1995. *Searching for a Niche: Vietnamese Music at Home in America.* Kent, OH: Viet Music Publications.

Nketia, J. H. Kwabene. 1974. *The Music of Africa.* New York: Norton.

Norfleet, Dawn. 1997. "'Hip-hop Culture' in New York City: The Role of Verbal Musical Performance in Defining a Community." Ph.D. dissertation, Columbia University.

Noss, Luther. 1989. *Paul Hindemith in the United States.* Urbana: University of Illinois Press.

Nyman, Michael. 1999 [1974]. *Experimental Music: Cage and Beyond.* 2nd ed. New York: Schirmer Books.

O'Brien, Lucy. 1996. *She Bop: The Definitive History of Women in Rock, Pop and Soul.* New York: Penguin.

O'Dair, Barbara, ed. 1997. *Trouble Girls: The Rolling Stone Book of Women in Rock.* New York: Random House.

Oka, Seizo. 1987. Interview by author. San Francisco, California, 21 July.

Oliver, Paul. 1998. *The Story of the Blues.* New Ed. Boston: Northeastern University Press.

Oliveros, Pauline. 1984. *Software for People.* Baltimore, MD: Smith Publications.

Olmstead, Frederick Law. 1976 [1856]. "Negro Jodling: The Carolina Yell." *The Black Perspective in Music* 4(2):140-141.

Otis, Johnny. 1993. *Upside Your Head! Rhythm and Blues on Central Avenue.* Hanover, NH: University Press of New England.

Otis, Johnny. 1984. Personal interview. 13 September.

Paredes, Américo. 1993. "The Folklore Groups of Mexican Origin in the United States." In *Folklore and Culture on the Texas-Mexican Border,* ed. Richard Bauman, 3-18. Austin: University of Texas, Center for Mexican American Studies.

Pareles, Jon. 1992. "On Rap, Symbolism and Fear." *The New York Times,* 2 February. 1-2, 23.

Parker, Charlie. 1945. *The Savoy Recordings* (Master Takes). Vol 1. Savoy Records ZDS 4402. Compact disc.

Parker, Deanie. 1984. Personal interview. 6 September.

Parks, H. B. 1928. "Follow the Drinking Gourd." In *Texas Folk-Lore Society Publications 7,* ed. J. Frank Dobie, Austin: Texas Folk-Lore Society.

Paton, Christopher Ann. 1981. "The Evolution of the Polka from 1830 to 1980 as a Symbol of Ethnic Unity and Diversity." Master's thesis, Wayne State University.

Patterson, Beverly Bush. 1995. *The Sound of the Dove: Singing in Appalachian Primitive Baptist Churches.* Urbana: University of Illinois Press.

Pavlow, Al. 1983. *The R & B Book: A Disc-History of Rhythm and Blues.* Providence, RI: Music House Publishing.

Peabody, Charles. 1976 [1903]. "Notes on Negro Music." *The Black Perspective in Music* 4(2):133-137.

Pegley, Karen. 1995. "'Places, Everyone': Gender and the Non-Neutrality of Music Technology." *The Recorder* 37(2):55-59.

Peña, Manuel. 1980. "Ritual Structure in a Chicano Dance." *Latin American Music Review* 1(1):47-73.

Peña, Manuel. 1985. *The Texas-Mexican Conjunto: History of a Working Class Music.* Austin: University of Texas Press.

Peña, Manuel. 1989. "Notes Toward an Interpretive History of California-Mexican Music." In *From the Inside Out: Perspectives on Mexican and Mexican American Folk Art,* ed. Karana Hattersly-Drayton, Joyce M. Bishop, and Tomás Ybarra-Frausto, 64-75. San Francisco: The Mexican Museum.

Peretti, Burton. 1992. *The Creation of Jazz: Music, Race, and Culture in Urban America.* Urbana: University of Illinois Press.

Perkins, William Eric, ed. 1996. *Droppin' Science: Critical Essays on Rap Music and Hip Hop Culture.* Philadelphia: Temple University Press.

Perlman, Marc. 1983. "Some Reflections on New American Gamelan Music." *Ear Magazine,* 7(4):4-5.

Peterson, Bernard L., Jr. 1993. *A Century of Musicals in Black and White.* Westport, CT: Garland Press.

Peterson, Richard A. 1990. "Audience and Industry Origins of the Crisis in Classical Music Programming: Toward World Music." In *The Future of the Arts: Public Policy and Arts Research,* ed. David Pankratz and Valerie B. Morris, 210-213. New York: Praeger.

Peterson, Richard A. 1992. "Class Unconsciousness in Country Music." In *You Wrote My Life: Lyrical Themes in Country Music,* ed. Melton A. McLaurin and Richard A.

Peterson, Richard, 1997. *Creating Country Music: Fabricating Authenticity.* Chicago: University of Chicago Press.

Pirkova-Jakobson, Svatava. 1956. "Harvest Festivals Among Czechs and Slovaks in America. In *Slavic Folklore: A Symposium,* 68-82. Philadelphia: American Folklore Society.

Pogue, David and Scott Speck. 1997. *Classical Music for Dummies.* Foster City, CA: IDG Books.

Porter, James, ed. 1978a. *Selected Reports in Ethnomusicology* 3(1). Special Issue. Los Angeles: UCLA Program in Ethnomusicology.

Porter, Lewis and Michael Ullman. 1993. *Jazz: From Its Origins to the Present.* Englewood Cliffs, NJ: Prentice-Hall.

Porterfield, Nolan, 1979. *Jimmie Rodgers: The Life and Times of America's Blue Yodeller.* Urbana and London: The University of Illinois Press.

Poschardt, Ulf. 1995. *DJ Culture.* Hamburg, Germany: Rogner & Bernard.

Potter, Keith. 2000. *Four Musical Minimalists: La Monte Young, Terry Riley, Steve Reich, Philip Glass.* New York and Cambridge: Cambridge University Press.

Potter, Russell. 1995. *Spectacular Vernaculars: Hip-Hop and the Politics of Postmodernism.* The State University of New York Series in Postmodern Culture. Albany: State University of New York Press.

Powers, William K. 1977. *Oglala Religion.* Lincoln: University of Nebraska Press.

Preston, Katherine. 1993. *Opera on the Road: Traveling Opera Troupes in the United States, 1825-60.* Urbana: University of Illinois Press.

Priestley, Brian. 1987. *John Coltrane.* Jazz Masters Series. London: Apollo Press.

Pritchett, James. 1993. *The Music of John Cage.* New York and Cambridge: Cambridge University Press.

Puccini for Dummies. 1997. EMI 7243 5 66404 0 5. Compact disc.

Racy, Ali Jihad and Simon Shaheen. 1991 [1979]. *Taqasim: The Art of Improvisation in Arab Music.* Ali Jihad Racy, *buzuq,* and Simon Shaheen,'*ud.* With documentary notes by Philip Schuyler. Lyrichord LYRCD 7374.

Racy, Ali Jihad.1992. "An Evening in the Orient: The Middle Eastern Nightclub in America." *Asian Music* 23(2):63-88.

Racy, Ali Jihad. 1997a. *Mystical Legacies: Ali Jihad Racy Performs Music of the Middle East.* With Ali Jihad Racy (*nay, buzuq,'ud,* and bowed *tanbur*) and Souhail Kaspar (percussion). Lyrichord LYRCD 7437.

Racy, Ali Jihad.1997b. "The Music of Arab Detroit: A Musical Mecca in the Midwest." In *Musics of Multicultural America: A Study of Twelve Musical Communities,* ed. Kip Lornell and Anne K. Rasmussen, 73-100. New York: Schirmer Books.

Radano, Ronald. 2000. "Hot Fantasies: American Modernism and the Idea of Black Rhythm." In *Music and the Racial Imagination,* ed. Ronald Radano and Philip V. Bohlman, 459-480. Chicago Studies in Ethnomusicology. Chicago: University of Chicago Press.

Rahkonen, Carl J. 1993. "Pan-Ethnic Polkas in Pennsylvania." Paper presented at the 32nd World Conference of the International Council for Traditional Music, Berlin, June 18.

Ramsey, Frederic. 1960. Notes to *Been Here and Gone.* Folkways Records FA 2659. LP disk.

Rasmussen, Anne K. 1991. "Individuality and Social Change in the Music of Arab Americans." Ph.D. dissertation, University of California, Los Angeles.

Rasmussen, Anne K., producer. *The Music of Arab Americans: A Retrospective Collection.* With 20-page booklet of notes, photographs, and song lyrics. Rounder CD 1122. Compact disc.

Reich, Steve. 1974. *Writings about Music.* Halifax: Press of Nova Scotia College of Art and Design.

Revill, David. 1992. *The Roaring Silence: John Cage: A Life.* New York: Arcade Publishing.

Reyes Schramm, Adelaida. 1979. "'Ethnic Music,' the Urban Area, and Ethnomusicology." *Sociologus* 29(1):1–21.

Reyes, Adelaida. 1999. *Songs of the Caged, Songs of the Free: Music and the Vietnamese Refugee Experience.* Philadelphia: Temple University Press.

Reyes, Luis I. 1995. *Made in Paradise: Hollywood's Films of Hawai'i and the South Seas.* Honolulu: Mutual Publishing.

Reyna, José. 1976. Tejano Music as an Expression of Cultural Nationalism. *Revista Chicano-Riqueña.* 4(3):37–41.

Reyna, José. 1982. "Notes on Tejano Music." *Aztlán: International Journal of Chicano Studies Research. Thematic Issue: Mexican Folklore and Folk Art in the United States,* 13:1 and 2 (Spring and Fall). Chicano Studies Research Center, University of California, Los Angeles.

Rhodes, Willard. n.d. Delaware, Cherokee, Choctaw, Creek. Library of Congress AFS L37. LP disk.

Rice, Timothy, Christopher Goertzen, and James Porter, eds. 2000. *The Garland Encyclopedia of World Music.* Vol. 8, *Europe.* New York: Garland Publishers.

Ricks, George Robinson. 1977. *Some Aspects of the Religious Music of the United States Negro.* New York: Arno Press.

Riemer, Mary Frances. 1980. Seneca Social Dance Music. Smithsonian Folkways Recordings FE 4072. Compact disc.

Riis, Thomas L. 1989. *Just Before Jazz: Black Musical Theater in New York, 1890 to 1915.* Washington, DC: Smithsonian Institution Press.

Riis, Thomas L. ed. 1996. *The Music and Scripts of In Dahomey.* Vol. 5 of *Music of the United States of America.* Madison, WI: A-R Editions.

Roberts, Chris. 1992. *Pow-wow Country.* Helena, MT: American and World Geographic Publishing.

Roberts, John Storm. 1972. *Black Music of Two Worlds.* New York: Praeger.

Roberts, John Storm. 1999 [1979]. *The Latin Tinge: The Impact of Latin American Music on the United States.* 2nd ed. New York: Oxford University Press.

Roberts, Robin. 1996. *Ladies First: Women in Music Videos.* Jackson: University of Mississippi Press.

Robinson, Linda. 1998. "Hispanics Don't Exist." *U.S. News & World Report.* 11 May, 26–32.

Rochberg, George. 1984. *The Aesthetics of Survival: A Composer's View of Twentieth-Century Music.* Ann Arbor: University of Michigan Press.

Rodman, Ronald. 1997. "And Now an Ideology from Our Sponsor: Musical Style and Semiosis in American Television Commercials." *College Music Symposium* 37:21–48.

Romantic Music for Dummies. 1997. EMI 7243 5 66561 0 9. Compact disc.

Root, Deane L. 1981. *American Popular Stage Music: 1860–1880.* Ann Arbor, MI: UMI Research Press.

Rose, Tricia. 1994. *Black Noise: Rap Music and Black Culture in Contemporary America.* Hanover, NH: Wesleyan University Press.

Rosenberg, Neil V. 1993. *Transforming Traditions: Folk Music Revivals Examined.* Urbana: University of Illinois Press.

Ross, Andrew and Tricia Rose, eds. 1994. *Microphone Fiends: Youth Music and Youth Culture.* New York: Routledge.

Rudhyar, Dane. 1961 [1933]. "Oriental Influence in American Music." In *American Composers on American Music: A Symposium,* ed. Henry Cowell, 184–185. New York: Frederick Ungar Publishing Co.

Russell, Albert "Diz." 1983. Personal interview. 27 September.

Ruymar, Lorene. 1996. *The Hawaiian Steel Guitar and Its Great Hawaiian Musicians.* Anaheim Hills, CA: Centerstream Publishing.

Ryan, John. 1985. *The Production of Culture in the Music Music Industry: The ASCAP-BMI Controversy.* Lanham, MD: University Press of America.

Sahl, Michael. 1986. "Thoughts on the State of Classical Music in the United States." *Musical Quarterly* 72(4):523-527.

Salazar, Max. 1991a. "Machito, Mario and Graciela: Destined for Greatness." *Latin Beat* 1(6):25-29.

Salazar, Max. 1991b. "Salsa Origins." *Latin Beat* 1(10):9-11.

Salazar, Max. 1992. "Who Invented the Mambo?" *Latin Beat* 2(9):9-12.

Sampson, Henry. 1980. *Blacks in Blackface: A Sourcebook on Early Black Musical Shows.* Metuchen, NJ: Scarecrow Press.

Sanjek, David and Russell Sanjek. 1996. *Pennies from Heaven: The American Popular Music Business in the Twentieth Century.* New York: DaCapo Press.

Savaglio, Paula. 1996. "Polka Bands and Choral Groups: The Musical Representation of Polish-Americans in Detroit." *Ethnomusicology* 40 (Winter): 35-47.

Saxton, Alexander. 1975. "Blackface Minstrelsy and Jacksonian Ideology." *American Quarterly* 29:3-28.

Schiff, David. 1997. *George Gershwin: Rhapsody in Blue.* New York and Cambridge: Cambridge University Press.

Schuller, Gunther. 1968. *Early Jazz: Its Roots and Musical Development.* New York: Oxford University Press.

Schuster, J. Mark Davidson. 1985. *Supporting the Arts: An International Comparative Study.* Washington, DC: National Endowment for the Arts.

Schwarz, K. Robert. 1996. *Minimalists.* London: Phaidon.

Seeger, Anthony. 1992. "Ethnomusicology and Music Law." *Ethnomusicology* 36(2):345-359.

Seeger, Charles. 1957. "Music and Class Structure in the United States." *American Quarterly* 9(3):281-294.

Seeger, Charles. 1961. "The Cultivation of Various European Traditions of Music in the New World." In *Report of the Eighth Congress of the International Musicological Society, New York, 1961,* 364-375. Kassel: Barenreiter. Reprinted in *Studies in Musicology 1935-1975,* 195-210. Berkeley: University of California Press.

Seeger, Charles. 1966. "Versions and Variants of the Tunes of 'Barbara Allen.'" *University of California, Los Angeles Selected Reports* 1(1):120-167.

Setian, Sosi. 1990. *"Kef-Time: A Prohibited Style of Armenian Music."* Paper presented at the joint meeting of the *Society for Ethnomusicology,* the *American Musicological Society,* and the *Society for Music Theory,* Oakland, California.

Shaner, Richard H. 1963. "The Amish Barn Dance." *Pennsylvania Folklife* 13(2):24-26.

Shannon, Doug. 1985. *Off the Record: Everything Related to Playing Recorded Dance Music in the Nightclub Industry.* Cleveland, OH: Pacesetter Publishing House.

Shapiro, Anne Dhu. 1975. "The Tune Family Concept in British-American Folk-Song Scholarship." Ph.D. dissertation, Harvard University.

Sharp, Cecil. 1932. *English Folksongs from the Southern Appalachians.* London: Oxford University Press.

Shaw, Arnold. 1978. *Honkers and Shouters: The Golden Years of Rhythm and Blues.* New York: Collier Books.

Sheehy, Daniel. 1997. "Mexican Mariachi Music: Made in the USA." In *Musics of Multicultural America,* ed. Kip Lornell and Anne K. Rasmussen, 131-154. New York: Schirmer Books.

Shepherd, John, Phil Virden, Graham Vulliamy, and Trevor Wishart, eds. 1977. *Whose Music? A Sociology of Musical Languages.* New Brunswick, NJ: Transaction Books.

Slobin, Mark. 1993. *Subcultural Sounds: Micromusics of the West.* Hanover, NH: Wesleyan University Press.

Small, Christopher. 1996. *Music, Society, Education.* Hanover, NH: University Press of New England.

Smith, Eric Ledell. 1992. *Bert Williams: The Pioneer Black Comedian.* Jefferson, NC: McFarland.

Solie, Ruth A., ed. 1993. *Musicology and Difference: Gender and Sexuality in Music Scholarship.* Berkeley: University of California Press.

Sonneck, Oscar G. 1921. "The History of Music in America." In *Miscellaneous Studies in the History of Music,* 324–344. New York: Macmillan.

Sonneck, Oscar George Theodore. 1983. *Oscar Sonneck and American Music.* Urbana: University of Illinois Press.

Sounds Like 1996: Music by Asian American Artists. 1996. AsianImprov Records, L 0002. Compact disc.

Southern, Eileen and Josephine Wright, comps. 1990. *African American Traditions in Song, Sermon, Tale, and Dance, 1600s–1920: An Annotated Bibliography of Literature, Collections, and Artworks.* Westport, CT: Greenwood Press.

Southern, Eileen, ed. 1994. *African-American Theater: Out of Bondage (1876) and Peculiar Sam; or The Underground Railroad (1879).* Vol. 9 of *Nineteenth-Century American Musical Theater,* ed. Deane Root. New York: Garland Press.

Southern, Eileen. 1982. *A Biographical Dictionary of African and African-American Musicians. Greenwood Encyclopedia of Black Music.* Westport, CT: Greenwood Press.

Southern, Eileen. 1997 [1983, 1971]. *The Music of Black Americans: A History.* 3rd ed. New York: Norton.

Spaulding, Norman W. 1981. "History of Black Oriented Radio in Chicago 1929–1963." Ph.D. dissertation, University of Illinois.

Speck, Frank G. and George Herzog. 1942. *The Tutelo Adoption Ceremony: Reclothing the Living in the Name of the Dead.* Harrisburg: Pennsylvania Historical Commission.

Speck, Frank Gouldsmith. 1949. *Midwinter Rites of the Cayuga Longhouse.* Philadelphia: University of Pennsylvania Press.

Spencer, John Michael, ed. 1992. *Sacred Music of the City: From Blues to Rap.* A special issue of *Black Sacred Music: A Journal of Theomusicology* (vol. 6, no. 1). Durham, NC: Duke University Press.

Spencer, Peter. 1992. *World Beat: A Listener's Guide to Contemporary World Music on CD.* Pennington, NJ: A cappella Books.

Spottswood, Richard K. 1990. *Ethnic Music on Record: A Discography of Ethnic Recordings Produced in the United States, 1893 to 1942.* Urbana: University of Illinois Press.

Stearns, Marshall and Jean Stearns. 1968. *Jazz Dance.* New York: Schirmer.

Stehman, Dan. 1984. *Roy Harris: An American Musical Pioneer.* Boston: Twayne Publishers.

Stevenson, William "Mickey." 1983. Personal interview. 20 April.

Stokes, Martin, ed. 1994. *Ethnicity, Identity and Music: The Musical Construction of Place.* Oxford and Providence, RI: Berg.

Stone, Jesse. 1982. Personal interview. 30 November.

Stowe, David W. 1994. *Swing Changes: Big Band Jazz in New Deal America.* Cambridge, MA: Harvard University Press.

Strasser, Susan 1989. *Satisfaction Guaranteed: The Making of the American Mass Market.* New York: Pantheon.

Strickland, Edward. 1991. *American Composers: Dialogues on Contemporary Music.* Bloomington: Indiana University Press.

Stuckey, Sterling. 1987. *Slave Culture.* New York: Oxford University Press.

Stuessy, Joe. 1990. *Rock and Roll: Its History and Stylistic Development.* Englewood Cliffs, NJ: Prentice-Hall.

Sudhalter, Richard M. 1999. *Lost Chords: White Musicians and Their Contributions to Jazz, 1915-1945.* New York: Oxford University Press.

Sugrue, Thomas. 1996. *The Origins of the Urban Crisis: Race and Equality in Postwar Detroit.* Princeton, NJ: Princeton University Press.

Suzuki, D. T. 1959. *Zen and Japanese Culture.* Bollingen Series. New York: Pantheon.

Sweeny, Philip. 1992. *The Virgin Dictionary of World Music.* New York: Henry Holt.

Szatmary, David P. 1996. *A Time to Rock: A Social History of Rock-and-Roll.* New York: Schirmer Books.

Takaki, Ronald. 1998. *Strangers from a Different Shore: A History of Asian Americans,* rev. Back Bay Books. Boston: Little, Brown.

Talley, Thomas V. 1922. *Negro Folk Rhymes: Wise and Otherwise.* New York: Macmillan Co.

Taquachito Nights: Conjunto Music from South Texas. 1999. Produced by Cynthia Vidaurri and Pete Reiniger, in collaboration with the Narciso Martínez Cultural Arts Center. Smithsonian Folkways Recordings SFW CD 40477. Compact disc.

Tawa, Nicholas E. 1990. *The Way to Tin Pan Alley: American Popular Song.* New York: Schirmer Books.

Tawa, Nicholas E. 1982. *A Sound of Strangers: Musical Culture, Acculturation, and the Post-Civil War Ethnic American.* Metuchen, NJ: Scarecrow Press.

Tawa, Nicholas E. 1987. *Art Music in the American Society: The Condition of Art Music in the Late Twentieth Century.* Metuchen, NJ: Scarecrow Press.

Tawa, Nicholas. 1995. *American Composers and Their Public: A Critical Look.* Metuchen, NJ: Scarecrow.

Taylor, Billy. 1982. *Jazz Piano: History and Development.* Dubuque, IA: William C. Brown.

Taylor, Timothy D. 1997. *Global Pop: World Music, World Markets.* New York: Routledge.

Texas-Mexican Border Music, vol. 1: *Una historia de la música de la frontera: An Introduction 1930-1960.* 1974. Folklyric Records 9003. LP disk.

The Arts and the Public Purpose. 1997. New York: The American Assembly.

Théberge, Paul. 1997. *Any Sound You Can Imagine: Making Music/Consuming Technology.* Hanover, NH: University Press of New England.

Thernstrom, Stephan, et al. eds. 1980. *Harvard Encyclopedia of American Ethnic Groups.* Cambridge: Belknap Press of Harvard University Press.

Thomas, Anthony. 1995. "The House the Kids Built: The Gay Imprint on American Dance Music." In *Out in Culture: Gay, Lesbian and Queer Essays on Popular Culture,* ed. Corey K. Creekmur and Alexander Doty, 437-448. Durham, NC: Duke University Press.

Thomas, J. C. 1975. *Chasin' the Trane: The Music and Mystique of John Coltrane.* Garden City, NY: Doubleday.

Thomson, Virgil. 1971. *American Music Since 1910.* New York: Holt, Rinehart and Winston.

Tick, Judith. 1997. *Ruth Crawford: A Composer's Search for American Music.* New York: Oxford University Press.

Tilzer, Harry Von. 1903. *In Dahomey.* London: Keith, Prowse.

Tirro, Frank. 1977. *Jazz: A History.* New York: Norton.

Tischler, Barbara L. 1986. *An American Music: The Search for an American Musical Identity.* New York: Oxford University Press.

Titon, Jeff Todd. 1985. "Stance, Role, and Identity in Fieldwork Among Folk Baptists and Pentecostals." *American Music* 3(1):16-24.

Tonooka, Sumi. 1987. Interview by author. Philadelphia, Pennsylvania, 10 November.

Tooker, Elizabeth. 1970. The Iroquois Ceremony of Midwinter. Syracuse, NY: Syracuse University Press.

Toop, David. 1991. *Rap Attack 2: African Rap and Global Hiphop.* New York: Serpents' Tail.

Townsend, Charles, 1976. *San Antonio Rose: The Life and Times of Bob Wills.* Urbana: University of Illinois Press.

Trigger, Bruce G., ed. 1978. Northeast. Vol. 15, *Handbook of North American Indians.* Washington, DC: Smithsonian Institution Press.

Tucker, Ken. 1986. "The Seventies and Beyond." In *Rock of Ages: The Rolling Stone History of Rock'n'Roll,* ed. Ed Ward, Geoffrey Stokes, and Ken Tucker, 467-624. New York: Summit

Tucker, Mark. 1993. *The Duke Ellington Reader.* New York: Oxford University Press.

Tucker, Sherrie. 1998. "Female Big Bands, Male Mass Audiences: Gendered Performances in a Theater of War." *Women and Music* 2:64-89.

Turino, Thomas. 1996. "Nationalism and the Spread of Cosmopolitanism in Zimbabwean Music." Unpublished paper.

Tweed, Thomas A. and Stephen Prothero, eds. 1999. *Asian Religions in America: A Documentary History.* New York: Oxford University Press.

Twitchell, James. 1996. *AdcultUSA: The Triumph of Advertising in American Culture.* New York: Columbia University Press.

Van Peer, Rene. 1999. "Taking the World for a Spin in Europe: An Insider's Look at the World Music Recording Business," *Ethnomusicology* 43(2):374-384.

Vander, Judith. 1988. *Songprints: The Musical Experience of Five Shoshone Women.* Urbana: University of Illinois Press.

Vander, Judith. 1997. *Shoshone Ghost Dance Religion: Poetry Songs and Great Basin Context.* Urbana: University of Illinois Press.

Veblen, Thorstein. 1899. *The Theory of the Leisure Class.* New York: Macmillan.

Vennum, Thomas, Elli Kongas-Maranda, and Marsha Penti.1983. *At Laskiainen in Palo, Everyone Is a Finn.* Washington, DC: Smithsonian Institution Film.

Verhoeven, Martin. 1998. "Americanizing the Buddha: Paul Carus and the Transformation of Asian Thought." In *The Faces of Buddhism in America,* ed. Charles S. Prebish and Kenneth K. Tanaka, 207-227. Berkeley: University of California Press.

Vincent, Rickey. 1996. *Funk: The Music, the People, and the Rhythm of the One.* New York: St. Martin's Griffin.

Visions. 1991/1992. *Time to Discover.* Mina Productions MPCD 75. Compact disc.

Waksman, Steve. 1996. "Every Inch of My Love: Led Zeppelin and the Problem of Cock Rock." *Journal of Popular Music Studies* 8:5-25.

Wald, Gayle. 1998. "Just a Girl? Rock Music, Feminism, and the Cultural Construction of Female Youth." *Signs* 23(3):585-610.

Walker, William. 1966 [1854]. *The Southern Harmony, and Musical Companion.* Rev. ed. Los Angeles: Pro Musicamericana.

Wallis, Roger and Krister Malm. 1984. *Big Sounds from Small Peoples.* New York: Pendragon.

Walser, Robert. 1993. *Running with the Devil: Power, Gender, and Madness in Heavy Metal Music.* Hanover, NH: Wesleyan University Press.

Walser, Robert. 1995. "Rhythm, Rhyme, and Rhetoric in the Music of Public Enemy." *Ethnomusicology* 39(2):193-217.

Ward, Brian. 1998. *Just My Soul Responding: Rhythm and Blues, Black Consciousness and Race Relations.* London: University College London Press.

Watada, T., ed. 1997. *Collected Voices: An Anthology of Asian North American Periodical Writing.* Toronto: HpF Press.

Watkins, Glenn. 1988. *Soundings: Music in the Twentieth Century.* New York: Schirmer Books.

Weber, William. 1975. *Music and the Middle Class: The Social Structure of Concert Life in London, Paris and Vienna*. London: Croom Helm Press.

Webster, Danny. 1997. Personal interview. 18 August.

Weinstein, Deena. 1991. *Heavy Metal: A Cultural Sociology*. New York: Lexington Books.

Welch, Chris. 1977. "Zeppelin over America," *Melody Maker* (25 June) :30.

West, Cornel. 1994. Radio interview. On "Profile of George Clinton, the Master of Funk." Weekend Edition, National Public Radio. 6 February.

Wheeler, Elizabeth. 1991. "'Most of My Heroes Don't Appear on No Stamps': The Dialogics of Rap Music." *Black Music Research Journal* 11(2):193-215.

Whitburn, Joel, 1994. *Top Country Singles, 1944-93*. Menominee Falls, WI: Record Research.

White, Shane. 1994. "It Was a Proud Day: African-American Festivals and Parades in the North, 1741-1834." *Journal of American History* 81(1):13-50.

Whiteley, Sheila, ed. 1997. *Sexing the Groove: Popular Music and Gender*. New York: Routledge.

Whitely, Sheila. 1992. *The Space Between Notes: Rock and the Counter-Culture*. New York: Routledge.

Wilgus, D. K. 1959. *Anglo-American Folksong Scholarship Since 1898*. New Brunswick, NJ: Rutgers University Press.

Williams, Martin T. 1967. *Jazz Masters of New Orleans*. New York: Macmillan.

Wilson, John S. 1996. *Jazz: The Transition Years*. New York: Meredith.

Wilson, Olly. 1986. "The Black-American Composer and the Orchestra in the Twentieth Century." *Black Perspective in Music* 14(1):26-34.

Wise, Sue. 1990. "Sexing Elvis." In *On Record: Rock, Pop and the Written Word*, ed. Simon Frith and Andrew Goodwin, 390-398. London: Routledge.

Wolfe, Charles K. 1976. *Tennessee Strings: The Story of Country Music in Tennessee*. Knoxville: The University of Tennessee Press.

Wolfe, Charles K. 1989. "Thomas Talley's Negro Folk Rhymes." *Tennessee Folklore Society Bulletin* 53(3):104–111.

Wolfe, Charles K. 1999. *A Good Natured Riot: The Birth of the Grand Ole Opry*. Nashville: Vanderbilt University Press and the Country Music Hall of Fame.

Wolfe, Richard J. *Secular Music in America: 1801-1825*. 3 vols. New York: New York Public Library.

Woll, Allen. 1989. *Black Musical Theater: From Coontown to Dreamgirls*. Baton Rouge: Louisiana State University Press.

Wong, Deborah. 1994. "I Want the Microphone: Mass Mediation and Agency in Asian-American Popular Music," *TDR* 38(3):152-167.

Writers' Program. 1940. *Drums and Shadows: Survival Studies among the Georgia Coastal Negroes*. Athens: University of Georgia Press.

Zheng, Su de San. 1993. "Immigrant Music and Transnational Discourse: Chinese American Music Culture in New York City." Ph.D. dissertation, Wesleyan University.

Ziporyn, Evan. 1992. "One Man's Traffic Noise: The Making of Kekembangan." In *Festival of Indonesia Conference Summaries*, ed. Marc Perlman. New York: Festival of Indonesia Foundation.

Index

Cox, Ida, 214
Creation, 60, 62
  stories, 141, 144, 158
Creoles, 111, 196
Crew Cuts, the, 349–350
Cries, 9, 12, 192–196.
Crooning, 39, 40
Crosby, Bing, 131, 342, 346
Crosby, Fanny Jane, 12
Cross-rhythms, 333
Crossover, 118, 232–234, 265, 349,
  371, 375
Crow Hop, 114–115
Crowley, Aleister, 356
Cuatro guitar, 258
Cuban music, 108, 245, 261, 262,
  263, 264, 265, 266
Cubop, 269
Cugat, Xavier, 15
Cultural dependency, 35
Cultural diversity, 299
Cultural patrimony, 25–28
Cultural preservation projects, 24
Cumbia, 260
Curing, 147, 149, 151
  rituals, 156
  songs, 152
Cylinder phonograph, 25
Cylinder recording, 29, 182
  invention of, 38, 40
Cymbaly/tsymbaly, 180

D

d'Indy, Vincent, 306
Dalai Lama, 100
Dance bands, 253, 268, 279, 323, 328
  "sweet" style of, 326
  European Americans and, 179
Dance hall music, 375
Dance halls, 262, 269
Dance music, 38, 41, 44, 52, 75, 354
  American Indians and, 156
  Asian Americans and, 293
  categories of, 42
  contemporary concert musics
    and, 315
  European Americans and, 161,
    164, 169–170, 173–180
  Latinos and, 245–246, 257–258,
    260–261, 265, 268–269
Dance skits, 219
Dance traditions, 13

Dances
  alligator, 157
  animal, 150, 157
  ball game, 150
  barn, 127, 178–179
  basket, 152
  bear, 26
  Bharata Natyam, 285
  brush, 151
  buffalo, 152
  butterfly, 143, 152
  Celtic, 11
  ceremonial, 150
  circle, 199
  cloud, 152
  Comanche, 152
  competitive, 361
  Congo, 189
  contest, 114
  contra, 189
  corn, 152
  crow, 112
  dog, 152
  drum or dream, 112
  exhibition, 114
  friendship, 150
  ghost, 112, 117, 139, 148
    ceremonies, 13
    defined, 116
    religion, 12
    songs, 152
  grass, 112–114
  Guinea, 188
  harvest, 152
  hoop, 114
  horse, 150
  Indian social, 119
  intertribal, 114
  line, 287
  losing, 150
  Negro, 187, 189, 218
  old man's cane, 157
  Omaha, 112, 114
  owl, 114
  partner, 143
  popular, 189, 190
  Pueblo, 217
  rabbit, 114, 143–144
  religious, 199
  round, 114
  Saturday, 250
  secular, 146

CD TRACK LISTINGS

1. "Song of Happiness" (1:06) Performed by a children's chorus, drum, and harmonica. From *Music of the Sioux and the Navajo* (1949), Folkways 4401 (1953). Courtesy of Smithsonian Folkways. Page 142.

2. Brush Dance Heavy Song" (Yurok) (1:01) Sung by Ewing Davis and recorded by Frank Quin in 1956. Courtesy of Richard Keeling. Page 151.

3. Iroquois "Women's Shuffle Dance" (1:20) Performed by George Buck and Joshua Buck. From *Songs from the Iroquois Longhouse*, Library of Congress AFS 16 (1942). Page 169.

4. "Gloucester Witch" (Old Meg) (1:23) Performed by John Allison. From *Witches and War-Whoops: Early New England Ballads*, Folkways F-05211 (1962). Courtesy of Smithsonian Folkways. Page 169.

5. "Chicago is a Polka Town" (2:26) Performed by Stas Golonka and the Chicago Masters. From *Deeper Polka: More Dance Music from the Midwest*, Smithsonian Folkways SF40140. Courtesy of Smithsonian Folkways. Page 172.

6. "Vigala reinlender" (Vigala Schottische) (1:56) Performed by Estonian Kantele. From *Tuuletargat* (Wind Wizards): Estonian Instrumental Folk Music Ensemble of Chicago. Copyright 2000 Innovative Mechanics, Inc. Page 181.

7. "Dortn, Dortn Ibern Vasserl" (There Across the Water) (2:02) Performed by Ruth Rubin. From *Yiddish Folksongs*, Folkways F08720 (1978). Courtesy of Smithsonian Folways. Page 182.

8. "My Little Annie, So Sweet" (2:08) Performed by Horace Sprott. From *Been Here and Gone: Music from the South, Vol. 10*, Folkways FA02659 (1960). Courtesy of Smithsonian Folkways. Page 195.

9. "Were You There" (2:03) Performed by the Fisk Jubilee Singers. From *Fisk Jubilee Singers*, Folkways 02372 (1955). Courtesy of Smithsonian Folkways. Page 201.

10. "In the Pines" (2:08) From *Lead Belly: Where Did You Sleep Last Night? Lead Belly Legacy, Vol. 1* (1996) Smithsonian Folkways SF 40044. Courtesy of Smithsonian Folkways. Page 211.

11. "Pea Patch Jig" (1:53) From *The Early Minstrel Show*, New World Records, 1985. Recorded Anthology of American Music, Inc. Used by Permission. Page 219.

12. "Los Arrieros" (The Muleteers) (4:43) From Viva *El Mariachi: Nati Cano's Mariachi Los Camperos*, Smithsonian Folkways 40459. Courtesy of Smithsonian Folkways. Page 248.

13. "Asi se baila in Tejas" (This is the Way They Dance in Texas) (1:32) Performed by Tony de la Rosa. From Rounder CD 6046 (1991) Licensed courtesy of Rounder Records. Page 249.

14. "Something About Me Today" (2:30) Performed by Chris Kando Ijima, Joanne Nobuko Miyamoto, and "Charlie" Chin. From *A Grain of Sand: Music for the Struggle by Asians in America*, Folkways 1020 (1973). Courtesy of Smithsonian Folkways. Page 280.

15. "Lam khon savane" (3:14) Traditional singing from southern Laos. Recorded by Terry E. Miller on April 24, 1987, in New York City. Used by Permission, Page 287.

16. "Saba Melody" (3:03) Live recording. From *Mystical Legacies: Ali Jihad Racy Performs Music of the Middle East*, Lyrichord LYRCH 7437 (1994). Used by Permission. Page 288.

17. "Puser Belah" (Unstable Center) (4:17) Field recording by Michael Tenzer. Used by Permission. Page 297.

18. "Raudra" (3:21) From Attacka Compact Disk, Babel 9158-1. Used by Permission. Page 312.

19. William Grant Still: "Danzas de Panama; Tamborito" (3:24) From *Louis Kaufman, Violin: Twentieth Century American Violin Works in Historic Recordings*, Music & Arts Program of America, CD 638. Used by Permission. Page 319.

20. Mary Lou Williams: "Gloria" (4:38) From *Mary Lou Williams: Zoning*, Smithsonian/Folkways 40811, 1974. Courtesy of Smithsonian Folkways. Page 336.